What a Beautiful Sunday!

Jorge Semprun

What a Beautiful Sunday!

Translated from the French
by Alan Sheridan

A Helen and Kurt Wolff Book
Harcourt Brace Jovanovich, Publishers
San Diego   New York   London

Library of Congress Cataloging in Publication Data

Semprún, Jorge.
What a beautiful Sunday!

Translation of: Quel beau dimanche!
"A Helen and Kurt Wolff book."
1. Buchenwald (Germany : Concentration camp)
2. World War, 1939–1945—Personal narratives, French.
3. Semprún, Jorge.
4. Prisoners of war—France—Biography.
5. Prisoners of war—Germany—Biography.
I. Title.
D805.G3S44813   940.54'72'43094322   82–47662
ISBN 0–15–195857–2   AACR2

Printed in the United States of America
First edition
B C D E

TO THOMAS,
that he may—later, afterward—
remember this memory

". . . man's struggle against power is the struggle of memory against oblivion."

MILAN KUNDERA

"In Russian captivity, as in German captivity, the worst lot of all was reserved for the Russians. In general, this war revealed to us that the worst thing in the world was to be a Russian."

ALEXANDER SOLZHENITSYN

"I persist in demanding names, in interesting myself only in books that one leaves ajar like doors, and for which one does not have to find the key. Fortunately, the days of the psychological novel are numbered."

ANDRÉ BRETON

What a Beautiful Sunday!

Zero

He thought he detected some movement. A crunching on the thin snow. Over there, under the wheels of a truck perhaps, at the fork in the road, by the barracks. A sheaf of snow sparkling in the sunlight, among the trees, perhaps under the wheels of some army vehicle. Wheels moving off in the fresh snow, soft under the wheels.

A brief crunching sound and it was over. The landscape resumed its dazzling stillness.

He took a few more steps, in the inertia of a walk so dogged that it had become automatic. A few steps, a few strides, an involuntary, or at any rate unconscious, movement. He then stopped in the middle of the avenue. For no reason, it seemed. Awakened from the dreamlike routine of that walk.

The silence could go on forever—such a thing was not unconceivable.

The landscape remained vacant, abandoned after that last sound of human life, of movement, a moment ago.

He saw the mist forming in front of his mouth. He

wiggled his toes, stiff in the rough leather of his boots. He thrust his clenched fists into the pockets of his blue pea jacket.

It could be that nothing would happen, nobody come. The avenue lead nowhere. The winter unfold its frozen, limpid solitude. Later, in some uncertain but foreseeable future, the snow would begin to melt. There would be streams, running water throughout the forest. The wood would set to work, the earth, too, the sap, the seeds. One day, it would be green. Verdant even, prolific. There is a word for all that: spring.

Then, to his left, in that snowy eternity, he saw the tree.

Beyond the slope, beyond the row of tall lampposts, beyond the long line of hieratic columns, there was a tree. A beech, probably. Or so he supposed. It certainly looked like one. Detached from the blurred mass of beeches, in the middle of a cleared space, in splendid isolation. Maybe it was the tree that kept one from seeing the forest, who knows? The supreme beech. He took three steps to one side, feeling very cheerful. But he suspected that this cheerfulness wasn't of his making, that he hadn't just invented it. No, it was probably some literary memory. He smiled, took another few steps.

It certainly looked as if he was going to cross the avenue, without thinking, in an oblique line.

He remembered no other tree. There was no trace of nostalgia in his curiosity, for once no childhood memory rising up in a stirring of the blood. He was not trying to rediscover something inaccessible, some impression from an earlier time. No long-lost happiness nourished this present bliss. Just the beauty of a tree, whose name, even if it was in fact what it seemed to be, had no importance. A beech, probably. It could just as easily be an oak, a sycamore, a weeping willow, a silver birch, an ash, a poplar, a cedar, a tamarisk.

A tamarisk in the middle of that snow, however,

wouldn't make sense. He was saying the first thing that came into his head. Carried away by sheer joy. A tree, just that, in its immediate splendor, in the transparent stillness of the present.

He had crossed the slope and was walking in the soft, immaculate snow.

The tree was there, within reach. The tree was real, one could touch it.

He held out his hand, he touched the bark, scratching the frozen snow that the wind had plastered on its trunk. He then stood back, to take stock, to get a better view. A whole minute landscape lay before his eyes. He warmed his fingers with his breath, then stuck his hands back into the pockets of the blue pea jacket. He just stood there, looking. The December sky was pale, a sheet of slightly tinted glass.

One could dream in the sunlight.

Time would pass. The beech would let fall its snowy mantle. With a silent tremor, the branches of the tree would drop lumps of the porous, crumbly stuff to the ground. Time would do its work, and the sun, too. They were already doing it. Time was still plunging into winter, with its gleaming magnificence. But at the very frozen heart of the still season, a future green bud was already feeding on secret stores of sap.

He thought, as he stood there motionless, his whole life turned to a meticulous gaze, that the bud negated the winter, and the flower the bud, and the fruit the flower. His face set in an ecstatic, almost beatific smile at the thought of this crude dialectic, for that delicate, still-impalpable bud, that green, vegetal dampness in the snow-covered belly of time, would be not only the negation, but also the fulfillment of winter. Old Hegel was right. The bursting snow would find its fulfillment in the bursting green.

He looked again at the snow-covered beech. He already

knew its verdant truth. December; how many more months to wait? He himself might be dead by then. The bud would burst, bringing to an end the profound truth of winter. And he would be dead. No, not even dead: he would simply have vanished. He would be absent, gone off in a puff of smoke, and the bud would burst, a ball full of sap. It was fascinating to imagine. He laughed at the sun, at the tree, at the landscape, at the idea of his own probable, pitiful absence. Things would take their course, in any case. Winter would be fulfilled in the profusion of the spring.

He wiggled his toes in his boots. The leather had become hard and sharp from the ice. He moved his clenched hands in the pockets of the blue pea jacket.

He had not actually read the Talmud. "If you see a fine tree, do not stop, go on your way," the Talmud apparently says. He had stopped. He had walked over to this fine tree. He had never felt the need to affirm his own existence by negating the ephemeral beauties of the world.

He had not read the Talmud, it was a superb beech, it seemed to him to be happy.

Then a metallic click attracted his attention.

He turned his head. He saw a warrant officer—he had not heard him coming. The warrant officer had taken out his revolver from its deerskin holster. He had cocked it. That metallic click became, retrospectively, explicit.

He looked at the revolver pointing at him. The warrant officer looked surprised. Even worried. There was a touch of outrage in his voice.

"*Was machst du hier?*" he asked.

The warrant officer was asking what he was doing there.

His voice shook with indignation or surprise. It was understandable. Standing in front of a tree, stupidly, ecstatically, his face set in a beatific smile, off the beaten paths—this was intolerable.

He thought for a second. He had to be careful what he said.

"*Das Baum*," he said in the end, "*so ein wunderschönes Baum!*"

It was the only possible explanation.

He was pleased that he had managed to express in German, with real conciseness, the true reasons for his presence in that unexpected place. The tree really was a miracle of beauty. In French, however, the explanation would have had something solemn or affected about it. "*C'est l'arbre*," he would have said, "*un arbre miraculeux de beauté.*"

The warrant officer turned his head to look at the tree; he, too, looked for the first time. He had not yet noticed the beech, this soldier. And even if he had, he would have gone on his way. Yet he couldn't have read the Talmud, either—that was hardly likely.

The revolver described a descending movement toward the snow-covered ground.

For a split second, he caught himself imagining that the warrant officer would see the tree as he had. The warrant officer's gaze had weakened, invaded perhaps by so much beauty. All that whiteness, turning to a steely blue in the depths of its mass, iridescent at its delicately jagged edges, had diluted the darkness of his gaze. He held the revolver loosely, his arm swinging slightly, as he looked intensely at the tree. A confused, perhaps disturbing possibility seemed to be emerging.

They were there, side by side; they could have talked together about that miracle of beauty.

He saw the stylized flash of the double S embroidered in silver on a diamond-shaped black ground on the tabs of the warrant officer's collar, and, curiously enough, this didn't seem to present an obstacle. The SS warrant officer took a few steps back, as he had done a little while ago. The warrant officer looked at the beech, the landscape, with eyes that had turned blue. Everything seemed so innocent; there was a vague possibility that it was, anyway.

It was possible that the warrant officer would come back to him, nodding. "*Tatsächlich, ja, Mensch, ein wunderschönes Baum,*" he would say. They would both look at the tree and nod. He would take the opportunity of explaining to the SS warrant officer as tactfully as he could the amazing ideas of one of his country's philosophers, in all their complexity.

They stood motionless in front of the tree. There was some sunlight, a pale sky; the snow deadened any sound, smoke rose in the distance. It was ten o'clock in the morning, in December, a Sunday. It would probably go on like this.

Suddenly it was all over.

The SS warrant officer came back. The revolver was pointed once again at his chest. The warrant officer's face grew red, with anger or hatred. He was going to shout.

But he stood to attention, clicking his heels. This wasn't easy, given the soft snow. He managed it all the same. He clicked his heels, impeccably. He snatched off his cap. Standing erect, his head up, his eyes on the blind nothingness of the pale sky, he began to shout. He had forestalled the SS warrant officer, who stood there gaping with astonishment. He was presenting himself as specified by the regulations, which were all the more meticulous for not being written, shouting out his number, the order he was obeying, the reasons for his presence outside camp boundaries.

"*Häftling vier-und-vierzig-tausend-neun-hundert-vier!*" he yelled. "*Von der Arbeitsstatistik! Zur Mibau kommandiert!*"

The smoke, rising calmly in the distance, was from the crematorium.

The SS warrant officer is named Kurt Krauss. Nothing more can be said about him.

No. 44904, who was caught by Kurt Krauss just off the main avenue, bordered by columns crowned by Nazi eagles, staring ecstatically at an isolated beech tree, has just announced who he is: No. 44904. The number is printed in black on a rectangle of white material sewn onto the left side of the blue pea jacket, over the heart. It is also printed on a second rectangle, sewn this time onto the right side of the right leg of the trousers, over the thigh. Above each of these rectangles is an isosceles triangle of red material. Printed in indelible ink on the red triangle is the letter S.

An uninformed observer might misinterpret this, might think that it was not mere coincidence. As if the stylized double S—a double zigzag, a double lightning flash —embroidered in silver on a black diamond on the warrant officer's collar, and the single black S on a red background on the clothes of No. 44904, revealed some hierarchical relationship. From the simple to the double, in some sense. But not at all. Hierarchy is no doubt part of it. Between SS Warrant Officer Kurt Krauss and No. 44904 there is all the distance created by the right to kill. Distance and hierarchy, however, are not symbolized by that passage from the simple to the double, from the S to the SS. In fact, instead of the single S, there might equally well have been any other letter. An *F*, an *R*, a *T*, for example, for *Franzose, Russe, Tscheche,* the letter sewn on the isosceles triangle being no more than an indication of the nationality of the bearer of the number. In the present case, the S stood for *Spanier,* Spaniard. Thus the hierarchical distance between the bearer of a number and SS Warrant Officer Kurt Krauss is not affected by the national origin of the bearer of that number. The right to kill may be exercised on any wearer of a number, independently of his nationality, no matter what letter is sewn on his clothes, for purposes of identification, for the convenience of the administration.

It is ten o'clock in the morning. It is Sunday. It is late December. The landscape is covered with snow.

The beech forest on the hill known as the Ettersberg, and which gives its name to the place in question, Buchenwald, is a few kilometers from Weimar.

Yet the city of Weimar had not had such a bad reputation until recent years. Founded in the ninth century, if usually respectable historical sources are to be believed, it belonged until 1140 to the counts of Orlamünde. In 1345 the city became the fief of the landgraves of Thuringia, and a century later, in 1485 to be precise, it fell as an appanage to the senior branch of the Saxon house of Wettin. After 1572 Weimar became the permanent residence of that ducal line. Under Charles Augustus and his successors, the city was a liberal center for the arts and letters.

This last aspect of the city's life was strongly emphasized, not without a certain overblown rhetoric, in a collection of documents on the Ettersberg concentration camp.

"Weimar," we read, "was hitherto known to the world as the city in which Lucas Cranach the Elder, Johann Sebastian Bach, Christoph Martin Wieland, Gottfried Herder, Friedrich von Schiller, Johann Wolfgang von Goethe, and Franz Liszt lived and created their immortal works. . . . Goethe walked on this hill, among these beeches. It was there that the *Wanderers Nachtlied* was conceived. Like Goethe, the whole of the intellectual society of Weimar was fond of going up to the Ettersberg, in search of rest and fresh air."

This bucolic vision of the life at Weimar is confirmed by Goethe himself. In his *Conversations* with Eckermann, under September 26, 1827, we can read a charming account of a walk on the Ettersberg.

Let us hear what Eckermann, a meticulous if uninspired transcriber, has to say:

"Goethe had invited me to take a drive this morning to the Hottelstedt Ecke, the most westerly summit of the Ettersberg, and thence to the Ettersberg hunting-lodge. The day was very fine, and we drove early out of the Jacob's Gate. . . . We were now upon the height, and drove quickly along. On our right were oaks, beeches, and other leafy trees: Weimar was behind us, but out of sight. . . .

" 'This is a good resting-place,' said Goethe. 'I think we may as well try how a little breakfast would suit us in this good air.'

"We alighted, and walked up and down for a few minutes upon the dry earth, at the foot of some half-grown oaks stunted by many storms; while Frederick unpacked the breakfast we had brought with us, and spread it upon a turfy hillock. The view from this spot, in the clear morning light of the autumn sun, was magnificent. . . .

"We seated ourselves with our backs against the oak, so that during breakfast we had before us the view over half Thuringia. Meanwhile we demolished a brace of roast partridges, with fresh white bread, and drank a flask of very good wine out of a cup of pure gold that Goethe carried with him on such excursions in a yellow leather case. . . ."

However, in spite of the refinement of these patrician memories, Weimar was, when Goethe arrived there, a township of no more than five or six thousand souls. Cattle wandered through its muddy streets. There were no roads in the country, nothing but bad tracks on which one embarked at the risk of breaking one's bones, if the best-informed authors are to be believed.

Five years later, in 1779, appointed by Duke Charles Augustus as privy councilor and director of the departments of War and Public Works, Goethe was to strive to remedy this state of affairs. But it would seem that progress was not particularly rapid. In any case, Stendhal, who crossed the region on his way to Russia with the Emperor, was still complaining, in a letter to his sister Pauline dated July 27, 1812, of the "German slowness" that held up his ride across the roads of Thuringia. The landscape, moreover, did not impress Stendhal, as it had Goethe and Eckermann, who found it quite delightful. "At Weimar," he wrote to Pauline, "one feels the presence of a prince who is a friend of the arts, but I saw to my sorrow that there, as at Gotha, nature has done nothing to help; it is as flat as Paris."

Nevertheless, even though there was disagreement among these illustrious minds, at least as far as the beauties of the landscape are concerned, the city of Weimar did not have such a bad reputation. In 1919, after the fall of the Hohenzollerns, it gave its name to the new Republic, whose first National Assembly met there.

It is often difficult, sometimes even impossible, to date in any precise way the real beginning of a story, of a series of events whose interrelationships, mutual influences, obscure links, if they appear at first sight to be contingent, even improbable, turn out in the end to be highly structured, and achieve such a degree of determinate coherence that they acquire the influence, however illusory it may be, of self-evident fact.

However, in the present case, the date of June 3, 1936, seems a decisive one.

That day, in Berlin, in his office on the Wilhelmstrasse,

the Inspector General of Concentration Camps and head of the SS Totenkopf Detachments, Theodor Eicke, initiated an official communiqué, stamped SECRET, that was to have decisive consequences for the rest of this story.

Let us take a look at it.

"SS Reichsführer Himmler has agreed to the transfer of the Lichtenburg (Prussia) concentration camp to Thuringia. A suitable site must therefore be found in the last-named state for a camp designed for three thousand prisoners, around which the barracks of the Second SS Totenkopf Division will be built. The cost of the operation is estimated at 1,200,000 marks."

This confidential communiqué of June 3, 1936, was addressed to Fritz Sauckel, who for a long time, it will be remembered, was *Gauleiter* of Thuringia and who, in 1942, became head of the Labor Service for the Reich and the whole of the occupied territories, a job that led him to organize the departure for Germany, on various pretexts, of several million workers. In 1946, at Nuremberg, he was found responsible for this operation, condemned to death, and hanged.

For his part, Theodor Eicke, the signatory of the directive, had been a mere *Brigadeführer* two years before. It was he who gained access to Cell 474 of Stadelheim Prison, where Ernst Röhm, the head of the SA, was confined. It was warm, and Röhm was stripped to the waist, according to usually reliable sources. Ernst Röhm, the head of the plebeian Nazis, was beaten to death by Theodor Eicke, on the personal orders of Hitler, who wanted once and for all to get into the good books of the gentlemen of big business and the army general staff. Later, in 1943, Eicke was killed on the Eastern Front.

But all these dead must not interrupt our story.

There is nothing to prevent us from imagining that hot, humid day in Berlin, in June 1936. Theodor Eicke is sitting in his office on the Wilhelmstrasse. He has just read over the letter he is sending to Fritz Sauckel, which his secretary has just put in front of him. In the top right-hand corner of the first page, under the date and usual references—*Berlin SW 68, den 3 Juni 1936, Wilhelmstr. 98/IV*—is written, in brackets, the word GEHEIM, SECRET, as I have already said.

Theodor Eicke picks up his pen and writes at the bottom of the letter, under the mandatory *Heil Hitler!* and the roll call of his titles and ranks—*Der Inspektor der Konz.-Lager u. Führer der SS-Totenkopfverbände, SS-Gruppenführer*—a capital E, his customary form of signature. The secretary then gathers the typed sheets and puts them back into the red leather portfolio for special administrative mail. After a few words with the Gruppenführer on the subject of the weather, their mutual health, or plans for holidays on the Baltic coast, she leaves the office.

One can imagine the scene.

In any case, on the day that letter was written and sent off, Léon Blum, leader of the Socialist Party and what came to be known as the Popular Front, could not possibly have known of its existence, still less suspected the impact that it was to have on his own destiny.

On that same day, June 3, 1936, in Paris, joint talks between employers and unions were in progress. They had been called on May 31 by the Minister of Labor, Ludovic-Oscar Frossard, who had lost his post as secretary of the Communist Party at the party congress in Tours; rather unflattering remarks about him can be found in the writings of Zinoviev and Trotsky. Frossard had called these joint talks with an eye toward finding a solution to social confrontation and the increasing takeovers of factories, but, despite the efforts of the General Confederation of Labor, the Communist-led trade-union confederation, to pacify the workers, the negotiations met with defeat.

In these circumstances, Léon Blum presented his Cabinet to President Lebrun on Thursday, June 4. "The outgoing Cabinet," Lebrun said to Blum, "regards the situation as so serious that it asks you not to put off the transfer of power until tomorrow. It begs you to take over the Ministry of the Interior and the Ministry of Labor by nine o'clock tonight." Léon Blum acceded to this request.

And so, on June 3, 1936, Léon Blum could have known nothing of the secret letter sent by Theodor Eicke to Fritz Sauckel, and even if by some miraculous chance he had, it is unlikely that he would have guessed the consequences it was to have on his own life.

Engrossed in the formation of his Cabinet, in preparing his speech to the Chamber of Deputies on the occasion of his investiture, which was planned for Saturday, June 6, and in trying to find a settlement for social conflicts, Léon Blum would hardly have had time to recall on that particular day that he himself had written, thirty-five years earlier, a book called *Nouvelles Conversations de Goethe avec Eckermann*. He is unlikely to have given a thought to that particular work of his at the very moment when Theodor Eicke was initialing the secret communiqué that was to result in the building of a concentration camp on the same charmingly rustic spot where Goethe once talked with Eckermann, and where he, Léon Blum, was eventually to be deported and interned.

As for the Narrator, another essential character in this story, he is only twelve years old on that June 3, 1936. He has just failed one of his end-of-term examinations. But don't worry: it was only in mathematics. In the humanities, the Narrator has never been anything but brilliant. What else? It is likely that the Narrator has spent the afternoon with two of his brothers in the Parque del

Retiro in Madrid. But the Retiro itself is no longer a quiet, enclosed space, sensuously laid out around the maternal waters of its lakes, around the rose gardens and museums of the Crystal Palace. The Retiro is constantly overrun by groups of excited, sometimes vociferous, workers, walking up its avenues toward the city center from their homes in the suburbs of Vallecas. It is, of course, the last June before the war, before the Spanish Civil War, before all the wars.

In short, on that Wednesday, June 3, 1936, as in every well-structured tragedy, fate has just made its appearance —absent-mindedly, even administratively—and none of the characters is yet in a position to recognize its face, its disillusioned smile, its ironic or pitying wink.

The letter sent by Theodor Eicke to Fritz Sauckel initiates an administrative correspondence too lengthy to be reproduced here in detail.

One thing is certain: the business of transferring the Lichtenburg camp to Thuringia dragged on.

Finally, on May 5, 1937 (almost a year will have gone by and the time envisaged by the original plan will have been exceeded), a note signed by Gommlich, counselor at the Ministry of the Interior of Thuringia, tells us that the choice of the Etter hill, the Ettersberg, just outside Weimar, was approved by Eicke. As a result, on July 16, 1937, the first group of three hundred prisoners was to be brought to the site to begin the clearing of the woods prior to the building of the barracks, under the command of SS-Obersturmbannführer Koch, whose wife, Ilse, it will be remembered, was later to make lampshades out of the skin of prisoners whose tattoos had particularly attracted her attention.

However, the first official name of the camp, K.L. Ettersberg, created something of a stir. In a letter to

Himmler dated July 24, 1937, Theodor Eicke mentioned that the National Socialist Cultural Association of Weimar had protested against this name, "for the name of the Ettersberg is associated with the life and works of Goethe," and invoking his spirit in the name of a re-education camp (Umschulungslager), in which the dregs of the earth would be assembled, could only sully the poet's memory.

Nor was it possible, Eicke pointed out, to name the camp after the nearest village, Hottelstedt, for this would result in considerable financial loss to the SS of the garrison, since their accommodation allowances would then be calculated in conformance with the cost-of-living index at Hottelstedt, as specified in the regulations, whereas a standard of living based on the higher prices prevailing in Weimar would be more in keeping with the dignity of the SS. For that reason Eicke suggested calling the camp K.L. Hochwald.

Four days later, Himmler announced his decision. The camp would be called K.L. Buchenwald/Weimar. In this way the cultural susceptibilities of the local burghers would not be hurt and the SS personnel would get accommodation allowances in keeping with their social role.

Blum's Nouvelles Conversations avec Eckermann was first published, anonymously, in 1901, in the Revue Blanche. But it is hardly likely that on Sunday, June 7, 1936, he had an opportunity of remembering that early work of his, though, some years later, interned in a villa in the Falkenhof of Buchenwald, on the very spot where Goethe took his walks with Eckermann, he must have thought of it more than once. No doubt he did recall, with silent, sorrowful anger, words spoken the day before in the Chamber of Deputies by Xavier Valla: "Your coming to power, Monsieur le Président du Conseil, is unquestionably an event of historical significance. For the first time this old Gallo-Roman country is to be governed by a Jew"—words that, in a roundabout way, bring us back to the distant origins of this story, to the letter of Theodor Eicke, so often mentioned, and of which none of the individuals sitting around the negotiating table at the Hôtel Matignon had the remotest idea. But Léon Blum, in his *Nouvelles Conversations de Goethe avec Eckermann*, thirty-five years before becoming the first Jew to govern France, forty-two years before finding himself on the very spot where those famous conversations took place, had written:

"*July 3 1898*,

"Dined at Goethe's. He told me an interesting story about Racine. When he had finished planning *Phèdre*, he said to a friend: 'My play is finished. All that remains is to write the lines.' "

Let us write.

One

"*Les gars, quel beau dimanche!*" he said.

He looked up at the sky and said to the other guys that it was a beautiful Sunday. But all you could see in the sky was the sky, the darkness of the sky, the night sky, full of snow swirling in the beams of the searchlights. A dancing, icy light.

As he said it, he let out a great, exaggerated burst of laughter, like someone who had just said "*merde!*" But he had not said "*merde*" He had said, "*Quel beau dimanche, les gars!*" in French, looking up at the dark sky at five o'clock in the morning. He had let out a great burst of laughter, just for his own benefit, and he had not said "*merde!*" In any case, if he had wanted to say "*merde!*" he would have said "*Scheisse,*" because the important words were not French, or, for that matter, Serbo-Croatian, Flemish, or Norwegian. They were not even Russian, except for *makhorka*, which was a word of considerable importance. He said "*Scheisse,*" "*Arbeit,*" "*Brot,*" all the important words, in German. Shit, work, bread: all the real words. Then there was *makhorka*, which was also a real word, which meant tobacco, or, rather, the acrid grass we smoked.

In any case, he would have looked up at the sky, at the night sky, at the snow-filled sky, at the electric glow of the sky, and he would have yelled out "*Scheisse*," had he wanted to say "shit." Since we said "*Scheisse*," everyone understood, and it was important to be understood when we wanted to shout out "shit" and be understood.

His laughter rose to the night sky, to the night of the beautiful Sunday at dawn, and he immediately turned around. He said nothing else. He must have said all he had to say about life and dashed off into the snowy night, in the direction of the *Appellplatz*. He was no more than a running shadow, bowing under the driving snow. Other shadows started to run behind the shadow of the guy who had said that it was a beautiful Sunday.

For whom had he spoken? Why was there such desperate contempt in his voice, in his cry toward the snow-filled sky?

He had been raising the collar of his greatcoat, which had traces of green paint on the back, the vague outlines of half-effaced letters; a *K* perhaps was still visible, *B* and *U* could be made out. Standing in front of the entrance to the block, protected from the swirling snow by the projection of the double outside staircase that led to the second floor, he stood there, outside, raising his greatcoat collar, looking at that Sunday dawn, that night penetrated by the reflections from the searchlights, listening to the confused din punctuated by the whistle blasts that summoned the guys to the first roll call of the day.

Then he shouted out, for his own benefit, in a loud, declamatory, desperate voice that was filled with contempt—or, rather, was turning itself into contempt— he cried out, *Quel beau dimanche, les gars.*"

It must have been the memory of other beautiful Sundays, at home, on the banks of the Marne, which suddenly invaded him as he was about to dash into the swirling snow, that made him cry out in that way, made him burst into such desperate laughter.

"*Quel beau dimanche, les gars.*" He had probably found the memory of a beautiful Sunday irrepressible, a Sunday long ago on the banks of the Marne, as he watched the swirling snow over the Ettersberg. Perhaps he felt the unacceptable stupidity of a world in which there are Sundays on the Marne—elsewhere, long ago, far away, on the other side, outside—and then this obstinate fleecy snow of the Ettersberg. He had probably cried out to revenge himself on that stupidity, at least to name it, if only in such a roundabout way. If he had cried out, "It's beautiful, the Marne, on Sundays!" no one would have understood what he was saying.

He waited, mingling with the group of latecomers, those who did not move till the last minute to join the crowd and stumble in the direction of the *Appellplatz*. He had looked up at the sky and cried out. For himself, for the memory that had come back to him, for the shadows around him, for the snow of the Ettersberg, for the half-day's work that lay ahead, for the kapos who would start yelling, for the Marne in spring, because only a memory of spring could suddenly have come to him like that, in that obstinate snow. He had cried out that it was a beautiful Sunday!

Then he had taken two steps to the side, and his face had been caught in a beam of light, in profile.

It was Barizon, Fernand Barizon.

He started to run under the driving snow, and his dash into the night got all the others moving as well, all the latecomers. Barizon was a shadow running toward the crowd of moving shadows, whose step soon turned into a rhythmic march, beating out the time of that beautiful Sunday.

Later, as he stands in line in the solid, rectangular formation of prisoners from Block 40, on the spot that belongs by right to Block 40 on the *Appellplatz*—even if most of the men who originally formed that solid, frozen, immobile rectangle, standing mechanically to attention, have died, gone up in smoke, leaving no other trace of their passage through here than the permanence of that solid, immobile, yet hollow form of Block 40 on the *Appellplatz*, an empty shape, endlessly filled up, as individuals disappear, by other, renewable, prisoners—later, standing in his perfectly straight line, Barizon must again be remembering the banks of the Marne.

In the muffled silence, broken only by the orders barked out through the loudspeakers, Barizon dwells lovingly on every detail of that memory: the weather, that spring Sunday long ago; the color of the leaves, and of the young women's dresses; the taste of the wine; the tepidness of the water swirling around the still oars, abandoned so that he could light a cigarette or take the hands of one of the young women. Under the impact of that freezing cold, as he remembers the banks of the Marne, Barizon must have thoughts on the fragility of human happiness, trivial thoughts on the lost happiness of life, outside. If only he had known how full life could be, full of all the mortal riches that lie hidden within it, he would not have been so stupid as to be satisfied with the petty happiness to be found on the banks of the Marne; he would have made some attempt to create a great happiness for himself, so great and so extreme that neither the snow nor the kapo of the Gustloff nor the SS Works officer with glasses could efface it.

In any case, the only clues we have to suppose that

Fernand Barizon was remembering the banks of the Marne are the words he yelled out before running off. It isn't much to go on, one has to admit:

"*Quel beau dimanche, les gars!*"

And that it was Sunday.

What were Sundays like?

It wasn't the Marne, in any case. Once I took a girl out boating in the Bois de Boulogne. Boating was a healthy and, what's more, not very expensive recreation. But not all girls appreciate fresh air, or being lectured, however brilliantly, by an intellectual in a boat. With that particular girl it didn't get me anywhere, as far as I remember. Maybe the banks of the Marne would have been more conducive.

I don't know. I don't remember the banks of the Marne.

I light my morning cigarette, which is rolled in newspaper. The acrid smoke of the *makhorka* burns my throat. I stand under the shelter of the outside staircase, my coat collar turned up. My toes are coming through the holes in my socks and rubbing against the rough leather of my boots. I tap my heel against the concrete flagstone at the entrance to Block 40.

Emil, the leader of Block 40, appears, wearing his sailor's cap; he's well built, sullen, with lavender-blue eyes. Emil will have checked that the dormitories are empty, that no one has stayed behind. He mutters a greeting as he walks past and plunges into the snowy night.

The Marne? Absolutely not, it doesn't remind me of anything.

I look at the snow sparkling in the beams of the searchlights. The dancing, icy light. Now I'll have to go to the *Arbeitsstatistik* hut; it will soon be time for the roll call. But I prolong the moment. Alone, with the harsh taste of the *makhorka* in my mouth. A sort of peace, no one looking at me: a hollow, padded, fragile space of total solitude.

For two years I even shared my sleep with others. I would wait for someone else to finish, pressed in on every side, to squeeze into a few centimeters of bench and eat the evening soup. Others, behind me, were waiting their turn, waiting for me to finish. I would crouch on the lukewarm porcelain seat, in a row with a dozen others, in the filthy promiscuity of the latrines. I would march in line, shoulder to shoulder, just one paw of some huge, stumbling, frightened insect. The water of the shower trickled over my body, over hundreds of hairy legs, soft, purplish-blue genitals, swollen bellies, hollow chests. For two years I had been thrown into a tightly packed world, sticky with breath, a-gurgle with the disgusting rumblings of guts.

So I would prolong those morning moments, with their solitude: the first cigarette, the dancing, frozen light, the temporary silence, the fabulous certainty of existing.

But why think of the Marne and its Sunday pleasures? I knew nothing of the Marne, in fact. When Fernand Barizon, just now, shouted out those words about Sunday, I remembered the banks of the Marne—or, to be more precise, my mind was swamped by a memory that did not belong to me. As if someone else had started remembering in my mind.

The last summer before the war, I mean the last summer of the years between the wars, the summer of 1939, I went to the movies every afternoon. It was not exactly a habit. It was something I decided to do, all over again, each day: the same feigned surprise, the same fascination.

I would walk up the Rue Soufflot and stop in front of

the doors of the Bibliothèque Sainte-Geneviève. I should have gone in. As the studious young man I pretended to be, I was expected to do so. I would stand there at the top of the steps, slyly breathing in the cool, toffee-scented air of the empty square, as if taking one last breath before plunging into the austere mustiness of the library. But my whole being was already veering from side to side, like dirty rainwater running along the gutters on the slopes that lead down to the Seine.

I looked across the square, breathing in the air. I looked to the left and saw the façade of Saint-Etienne-du-Mont in the precise, flat August light. One more moment and I would walk into the library. Suddenly my mind was made up: there was no going back. With beating heart, I dashed down the Rue Valette, throwing one last glance, guilty but relieved, at the blind façade of the Panthéon behind me.

On the Rue de Rivoli all the movie theaters were showing double features. Sometimes I left one theater and went into another: four films in an afternoon. I often saw Arletty, and the banks of the Marne seemed to be the chosen place for pleasure. The Marne, dancing in the open air, Pernod, hands wandering naughtily over rounded flesh: that was the filmic image of happiness, apparently.

The Marne of the movies was a very pale, brilliant gray, with spots of shadow where boats were grounded. A sort of Lethe, but one that led to a brief Sunday paradise. So just now, when Barizon's mocking voice had expressed his yearning for beautiful Sundays gone by, I, quite naturally, thought of the banks of the Marne. The waltz, the boats, and the Pernod. A woman's shrill laughter. A hand under skirts, the game of the little beast that rises, rises.

So I remembered the Marne through the memory of

others, and not even that of real people I might have known, but of the colorless, flickering characters of the films of that summer. As if the ghosts of Michel Simon and Arletty had got off their tandem and begun to have memories in my mind, on that Sunday of late December 1944, under the snow of the Ettersberg. Arletty, with her beautiful, rather rough voice, would have answered Barizon on the subject of beautiful Sundays gone by. She would have had something to say about them, no doubt.

But I'm burning my lips on the last puff from the *makhorka* butt. A dull rumble comes from the top of the hill. Everyone must be on the *Appellplatz*, given the time—everyone, that is to say, who doesn't answer the roll call at his place of work. I answer the roll call in the *Arbeit* hut. That's one of my privileges. I ought to go now: the detailing of the prisoners will start soon.

I take a last look at the night, at the sparkling snow swirling in the searchlights. I take my hands out of my pockets and start to run. How beautiful it all was, the Marne and the spring! I laugh to myself, as if I had been there.

They were talking about it, of course. For some days now, we had talked of nothing else.

They were talking about it in small groups, as they stood around waiting for the roll call, when I entered the office of the *Arbeitsstatistik*. At the entrance to the hut, right on top of the hill, almost opposite the crematorium, I tapped my boots against the iron bar at the bottom of the steps. I shook off the snow from my blue pea jacket. I went into the hut, turning to the left. To the right were the premises of the *Schreibstube*, the secretariat. Opposite was the library. On the left was the *Arbeit*.

They were all there, talking. Except Meiners, the black triangle, who probably couldn't care less.

At first some of us had thought it was a lie. It had to be.

An invention of Nazi propaganda, to raise the morale of the people. We listened to the news bulletins on the German radio, broadcast by all the loudspeakers, and we shook our heads. A trick to raise the morale of the German people, it had to be.

But we soon had to face up to the evidence. Some of us listened in secret to the Allied broadcasts, which confirmed the news. There was no doubt about it: British troops really were crushing the Greek Resistance. In Athens, battle was raging, British troops were retaking the city from the ELAS* forces, district by district. It was an unequal fight: ELAS had neither tanks nor planes.

But Radio Moscow had said nothing, and this silence was variously interpreted.

We had talked of nothing else for days. In December 1944, under the swirling snow of the Ettersberg, we talked about nothing but Greece. The war wasn't over yet and another battle was beginning within the anti-Nazi coalition. British tanks were crushing the Communist partisans, even before Hitler had finally been beaten. That was certainly something to talk about.

For days we talked of nothing else.

"Hey!" says Daniel.

"Yes?" I say.

"Just a couple of words," says Daniel.

"Yes," I say.

"Later," says Daniel.

He makes a gesture to show me that there are too many people around, that he wants to talk to me alone.

I know what it's about. I nod to show him that I understand.

We're all there, awaiting the arrival of the SS warrant

*ELAS was the People's Liberation Army, created in December 1941 on the initiative of the Communist Party of Greece. —ED.

officer, for the roll call, in the open space at the entrance to the offices of the *Arbeitsstatistik*.

When you enter you find yourself in an open space. Farther on, a barrier separates this empty space from another, larger, space, full of tables, chairs, card indexes, shelves, files, cabinets. There is also a stove in the middle, a great round stove in which dry wood is burned. An office, in fact. The silent mustiness of a bureaucratic place.

At the end of the office area filled with office equipment are two doors. The right-hand one leads to a room used by Willi Seifert, the *Arbeit* kapo. In principle, that room is just an office: the manager's office, if you like. But Seifert has set up his bed there. He sleeps there, in peace. The SS turn a blind eye to this stretching of the regulations.

The left-hand door leads to a sort of common room or mess where we can retire if we like, to smoke a cigarette, chat for a moment with a pal, dream, look out at the snow or sun, or the rain, through the window.

That's it; there is nothing else to be said about that particular setting.

I first came to work in the *Arbeit* offices after some weeks in Block 62, in the quarantine of the Little Camp. It just happened like that. I had nothing to do with it: a sort of objective mechanism.

Two days after my arrival, I was lying on my bunk in the quarantine block, not even trying to sleep or to protect myself against the vermin crawling in the mattresses, when my name was called out. My real name, I mean, my Spanish name, the one printed in the official records. Usually, the Frenchmen who had been with me since Compiègne, some of them even from prison at Auxerre and Dijon, called me Gérard. It was my *nom de guerre*.

I had a place on the edge of the bunk—the third spot on

the top deck—and I leaned over to see who was calling my name.

There was a guy standing there, looking up, talking up at me in Spanish. Yes, that's me, I told him. A guy with a shaven head, wearing a medley of different clothes, all too tight, like the rest of us. A bony face, with pale eyes.

This guy wants to talk to me.

I swing myself over the edge of the bunk and get down. We take a few steps into the central corridor of the block. There's the usual commotion. The guy talks to me. Just like that, questions, sentences that don't seem to make any sense.

A contact, I know what that is. I recognize that look, that circumspection, that obstinate fervor. The organization is there already. We go on talking, though we seem to be going in circles. But no, it's getting clearer—where one has come from, what one has done—a bit here, a bit there. And then, quite naturally, one puts one's cards on the table. It's my turn now, take it or leave it. I pick up the cards, give a few references, not all at once. We'll see what comes of it. It's a rule, a ritual, a game. The other guy makes up the rest, on the basis of the few data.

That's the Party!

I was alone, I had only two eyes: the Party has thousands. I was alone, I had only an hour to live, the present: the Party has all the time in the world, the future. I was alone, I had only my own death to live through: the Party could live through all our deaths, it would never die. It's all in Brecht, more or less. But I hadn't read Brecht at that time. Things were less literary then. Quite simply, I'd been taken back into the Party organization.

The guy took three cigarettes out of his pocket and gave them to me. He gave me a password. Three cigarettes, a password, nothing else. He might disappear; someone would come in his place; we would recognize each other.

Later, when I knew him better, I forgot to ask Falco—who belonged to the leadership of the underground Spanish Communist organization—how, by what round-about means, they had found out about me: "There's a guy, about twenty, a Spaniard in Block 62, who's come from a *maquis*, a resistance cell, in Burgundy and who looks like a comrade. Anyway, he worked with our partisans. Go and see him." I forgot to ask that question because it had something personal about it.

What followed was so simple.

I was the only one, among all the Spaniards, who spoke German. Thanks to Fräulein Grabner and Fräulein Kaltenbach, German governesses from my privileged childhood! So the organization of the Spanish Party had asked the German Communists to have me transferred to the *Arbeitsstatistik*, as its "representative." One day, when the camp was covered in snow, I was summoned. It was the end of my quarantine. I was sent to see Seifert, the *Arbeit's* kapo. He saw me in his own office—behind the right-hand door at the back—and talked to me for a long time.

Seifert was quiet, precise, authoritative. Or, rather, he radiated an authority that derived not only from his job but also from his character. In this universe of the camp he was a lord; that was obvious. He must have been twenty-six or twenty-seven. Over the red triangle on his well-cut jacket, there was an extra little red band. *Rückfälliger*: recidivist. Having the job he did and wearing that extra band of red material, at his age, told a story, a biography.

Later, bit by bit, I found out about him. A member of the Communist Youth Movement, underground work, prison, temporary freedom, more underground work, the camps. At one point I came to realize how Seifert had got that authority that had become so natural to him.

It was a spring day. An SS warrant officer, in charge of one of the work kommandos of the German armament industry, came into the office. It was after the morning roll call. We were quietly working away at our card indexes and lists. There were also, in the open space in front of the barrier, about ten deportees of various nationalities, summoned to be transferred to new work. As the SS warrant officer came in, someone shouted: "*Achtung!*" Then, mechanically, we all jumped to attention and stood frozen beside our chairs. That was the regulation. Willi Seifert came out of his office, relaxed. He made the necessary report. The SS warrant officer ordered us to resume our work: "*Weitermachen!*" Seifert stood leaning with both hands on the barrier, facing the warrant officer. The German had come to complain. In an angry, staccato voice, he complained to Seifert that the *Arbeitsstatistik* was not sending enough prisoners to his armament kommando. There weren't enough men, this wouldn't do. He was still behind on his production schedule.

Seifert let him say his piece, without a trace of emotion. Then, in the same tone of voice as the SS warrant officer, with the same anger, the same violence—but contained, controlled—he explained that the SS officer would never have enough men as long as he spent his day bludgeoning them.

"Why should I send men to you just to have them knocked senseless? There are plenty of kommandos in places where they are allowed to get on with their work. Stop beating up guys and we'll fulfill your numbers!"

Seifert was shouting, and I said to myself that it would end badly.

But the SS let him shout. He nodded. He could find nothing to say. He turned on his heels and left.

Seifert yelled: "*Achtung!*" Again we lifted our backsides off our chairs. It was the regulation. The SS shut the office door behind him. We all looked at Seifert and

Seifert smiled. That day, I realized where his authority came from. Years of underground fighting, in the jungle of the camps, had tempered that fierce will of iron. We were standing, but Seifert looked down at us all from his height. A lord, there was no doubt about it.

Later, much later, however, I saw his face break up.

That time, I was part of the night shift. The night shift was one of Seifert's inventions. Actually, with our twelve hours of work a day, they were making out very well anyway. The administration of the whole work force in the camp was on a secure basis: a good administration, which bore the imprint of Teutonic efficiency. But Seifert had set up this night shift, which came around for each of us every three weeks, so that we could rest in turn. After the morning roll call, we could go back to the dormitory blocks and sleep in peace, in unimaginable silence, each man having the whole width of the bunk to himself, for the dormitories were practically empty during the day, until the return of the work kommandos.

So, that time, I was part of the night shift. I was talking to Seifert and Weidlich, his assistant. Herbert Weidlich had managed to leave Germany after 1933. He had lived in Prague, in exile. That night, I don't remember why, Weidlich was telling us about his time in Prague. There was probably no reason, for Weidlich would tell anyone about his time in Prague at the slightest opportunity. He had very good memories of Prague—up to the Nazi invasion, anyway.

I was smoking a cigarette that Seifert had given me, and it wasn't *makhorka* rolled in newspaper. It was a real German cigarette made of Balkan tobacco. I was listening to Weidlich attentively. It was Weidlich's stories that made me like Prague, most definitely, and that made me find that town strangely familiar when I walked through it for the first time, ten years later, in 1954.

Herbert Weidlich had lived in Prague, at one point, in a room overlooking a courtyard. It was summer, and most of the neighbors had gone away on vacation. At night, after a day of stifling heat, Weidlich would turn off the lights and lean out of the window, to get some fresh air. Once, as he was musing in the darkness, a bedroom lit up on the other side of the courtyard. Neighbors who had come back from their vacation, perhaps. Not a young couple. He must have been about forty, she a bit younger. A room with all the lights on, curtains open, to get the cool night air, he thought. The curtains stirred in the breeze that rose from the river, which was nearby.

Weidlich had watched the man and woman go to bed, unaware of his presence in the darkness. In their twin beds, the man opened a newspaper, the woman a book. They stayed like that for some time, without saying a word. Then the man folded his paper, carefully. He turned toward his wife and she to him. They may have said a word or two to each other; Weidlich was too far away to hear. But in any case it must have been a very brief exchange: a signal, an order, a call. The man carefully folded his newspaper and folded back the light summer eiderdown in its white cotton cover. At the same moment, the wife did likewise on her bed. The man stood, facing his wife, in the gap between the two beds, already half naked. Tall, solidly built, his backside and his genitals in the lamplight. She, in the bed, stretched out and, having exposed her legs and belly, arched the small of her back to slip off her nightgown. In silence, it seemed. Or maybe he was whispering something as he leaned over her. In any case, said Weidlich, with a rough laugh, she soon wouldn't be in a position to say anything. Naked now, she had half raised herself, leaned on one elbow, and plunged her face between the man's thighs, he having flexed his legs and rested his knees on the edge of his wife's bed, with his belly stretched forward. "She wasn't in a position to say anything," said Weidlich with his coarse laugh. "She must have had her mouth full!"

I listened to Weidlich dreamily: it brought images to my mind.

Weidlich described everything in minute detail. The work of that mouth on the man's cock, the woman's hand gripping her husband's hips, the man's short, raucous cries. And then the woman's postures, and suddenly her interminable, grave, heart-rending, ecstatic laughter.

I was listening to him dreamily when my gaze landed, quite by chance, on Seifert's face. Under the impact of some pain, some unnamable sorrow, it seemed, Seifert's face had broken up.

I was daydreaming, operating my own private movie in that obscure complicity of male stories made desperate by privation, when I saw Seifert's face drained of blood. Such obvious distress. One could imagine everything.

As Weidlich continued his meticulous but comic account of his voyeuristic adventure, Seifert must have sensed that I was looking at him. He turned his head away and rubbed his hand over his face: it was over.

Fifteen years later, in 1960, I remembered again how Seifert's face had looked that night.

I was a member of the Politburo of the Spanish Communist Party at the time. I had a pseudonym that I was very fond of, because it was so commonplace. I was called Sanchez—the Spanish equivalent of Dupont or Smith. I don't know who had chosen the name for me, in 1954, when I was co-opted onto the Central Committee. Probably Carrillo, the head of the party, himself. But I liked it, that commonplace, almost anonymous name. Working underground, in Spain, I often came into contact with comrades who had a lifetime of activism behind them. They had fought during the civil war, they had sustained the party organization with their ebbing strength during the terrible years, they had been in prison. They were shrouded in glory, secrets, and doubts. They would look at me. They knew that I was "Sanchez" of the Central Committee and the Politburo. They listened to me. But when they first met me, I could see by the look in their eyes that they were wondering who I was, where I'd sprung from. "Sanchez"? What was this "Sanchez"? I was not a leader out of history. Nor was I old enough to have taken part in their civil war. I didn't share the same experiences, the same obscure, tragic complicities, the same glorious or wretched memories. Nor did we have the same things to forget—I mean the same wish to forget certain episodes in a long, bloody history.

"Sanchez"? The veterans would shake their heads. That didn't bother me. I liked to listen to their stories, to build up with their help a collective memory. But even better I liked to be "Sanchez," with no links to their past, linked, rather, to the future of our struggle.

Anyway, I had gone to East Berlin in 1960 to straighten out certain problems. I was alone. I was staying at the hotel reserved for guests of the German Party. A black limousine collected me each morning to take me to the meetings. It was not very exciting. On the last day, the official from the German Central Committee who had been put in charge of me asked me if there was anything I particularly wanted. Then, suddenly, the memory of that night long ago came back to me. I asked if I could meet Willi Seifert or Herbert Weidlich. At first he didn't understand. I had to explain to him that I had been deported to Buchenwald. I had to talk to him about Seifert and Weidlich and about the *Arbeitsstatistik*.

I had been at Buchenwald? he exclaimed. He was as excited as an Englishman who has just been told, in the middle of some ordinary conversation, some polite chitchat about this and that, that one had been at Oxford. Buchenwald! Why didn't I say so earlier? He immediately suggested organizing an excursion by car to Weimar to visit the camp.

Oh, no; shit! I had spent fifteen years trying not to be a survivor. I had managed to keep out of the associations of former deportees. The pilgrimages, as they called the trips organized for the deportees and their families to the sites of the former camps, had always filled me with horror. So I muttered, in a toneless voice, some vague excuse. I had to get back to the West. I was in a hurry. Party work, yes. But the Central Committee official insisted, determined to do his best for me. You don't mean to say you've never been back to Buchenwald? No, never. He shook his head. He described for me all the work that had been done to the camp since. A memorial: the German Democratic Republic had built a memorial there of great artistic value. I nodded, but I had seen the photographs of it, I knew: it was disgusting. A tower, groups of marble sculptures, an avenue bordered with walls covered with bas-reliefs, monumental steps. In short, disgusting. I didn't tell him what I thought, of course. Shyly, I just told him my old dream: that the camp should be left to the slow work of nature, to the forest, to the roots, to the rain, to the irreversible erosion of the seasons. One day, people would rediscover the buildings of the old camp overgrown by the irresistible profusion of trees. He listened to me, surprised. But no, a memorial, something educational, political, that's what they had built. In any case, it was Bertolt Brecht's idea. It was he who had suggested that they build this majestic memorial, opposite the old Buchenwald concentration camp, on the slope leading to Weimar. He had even wanted the figures to be larger than life, carved in stone and placed on a pediment devoid of ornament, taking in with their gaze some majestic amphi-

theater. In this amphitheater a festival would be organized each year in memory of the deportees. Oratorios,
works for massed choirs would be performed there. There
would be public readings and political appeals.

I listened to the Central Committee official, non-
plused. I was well aware that Brecht had often displayed
bad taste, but to such an extent, it was unbelievable!
However, I said nothing. I felt uncomfortable discussing
all that with him. No, I didn't have time to go to Weimar,
that was all. I was sorry. On the other hand, if he could
arrange for me to meet Willi Seifert or Herbert Weidlich,
I'd be grateful. Providing it wasn't too much trouble, I
added.

He became once more vague, cold, administrative. He
would have to look into it, he told me. He didn't know, he
told me. He would let me know, he told me.

The Central Committee official came back early that
afternoon. I was sitting in the lobby of the party hotel,
reading a two-week-old copy of *L'Humanité*, sipping my
coffee. It was not the most exciting thing to be doing, but,
apart from the fabulous performances of the Berliner
Ensemble, what else was there to do in East Berlin, at
least when one was being looked after by the party
machine?

The German comrade beamed with pleasure. However,
the news he brought me was that I would not be able to
meet either Seifert or Weidlich. They were both absent
from Berlin.

His pleasure had quite a different source. When I
mentioned Seifert and Weidlich to him, I could tell from
his eyes that he did not know their names. And what if I
had asked to meet two individuals who had fallen from
grace? After all, several years in a concentration camp
under the Nazis was no guarantee against political deviation. And what if I had asked to meet two individuals

whom the Party had had to expel from its paternal bosom (or maternal bosom; maybe the Party is androgynous or hermaphroditic, who knows)? Whom the Party may even have had to imprison, or get rid of? I had seen in his eyes the embarrassment he had felt. It was always a delicate matter, stirring up the past. Always rather embarrassing when you have to explain why this or that individual turned out badly.

As it happened, his fear turned out to be unfounded. The Central Committee official had been able to check that Seifert and Weidlich had both had brilliant careers in the German Democratic Republic. Of course, in Seifert's case especially, that was hardly surprising. Brilliant careers, no doubt about it. Weidlich was an inspector in the criminal police. As for Seifert—the official's voice took on that inimitable tone of administrative delight that we know so well—Willi Seifert had become a major-general in the *Volkspolizei*. Unfortunately, neither of them was in Berlin at the moment. He could tell me, in confidence, that Weidlich was away on a mission, somewhere in the provinces, and that Seifert—here the administrative delight was tinged with political satisfaction—was attending a seminar on historical (and, no doubt, dialectical) materialism for senior officers of the People's Army and People's Police.

I remembered Seifert's face, that unspeakable distress. A night, long ago, in the *Arbeit* hut in Buchenwald when Herbert was recounting in his coarse voice the frolics of that couple, and on Seifert's face had appeared that devastated light. A truth about himself, perfectly visible, the obscene evidence of which suddenly shattered his lordly mask.

One had only to do one's arithmetic, of course. Seifert must have been fifteen when he was arrested for the first time. He had probably never known a woman. Through years of prison and camp, he had always lived in the arid, opaque, murky world of masculinity. The images that Weidlich had evoked, in his hearty way; that unexpected explosion between that unknown man and woman, quietly stretched out in their twin beds, under that conjugal, serene lamplight; that unexpected explosion of sexual pleasure, freed from all restraint, in which the brutal submission of two bodies to each other, the sweet domination of one by the other, had as its object nothing but that pleasure, in a sort of crude joy punctuated only by the man's gruff words and the woman's ecstatic laughter; those images of Prague that Weidlich's account evoked were quite simply those of life outside.

The heart-rending, fabulous evidence of life outside.

But Seifert did not ultimately rediscover the evidence of life outside. Or, rather, he had refused that evidence, with all its attendant risks and contradictions.

He had no sooner left Buchenwald than he joined the police organized by the Russians in their occupied zone. He remained in the familiar comfort of the same world of constraint. He had chosen to stay there, but this time on the right side, at the right end. The young Communist from Buchenwald was now just a policeman. And, what was more, a policeman who had done well for himself. He had become a major-general in the People's Police. Now, to have a successful career in East Berlin, under the eye of Ulbricht and the Russian secret service, in the midst of all the intrigues, plots, and purges of the final period of Stalinism, followed by the meanderings of bureaucratic de-Stalinization, one really had to be ready for anything. Ready for every kind of baseness, every kind of rotten compromise, to stay on the right side, so as not to fall off the cart at some sharp corner.

In 1952, then, Seifert must have felt very close to

danger. He must have gone through weeks of fear, no doubt expecting the worst every night. He must have tried to get himself forgotten, to ignore the looks cast in his direction by his colleagues in the People's Police, whether suspicious, bemused, or sympathetic. He must have begun to breathe freely only after Stalin's death.

In November 1952, Josef Frank stood in the dock in Prague. The trial that was taking place, in which he and Rudolf Slansky were the star performers, was the last great show trial of the Stalin period. The almost perfect culmination of twenty years of investigation on the part of Stalin's security services. But the culmination, too, of twenty years of unconditional submission, of feeble fascination on the part of the Western Communist movement. They go together, of course.

He was one of our comrades at Buchenwald, Josef Frank. We had worked together at the *Arbeitsstatistik*. His Czech friends called him "Pepikoou." I myself didn't call him by this diminutive. Frank was not an extrovert; it wasn't easy to cross the barriers of his natural reserve. Nevertheless, we were on very good terms. I liked him, Josef Frank. He didn't bore us with his veterans' stories. He did not, like most of the other Communist leaders in the camp, display the arrogance of the bureaucratic big shot who lorded it over the rest of us.

Later, after the liberation, Josef Frank became deputy general secretary of the Czechoslovak Communist Party. But in November 1952, in Prague, he stood in the dock. A few days later he would be hanged. His ashes would be cast to the wind, on a snow-covered road.

Standing opposite the judges, reciting the text that he had learned by heart, Josef Frank declared: "During my time in the concentration camps, from 1939 to 1945, I sank still deeper into the bog of opportunism and betrayal. While there, I also committed war crimes."

But the prosecutor required details, of course. The scenario of the public interrogation, perfectly rehearsed, several times repeated, skillfully graduated its effects. So Frank gave the details expected of him, after this general opening.

"During my time in the Buchenwald concentration camp," he said, "I obtained in 1942 the post of secretary and interpreter in the service of the *Arbeitsstatistik,* and from then on I carried out my duties in the interests of the Nazi command of the camp."

But it still wasn't enough. Frank had to go further. The public trial had to play to the full on the pedagogical mechanisms of terror, the shame of confessions, scandals. The good people had to understand to what extremes you can allow yourself to go, once you depart from the straight and narrow path lit by the shining certainties of Correct Thought. The text of the show had been carefully written, revised, rehearsed to this end.

Thus, if Frank yielded the concrete content of his "war crimes" only gradually, bit by bit, as if the prosecutor were dragging them out of him, it was because the scenario of the trial played on the mechanism of suspense, on the mythology of some horrible truth buried in the criminal's conscience, a truth that the wise maieutics of the Party would soon bring out into the light of day. These were the *Mysteries of Prague,* a serial novel on the trial, released to the public episode by episode and transmitted by all the radio stations.

And if Frank sometimes seemed to have difficulty in speaking his text, if he stumbled over certain words, everyone would think that it was because of the shame he felt at the recital of his crimes. Everyone would think that it was shame at having to admit this truth that made him stammer in this way at certain moments—whereas, in fact, it was shame at having to speak those lies.

And so the prosecutor, on that November day in 1952, asked Frank to add further details to this tissue of lies. "What war crimes did you commit?" he asked.

Josef Frank replied: "In the exercise of my duties, I helped the Nazis make up the lists of prisoners to be sent out to the various outside kommandos. In these kommandos, living and working conditions were basically harder than in the camp itself. Thus many prisoners sent out never came back. Furthermore, in the exercise of my duties, several times I struck prisoners, thus committing war crimes."

The prosecutor required still more of Frank. The prosecutor asked one more question. It was, we may be sure, a decisive question: "On whose instructions and in what way did you send the prisoners to their deaths?" And Josef Frank replied to this decisive question: "The instructions concerning the transports came from the Nazi camp command. They were given to me through kapo Willi Seifert, who gave me the lists of prisoners to be sent out. . . ."

So, it was out.

That was why Willi Seifert must have felt that he had had a close shave in November 1952. Every newspaper in Eastern Europe was publishing accounts of the Prague trial, which was intended to be exemplary. So, one day, Seifert saw his name in the papers. And in what a context! He, a senior officer of the People's Police, there he was, indirectly accused of having passed on to Frank Nazi orders for the extermination of prisoners at Buchenwald. Seifert was sufficiently well placed to know what this meant. He knew very well that it was useless, presumptuous even, to try to re-establish the truth. What good would it do to recall the real situation in Buchenwald, the real possibilities for responding to Nazi demands, concerning which a strategy had been worked out, with the agreement of the various national resistance organizations? What was the point of recalling that Josef Frank had never had anything to do with the organization of the transports at the *Arbeitsstatistik*? What was the use of declaring that never, but never, had anyone seen Josef Frank strike a prisoner? Seifert knew very well that the Prague trial was a work of fiction, in which what mattered was not the truth but verisimilitude. He knew very well why Frank had been asked to cite his name: it was a tested method employed by Stalin's security services. Militants were cited who were not directly accused in the current trial, in order to leave the door open for new trials that would take up the story where it had left off. In order to let terror hover over those who had been named.

Thus, in that particular case, having the name of Seifert cited in November 1952 meant that Stalin's security services were keeping open the possibility of triggering a new purge in the state apparatuses of the German Democratic Republic. But when? Any time, at the slightest opportunity. A new twist in the international policy of the USSR? A change of direction in the countries of the Eastern bloc? Why? For no particular reason—or, rather, to prove that an absolute power has no need of a rational, legal justification of its abuses of power. To have it made quite clear that there will never be an end to terror, that it should be self-evident that terror, from a certain moment on, feeds upon itself, upon the endless exercise of its own arbitrary power.

Anyhow, Willi Seifert must have begun to breathe freely again only five months later, on the day Stalin died. Meanwhile, he must have emphasized still more than before, I imagine, his docility, his respect for Correct Thought, his vigilance toward deviationists of all kinds. Five months later, on the day of Stalin's death, he no doubt drank himself silly—as the people pressed in, crushing one another, literally walking over one another, to contemplate for the last time the waxy face of the Master, in the Hall of Columns, in Moscow—how they all must have drunk themselves silly, the survivors of the Russian Politburo. In fact, these individuals did not have a great deal of time to celebrate the Georgian's death. They must have been plunged at once into the intrigues, surreptitious coups d'état, executions, alliances, and overturnings of alliances of the succession period.

It was Seifert who saw me the first time I went to the *Arbeitsstatistik*, in February 1944, after my quarantine period.

From the window of his office, one could see the armament factories, which were placed inside the electrified boundary. If one leaned over a little, one could also see the crematorium chimney. It was smoking steadily.

Seifert was behind his desk, playing with a long ruler. He motioned me to sit down. He looked at my outfit with a trace of disgust. I didn't know what to do with the limp, filthy felt hat that had been stuck on my head the day I arrived at the camp, after the disinfection. I rolled the hat between my fingers. In the end I put it on the desk.

Seifert looked at the felt hat with disgust.

Several moments passed; nothing was said. I didn't feel embarrassed—I don't dislike silence. I looked outside. Sunlight on the snow. The beech forest, beyond the armament factories. I craned my head a little; yes, that was it: I could see the crematorium. Pale-gray smoke was rising into the sky.

Then Seifert spoke.

"Yes, the crematorium," he said. "We built it. We built everything here."

He shrugged his shoulders.

"This camp is nothing but a sanatorium now!"

It was shorthand, a way of putting it. That didn't bother me. I understand shorthand, ways of speaking, putting things.

Seifert mechanically sorted the papers on his desk.

After his opening sentence about the camp's being nothing but a sanatorium now, I expected him to go on to express all the anger and contempt of an old-timer. *Ein Sanatorium! Das Lager is nur ein Sanatorium, heute!* For a month now the old-timers had repeated those words to us, over and over. OK, so the camp was nothing but a sanatorium now. You should have known it in the old days, the old-timers would say, contemptuously. And the stories of the old days fell on us, like hail at harvest time.

So I continued to sit before Seifert. Finally I put my filthy hat on his desk and waited for him to repeat that the camp was nothing but a sanatorium now and that it was quite different in the old days. But no.

"I think this is the first time I've interviewed a philosophy student here," he said. "Usually the pals sent to me are proles."

Die Kumpel die zu mir geschickt werden sind Proleten.

There were two German words in this sentence that I heard for the first time, *Kumpel* and *Proleten*. But to me they were at once identifiable, recognizable: transparent. Words that immediately placed you in a familiar world, one with an esoteric, universal language. Passwords that opened up a world.

In the night train that took us to Laroche-Migennes, in the cafés around the Contrescarpe, in the woods around Semur, we, too, had stopped using the word "comrades" when we spoke of our own people: we said "copains," "pals." And when we felt the need to identify with that obscure, impenetrable, radiating force, the working class, whose mission, we thought, was to change the world, when we spoke of the representatives of that class that we had known in the resistance, we, too, said "proles."

Kumpel and *Proleten*, pals and proles: they were the same words, they evoked the same ideological will to cohesion, the same pride in a secret society, which, one day soon, would become universal.

On Seifert's lips, as the sunlight outside laid blue reflections on the snow, as the calm, routine smoke rose from the crematorium, those words seemed to forbid me access to that fraternal yet hierarchical, open yet ritualized world of Communism. I was no longer just a philosophy student: my social background had suddenly risen to the surface, just as a corpse, bloated with water, swathed in weeds and mud, sometimes rises after an obscure drowning near an ocean beach. My corpse rose to the surface, in the form, suspect on more than one count, of a philosophy student: a young corpse of the old society.

Until that sunny, snowy February day in 1944, I had lived out my relationship with my social background in total innocence. I did not think to feel guilty, not at all. On the contrary, my self-awareness was not without a certain self-satisfaction. I was quite pleased to be who I was, to be where I was, to have come from where I came from.

The Spanish war had broken out over my childhood. It had apparently solved in one blow all the problems that I would otherwise have had to settle individually by myself. It had marked out the camps, in the harsh light of great historical crises. It was history, with its cunning and its violence, that had taken over my problems, and temporarily settled them for me. The crisis of history had saved me from the crises of adolescence, as it would later, in 1956, bring on the crisis of manhood. The critical history of those years had rid me of the faith of my ancestors, with their moral values, in the temporary innocence of storms and cataclysms.

No, really, I had no sense of guilt. At twenty, I thought rather highly of myself.

But that day Seifert had quietly thrown me back into my singularity—that is, into the suspect universality of my class background. I might at most be a pal, *ein Kumpel*, but I would never be a prole, *ein Prolet*. Never, that much was certain. Thus those passwords that had seemed to me to open up the doors of a fraternal world, in which each individual would be judged by what he did and treated according to his needs suddenly turned against me. I was sent back by those words into the sulfurous hell of ontology. Here I was, no longer to be judged by my actions, but classified according to my being, and, what was more, that part of my being that was most external to me, that most inert, adhesive part of me, for which I could never assume responsibility: my social being.

As I listened to Seifert talk to me quietly, all my ancestors, who had been landowners, warring small-holders, bourgeois adventurers who had made their fortunes in precious woods, distant spices, or the exploitation of Indian mines, all my ancestors who had fought for the wretched baroque glory of Spain—or for its liberty, for the progress of Enlightenment and Reason, there had been those among them, too—all my ancestors seemed to rise from the shadows of oblivion, from the sepia-colored sadness of old photographs, with their mahogany and rosewood furniture—*caoba y palosanto!*—their pale-faced women, with their languid gestures, their barouches, their Hispano convertibles, their sharp, clear sentences, spoken in provincial cafés on white, arcaded squares—they all seemed to rise and pull me by the feet down into some ontological hell from which I had mistakenly thought I had escaped. All my ancestors sniggered as they listened to Seifert: We told you you would never be one of them!

I listened to Seifert explaining to me how unusual my case was. Never, no, never, had the party organization sent him a philosophy student to work in the office of the *Arbeitsstatistik*. I felt that he was asking me how a philosophy student could *really* be a Communist.

I looked out at the snow. I knew that if I leaned my head a little I would see the crematorium chimney and its routine smoke. But I couldn't feel guilty. I don't seem to be very good at feeling guilt.

Two

Fernand Barizon is on the *Appellplatz*.

He is in the middle of the Block 40 formation, perfectly anonymous in the crowd of prisoners, well protected by the rows of men moving outward in front of him, behind him, and on either side of him.

He's beginning to learn a few tricks, is Barizon.

He knows that you should never put yourself forward, in either the literal or the figurative sense. If you are in the front row, the SS who does the count of the prisoners may stop in front of you, notice that you're missing a button, that the number sewn on your chest is not perfectly legible, that your posture doesn't exactly conform to the regulations. If he is in a bad temper, or just wants to take it out on someone, he may pick on anything at all. There will always be something to pick on. Then it's a fist in your face, a few truncheon blows, perhaps even some extra job to do, some punishment or other.

Fernand Barizon is hiding himself in the middle of the crowd of prisoners, melting into it, losing himself in it, forgetting himself in it. He's learned a few tricks.

It's still snowing, this lousy Sunday.

The Spaniard, lucky devil, is spending the roll call snug and warm in the *Arbeit* hut. A little while ago, when he turned around in front of the entrance to Block 40, before starting to run, Barizon noticed the Spaniard behind him, in the angle of the flight of steps that leads to the floor above.

The Spaniard has come from the Burgundy *maquis*, it seems. In any case, he's in the Party. He's called Gérard. It's the name he had in the *maquis*, apparently. Anyway, as far as Barizon knows, he doesn't have any other name.

In fact, Barizon never did know him by any other name. When he saw Gérard again, years later, fifteen years after Buchenwald, I was no longer called Gérard, I was called Sanchez, but it was obvious that Barizon didn't recognize me.

Fifteen years later, I went out onto the castle steps. The castle was a huge brick construction, with cornerstones in the right places: mock Louis something-or-other. But good-quality mock, sturdy, expensive mock. Set in the midst of a wooded park of several hectares, the castle was to serve as a vacation camp, at vacation times, for the children of a Communist-run municipality in the Paris suburbs. The French comrades had put the estate at our disposal for a meeting of several days' duration with the cadres and instructors of the Spanish Party who were working underground in the rural regions of Andalusia and Estremadura.

Night was falling. I went out onto the steps and smoked a cigarette. The meeting had been fascinating. "They were the most valiant of valiant Spain. . . ." A few lines from Hugo floated around in my memory. There were always a few bits of poems lying around in my memory, like morning mist over the meadows, for every occasion and on every subject. Or without any occasion. An innocent enough idiosyncrasy. Could be useful, too. In prison, or during the long waits on expeditions for the underground, it had often proved useful to be able to recite poems to myself.

I was standing on the steps, smoking a cigarette, and night was falling. In the drive at the foot of the steps, a few cars were waiting to take the comrades back to Paris in small groups. The drivers were there, too, chatting. I saw their cigarettes glowing in the half-light. And suddenly I heard Barizon's voice, Fernand Barizon's voice. He was grumbling about something or other. He was protesting to some Spanish comrade who was in charge of the technical organization of the meeting. He didn't agree with the timetable drawn up. So he protested.

He hadn't changed, Fernand.

Fifteen years after those Sundays in Buchenwald, in one silent pulse of my blood, I recognized Barizon's grumbling voice. I went down the steps and walked a little along the drive. An electric light dimly illuminated the group of drivers. I looked at Fernand Barizon's face, which stood out in the feeble light of that distant lamp. I wanted to go up to him, take him in my arms, tell him that he hadn't changed. "You really haven't changed, Fernand!" I wanted to remind him of those Sunday conversations of ours in Buchenwald. Did he remember Zarah Leander's singing during those Buchenwald afternoons?

Later, it so happened that I found myself in the car that he was driving back to Paris. I got out at one of the city gates. Before walking off to the métro station, I shook Barizon's hand. He looked me straight in the eye and said, "Good-bye, comrade!" but quite obviously he had not recognized me. When I happened to see an old photograph and saw what I looked like at twenty, I didn't recognize myself.

• • •

A few months after this meeting, I bumped into Fernand Barizon again.

I had to go to Prague, for some urgent business or other, though I haven't the slightest recollection what it was. But at that time everything we did seemed urgent. There was never a minute to lose. Underground political work secretes that ideology of the urgent, as the liver secretes bile.

So I had to go to Prague. It was urgent.

It had been decided that a car would take me to Geneva. From there I would travel to Zurich by train. From Zurich I would fly to Prague. I would enter Switzerland with a French identity card. I would leave Zurich by plane with a South American passport. This would throw anyone off my scent.

Pretty routine stuff.

Fernand Barizon had been chosen to drive me to Geneva.

Fernand drove very fast. We exchanged no more than a few words. I told him what identity I was traveling under. If my memory serves me right, I was called Salagnac that time, Camille Salagnac. We worked out our story as to why we were traveling to Geneva, in case anything went wrong at the frontier.

Then I sank back into my usual reveries.

As we entered Nantua, Fernand took his foot off the accelerator. He turned around to me with a broad, friendly smile.

"What about stopping for a bite to eat?" he said.

I nodded. "Why not?"

"Ever tasted Nantua sauce?" Fernand asked.

No, I never did taste Nantua sauce, but Nantua reminded me vaguely of something, or someone.

Shortly afterward, sitting in the restaurant of the Hôtel de France, as Barizon ordered crayfish in Nantua sauce, I vaguely remembered that I had known someone who had taught English in a school at Nantua. But who on earth could I have known who had been an English teacher at Nantua? It was rather incongruous to recall so precise a detail and yet not know to whom this detail related. I racked my brains. But no image, no name, emerged.

In any case, I did not associate Nantua with the sauce of the same name, which I discovered for the first time that day. With delighted anticipation, Barizon was explaining in great detail exactly how the sauce was made and exactly how it should taste. This reminded me of those arithmetical problems put to schoolchildren: make one liter of Béchamel sauce, add two deciliters of cream, reduce by a third, etc.

I was amused to think that Barizon had been clever enough to arrange this gastronomic stop-over at Nantua, probably calculating the speed of the car from the time we left Paris, so that he could turn to me, smiling innocently, just as we came into Nantua, and say, as if the idea had just occurred to him, "What about stopping for a bite to eat?" And, of course, it just happened to be lunchtime.

But then, in the dining room of the Hôtel de France at Nantua, Barizon was no longer talking about Nantua sauce. Suddenly he had started to talk about the great hunger he had felt in Buchenwald. Suddenly Nantua sauce was no longer the accompaniment of the dish about to be served to us, but the realization of a dream he had had in Buchenwald. A dream of cream, Béchamel, and crayfish butter that was to be poured over the nostalgic, delirious stories aroused by the hunger he had felt in Buchenwald.

As the smell from the sauces rose to his nostrils, Barizon became more voluble. He told me about his life in Buchenwald. I nodded, listening to him recount a life that was also my life. Barizon had still not recognized me. All he knew was that I was a Spanish Communist leader traveling under the pseudonym of Camille Salagnac. He was to drive me to Geneva, that was all he knew. Stimulated by the rich, heavy Nantua sauce, Barizon told me about our life in Buchenwald.

But was it really our life?

I listened, nodded, said nothing. Yet I wanted to interrupt this account, correct certain details, remind him of episodes that he seemed to have forgotten.

For example, Barizon had said nothing about Zarah Leander. And, after all, Buchenwald wasn't really Buchenwald without Zarah Leander!

When we happened to be on the night shift at the same time, Barizon from the *Gustloff* Works, I from the *Arbeitsstatistik*, we would sometimes have long chats together in the afternoon, in the quiet of the empty mess, after we'd slept all morning. We'd eat a slice of black bread smeared with a thin film of margarine. We'd talk. The loudspeakers poured out sweet music.

The SS officer in the watchtower must have had a weakness for Zarah Leander's songs. He put on nothing but her records.

One can imagine the SS warrant officer on duty in the watchtower. From where he's sitting in an armchair, his feet on the table, he can see the entire camp spread out across the hillside. Beyond the outer wall with its electrified barbed wire stretches the plain, dotted with white farmhouses and peaceful hamlets.

He has a perfect view, that warrant officer on duty. Even Goethe could not have had such a fine view, for the trees that were cut down to build the camp must have blocked the view in his day. So, as he sits facing the blue mountains that rise beyond the Thuringian plain, and since he has no Eckermann next to him to jot down any immortal reflections that may occur to him, the warrant officer on duty puts on Zarah Leander's records. All the camp loudspeakers are transmitting that deep voice, with its vibrant tremolos, the voice that talks only of love:

Schön war die Zeit
da wir uns so geliebt. . . .

The record gets played over and over again during the quiet Buchenwald afternoons.

Barizon and I are sitting together in the empty mess in Block 40, upstairs, in C Wing. We are eating the thin slice of black bread that we have kept for this special moment, in the relative silence of these wonderful leisurely afternoons when we are on the night shift. We listen vaguely to Zarah Leander's voice, which tells of love, as if life were nothing but a succession of tiny joys, heart-rending memories, feelings that tinkle like crystal.

So stelle ich mir die Liebe vor,
ich bin nicht mehr allein. . .

We talk while listening vaguely to the deep, vibrant voice of Zarah Leander.

Sometimes I translate for Barizon an article in *Völkische Beobachter* or the weekly *Das Reich*. We talk about the war, and the future of the revolution. Sometimes, too, on days when the slice of bread is really too thin, when we can do nothing to make it last longer, when there's no use chewing it slowly, meticulously, rolling it into tiny crumbly balls under the tongue, between the teeth, no good, the bread has melted, it's as if one had never had any bread, on such days we recount meals we have eaten.

Barizon does most of the talking. Where food is concerned, I don't have much of a memory, not much imagination.

I don't really have memories of what I eat. I only have some childhood memories in which the issue of food is secondary. The meringues on Sunday in Madrid. The fritters at breakfast, on feast days, after Mass at San Jeronimo's. Or, and this never ceases to amaze Fernand, the tender memory of the chick-peas in a stockpot which were cooked every week, without fail. The fact that one can remember with tenderness and satisfaction the chick-peas in some pathetic stockpot is beyond Barizon's comprehension, and he doesn't hesitate to tell me so. His own memories of food are somewhat more refined. And yet it's Barizon who is the prole and I who come from a bourgeois family. That's obvious enough, anyway. And Barizon never lets me forget it. When the subject of my father's cars comes up, in the course of some conversation or other, they are De Dion–Boutons, Oldsmobile convertibles, Graham-Page saloons, and even Hispano-Suizas. The fact that one can have such a luxurious childhood and yet remember with nostalgia chick-peas in a pathetic stockpot opens up for Barizon new horizons on the complexity of the human soul.

Fifteen years later, in the dining room of the Hôtel de France at Nantua, as I listen to Barizon's stories, I nod and say nothing. I pretend to be interested, but actually I am disappointed. He doesn't talk about his life very well, Fernand. The memories are all jumbled up and come out every which way. There's no subtlety in his account, and he forgets some of the most important things.

He forgets to tell me about his escapade in Brittany, for instance. He forgets to tell me about his joy ride with Juliette.

Yet in Buchenwald, on those afternoons when we found ourselves in the deserted mess of Block 40, because we had both been on the night shift, the *Nachtschicht*— those afternoons when the piece of black bread was so thin that there was no use chewing it, no use sucking it like a sweet to make it last longer, because it still wouldn't last—on those afternoons, floating in the sickly-sweet crooning of Zarah Leander's songs, there was always a moment when Fernand remembered his escapade in Brittany with a young woman named Juliette. It was Barizon's favorite memory, his fetish in the vague, distant world of imaginary experience.

It always happened the same way.

Excited by hunger, by the frustration of that piece of black bread almost devoid of real consistency, which melted as soon as it was in his mouth, Barizon turned to that joy ride in Brittany with Juliette. This was understandable. They had both had a few days of total freedom, divided between the bed and the table. Thus, through that memory of unbounded pleasure, Fernand exorcised his most insistent desires. The stories of great meals long ago always ended up with crazy descriptions of his frolics with Juliette, who officiated in Barizon's memory as the emblem of past happiness.

In the end, I knew all there was to know about Juliette. I knew her as if I had created her myself—or, rather, as if I had created her for myself. Her long legs, the full curves of her breasts, the greedy, skillful sweetness of her mouth, her laughter and her cries at the moment of pleasure. Juliette had become the companion of our dreams; her body was a pure, magnificent gift that Fernand had given me in those Buchenwald afternoons, as Zarah Leander's voice crooned on.

But fifteen years later, at Nantua, as we were finishing our crayfish in Nantua sauce, Barizon left out both Juliette and Zarah Leander from his account of Buchenwald. And so, with some anxiety, looking across at Barizon, who seemed not to wish to recognize me, who had skipped Juliette and Zarah Leander, I began to wonder whether I had really lived through all that.

Once again, the insidious interrogation rose inside me.

Had my life at Buchenwald been a dream? Or, on the contrary, was my life since I had come back from Buchenwald just a dream? Had I quite simply died, fifteen years ago, and was all this—Nantua, the crayfish in Nantua sauce, and Prague, the old Pinkas Jewish cemetery, and that whole delicate fabric of political activity, whose stitches unraveled as soon as they had been made—just a dream of gray, premonitory smoke on the Ettersberg?

I looked at Barizon, I listened to his story, nodded; I really did not know what to reply to that wounding final question. Why had there been all this, rather than nothing? Rather than the smoke from the crematorium in the blind emptiness of a transparent winter sky?

Probably Juliette—at least I hoped so, I desperately hoped so—could have answered this question. She would have had something to say. But at Nantua that day, Juliette seemed to have deserted us. And I had nothing to say. I had no answer to that question.

As I nodded and listened vaguely to Barizon's account, I reflected that I had found myself, not long before, in a similar situation.

In Madrid, at the time of that 1960 trip to Geneva with Barizon, I was living in a safe house belonging to the PCE, the Spanish Communist Party. It was in a working-class district, at Ventas, on the Calle Concepción-Bahamonde. In my childhood, the city came to an end there. Beyond was a desolate landscape, gray and ocher, the high Castilian plateau hollowed out by the ridges, or, rather, the scars, of the landscape, covered with the sores of shantytowns, the pustules of huts with mud walls and rusty corrugated iron roofs, packed with farm laborers looking for work on the building sites. There were also, in that dusty landscape, a few oases: the gleaming-white buildings of market gardens, built next to some spring or artesian well, surrounded by vegetable gardens and orchards tenaciously maintained against the rigors of the climate.

But Madrid had changed since my childhood.

In 1960, when I lived on the Calle Concepción-Bahamonde, in that suburb of Ventas, only a few leprous stains from the shantytowns and a few market-garden buildings remained. But the urban sprawl had begun. New, anonymous districts surrounded these vestiges of the past on every side.

The Calle Concepción-Bahamonde was a quiet little street, away from the circular road thar marked the boundary of the old urban center. The buildings had three stories, with wrought-iron balconies.

In the evening, when I came back to the Calle Concepción-Bahamonde, I did not get off at "Manuel-Becerra," the nearest subway station. I would get off at a station farther on. At "Goya," for example. If I came back by taxi, I did the same thing. I asked the driver to stop some distance away from my street. Then, each time, I improvised some different, capricious itinerary. I would go back partly the way I had come and stop at one of the cafés in the neighborhood. This enabled me to check that I had not been followed, that nobody was showing any interest in me.

The apartment on the Calle Concepción-Bahamonde in which I occupied two small rooms had been bought in behalf of the PCE by a couple of party members, Maria and Manuel Azaustre. In 1939, at the end of the civil war, Maria and Manuel went into exile in France. But they had come back to Spain quite legally, being unknown to Franco's police. In Spain, they did not take part in any political activity. The mission that they had agreed to carry out consisted of buying an apartment in Madrid in behalf of the Party and keeping it at the disposal of our underground apparatus. Manuel worked as a private chauffeur, and Maria took care of the apartment.

Sometimes, in the evening, I dined with Manuel and Maria. It was during those evenings, over coffee and the inevitable recounting of memories, that Manuel told me about his time in Mauthausen. He had spent five years there, one of the harshest Nazi concentration camps.

On January 2, 1941, Reinhard Heydrich, head of the Gestapo and of the Nazi security service, wrote a memorandum marked secret (GEHEIM!) entitled "Einstufung der Konzentrationslager," a classification of the concentration camps. The first category, envisaged for the least serious cases, prisoners capable of re-education and improvement *(unbedingt besserungsfähige Schutzhäftlinge)*, comprised the camps of Dachau, Sachsenhausen, and Auschwitz 1. The second category, envisaged for more dangerous prisoners who were nonetheless capable of being re-educated and improved *(jedoch noch erziehungs-und besserungsfähige Schutzhäftlinge)*, comprised the camps of Buchenwald, Flossenburg, Neuengamme, and Auschwitz 2. The third category was reserved for the most serious cases, prisoners regarded as beyond re-education or improvement *(kaum noch erziehbare Schutzhäftlinge)*; they were to be confined in a single camp, that of Mauthausen.

Of course, this insane, typically bureaucratic rationalization of offenses and punishments was not applied literally. On the one hand, the organization of the final solution of the Jewish question, with the transfer of the Jewish deportees to the camps in Poland and the establishment in those camps of the means of mass extermination; on the other hand, the requirements of the war industry and a consequent distribution of deported labor —these two factors, especially after 1942, constantly interfered with the application of Reinhard Heydrich's directives. This did not prevent Mauthausen, however, from being one of the harshest of Nazi camps, always.

So we drank our coffee on the Calle Concepción-Bahamonde, and Manuel Azaustre told me about his life in Mauthausen.

Manuel knew nothing about my past, of course. All he knew was that I was one of the party leaders. He knew me under the name of Rafael. Rafael Bustamonte, probably, or Rafael Artigas, I don't remember. He did not know that I, too, had been deported. Without saying a word, I listened as he recounted to me, awkwardly, interminably, with the prolixity natural to that sort of narrative, his life in the camp, the life of the camps. Sometimes, when it became too confused, when it went off in all directions, I wanted to chip in. But I could say nothing, of course. I had to preserve my anonymity.

Some months later in the autumn of 1960, I was at Nantua. We were finishing lunch at the Hôtel de France and I was listening, nodding occasionally, as Fernand Barizon recounted his life in Buchenwald.

But it seemed to me that he described Buchenwald no better than Manuel Azaustre had described Mauthausen, in the little dining room on the Calle Concepción-Bahamonde in Madrid. Perhaps that isn't the problem for them, recounting convincingly the life of the camps. Perhaps the problem for them is quite simply that they have been there and survived.

Yet it isn't so simple. Has one really experienced something that one is unable to describe, something whose minimum truth one is unable to reconstruct in a meaningful way—and so make communicable? Doesn't living, in the full sense of the term, mean transforming one's personal experience into consciousness—that is to say, into memorized experience that is capable at the same time of integration into the future? But can one assume any experience without more or less mastering its language? The history—the stories, the narratives, the memories, the eyewitness accounts in which it survives —lives on. The text, the very texture, the tissue of life.

At Nantua, as I listened to Fernand Barizon's rigmarole, I wondered why it is always the same people who tell stories, who write history. Oh, I knew very well, at Nantua, that it is the masses who make history! It had been repeated to me so often, in so many different tones of voice—sometimes in cutting, not to say decapitating tones, but also in soft, gentle tones, during the times of broad alliances and outstretched hands, of a hundred flowers blooming, though after that it's back to the shears and the sickle, to cut flowers, and cut hands—that the masses make history, and better still, *their* history, that I ended up repeating this nonsense, pretending to believe this collossal confidence trick. When I felt disillusioned or just ideologically subtler, I could always cling to one of Marx's more cynical, less triumphal formulas, to the effect that men make their history but don't know the history they are making. Which means, quite crudely, for him who has ears to hear, that men don't make the history they want, dream about, and *think* they are making. They do not therefore make their history: they always make something else. This brings us back to the beginning of my interrogation, which is really more tautological than metaphysical: who makes real history?

At Nantua, savoring the *écrevisses à la sauce Nantua,* which Barizon had so cunningly ordered for us, I ended up by putting the question in parentheses, thanks to a temporary, compromise formula: The masses may make history, but they certainly don't write it. It is the domi-nant minorities—which on the left are called "van-guards" and on the right, and even in the center, "natural élites"—that write history. And rewrite it, if need be, if the need is felt, and, from their dominant point of view, the need is often felt. But to return to the confused accounts of Manuel Azaustre and Fernand Barizon, describing life in the camps is no easy matter. I haven't solved the problem myself. I, too, get confused. What exactly am I recounting, anyway? A December Sunday in 1944 at Buchenwald, while the British troops were crushing the Greek Communist resistance under Stalin's jaundiced, impassive eye? Or that drive with Barizon in 1960 that took me from Paris to Nantua, and from Nantua to Prague, with all the memories that it conjures up for me?

At that very moment, at Nantua, for example, as I listened absent-mindedly to Fernand Barizon, I remembered who had been an English teacher at a school in Nantua. It was Pierre Courtade—unless I was mixing reality and fiction. Perhaps it was a character in some story by Courtade who had been a teacher at Nantua. Anyway, through a story by Pierre about himself, or about some fictitious character who was more or less himself, Nantua was intimately associated in my memory with Pierre Courtade.

It was, of course, impossible for me to say exactly what I thought of Courtade during those few fleeting moments of our gastronomic stop-over at Nantua. I am writing this fifteen years later. The ideas, the sensations, the judgments are superimposed in a chronological layer restructured by my present opinions. In 1960 I probably didn't think the same of Pierre Courtade as I do today. In any case, in 1960 I didn't think, or didn't think I thought, the same about myself as I do now. What I think now may even be fundamentally different from what I thought then.

So I am not going to try to recount our stop-over at Nantua as if we were there, as if you were there. We are not there, we shall never be there in the same way. Pierre Courtade is dead. I, too, at least as Federico Sanchez, that distant ghost who accompanied Fernand Barizon, am dead. And what about Barizon himself? I have heard nothing more about Barizon for the last fifteen years. And yet, the last time I met him, in 1964, we promised to see each other again.

I was listening to Barizon absent-mindedly, thinking of Pierre Courtade.

That summer, I had earned the right to a vacation in the Soviet Union. It was a privilege given us every two years in the higher circles of the PCE. ("Higher circles": not a bad phrase! You can almost hear the music of the celestial spheres, of closed, smooth worlds gliding majestically through the eternal space of knowledge and power!)

So I spent July in the Crimea, at Foros, in a house reserved for the staff of the Central Committee of the Russian Party and for the leaders of foreign parties. "Brother Parties," as they used to say: in the sense, I suppose, that Cain and Abel were brothers.

The main building of this house, at the farthest tip of the Crimea, southeast of Sebastopol, was a former dacha, luxuriously appointed in a rather stuffy, old-fashioned kind of way. It had been the vacation home of some nineteenth-century Russian landowner or industrialist. At the time of my visit, the bath water was still heated by means of huge wood fires, lit under enameled cast-iron tanks by silent old women servants, wearing gray linen uniforms. It was said that Gorky had spent long rest periods here toward the end of his life. One could see why: the setting and climate must have reminded him of Capri.

So, in July 1960, we and our families found ourselves once again at Foros for the summer vacation—Dolores

Ibarruri, Santiago Carrillo, Enrique Lister, and me—in other words, Federico Sanchez.

The functionaries of the Russian Central Committee were watching from a distance the black-clad figure of "La Pasionaria," who never went to the beach, but wandered through the enormous, romantic park, with its lakes, rock gardens, and water lilies. The night before, Lister had kept us up, recounting for the thousandth time, with all his usual self-satisfaction, the military exploits of the 11th Division or 5th Corps of the Republican Army, which he had commanded during the civil war. As for Carrillo, he was particularly relaxed that summer. The Sixth Congress of the PCE, at which he had been made general secretary, replacing La Pasionaria, for whom we had invented an honorary post as president of the Party, had already taken place. One of the major ambitions of his life had been achieved (the other, that of being accepted, recognized, by society in general, and good society in particular, had not yet made its appearance).

That summer, the latent conflict between the Russians and the Chinese had broken out into the open, or at least into the higher circles (again!) of the Communist movement. In June, at Bucharest, during the congress of the Rumanian Party, Peng Chen and Khrushchev had almost come to blows. "If you want Stalin's sword," Nikita Sergeevich had yelled, "take it! It's covered in blood. And we'll give you his corpse as a bonus. Take Stalin's mummy back with you!" It was Lister who told us about this confrontation. He had been the representative of the PCE at the congress of the Rumanian Party.

Again, in Peking, in the corridors at a meeting of the World Labor Federation, the Chinese had taken the offensive, attacking Khrushchev's general line and advocating a "return to Leninism."

We had hardly arrived in Moscow, where we were to

spend a few days before leaving for the Crimea, when Kolomiez, the functionary of the Russian Central Committee who at the time dealt with Spanish matters under the direct responsibility of Zagladin and Ponomarev, had come to meet us with the first documents of the polemics exchanged between the Russian and Chinese parties. They were, of course, confidential documents. We were shut up in a room to read them and were refused permission to take notes. As soon as we had finished reading them, Kolomiez took the documents away.

Kolomiez was a jolly individual, and an inexhaustible vodka drinker. I had first met him in 1954, during the Fifth Congress of the PCE, which had taken place in secret on the banks of Lake Machovo, in Bohemia. Kolomiez spoke Castilian fluently, and was relatively well informed about the situation in Spain. He was the first member of the Russian Party with whom I had been able to exchange opinions since my disconcerting experiences with the Russians in Buchenwald.

It was a decisive meeting, certainly, one that enabled me to understand in a flash the appalling political level, the dull, petty mental world of the Russian Communists, thirty-three years after the October Revolution. We were talking about the strikes that had taken place in Catalonia in 1951, after a long decade of defeats for the working class. Suddenly Kolomiez asked me what role, in my opinion, had been played in these massive strikes of Catalan workers by British intelligence agents. Stunned, I asked him to repeat his question. Yes, I had heard him correctly. According to Kolomiez, British intelligence agents must have played a role in those strikes, or the strikes could never have taken place. I tried, politely and politically, to show him the absurdity of this notion. But I failed to convince him. We were speaking two different languages, even though the words were identical. We lived in two different worlds. For Kolomiez, the social classes, the masses, the forces of production, the groups structured around the subjective determination to struggle, all that was no more than an inert, shapeless magma, ready to be manipulated by the apparatuses, but incapable of creative spontaneity. Thus, since the apparatus of the Catalan Party had obviously been too weak to cause and direct the strikes in 1951, it followed that some other apparatus must have been responsible for them. Why they had concluded that it was a British intelligence network—rather than the Catholic Church or the Freemasons—was a mystery that I never tried to solve.

I had seen Kolomiez again on the final evening of the Sixth Congress of the Spanish Party, the same congress at which we had made Carrillo party general secretary. To celebrate the event, Carrillo had been invited to dinner by a group of delegates ("fraternal" delegates, of course!) from the Eastern European parties, and he asked me to go with him, fearing perhaps that he might be bored if he went alone, unless his choice had some political significance. I was by far the youngest member of the Executive Committee of the PCE. What is more, I was an intellectual of bourgeois origin who had worked underground in Spain. By favoring me with this invitation, Carrillo wanted perhaps to show all those Rumanians, Russians, East Germans, Bulgarians, etc., etc., that the ruling group of the PCE possessed the correct breadth of vision and determination to rejuvenate itself.

For the enlightened despotism of the Great Helmsmen needs the "light" cast by intellectuals, as the epithet itself suggests. And when the Great Helmsmen are autodidacts made in the image of the party apparatus itself, like Carrillo, it is usually intellectuals who hold the candle, in the corridors of power and at the bedsides of the enlightened despots. Some hold it to the end of their days, voyeurs fascinated by the spectacle of their own fascination, offering as an excuse fidelity to the Cause (of the working class, of the people, of the wretched of the earth), whereas they are faithful only to the successive despots and to their own lack of fidelity to what really matters. Others decide, one fine day, always too late, to save their souls, and to become once again what they really are. They snuff out the candle and return to the night of their solitary question.

In any case, that evening at the Sixth Congress, the vodka and wine flowed, and Kolomiez was already pretty drunk before we reached the main courses. His speech was getting more and more incoherent. Or, rather, oddly coherent. With perverse pleasure, a comrade from the Rumanian Politburo kept refilling the Russian's ever-empty glass. Then, near the middle of the meal, the brakes off, all inhibitions lifted, Kolomiez began to harangue us. He began, in a slurred voice, to deliver a speech in praise of Stalin, even threatening us with his return. Yes, Stalin would soon be back, ready once again to guide the masses, who, ever since he had left them, had languished in confusion and disarray. Comrade Stalin, that giant among men, would come and put us all in our places. We were no more than straws in his almighty hand. He was the soaring eagle and we were no more than blind kittens.

A deathly silence had fallen over all of us as we listened to this voice from the past, this still-present voice. The comrade from the Rumanian Politburo stared back at Kolomiez, stony-faced. In his look were mingled contempt, horror, and a sort of desperate, fascinated fear that made his eyelids twitch. The Rumanian comrade turned toward us. "There!" he seemed to be saying to us. "These are our masters. These are the men who decide our future!" The Rumanian comrade remained stony-faced; his fingers tightened around a glass. Suddenly Kolomiez collapsed and rolled off his chair. Then, pushing Kolomiez with his foot under the table, the Rumanian comrade raised his glass and said, in a flat voice, with all the incisiveness of despair, "A long death to Comrade Stalin!" And we raised our glasses to the death of the Georgian, to his eternal death.

Among the foreigners invited to Foros, in addition to our Spanish group, was Adam Schaff and his family. At the time this Polish philosopher was still a member of the Central Committee of the United Workers' Party, as the Polish Communist Party was called. He had brought with him, as vacation reading, the same book as I: Sartre's *Critique of Dialectical Reason*. That brought us together. For hours, on the beach, we had talked very freely about the problems of our respective parties and about the situation of the Communist movement in general. I thought rather naïvely—not having yet emerged from the illusions about possible reforms created by the Twentieth Congress of the Soviet Communist Party—that the Russo-Chinese dispute would have the effect of loosening the ideological grip on the European Communist parties. I thought that these parties would be able to exercise a more decisive influence over the movement as a whole. But Adam Schaff, who was more aware of what was going on than I was, thought the opposite. He thought that the Russo-Chinese conflict would usher in a new ideological ice age. Certainly the dominance of the One would be broken. But by dividing into Two, this One would not produce the conditions for a dialectical supersession: it would simply produce a double discourse, monolithic and monotheistic, a duplication of the orthodox monism. The first consequence of this would be a more or less severe tightening of control in both camps. Poland, of course, was in the Russian camp and would know the consequences soon enough.

He was not very optimistic.

On the third day of our interminable discussions, Carrillo took me to one side. Rather embarrassed, he told me that the Soviet comrades did not view too kindly my conversations with Adam Schaff. Was I not aware that, during the Polish October of 1956,* Schaff had taken up clearly anti-Soviet positions? Of course, he was a member of the Central Committee of the Polish Party, but that was not a sufficient guarantee. Since 1956, the leadership of the Polish Party had done well for themselves. That was what the Soviet comrades had said. I asked Carrillo what he himself thought about the matter. Carrillo did not have a personal view of the matter; he was simply passing on the views of Soviet comrades. Personally, he said, he could understand very well that I should get along so well with Schaff—after all, Schaff was, like me, an intellectual. However, we had to take into account that we were in the USSR, at the invitation of the Soviet comrades. There was no point in provoking conflicts and misunderstandings over what, after all, was only a minor matter. In any case, it was up to me to decide, Carrillo concluded with an ambiguous smile.

So I decided to look for Schaff and tell him in detail what had happened. He was not particularly surprised, I must admit. Such an intervention on the part of the Russians struck him as perfectly logical. They'd never change, he said. He thought, nevertheless, that it might be better to break off our conversations. There was no point

---

*In October 1956, after widespread expressions of popular discontent with Soviet rule in Poland, Wladyslaw Gomulka was made secretary general of the Polish Communist Party. Gomulka, perceived as a nationalist, succeeded in wresting some degree of independence from the Soviet Union. —ED.

in causing misunderstandings and conflicts, however minor. In any case, we had said what we had to say.

But I'm not going to recount in detail everything that happened that summer in the Crimea. That is not at all my purpose. My mind was carried back to that vacation in the Crimea, my last stay in the Soviet Union, only because of Pierre Courtade. In a moment I shall come back to Pierre Courtade.

Not that I've said all I have to say about Russia. On the contrary, I could talk for hours on the subject. For whole nights. Until I have lost voice, breath, and reason. Anyway, there's no need to raise one's voice, or pile on adjectives, when talking about Russia. My account will be restrained, in a way almost grim, certainly gray—that same thin, transparent, silver-gray of the Russian skies over the endless plains, over the immense rivers—an account in *grisaille*, at least on the surface, but with iridescent depths, unexpected variations of pattern, tiny fireworks of feelings and language.

But I am not so naïve, so spontaneously sincere, and therefore so crude, as Fernand Barizon or Manuel Azaustre. My account of Russia, if I wanted to tell it now, would not just pour out. It would be constructed like a narrative. Nothing is less innocent than writing. So I would place at the center of the narrative, like a magnet that would attract all the iron filings of the secondary episodes, an outdoor party. The setting would be one of the rest houses that surrounded our place at Foros, situated in a zone cut off from ordinary mortals by barbed wire and the armed soldiers of the security forces.

A party, then. There would be dancing.

In the heady, resinous evening air, on a huge terrace surrounded by the beseeching candles of tall, motionless cypresses, a band would be playing dance tunes. Not just any dance tunes, of course. No music requiring physical contact would be played. The passions and dreams of the body are incompatible with the requirements of socialism, as everyone knows. The body is no longer anything more than a cog in the productive machine, and as such it is fed, developed, given medical care that is theoretically free and, though incompetent, sufficiently renews its capacity for work. But the crazy fantasies of the body must not be aroused; nothing must be done to provoke an uncontrollable lurch toward the waste of desire. So, no sexy dancing. No physical contact.

The dance music that was played endlessly through the bluish, odoriferous Crimean night had been chosen according to the strict criteria of that Victorian morality that always accompanies—and idealizes—the crude imperatives of productivity. I thought of the Spanish priests who, during that same period, for no doubt very different reasons, were writing illustrated pamphlets directed at the young, condemning the *baile agarrado*, body-to-body dancing, a source of diabolical temptations. They would have been pleased, those Spanish priests. There was no body-to-body dancing at the Crimean parties.

In 1960, the favorite dance seemed to be a sort of minuet called—I'm not making this up—the *pas de grâce*, a name that the Russians pronounced in a rather approximate way, often without knowing the exact meaning, the real origin, as one would say "polka," "tango," or "Charleston." Those responsible for ordinary people's, and therefore organized, leisure had discovered in the past of monarchical France this collective dance, whose charming figures unfolded chastely, interminably. Of course, those prudish, reverential dance steps were so much dust in the eyes, a way of asserting hypocritically— another Victorian characteristic—the virtues of the society in which the qualities of the new man had to blossom.

In fact, man—old or new—and the Eve of his chaste, productive paradise bedded down in the rest houses with all the frenzy of the old order. For the holiday eroticism of the upper cadres of the bureaucracy could only be practiced outside the legal limits of the matrimonial couple. With few exceptions, husbands and wives could not enjoy their paid vacations together, since the vacations were organized by their respective employers, in different rest houses. Thus those few weeks of summer vacation on the beaches of the Black Sea or the Baltic were devoted to a sort of institutionalized adultery, most likely conceived by the system of organized leisure as a harmless, even positive, distraction from the difficulties of everyday married life. Even adultery became one more mechanism of the gratifying reproduction of the labor force and of social discipline.

And so, one evening, I was watching the swirling figures of the *pas de grâce*, danced by dozens of disunited couples on a paved terrace, surrounded by cypresses. Suddenly it seemed to me that I understood it all.

I looked at those men and women striving to execute the *pas de grâce*. They were quite obviously happy. They were fat and strong, obviously healthy. They were functionaries of the Party, the trade unions, the state or industrial administration. There were no scientists among them, no artists or writers of note. For a long time now, such individuals lived in quite a different universe, in another enclosure. They had private dachas. They consumed individually their portion of the surplus value produced by the Russian workers. The vacationers in the rest houses, on the other hand, consumed collectively their share of this surplus value, their share of the surplus labor of the Russian workers. It was their function, their rank in the hierarchy of the apparatuses, that gave them this right of collective, privileged, but anonymous consumption. If they fell into disgrace tomorrow, they would lose their right, and others, as anonymous and interchangeable as themselves, would take their place. Meanwhile, they danced the *pas de grâce*. They were happy.

Through their discipline, their silence, their pragmatism, their submission to Correct Thought—taken up in all its contradictory twists and turns—they had won this right to be happy. Through their courage, too, no doubt. They had fought fearlessly to defend the society that had given them these privileges.

First they had fought against the Whites and interventionists, to defend this nascent society, its outlines still blurred. And then they fought against the left-wing deviationists, who understood nothing of the problems of the peasants and the "nepmen,"* they were told. And then they fought against the right-wing deviationists, who understood only too well, it seemed, the problems of the peasants and the *nepmen*. And then, in a second civil war, even bloodier than the first, they had decimated the peasants and the *nepmen*, which was an expeditious but illusory way of liquidating their problems. And then, when they had been victorious through blood and iron over all those enemies, when the new hierarchies of their society seemed to have been consolidated, in the mid-thirties, they had to take up the struggle once more to exterminate—this time, the Communists themselves. The mysteries of the dialectic had been explained to them and they had understood. Since the enemy classes had been liquidated, it was within the Party itself that the class struggle would now take place. It was necessary, therefore, to exterminate the Party itself. It was simple, if you just thought about it. Anyway, it seemed clear enough

---

*New Economic Policy, a reintroduction of private enterprise, suppressed by Stalin. —ED.

that the Party as a whole had agreed with this analysis: it had quietly gone to its own extermination. And then they had to fight against the German invaders, who had spat at the dialectically fraternal hand extended to them by Stalin. So they had fought hard, often courageously. One had only to see, on the Crimean beaches, the scars that marked the bodies of most of the men between thirty-five and fifty to understand that they had fought hard. The other scars, those of earlier battles, were not visible.

I watched them dance the *pas de grâce* in Crimea, in that summer of 1960. They were the "little screws" and "little cogwheels" of the Great Mechanism of the State and Party, and it was to their health that Stalin had raised his glass, on the day that victory over Germany was celebrated. Yet that victory had not been enough. There now rose up new enemies, all the more dangerous in that they were more underhanded, in that they themselves did not know in what their hostility, their dissidence, or their reservations with regard to Soviet power consisted. They were enemies, pure and simple. Prisoners of war, in hundreds of thousands, who had survived the Nazi Stalags, who were to perish in the Gulags, and who were so devious that they did not even wish to understand the crimes they had committed. Political deportees and labor deportees, who had struggled and suffered out of reach of the paternal hand of Soviet power too long to be recoverable. Ukrainians, Latvians, Lithuanians, Estonians, Tatars, imbued with their pernicious, reactionary notion of the nation that had to be defended, preserved, constructed. And, lastly, the Jews, the eternal enemy, who were now insolently raising their heads.

As I watched the little screws and cogwheels of the Great Mechanism dance away the night, I suddenly seemed to be living through the reality imagined by Adolfo Bioy Casares in his novel *Morel's Invention*. It seemed to me that all these people had been dead a long time, that their gestures and laughter as they danced the *pas de grâce* were merely an illusion produced by some machine for reproducing the past, rather like Bioy Casares's fictional inventions. Suddenly I felt as though I were witnessing a dance of death. Perhaps Russia itself was dead and this music, this dancing, this futile happiness founded on oceans of blood, those pure, affecting voices that sometimes rose in chorus of an evening, perhaps all that was merely the last twinkle of a dead star.

But that evening, in 1960, I stopped on the threshold of a final question, an ultimate interrogation. If Russia was dead, who had killed her?

But I promised to get back to Pierre Courtade. Two or three days before we left Foros, we had been told that Pierre Courtade was coming. At the time he was the Moscow correspondent of *L'Humanité*, the French Party newspaper, and apparently he was coming to Foros for a vacation. I was delighted at the prospect of seeing Pierre again. I had known him since 1945. I had seen him in all sorts of places, but this was the first time I would see him in the Soviet Union, in a rest house of the Russian Central Committee. I looked forward to some lively conversations.

But for some reason or other, his arrival was postponed. We left Foros without seeing him. Indeed, I don't think I saw him again before he died.

I had been introduced to Pierre, shortly after I came out of Buchenwald, by a Hungarian comrade, Georges Szekeres.

And how did I meet Szekeres?

Still listening rather absent-mindedly to Fernand Barizon's monologue, I was in the spring sunshine, in Paris, fifteen years before, on the sidewalk of the Boulevard Saint-Germain. I was walking toward the Café de Flore with Michel Herr, two or three days after I had got back from Buchenwald, in 1945. It was Michel Herr who introduced me to Georges Szekeres.

Michel was wearing the uniform of a captain of the First Army. He was in Paris for a few days, on some mission or other or on leave, I don't remember. The evening before, we had sat up late, talking endlessly about the last two years, since my arrest at Joigny. I had found Michel nervous, painfully tense, beneath the mask of virile assurance he had worn in the bars and clubs of Montparnasse, where we had hung around until dawn. At the Petit Schubert, they played the same brassy, raucous music that had graced our parties in 1942. At Jimmy's, Michel had called two girls over to our table. They drank heartily, but they must have been pretty bored, for Michel talked the whole time of Hegel and the meaning of history. The night drew to its end, stars twinkling through the mist of my tiredness. Suddenly one of the girls started to stroke my hair lightly. "Did they shave your head?" she asked. "Did you sleep with the Boches?" Michel looked at me and we burst out laughing. My memory of what followed is rather confused. I'm not sure I can give a proper account of it. I'm not even sure I could give any account of it. No, I have not the slightest intention of giving an account of how that night with Michel and the girls from Jimmy's ended up.

But some hours later, outside the Café de Flore, Michel introduced me to Georges Szekeres.

I saw Szekeres again, at the same place, four years later, almost to the day, in the spring of 1949. In the meantime, we had become friends. But one day in that spring of 1949, Roger Vailland* had telephoned me. He was calling in behalf of Courtade. He had been told to warn all the pals, he said. Szekeres was in Paris, but we must refuse to

---

*Writer, fellow traveler, and thereafter member of the French Communist Party. —ED.

speak to him, he said. Szekeres was a traitor, Vailland said. He had deserted his post as counselor at the Hungarian embassy in Rome and, when summoned back to Budapest by the Hungarian Party, had refused. When he had conveyed the information as directed, Vailland added a few words of his own. Szekeres's attitude did not really surprise him: hadn't I noticed that Szekeres had always had a rather aristocratic outlook, that deep down he had always despised the people?

In fact, at this time, the trial of Laszlo Rajk was already being planned in Hungary.* And Georges Szekeres, as a Communist who had emigrated to the West, and during the resistance in France had had contact with groups of all kinds and agents of Allied networks, was an ideal candidate for a role in the trial to come. Szekeres, understanding what was happening, had left his post and asked for political asylum in France. The French police had worked out the deal: he was granted political asylum on condition that he become an informer for the French secret service. Otherwise, he would be expelled from France and handed over to the authorities in his own country. Szekeres refused the deal. He was taken to the frontier of the Soviet occupation zone in Germany and handed over to the Russian security forces.

Szekeres himself told me how this story ended when we met again, years later.

But in 1960, at Nantua, I have not yet seen Georges Szekeres again. I don't know in detail how that story ended. All I know is that he was freed in 1956 and is working in Budapest. In 1960, at Nantua, I remember my last meeting with Szekeres, in the spring of 1949, near

*Laszlo Rajk, a leading figure in the Hungarian Communist Party, minister of the interior, was accused of conspiracy against the state in a show trial, condemned and executed in 1949. Posthumously rehabilitated in October 1956, he was given a state funeral. —ED.

the newspaper kiosk, on the Boulevard Saint-Germain.

A few days after Vailland had called me, while I was buying a newspaper, I turned around and found Szekeres standing beside me. I stared at him for a long time, looking him in the eye. I didn't want to pretend that I hadn't seen him. I wanted him to know that I had seen him and that, having seen him, I would ignore him. I wanted him to understand that my stare and my silence were sending him back to hell. Better still, to nothingness.

I felt like the Archangel Michael. I gently beat my wings on the sidewalk of the Boulevard Saint-Germain and flew up toward the bright silver sky of Bolshevism. For a few seconds, I was no longer an intellectual of bourgeois origin, liable to all the temptations of humanism. I was a party man and I was resolutely assuming, without false sentimentality, true proletarian positions. I was suddenly at one with the immense crowd of the oppressed who had nothing to lose and nothing to forgive. I measured all values by the yardstick of the party spirit. It was all so simple. Hadn't I been this man's friend? Exactly. This friendship meant that I must be all the more severe in my judgment. And if someone had criticized me for my attitude, tried to make me feel ashamed, I would not even have had to look for words. The words that I would have thrown in the face of my critic had already been written! I had only to repeat them. I would have yelled in his face that the Party would become stronger by purging itself! That the revolution was not a gala dinner! Or, since I was a sensitive, cultured intellectual, I would have thrown in my critic's face a few lines from Mayakovsky. Or a few lines from Aragon. Or, hammering out the syllables for his better understanding, I would have thrown in my critic's face Bertolt Brecht's words: "He who struggles for Communism / must know how to fight and how not to fight / to tell the truth and not tell it / to serve and to refuse his services / to keep his promises and not to keep them / to expose himself to danger and to flee danger / to be recognized and to remain invisible / He who fights for Communism / possesses, of all the virtues, only one / that of fighting for Communism." That's what I would have yelled at my critic. And since I was not only a sensitive and cultured intellectual but also a polyglot, I would have yelled it to him in German.

> *Wer für den Kommunismus kämpft*
> *hat von allen Tugenden nur eine:*
> *dass er für den Kommunismus kämpft*

But there was no such critic.

We were alone, in front of the newspaper kiosk on the Boulevard Saint-Germain, Szekeres and I, almost on the same spot where we had met four years before. We looked at each other in silence. What would I have done if Szekeres had spoken to me? I trembled inside at the very idea. I trembled at the idea of hearing Szekeres's voice. For my superb assurance would no doubt have melted. I would have come down pathetically, at the sound of his voice, from my archangel's pedestal.

At more or less the same time, in similar circumstances, Robert A. had walked up to me on the Rue de Rennes. He had taken me by the arm. "Don't look at me like that," he had said. "Kill me or speak to me." I spoke to him, of course. We went into the Café Bonaparte and talked for a long time. I told him why I placed the requirements of the party spirit above everything else, even above those of a long friendship. Robert A. listened to me, in despair. Despair not at losing my friendship, which was, after all, of minor importance, but of losing, through me, because of me, part at least of the hope that he had put in Communism.

Robert A. tried to find a chink in my archangel's armor. He tried to convince me that it was rationally impossible to believe in Rajk's guilt. But, of course, I did not let him get me onto that ground. To begin with, Rajk was guilty. Pierre Courtade had been at the trial and assured me that Rajk was quite obviously guilty. I knew very well that he had not been so positive in his talks with some of our mutual friends. But I could only speak for myself. To me, Courtade had confirmed Rajk's guilt when I questioned him on his return from Budapest. But I was not going to let Robert A. get me to argue on that ground. For even if Rajk were innocent, one should still not leave the Party, I told Robert. We had a phrase to justify this attitude, dialectically. We said that it was better to be wrong with the Party than to be right outside it or against it. For the Party embodied overall truth, historical reason. An error on the part of the Party could only be partial and temporary. The very course of history would correct it. A truth against the Party, by the same token, could only be partial and temporary. Sterile, therefore, and pernicious, since it ran the risk of obscuring, obliterating, the overall truth of our historical reason. The tree that kept you from seeing the forest, the truth that hid the Truth and thus became a lie, the baby one threw out with the bath water. Q.E.D.

Years later, in the great hall of the former castle of the kings of Bohemia, where I had been excluded from the Politburo of the PCE, Santiago Carrillo threw the same words in my face: "It is better to be wrong with the Party than to be right outside it!" I nearly exploded with laughter. I had looped the loop, the screw had tightened, the rope of the dialectic had been tied around my own neck.

But in 1949, in front of that newspaper kiosk on the Boulevard Saint-Germain, Szekeres said nothing. We looked at each other in silence. His mouth curled into a small bitter smile; there was a sad look in his eyes. I turned away, I let Szekeres fall back into nothingness. I was a Bolshevik. A man of steel. A true Stalinist, in short.

And so, at Nantua, in 1960, angered by this memory, I turn to Fernand Barizon and interrupt his monologue:

"You didn't know any Spaniards at Buchenwald, I suppose?"

Fernand stares at me.

"Come off it, Gérard," he says in a toneless voice, "come off it!"

I look at Barizon, amazed.

So he has recognized me. How long has he recognized me?

"Ever since that first evening I saw you," he says, "the moment you appeared on the castle steps, six months ago!"

"But why didn't you say anything, Fernand?"

He shrugs his shoulders.

"It was up to you to make the first move," he says. "You're a big shot now!"

I give a short, embarrassed laugh.

"A big shot? Shit!"

"Well, aren't you a big shot?" he insists.

"A damp squib," I retort.

He shrugs his shoulders again and lights a cigarette.

"Funny as ever," he says. "And what's that supposed to mean?"

"It means that I spend most of my time in Spain, underground."

He looks at me, nodding.

"I'm not surprised," he says. "You've always liked to play the smart guy."

That is a way of looking at it. I can't help laughing.

In the warmth of long-lost friendship, Fernand orders brandy.

"As for me," he says, "for a long time now I've practiced one of your country's proverbs: *Del amo y del burro, cuanto mas lejos mas seguro!*"

The pronunciation left something to be desired, but it was comprehensible at least. From the master and the donkey, the farther you are the better off you are!

But he is suddenly talking about something else.

"You took long enough, didn't you? I've been talking about Buchenwald for an hour, trying to get some reaction out of you!"

"Don't get angry at me, but you're not a very good storyteller," I say to him. "You forget the most important things."

I don't think he's annoyed, but he looks surprised.

"What did I forget?" he asks.

"You forgot Juliette, for example."

The blood drains from Fernand's face.

"You remember Juliette?" he asks, in a voice that suddenly trembles with emotion.

Of course I remember Juliette. How could I ever forget Juliette? I've spent years of my life comparing the more or less real pleasures that young women of flesh and blood have brought my way with those imaginary, voluptuous pleasures available through my fantasy of Juliette. I begin to explain to Barizon why I remember Juliette, but Barizon is no longer listening to me; Barizon looks at the Spaniard who is talking to him about Juliette, but Barizon is no longer listening to what the Spaniard is saying; Barizon has plunged back into his own past, as one plunges into a dream, dizzily. Barizon is on the *Appellplatz* at Buchenwald, one December day in 1944, under the persistent snow of the Ettersberg.

He has just thought that the Spaniard spends the roll call warm and snug in the *Arbeit* hut.

Barizon is saying to himself that he doesn't always know where he stands with that Spaniard he calls Gérard. Gérard is twenty years old, and it's good to have a twenty-year-old friend who takes things as they come. No, what he sometimes finds irritating about the Spaniard is a certain mixture—how shall I put it—yes, that's it, a mixture of frivolity and secret knowledge. The frivolity takes the form of pouring scorn on everything, on principle. Everything is a laughing matter, nothing is too sacred. The worst of it is that he, Barizon, can't help laughing at Gérard's jokes, even if, invariably, he could kick himself for doing so. Fortunately, Fernand remembers one of Lenin's sayings, which he brandishes at the Spaniard like a truncheon: the anarchism of a *grand seigneur*, a kind of aristocratic eccentricity, that's what is at the bottom of that ironic attitude toward anything and everything.

The secret-knowledge side of it is more difficult to define. It's not that Gérard is an intellectual show-off. He's had a good education, of course, but he doesn't boast about it. On the contrary, he tends to apologize for the privilege. He's a good listener, too.

No, it's more complicated than that. It is, rather, that at certain moments during their afternoon discussions, as they are listening vaguely to Zarah Leander singing about love and its delicious despair, Gérard comes out with some quotation from Marx or Lenin that not only is unknown to Barizon, but that he also finds actually disconcerting. Does Gérard perhaps make them up to support his argument? No, Barizon would not go that far. But it's irritating, all the same. What's more, Gérard seems to possess the keys to a kind of knowledge—

words, formulas, a way of talking that is organized according to a coherence beyond Barizon's reach—that allows him to play with ideas, that gives him tremendous self-assurance. Not that Gérard adopts a superior or contemptuous tone. It's a sort of objective self-assurance that he isn't aware of. That's even worse. It makes one feel stupid, with no arguments to back up one's beliefs. It's profoundly irritating, for that unquestionable, unattainable knowledge, whether true or false, derives not from any experience that might be questioned, but from knowledge itself. It's a knowledge that reproduces itself by the operation of the Holy Spirit, as it were. It's the privilege of an intellectual, a sort of class privilege that can be passed on, that may even be hereditary.

On the *Appellplatz* Fernand Barizon stamps his feet to keep warm. He rubs his hands.

The Spaniard must have gone into the *Arbeit* hut, taking his time, the lucky devil. All warm and snug, during the roll call. He's got a cushy job, that one, no doubt about it.

But it's not so simple as that. He must think about it.

"You must think about it, Fernand," he says to himself, half aloud.

This is a habit he picked up when working underground—he would talk to himself under his breath, to keep himself company.

The guy on his right glances at him, then looks away to resume the corpselike rigidity of standing to attention, his eyes fixed on the watchtower. The guy on his right couldn't have understood what Fernand had said to himself under his breath, because he's a German. In Block 40 nearly everyone is German. In fact, they are the cream of the German prisoners. The senior cadres of the Communist apparatus, the leaders of the strikes of the 1920s, the survivors of the International Brigades. The pick of the bunch, in fact. In Block 40, apart from the old German Communists—I mean the original ones, those who built the camp and who now run it, those who have survived from the good old days—there is only a handful of foreigners. Mainly Westerners, too. A few Frenchmen, a few Spaniards, one or two Belgians. And not just any Belgians. To be in Block 40 and be Belgian, you have to have been a member of Parliament, or a member of the Central Committee, or general secretary of the miners' union at least. There are very few Poles, almost no Russians, let alone Hungarians, in Block 40. They are the plebs of the camp.

So, you see, it's complicated. You have to think about it, Fernand.

Every morning on the *Appellplatz*, during the few minutes before the SS officer who is to count the prisoners turns up, Fernand Barizon indulges in the pleasures of his inner life. He dreams, he remembers, he thinks about things. He is alone, lost in the crowd, protected by it. He allows himself this luxury of meditation. There aren't many other moments when it's possible. After the roll call the din will start, the shouts of the kapos, the military music, the departure of the kommandos, the trek to the Gustloff factories, work on the assembly line, and then, fourteen hours later, the journey back, with everyone yelling and screaming, the evening soup, and bed as soon as possible, except on those days when there is a meeting of the party cell or some secret exercise by the self-defense groups of the international military apparatus.

And so, every morning on the *Appellplatz*, Fernand Barizon lets his thoughts drift. It's like an internal breathing.

Whatever one may think, it's the winter that makes this morning meditation possible. Even when it's snowing.

There you stand, numb with cold. Your body begins, all by itself, to live through a gentle, diffuse agony. Before long, you can hardly feel it any more. Or you feel it at a distance, detached from yourself.

Your body has become a magma of tissues and placental vessels. It has become maternal. It keeps you warm, paradoxically, in a cocoon of protective numbness. And you yourself are no more than a single solitary flame of meditation, of memory: a darkened residence where only a single, tutelary lamp burns. It is what is called the soul, no doubt, if one cares for ready-made words.

Anyway, in winter, despite the cold, despite the numbness, the inner life seems practicable for a few minutes each morning. For the time it takes the SS officer to arrive in front of the ranks of prisoners from Block 40 to start the count.

In spring it's no longer possible.

At five in the morning in May, let's say, the sun is already touching the treetops. The beech forest that surrounds the camp on three sides is awakening in the sunlight. You can just smell the woodland scents. If there is a second of silence, a fraction of a second even, between the yelling of the loudspeakers, the sound of boots, and the military music, you can hear the innumerable sounds of nature. It pulls at your heartstrings, it breaks you into tiny pieces of diffuse, disturbed sensations, it beats in your arteries, it mounts like sap through your motionless limbs, it tightens around you and stifles you, like ivy, like Virginia creeper, wistaria, it takes possession of you vegetally, it makes you soft inside, stupid, it roots you in the nostalgic leaf mold of distant childhoods, it stops you from thinking.

In May, at five in the morning, with the sun rising over the forests of Thuringia, the misery of being alive, the joy of being alive, make you incapable of thinking clearly.

Your body is no more than a damp, confused mediation that binds you through a thousand roots and rootlets to eternal nature, to the cycle of the seasons, to the immensity of death, to the organic stammerings of renewal.

Let's put it like this: you become quite simply mad at Buchenwald under the diabolical warmth of the sun.

But we are in December. Fernand can think about things.

All right, the Spaniard spends the roll call snug and warm in the *Arbeit* hut, but, then, the Spaniard did not put himself there, at the *Arbeit* hut, on his own. It was the party organization that put him there, and for a particular purpose: to defend the interests of the Spanish collectivity of the camp.

Here, on your own, you don't get out. Or at least you have to have a lot of strength, a lot of luck, and be very, very clever. Tough, cunning, ruthless. Ready to lick the ass of the kapo or the civilian foreman; ready to work faster than anybody else, so as to get noticed, with the risk of being struck on the hands with an iron bar because you are working too fast and everyone is watching; ready to wangle anything you want, and, of course, to steal anything you want.

Here, stealing is called *organisieren*.

In the silence of his thoughts, in the falling snow, waiting for the roll call to end, Barizon says the word *organisieren* to himself. There is no other word for stealing.

He isn't interested in etymology. How could he be? He takes words as they come, the German words for the important things, the words without which one is lost, that mark out everyday life with comprehensible signals. *Arbeit, Scheisse, Brot, Revier, Schnell, Los, Schonung, Achtung, Antreten, Abort, Ruhe.* All the necessary words. And *organisieren*, too.

Barizon takes words as they come, but the first time he heard *organisieren* and realized that it meant "to steal," he couldn't help feeling a slight twinge inside. *Organisieren*—shit, what a lack of respect! Until that day, the word "organize" meant for him only serious, sometimes even dangerous, but in any case positive things. In fact, the whole of Barizon's political memory turned around this word.

Wasn't it Maurice Thorez* who had said that organization decides everything, once the political line has been laid down? Perhaps, in fact, it wasn't Maurice, but Stalin, who said that. Yes, it was probably Stalin who said it first. Anyway, Stalin always said everything first. Come on, Fernand, think hard: on what occasion did Stalin say that organization decides everything?

Images explode, fragments of memory, as the snow falls on the Ettersberg.

In 1929, at the time of the slogan CLASS AGAINST CLASS, Barizon had gone to a lecture in the Saint-Denis section. What he remembers from that lecture was that it was necessary to struggle against the social-democratic tradition and against that of anarcho-syndicalism, both equally dangerous to the Party. And the demarcation line, the breaking point with both these pernicious traditions, which were, nevertheless, deeply rooted in the thinking of the proletariat, was the Leninist view of organization.

Anyway, that, more or less, is what he remembers from the lecture.

But was it at Saint-Denis that Stalin's phrase about organization deciding everything came into the discussion? Barizon isn't quite sure. Perhaps he has mixed up the dates and the meetings. There was also, at about the

---

*1900–64, secretary general and later president of the French Communist Party. —ED.

same time, a regional assembly on the results of the Sixth Congress of the Communist International.

As he stands on the *Appellplatz* at Buchenwald, Barizon is smiling ecstatically. You will know why in a moment!

He can remember perfectly the pamphlet that was put out by the Publishing Bureau. A red cover, a title in black capital letters: CLASS AGAINST CLASS. The pamphlet contained the speeches and resolutions concerning the French question at the Ninth Executive and at the Sixth Congress of the International.

What had struck Barizon in the speeches at the Ninth Executive was something Maurice had said. On that occasion, there's no doubt about it. It was definitely Maurice who had said it, not Stalin. Enumerating the causes of the mistakes made by the French Party, Maurice had said that Communists remained too strongly attached to democracy, that they were not managing to loosen the grip that democracy still had on the Party. That was it: one of the major obstacles to the action of the Party was that it had grown up in a country infested with democracy—it was Maurice himself who had said that.

At the time, Barizon had thought the remark very true and perceptive. What, after all, is bourgeois democracy? It's the bourgeois state, the dictatorship of the bourgeoisie. That's what has to be overthrown and destroyed. That's what one can in no way arrange to one's own satisfaction, reform from within, if one doesn't want to get bogged down in it. But it is precisely this obvious truth that is not immediately visible. It acts as a screen, it eludes the everyday social experience of the masses. The masses float in bourgeois democracy like potato chips in the oil in which they are about to be fried.

Later, at the time of the Popular Front, and above all after the Arles congress, democracy seemed no longer to be an obstacle to the Party's action, but, on the contrary, a springboard. It had been explained to Barizon that this reversal of position was dialectical. In any case, at that time, in 1937, Fernand Barizon scarcely had time to ask himself theoretical questions. He was fighting in Spain, in the Brigades.

But, of course, it is not remembering the speeches made at the Ninth Executive, or even Maurice Thorez's words, that made Barizon smile so ecstatically a moment ago. It is Juliette.

Juliette was sitting opposite him at the long table, during the meal break at that assembly of the Paris region. Juliette was talking to him seriously about her work in the garment union. She was peeling an apple, looking him straight in the eye, talking of her union work. And suddenly Barizon felt, under the table, Juliette's foot rising along his left leg, slipping between his thighs, parting them, and ending on his cock, which hardened under the unusual caress. For Juliette's foot was bare. And yet, Fernand had noticed, Juliette had been wearing stockings a little while ago: that is, he had noticed Juliette's long legs clothed in artificial silk. Had she rolled down one of her stockings, under the table, so that she could stroke Fernand's cock all the more effectively? The pretty little bitch was quite capable of it. In any case, Fernand felt the living warmth of that bare foot through the cloth of his trousers.

Juliette was eating an apple, cut into small sections; she was talking about the union in a very balanced, sensible, thoughtful way. She was not saying just anything. But her bare foot, living and warm, was stroking Fernand's cock. At one moment, her big toe got between two buttons of Barizon's fly. He could no longer resist the invitation. He adroitly undid his fly, under the table, as the pals were finishing their meal amid the commotion of voices. He took out his erect cock, which Juliette then set about stroking with her bare foot.

She was still talking about the union, but her words seemed to pour out of her ever more rapidly. Barizon was quite incapable of uttering a word.

Anyway, Barizon has always had his doubts about the question of organization-decides-everything. He doesn't know why, but he has always found it vaguely disturbing.

Yet you have to admit that questions of organization always come to the fore when there are difficulties, never when things are going well. When the Party is isolated, when our slogans don't seem to reach the masses, in a period of ebb (that was a word Barizon liked, because it said just what it meant, despite the abuse that certain people made of it, "the ebb and flow," a little catchword in the mouths of area secretaries; a precise word, "ebb," suggesting precise images; when he heard the word "ebb" at the meeting his thoughts took off; images broke out in all directions; the word "ebb," even if the meeting was a serious one, reminded him of an escapade he had had for a few days with Juliette, in Brittany, a really crazy time; when he got back, he got fired, and was out of work for two months; but what a trip, the memories went round and round in his head like the big wheel at a fair; five days to sleep together, eat, walk on the sandy beaches that the ebbing tide uncovered, in all their immensity; the bed, the table, the ocean; afterward, down to earth, unemployment, but so what: he'd had five days that the bosses would never have; the word "ebb" made him feel warm inside when someone spoke it at a meeting, and somebody always did, it was as if one would never be able to do without it)—and so in a period of ebb, questions of organization came to the fore, they seemed to decide everything.

In fact they decided nothing, though he might have to keep this painful truth to himself. Barizon couldn't remember a single instance when bringing the question of Leninist organization firmly to the fore, comrades, had benefited the Party in any way. Whereas when things were going well, when the wind was behind one, everything became easy. Careful, Fernand, beware of tagging along with history! The Party has never been driven by the wind, it has always preceded it. One step forward, no more, so as not to lose contact with the masses, the vanguard and the masses. Let's see: we learned that at the section school! But, damn it, there was nothing wrong with being borne along, driven from behind by the movement that unfurls like a wave, a flow, comrades, a flow!

At such times—around '35 and '36, for Barizon had known no other times of flow than those—at such times, then, questions of organization suddenly became secondary. The Party managed to organize itself, with the masses, at the same time as the masses, for them and through them, and there was no need to go over the Leninist theory of organization. Anyway, between April and October 1917, how often had Lenin mentioned the Leninist conception of the Party? Not once, comrades! Maybe that will give you something to think about.

It was this that wasn't too clear, this that vaguely disturbed him. It seemed, in fact, that at moments of offensive, when the masses were moving, the Party ceased to be the vanguard. One no longer preceded the masses, even by one step; rather, one ran after them. And one ran after them to hold them back, rather than to drive them on. "Not everything is possible." "One has to know how to end a strike." The Party, it seemed, was in the vanguard only at times when nothing was moving, or at any rate when things were not moving in the direction laid down by the Executive of the Communist International. In October 1936, Barizon was sufficiently disturbed to drop everything, leave for Spain, and join the Brigades.

All the same, the first time he heard the word *organisieren* at Buchenwald and understood its meaning had come as a shock. There was nothing to be done about it after that. It had become part of the routine of their language. You have to take words as they come.

Fernand Barizon is standing on the *Appellplatz*.

It has stopped snowing. The night is even darker above the blocks, now that the searchlights no longer make the whirling snowflakes glitter.

The roll call of prisoners is drawing to an end.

The SS warrant officers have verified with the block leaders that the figures on the report tally with the number of prisoners actually present on the *Appellplatz*. The SS warrant officers have now gone up to the watchtower. The *Rapportführer* will now collate all the figures and add them up, to obtain the overall numbers for today, duly checked, block by block, kommando by kommando. There will then be only one final operation to perform: the subtraction from the overall number of the last roll call, the night before, of the number of entrants reported by the crematorium. If the results tally, that will be the end of it. When the living and the dead have been calculated, when all the figures produce, correctly added or subtracted, the correct result, the roll call will be over. The kommandos will set out for work amid the clamor of military music. The camp orchestra is already in place near the main gates. The musicians wear a rather flamboyant uniform: red riding breeches with green facings, green jackets with yellow frogs and loops, black boots. They are prisoners, of course.

In the middle of the Block 40 formation, Barizon snorts to keep warm.

One might have known he wasn't thinking about the banks of the Marne. The banks of the Marne, spring Sundays on the banks of the Marne—that was just an assumption on the part of the Spaniard who had seen him run toward the *Appellplatz* and heard him shout, *"Les gars, quel beau dimanche!"* An invention, that's all: fiction. Barizon wasn't thinking at all about the Marne, about its charms, natural or human. Whatever the Spaniard may think, Barizon shouted, *"Les gars, quel beau dimanche!"* Just like that, no more. As one might say "shit!"

And now Fernand Barizon is snorting to keep warm.

It all started with the passing thought that the Spaniard was spending the roll call snug and warm in the *Arbeit* hut. All right, a cushy job. But it wasn't so simple as that. He'd been planted there by the Party, to work for the Party. And anyway, hadn't he, Barizon, been planted, too? Also by the Party. Of course, there was the roll call on the *Appellplatz*—in the snow, as it happened. But then after that it was the Gustloff Works, which were like all the other firms he'd ever worked for, where he finished parts of G-43 automatic rifles. Barizon was under no illusions: whether he worked for Citroën or for Göring— yes, the field marshal was one of the shareholders in the Gustloff factories—what did it matter once one was at the machine, amid all the din? Well, yes, it did matter, there was a difference, but it was in your head, not in the work itself. He had known worse, much harsher rhythms of work. Diabolical, they used to call them.

At the Gustloff, the underground organization kept the situation well in hand: there was no chance that some idiot or ass-licker might take it into his head to fulfill the quotas. The factory worked at a low output: 40 percent of the production plan, in a good week (or, rather, in a bad one, depending on one's point of view). The German *Meister*—the civilian foremen—had long since abandoned any hope of fulfilling the production plan, the output quotas.

So Barizon had also been planted.

Planted, what did that mean exactly? It meant that you worked in one of the factories (Gustloff, MIBAU, D.A.W., etc.), dry and warm, relatively well off, at least when you were a steelworker, when you were used to working on an assembly line. It meant that you would not be put on a list of prisoners to be sent on one of the extermination kommandos. It was quite simple. You arrived from Compiègne, terrified out of your wits to find yourself in that incredible, unimaginable world of Buchenwald. You were quite alone, it seemed, ordered to do this and not to do that. The quarantine, the fatigues, the vermin, the floggings administered by the SS and the green kapos, and even by some of the red kapos. The slice of bread that you often had to defend from your neighbor with your fist. Shit! Your neighbor, an honest office worker, a colonel in the French army, a law professor, a man who, quite simply, had become a greedy, voracious, ruthless animal, concerned only with his own survival, ready to do anything, apparently, for a mouthful of bread, or an extra spoonful of soup! And then, two days, three days, a couple of weeks later, contact.

The Party took charge of you again.

That was the great surprise about Buchenwald: the existence of an underground party organization. It was the work of the German comrades, of course. Even if they seemed brutal, arrogant, and sectarian, even if most of them had gone mad, the fact remained that the German pals had preserved and reconstructed the Communist organization, the one thing that made solidarity and a common strategy possible. Individually, maybe they didn't amount to much, but their organization had kept going.

And so Barizon was transferred to the Gustloff, after his quarantine period. Dry and warm, the lucky devil, working happily at finishing as badly as he could parts for the G-43 automatic rifle, with pals all along the assembly line to give him support, to cover him, against the resigned looks, the powerless shakes of the head of the German *Meister*.

That's what organization means.

Of course, you don't get anything for nothing. In exchange for this relative peace and quiet, you had to take part in the systematic, rational sabotage of production. There was always a chance you might be caught red-handed, ruining some part, especially if you weren't really a skilled worker. You might be denounced by a common-law prisoner or a civilian *Meister* to the SS supervisors. One chance in how many? At the Gustloff, because of the way everything was arranged, organized, from the beginning of the assembly line to the firing range, where other pals checked the weapons, the risk of getting caught was minimal. You really had to be as crazy as a Russian to get caught.

The Russians!

Barizon didn't understand the Russians, didn't know how to handle them. The inhabitants of the Fatherland of Socialism seemed to come from another planet. They were a massive, distant, hostile crowd of young savages who did not accept the rules of the game. When they felt like sabotaging they sabotaged, in their own way, on their own account, impudently: almost for the fun of it, you might think. No respect for the rules of organization. Whenever some guy got caught sabotaging for no apparent reason, he had to be a Russian. Often a teen-ager, all worked up, spitting insults in the faces of the *Meister* and the SS supervisors who took him away, yelling at them to go fuck their mothers, to go get fucked by their fathers. (These were the only sentences in Russian that Barizon managed to understand, by dint of hearing them over and over again, always involving the sexual act between parents and children, brothers and sisters.) Whenever a guy was hanged on the *Appellplatz* before all the assembled prisoners, he had to be a Russian.

You had to accept the fact. Apart from the Soviet prisoners of war, who lived on their own in a special enclosure in the camp, the Russians seemed to have no sense of organization, or respect for it. They were more like anarchists than anything else.

Although they had no sense of organization in the true sense of the word, they were unbeatable when it came to *organisieren.* They pinched scraps of metal in the workshops and turned them into forks and spoons, which they then exchanged for bread and tobacco. They pinched scraps of leather, felt, and cloth, in the inside kommandos that handled the repair of prisoners' clothes, and turned them into boots, hats, or padded jackets that were easy to exchange on the underground market.

In fact, all the petty trafficking that went on in the camp was controlled by the Russians. The big stuff was in the hands of the SS themselves.

Grouped into bands under the command of twenty-year-old leaders who were easily identifiable by their dress—riding breeches, good leather boots, army tunics, and, in the case of the real gang leaders, helmets, obtained from the camp clothing stores, that had once belonged to frontier guards or NKVD troops—the Russians had a grip on all bartering, imposing an obscure and ruthless authority throughout the Little Camp. At night, up until curfew, in the huge smoky building of the collective latrines, in the *Stubendienst* huts, in the most distant beds of the invalid blocks, the Little Camp was mysteriously alive with the feverish, unremitting activity of exchanges, settlements, distributions of strong liquor secretly manufactured with 180-proof alcohol stolen from the hospital.

The Russians, strangely indifferent to political problems, did not seem at all out of place in the world of Buchenwald. It was as if they already knew its secret keys, as if the social world from which they came had prepared them for this experience. And they allowed no other forms of organization but those bands of wild teen-agers, whose mysterious hierarchy seemed to maintain their national cohesion. Confronted by these youth bands, the tiny organization of the Soviet Party— tolerated by the mass of Russian deportees with the sort of mistrust that does not exclude the prudent respect or even the servility one usually accords police authorities in countries where civil society is somewhat amorphous, lacking in structure—found itself constantly forced to swing from compromise to deal, in order to maintain a semblance of ideological authority.

Yet, to Barizon's stupefaction, these same little bosses, these same leaders, were to erect huge portraits of Stalin on all the huts occupied by the Russians, on April 12, 1945, just prior to the liberation of Buchenwald.

An astonished Barizon was to observe this profusion of huge portraits of Stalin, drawn in the night, in the most accomplished Socialist Realist style. Not a hair was missing from the marshal's mustache, not a button from his generalissimo jacket. During the night, the little bosses with their ice-cold blue eyes, all spick and span in their NKVD caps and their gleaming boots, set about manufacturing this profusion of portraits of Stalin, in homage to the Great Leader, to the Great Boss, who was soon to take them back into his paternal hand and send them to the labor camps of the Great North to complete the re-education that they had begun in the Nazi camps.

But that, of course, Barizon could not guess. Nor, in all probability, could the little leaders themselves. So, when he thought about the Russians, Barizon did not know exactly what to think.

"Do you remember the Russians?" says Barizon, sixteen years later, at Nantua.

He has just emerged from the long meditative silence brought on by the memory of Juliette. He had been sipping his brandy in silence for several minutes and the Narrator had taken advantage of that to continue his account of events one Sunday long ago, sixteen years ago, to be precise.

"Do you remember the Russians, Gérard?" Fernand Barizon asks.

I was already startled some time earlier, when Barizon called me Gérard. Gérard? It's a long time since I was called Gérard. I go under all kinds of false names that do not startle me. Gérard is a false name that does startle me. Why? Perhaps quite simply because it's a false name that hides more truth than others. More important truth. Or the reverse: because it's the false name that is furthest removed from me.

In any case, Gérard did not choose this Christian name. One day, a comrade from the *maquis* who was my contact, as we said, had given me this pseudonym. "You will be called Gérard," he had told me. All right, he would be called Gérard. Later, at Joigny, when a false identity card had been made for me, a surname had to be added to this Christian name. There again, it was not Gérard who chose it. It was Michel Herr. "Sorel," Michel said. "Gérard Sorel." Why not? So I wandered about the region with a false identity card in the name of Gérard Sorel, gardener.

He liked that, gardener.

(I would have been quite incapable of distinguishing between the fuchsias and the petunias, dahlias and begonias in a garden; but, as it happened, this hardly mattered: at Auxerre, in the garden attached to the Gestapo villa, there was nothing but roses, and I knew what a rose looked like).

I rode my bicycle from Joigny to Auxerre and from Auxerre to Toucy, with my gardener's bag, in which I carried a Sten gun.

At Buchenwald he had ceased to be Gérard Sorel, except with the Frenchmen who had known me since my time in the prisons at Auxerre and Dijon, and in the sorting camps at Compiègne.

The night I arrived in the camp, I ended up in front of a guy sitting at a table, with pencil and files in front of him. Two minutes before, I had been running naked—with hundreds of other funny men, who were also naked— along the concrete corridors and labyrinthine staircases. We ended up in the *Effektenkammer*, the clothing stores. They threw various assorted rags at us, and pairs of clogs with laces. My clogs resounded on the concrete floor of a new room, and I found myself standing in front of the table in question.

The guy asked me for the usual identity information, which he wrote down on a card. He was delighted to observe that Gérard spoke fluent German. It made his task easier. I answered mechanically. I was no longer clear where I was, after the long series of brutal initiation ceremonies of that first night in Buchenwald: the undressing, the shower, the disinfectant bath, the shaving of the head, the long run naked through the echoing corridors. I looked at the guy who was asking me questions and answered them mechanically. In the end, the guy asked me my occupation: *"Beruf?"* I told him I was a student, because I wasn't a gardener any more. The guy shrugged his shoulders. *"Das ist doch kein Beruf!"* he exclaimed. That was not an occupation, it seemed. *"Kein Beruf, nur eine Berufung!"* I nearly said. Not an occupation, just a vocation. In German, as you will have guessed, the pun worked better, at least on the semantic and phonetic levels. But I restrained from perpetrating such an erudite witticism. First because it was not entirely true: being a student was not so much a vocation as the consequences of a certain sociological weight. And anyway, I didn't know exactly who the guy asking me questions was. Not an SS officer, that was obvious enough. But it was better to tread carefully.

So I didn't make my witticism and I insisted on my status as a student. Then, taking his time, the guy explained to me that at Buchenwald it was better to have a manual occupation. Didn't I know anything about electricity, for example? Not even the basics? I shook my head. What about mechanics, did I know anything about that? I shook my head again. And wood, did I know how to handle wood? Surely I at least knew how to hold a plane. The guy almost sounded angry. I got the impression that he wanted at all costs to find some ability in this twenty-year-old student who shook his head like an idiot. It then occurred to Gérard that the only manual work he knew anything about was terrorism. Weapons, light arms at least, up to the machine gun of the French army, that I did know about. How to handle them, take them apart, clean them, put them together again. And I knew about plastic. Explosives in general, with their detonators, their Bickford fuses, everything you needed to organize a derailment. And magnetic mines to blow up trucks, locomotives, or canal locks, I knew about them, too. Really, the only manual occupation I could have mentioned to this guy who was beginning to get annoyed was that of terrorist. But I said nothing about this, and the guy, in desperation, put me down as a student.

So I was no longer a gardener at Buchenwald. I was no longer Gérard Sorel, either. The day of my arrest, at Epizy, a suburb of Joigny, I was carrying my real Spanish identity papers on me. I was supposed to go to Paris that very evening, to meet "Paul," the head of my network. And in Paris, my card as a gardener from the Yonne would have been suspect. I didn't really look like a gardener from the Yonne.

And so, quite by chance, I had been arrested under my real name. But Fernand Barizon, like the other French prisoners at Buchenwald, called me Gérard.

Sixteen years later, though, at Nantua, I'm startled that Barizon should still call me Gérard. It's as if I were no longer myself and have become a character in a novel. As if I were no longer the "I" of this narrative, and have become a mere Game, or Stake, a He. But which He? The He of the Narrator who holds the threads of this story? Or the He of a mere third person, the character in the story? In any case, I'm not going to allow myself to be led, since I'm the cunning God the Father of all these threads and all these He's. The First Person by antonomasia, then, even when it hides itself in the Hegelian figure of the One splitting into Three, for the greater pleasure of the reader who enjoys narrative tricks, whatever opinion he may hold on the delicate question of the dialectic.

"Can you really remember, Gérard?" Fernand Barizon asks me, at Nantua, sixteen years later.

"At the Swiss frontier," says Gérard, "do you remember how I stopped being Gérard and became Camille—Camille Salagnac?"

Barizon shrugs his shoulders impatiently.

"I don't give a damn what they call you! To start with, I've never discovered your real name, if you have one! Today you're called Salagnac, tomorrow Tartempion: I don't give a damn! I call you Gérard, I've always called you Gérard and I always will. But don't worry about the frontier; I'm used to it!"

He drains his glass of brandy, angrily.

"My real name is Sanchez," says Gérard.

"Yes, yes," says Barizon. "And of course you know mine—Dupont de Mes-Deux!"

We both laugh.

"What do you think I really should have remembered?" Gérard asks him.

Barizon stares into his empty glass.

"Now that you're a big shot," he says, "do you think you could buy me a second brandy out of your traveling expenses?"

I nod and call the waiter over.

"The camp," says Barizon. "Do you really remember it as something that really happened to you? Don't you sometimes have the feeling you dreamed it all?"

I look at him.

"Not even dreamed it," says Gérard. "I have the feeling it's all a dream, yes, but I'm not sure I dreamed it. Perhaps it was someone else."

I don't say everything I'm thinking. I don't say that this someone else might be someone who is dead.

Barizon takes a long sip of the second brandy, which has just been put on the table. He leans forward.

"That's it," he says, "that's exactly it! But why?"

"Perhaps because it's true," says Gérard.

I give a quick laugh and light a cigarette.

Perhaps it is true, after all. Perhaps I am just the dream of a young man called Gérard, who died at Buchenwald at

the age of twenty, and who went up in smoke on the
Ettersberg. But such things are not very easy to say.
Anyway, I say nothing to Barizon.

I look at him.

"Yes, I remember very well," says Gérard.

The memory is the best recourse, even if it seems
paradoxical at first. The best recourse against the pain of
remembering, against the dereliction, against the unspo-
ken, familiar madness. The criminal madness of living
the life of a dead man.

"Could you tell it?" Barizon asks.

Could I tell it?

During the previous few months, at Madrid, on the
Calle Concepción-Bahamonde, listening to the rambling
accounts of Manuel Azaustre, I had the feeling I could tell
it. Better than he could, anyway. Today, too, at Nantua,
listening to Fernand Barizon, I have the same feeling. At
least I wouldn't forget Juliette, or Zarah Leander. But I
mustn't kid myself: one will never be able to tell everything. A lifetime would not be enough. All the possible
accounts will never be anything but scattered fragments
of an endless, literally interminable, account.

"I think I could, yes," says Gérard.

"Of course," says Barizon, rather bitterly. "It's always
the same guys who tell it."

"Even if that were true," says Gérard, "it's only part of
the problem."

"There you are, you see!" Barizon exclaims. "There you
go again! You may be a big shot, but you haven't changed!
You're still splitting hairs and splitting them again. But
that's probably why you've become a big shot. Pro and
con, positive and negative, on the one hand, but on the
other! And what's the other part of the problem?"

He's a comforting soul, Barizon. I can't help smiling,
feeling comforted.

"The other part of the problem," says Gérard, "is this: to whom can one tell it?"

Barizon shakes his head and raises a categorical finger.

"Nobody," he says. "Nobody can really understand. Have you already tried?"

"You would understand," says Gérard.

Barizon shrugs his shoulders, obviously exasperated.

"Of course," he says, "but what's the point of that? If you tell me all about it, it's not an account. It's going over the same old thing. And vice versa!"

I'm forced to agree. If I tell him all about it, it won't be an account, but going over the same old thing. If he tells me all about it, it will also be going over the same old thing, and badly done, to boot. And it's surely because I hate going over the same old thing that I don't have much to do with war veterans.

"And what about Juliette," says Gérard. "What if you told it to Juliette?"

I know very well that Juliette is dead. Fernand told me, just now, before sinking into a commemorative silence. In the resistance, Juliette was the liaison agent of an interregional leader in the Southeast. But Barizon did not seem very anxious to say what he had learned about Juliette's death when he got back from Buchenwald. Just now, he brushed the whole matter aside. OK, he said, Juliette's dead, that's all there is to it! Since Juliette was dead, Barizon had gone back to his lawful wife, his life-long companion, the mother of his children, when he got back from Buchenwald. OK, Barizon said, bringing the matter to a close, that's the way it is!

So I know Juliette is dead. But I conjure up her ghost, at Nantua, as Fernand warms his glass of brandy between the palms of his hands; I conjure up Juliette's ghost as you might conjure up the ghost of a woman who loves you, whom you love, who is awaiting you, on your return from the lethal adventure of life. As one might conjure up Beatrice, or Penelope, or Laura, or Dulcinea.

Barizon understood.

"Perhaps," he says, very quietly. "Perhaps I could have told Juliette."

And whom could I have told? You, Gérard, whom could you have told? Was there a Juliette in your life?

But Barizon interrupts this secret interrogation. He brings his fist down on the table.

"That's you!" he exclaims. "I had a very precise question to ask. And now I've forgotten it! You muddle me up, you lead me up the garden path, you send me off into metaphysics!"

I can't let the opportunity slip by.

"What is metaphysics, Fernand?" Gérard asks.

Barizon looks at me, suspicious. He must suspect a trap. Then, risking all, he suddenly looks sure of himself.

"Come on!" he says. "In my day, we learned that in the political education classes. It's the opposite of the dialectic. And vice versa!"

"Of course!" says Gérard, conciliatory. "But what is the dialectic?"

Fernand doesn't hesitate. He looks me straight in the eyes.

"It's the art of always falling on your feet!" There is a twinkle in his eye and he raises his glass of cognac, as if drinking to my health.

I nod; it's not a bad definition. The art of justifying the ways things are going, no doubt.

"And what was your precise question?" Gérard asks.

"The Russians," says Barizon.

At Buchenwald, sixteen years earlier, you certainly had to consider—and grasp—the Russian question. You certainly had to find an explanation—and a dialectical one, if possible, as Barizon would say, involving, therefore, a plausible hierarchy of negative and positive factors, in which the latter, certainly, had to predominate in the end, so that the dialectical spiral should not end up in the pessimism of negation, but in the optimism of the negation of the negation—you certainly had to try to justify that Russian barbarism, juvenile and massive, structured according to an unwritten but coercive code, around nuclei of brute force.

Several theories had circulated among us. One held that the Russian problem was in fact a Ukrainian problem. The trouble was apparently that the great majority of Soviet citizens interned in Buchenwald were Ukrainians. Later, I saw that Eugen Kogon took up this explanation in his essay on the Nazi camps, *Organized Hell*. "The Russians," he wrote, "were divided into two absolutely distinct groups: the Russian prisoners, whether civilians or soldiers, on the one hand, and the Ukrainians on the other. The latter formed the overwhelming majority. Whereas the prisoners of war formed well-disciplined teams who, with great skill but also with justice, looked after their collective interests (the selection that had been made in the Stalags had brought into the camps Communists who were conscious of the cause they represented), the mass of Ukrainians were a breed that defied description. At the beginning, they were so favorably treated by their German comrades that it was almost impossible to make the slightest complaint against a Russian. But the insolence, the laziness, and the absence of comradeship of a large number of them worked, with great rapidity and thoroughness, to block their access to important posts. During the last year at Buchenwald, the Russian prisoners of war, like a few remarkable young Ukrainian Communists, set out to educate and to incorporate into the whole body the useful part of that very mixed society, which generally speaking knew no check on its inclinations."

Eugen Kogon was a meticulous observer of the Nazi concentration-camp system. Moreover, his position in Buchenwald enabled him to know a great many secret aspects of the life of the camp and of the anti-Nazi resistance. And, lastly, because he was not a Marxist but a Christian Democrat, his observations and analyses did not have to correspond to the pre-established canons of the dialectic. They could be objective. They were not necessarily so, but at least they could be. It is clear, however, that his explanation of the strange Russian barbarism of Buchenwald is not satisfactory. Why should the Ukrainians be worse than the other citizens of Stalin's multinational empire? Besides, if one examines in detail his own arguments, one will see that he himself provides the basis for a different explanation, not the one based on nationality—almost to the point of racism—but a social one.

In effect, the distinctive feature by which Kogon compares the Russian prisoners of war with the Ukrainian deportees is not really their nationality. It only looks that way. The main factor is that they constituted "well-disciplined teams," led, moreover, by "Communists who were conscious of the cause they represented." In fact, the question was not of the difference between Russians and Ukrainians, but of the opposition between cadres (or the élite) and mass (or plebeian collectivity) in a certain social structure peculiar to Stalinist Russia.

The second theory prevalent among us took into account and explained this social differentiation. According to this theory—in which the dialectic à la Barizon, the art of always falling on one's feet, came into its own—the revolution had not yet had time in Russia to create the new man, a man who has internalized and individualized the new moral values of socialism. It had to be admitted, the new man had not yet been born. The revolution had begun to set up new social structures, new relations of production, but these had been embodied and personified as yet only by the cadres of the new society: shock workers, intellectuals, officers of the Red Army, etc., etc. Now, this social structure had been destroyed in the territories occupied by the Germans, and the mass of Russian deportees from those territories, when left to themselves, fell back into a state of disorganization in which the old still predominated over the new man, partly on account of their youth.

And so we fell on our feet, as Barizon would have said.

However safe and comforting this theory may have been, I don't think it would have satisfied the zealots of Marxist science. They would no doubt have regarded it as still insufficiently dialectical, because it failed to justify reality completely, because it claimed to explain it in its contradictions and not to glorify it in the resolution or supersession (*Aufhebung*, comrades, *Aufhebung!*) of the afore-mentioned contradictions. Anyway, this explanation, which we worked out for ourselves in Buchenwald to try to rationalize the terrifying real Russian, was never formulated publicly at a later date, as far as I know. We kept it to ourselves, as we kept in the secrecy of our hearts all our doubts and all our questions about the Russians in Buchenwald.

Today, of course, those obscure signs are becoming legible, becoming part of a coherent whole. They enable one, through an analysis of the behavior of the Russians in Buchenwald, to obtain a real, nondialectical, idea of the Russian society of the time. Perhaps those signs were already decipherable in 1944; perhaps it was already possible to construct a concept of Russian society in Buchenwald. Perhaps. But one would have had to abandon the sermons of the dialectic and fall into the vile error of rationalistic, critical empiricism. *Horribile dictu!* One would have had to regard those young Russians as what they were, human beings, necessarily mysterious but accessible to communication, and not as the generic bearers of the new relations of production and the new values of socialism. One would have had to question them, listen to what they had to say, to the truth they spoke through their gestures, their bodies, their clothes, their brutal laughter, their infinitely nostalgic accordions, their respect for strength, their masculine tenderness, their springtime madness, which made them break loose anywhere, anyhow, any time, as soon as the wind from the East reached them from the great rivers of their country; one would have had to listen to them, instead of giving ready-made answers to a badly phrased question. Today, of course, I think I know what the Russian barbarism of Buchenwald meant. "The insolence, the laziness, and the absence of comradeship" of the young Russians and Ukrainians of Buchenwald, referred to by Eugen Kogon—I think I know what they meant.

But we haven't got there yet. We are still in 1960, at Nantua, and I had decided to tell this story in chronological order—perhaps I forgot to tell you that. So I had better note, out of respect for chronology, that Fernand Barizon has just come back from the toilets at the Hôtel de France.

"Well," he says, "if you want to get to Geneva before nightfall, maybe we ought to get moving."

I agree. So we leave the Hôtel de France at Nantua and continue on our way.

Two hours later, we were in Geneva, or, more precisely, in the refreshment room at the Gare de Cornavin. I was waiting for the Zurich train.

If I told you the story of my life, instead of narrating

more simply, and more modestly, a Sunday long ago at Buchenwald, this would be the perfect opportunity for a digression—an unquestionably moving, perhaps even brilliant digression—on the city of Geneva. For it was at Geneva, for me, that exile began, *die schlaflose Nacht des Exils,* as Marx called it. It was at Geneva that my sleepless night of exile began, in late 1936. A night that has still not come to an end, despite appearances to the contrary, and which will probably never come to an end. I'm only speaking for myself, of course.

Perhaps I should be more specific; chronological order has nothing to fear from specificity. Perhaps I should say that my exile really began at Bayonne, with the landing at Bayonne Harbor of the Basque trawler *Galerna* with its cargo of refugees from Bilbao, fleeing Franco's armies. But the memory of Bayonne has been exorcised. Since 1953 I have been to Bayonne so often, walked so often through those same streets, that same square on the Quai de l'Adour, with its same flower beds, that the wounding childhood memory has been exorcised. Since 1953 I have been through Bayonne several times on my way back into Spain. I would cross the bridge over the Adour, and then the second bridge, over that other river whose name I never learned. After that, the road ran along the great square, with its flower beds and bandstand. Exactly as it used to be. And under the same autumn sun, when it was autumn. There was a roadsign that said: Spanish frontier so many kilometers. We were nearly there. I was going home. The childhood memory of Bayonne, of the day my exile began, when I discovered that I was a Spanish Red, this memory was exorcised. I was going home, I was still a Spanish Red, but Barizon was not driving the car that was taking me back to my own country. In fact, he was sorry he wasn't. He told me between Nantua and Geneva, that day in 1960, that he would have liked to go on that journey with me for once.

After Bayonne, if I am to be specific and keep to chronological order, there was Lestelle-Bétharram. This tiny Béarnais village was a place of pilgrimage. There was a collegiate church, a wayside cross, several religious buildings: school, monastery, etc. Then there was a grotto where some miraculous event is supposed to have taken place long ago. I don't remember what, but, given the statistical frequency of the Virgin's apparitions in Béarnais grottoes, I suppose the event that made Lestelle-Bétharram a place of pilgrimage must have been some Marianic apparition. But it's not because of that miraculous event that the second stage of my exile—the first, in Bayonne, was actually very short, hardly a day—was the village of Lestelle-Bétharram. It is because the Soutou family owned a house there. We had lost everything when we arrived in exile, and the Soutou family took us in. Jean-Marie was the younger son of the Soutou family. He belonged to the Esprit movement,*as did my father, who was the general correspondent for the movement in Spain. At the beginning of the civil war, Jean-Marie Soutou, from Bayonne, had appeared at Lekeitio, the Basque village where events had overtaken us during the summer holidays in 1936, and made contact with my father on behalf of the Esprit movement. He was quite a young man, with a singsong, rough accent, like a mountain stream rushing over pebbles toward the Adour and the Garonne. The accent has gone with the passing of time, but not the Béarnais ardor of his youth. Anyway, we arrived at Bayonne with nothing, staring rather vacantly at the spectacle of French peace before us, the bandstand, the colored flower beds, the bakery windows, the *jeunes filles en fleur*—and we called on Jean-Marie Soutou for help. He came at once. He had already taken the situation in hand.

*Left-wing Catholic movement. —ED.

Our stay at Lestelle-Bétharram was quite long. We wandered the highways and byways, my brothers and I, while the lizards warmed themselves in the autumn sun, on the low, dry-stone walls. One day, as we were walking along a sunken road beside the torrent, one of the monks from the monastery at Bétharram called over to us. He recognized us from church, he said. Since he had seen us at church, he could not imagine that we were anything but Francoists. No, that's not quite the word; "Francoist" is an anachronism, and anachronisms don't fit into accounts in which one respects chronological order. The word "Francoist" was used only much later. At the time, people on the right called themselves Nationalists, and those on the left called them, quite simply, Fascists. Or Rebels, since they had risen in armed revolt against the legal government of the Republicans or Loyalists. I remember very well how stupefied, or at least embarrassed, we were by all these names. The confusion of tongues is one of the first experiences of exile. The sleepless night of exile is a night of Babel.

Anyway, this monk who presumed that we were Nationalists called over to us happily, proudly, in the sunken road where we practiced with delighted sadism the systematic stoning of lizards. He congratulated us on being Spanish, on belonging to that valiant people who had risen in defense of the state, in a crusade against the Marxist Infidel. His bluest of blue eyes shone with anger, with divine but deadly love for the lost sheep that had to be brought back into the fold through iron and fire. We listened to his diatribe, heads bowed. He terrified us. We didn't dare to say anything to him. We didn't dare to disabuse him, terrified by the holy thunderbolt from his fanatical eyes. Later, we were furious with ourselves. We were ashamed of our childish fear before this pathetic personage, brandishing, in a sunken road of the Pau torrent, the verbose, exterminating sword of the Faith.

But if I were telling the story of my life instead of recounting one Sunday in Buchenwald, some eight years after this meeting with the monk from the monastery of Bétharram, I would be forced to admit that the most important incident during my stay at Lestelle-Bétharram was not that encounter. It was reading Joseph Kessel's *Belle de jour*. I am well aware that an edifying story should avoid any allusion to that equivocal episode. I am well aware that I should have eliminated that episode and kept to the touching image of the child discovering the fears and perils of political exile, of uprootedness. But that child was beginning to experience the problems of early adolescence. He would soon be thirteen, and, at the same time as he was losing—perhaps forever—the signs of his identification with a nation, a family, a cultural world, he was discovering through the needs of his body his identity, his masculinity, the disturbing, compulsive expression of his true self. He became himself, an I, a Subject, an I-am, in the fascinated discovery of his sexual body, in the autonomy of a desire that did not yet have an object, at the moment when the violence of history tore him from the roots of that same possible identity. And so the child, unaware of all this, of course, but nevertheless afflicted by lascerating images, suffocating dreams, unnamable physical anxieties, had discovered in the Soutou family library, at Lestelle-Bétharram, a copy of *Belle de jour*, which he whisked away every now and then for moments of passionate, instructive reading in the relative quiet of the lavatory.

It may not have been very suitable reading. Indeed, the first impulse of the Narrator, once the child of Lestelle-Bétharram, now the Narrator of this story and of other stories that always return, obsessively, like the merry-go-rounds of the Luna Parks of memory, to the same themes —the Narrator's first impulse was to succumb to the temptation to forget that episode, to censor once again the memory of reading *Belle de jour*. Sometimes, when asked about his childhood, about his apprenticeship in the language of Claudel and of the monk from the monastery at Bétharram, the Narrator has replied that the first books he read in French were Cocteau's *Les Enfants terribles* and *Fils du peuple*, attributed to Maurice Thorez. The reading of these two books, though real enough, took place only later, some months later. It was when I was living in The Hague, another stage of my exile, when the magnolias were in bloom in the garden of the Spanish Republican legation in Holland, in 1937. But there is a link between my reading of *Belle de jour* and my reading of *Fils du peuple* and *Les Enfants terribles*. That link is Jean-Marie Soutou. It is, of course, an indirect, even involuntary link, of which the agent was quite unaware. Jean-Marie Soutou, at The Hague, got me to read the last two books I mentioned. He was not responsible, however, for my reading *Belle de jour*: I had simply stumbled across it, quite by chance, but with remarkable prescience, in the Soutou family library at Lestelle-Bétharram.

But I am in Geneva, in 1960, and I am not telling the story of my life, the life of that thirteen-year-old child that I finally became, rediscovering the disturbing and extraordinarily fertile memory of Kessel's novel. I am recounting one Sunday in Buchenwald, in 1944, and only incidentally a journey from Paris to Prague in 1960 that took me through Nantua, Geneva, and Zurich, with several halts which are of indeterminate duration in my memory. In the memory, rather, of that Sorel, Artigas, Salagnac, or Sanchez whom I finally, eventually, became, at once plural and univocal.

I have just returned to Fernand Barizon in the refreshment room of the Gare de Cornavin. He is drinking a beer, looking at me, frowning.

"And what do you call yourself now?" he asks.

"I call myself Barreto," I reply, "Ramón Barreto. And I'm Uruguayan."

He laughs briefly, sarcastically.

"Can you explain to me what I, Barizon, a prole from La Courneuve, am doing with a Uruguayan gentleman in this asshole of a city, Geneva?"

I shrug my shoulders.

"They won't ask," I say.

"Probably not," says Fernand. "No one is ever interested in us. But I'll bet you don't know who you are any longer, with all those changes of identity!"

I want to tell Fernand that sometimes I don't know who I am, even when I haven't changed my identity. Indeed, do I ever stop changing my identity? When I find my own again, isn't it in fact someone else's? But I say nothing. I would only be accused again of metaphysical complication. Not without some justification.

And so, at Geneva, as I was leaving Barizon, before getting on the train for Zurich, I wasn't thinking of Lestelle-Bétharram or Bayonne. I just went to the toilets, slipped my French identity card in the name of Camille Salagnac into the false bottom of a traveling bag, and took out a Uruguayan passport in the name of Barreto. The worst thing about these South American passports is the signature. The authentic, original holders of these passports often have complicated signatures that are difficult to imitate when one has to fill up police forms in airports or hotels. The elaborate flourish is a Spanish vanity that complicates the lives of secret agents.

I was not sad, that day in 1960, in the toilets of the Gare de Cornavin. Why should I have been? The day with Barizon had been pleasant enough. I was doing what I had chosen to do. No one had forced me to be what I was. I had freely decided to give up my freedom as an individual in the service of the underground community

of the PCE. And I still thought, in 1960, that the Russian
political system was reformable, and that we would soon
overthrow Franco's regime. I was thinking of the end of
my exile rather than its beginning twenty-four years
before. I had forgotten *Belle de jour*, the anguish of that
discovery of myself, long ago. And so I was not sad, nor
desanimado, as I would have said in Spanish—lacking in
animation, lacking in soul or *anima*, having lost the taste
for life. No, I was not yet *desanimado* in 1960.

"How would you tell it?" Barizon suddenly asks.

I look at him.

I had already asked myself the same question, at
Madrid, some months before, listening to Manuel
Azaustre's repetitive, confused account.

"I would tell about a Sunday at Buchenwald," I say.

"A Sunday?"

"Yes! Don't you remember, Sunday was the craziest day
of all. I'll tell about one Sunday, a Sunday like any other,
when nothing unusual happened. Waking up, work, the
Sunday noodle soup, Sunday afternoon with a few hours
to spare, conversations with one's pals. That's it, I'll tell
about a Sunday in winter when the two of us had a long
talk."

"What?" says Barizon. "You'd put me into your story?"

I nod. "Of course! That Sunday, I remember, at five
o'clock in the morning, just before roll call, we were both
standing in front of Block 40. It was snowing, and the
snowflakes swirled in the beams of the searchlights. A
dancing, icy light. And you cried out, '*Les gars, quel beau
dimanche!*' or something of that kind, before running off
to the *Appellplatz*. Yes, that's what I'd do. I'd begin my
story there and describe the whole day. But don't worry,
I'd change your name: then if you didn't recognize yourself in my story, you could always say you had nothing to
do with it."

"What would you call me?" he asks, warily.

"I'd call you Barizon," I say. "But I'd keep your real Christian name—Fernand Barizon."

He thinks for a second, then nods.

"Not bad," he says

A loudspeaker has just announced that the express for Zurich is standing at Platform 2. But Barizon is not leaving for Zurich. And he hears, not the loudspeaker of the Gare de Cornavin announcing the Zurich train, but the loudspeaker at Buchenwald announcing the end of the roll call. He hears the voice of the *Rapportführer* from the loudspeaker in the watchtower, and today, on that Sunday long ago, on the *Appellplatz*, Barizon is not thinking particularly of the Russians, any more than of the banks of the Marne. That much is obvious.

Today, what is bothering him—something quite absurd, something that he has just become aware of, with a sudden, insidious anxiety, or at least a certain discomfort —is of a quite different sort. He has just discovered, in the luminous numbness of the roll call that goes on and on, interminably, that being a Communist at Buchenwald immediately puts you in a privileged position. In the heart of Nazi Germany, under the eyes of the SS, being a member of the Party puts you in a privileged position. Of course, it involves certain risks. But that's only to be expected: any privileged position, to the extent that it expresses a social function, involves a corresponding number of obligations and risks. You don't get anything for nothing. And yet being a privileged individual in a Nazi camp by virtue of being a Communist is at first sight paradoxical.

Barizon has just stumbled upon this realization.

For this is the first time that being a Communist has put him in such a position. Barizon suddenly remembers Spain.

During the battle of the Jarama, when the front had crumbled under the charges of the Moorish cavalry, the day when the circle had nearly closed completely around the lines of communication of the Republican Army that was holding Madrid, the political commissar of the brigade had jumped up like a jack-in-the-box and yelled over the furious noise of machine-gun fire: "Communists to the front line!" And the Communists, hiding in shell holes, shivering with fear, rose, from one end of the landscape to the other, stood up among the smoke, fog, and corpses; the Communists had started to advance toward the Moorish cavalry and Italian tanks; the Communists, standing in the smoke-filled landscape, standing in the winter mist, charged through the Moorish cavalry and the Italian tanks, till they were in hand-to-hand combat with the enemy infantry, mouths agape in a cry that no one would hear, not even they themselves; the Communists carving out their passage with grenades and bayonets in the valley of the Jarama. The Communists to the front line.

Well, what do you expect, that's what they were there for.

But where is the front line today? In the Gustloff, snug and warm, quietly sabotaging parts of the G-43 automatic rifle? Or in the toughest outside kommandos, where the prisoners transferred from the main Buchenwald camp were often left to their fate, under the direct domination of the green kapos and SS warrant officers, precisely because the underground Communist organization that controlled the administration of labor in Buchenwald arranged matters so that members of the Party, the true resisters, didn't end up there, except in the event of some unforeseeable accident.

Barizon shakes his head. There is something to talk about in all that. It isn't at all clear. He must talk about it with the Spaniard.

But the voice of the *Rapportführer*, coming from the loudspeakers in the watchtower, has just brought them to attention. *Das Ganze, stand!* Barizon automatically corrects his position, thirty thousand prisoners packed into the *Appellplatz* automatically stand to attention. They stand impeccably to attention. *Mützen, ab!* Thirty thousand prisoners bare their heads, in a single, precise gesture, to salute the new day. *Mützen, auf!* Thirty thousand prisoners, now that they have saluted their own deaths, bared their heads before their future corpses, put their berets back on their heads.

The roll call is over.

Then the music breaks out with a clash of fife and drum, cymbals and trumpets: it's like being at the circus. The block formation falls apart in a sort of vortex.

Fernand Barizon runs to the place where the Gustloff kommando stands: it's one of the first to leave the camp compound. The musicians are beside the main gates, under the watchtower. They wear riding breeches, red with green facings, and long-sleeved pelisses. They blow into the brass, they beat the drums, they clash the cymbals. It's better than at the circus! Juliette, of course, didn't like the circus. She liked making love, but clowns made her cry, and the tigers frightened her. As for the acrobats, don't mention them: she'd shut her eyes. All right, Juliette would not have appreciated the funny side of the situation.

All the same, it's a shitty Sunday.

Three

I decided to tell this story in chronological order. Not because I thought it would be simpler that way—there's nothing more complicated than chronological order. And not because I was striving after realism—there is nothing more unreal than chronological order. It's an abstraction, a cultural convention, a victory for the geometrical mentality. It was that I had come to find it natural, like monogamy.

Chronological order is a way of demonstrating your grip on the disorder of this world, of making your mark on it. You pretend you're God. On the first day He created this, on the second day He created that, and so on. It was Jehovah who invented chronological order.

I decided to tell this story in chronological order— every hour of a particular Sunday, one after another— precisely because it is complicated. And unreal. I was attracted by the artifice of it, in both senses of the word according to the dictionaries: in the sense of "display of skill and ingenuity" and in that of "a pyrotechnic mixture intended to burn out fairly quickly"—what in French they call *feux d'artifice*. I liked the idea of the artifice of chronological order exploding in a shower of fireworks.

So it was really out of pride that I decided to tell this story in chronological order, and it's nine o'clock in the morning, this December Sunday in 1944, as I show up at the watchtower with Henk Spoenay.

Henk is twenty, like me. He's Dutch. He's always good-tempered, never gets excited. At the *Arbeitsstatistik*, he's got one of the most delicate jobs: he carries out daily liaison between our staff and the *Arbeitseinsatz* of the SS, the SS office that supervises and checks our work. In fact, Henk acts as liaison between Seifert, who is our kapo, and Schwartz, the *SS-Arbeitseinsatzführer*.

We get along well together, Henk and I.

It's nine in the morning and pretty cold. But the sun is now shining. The wind has dispersed most of the clouds. Henk and I are reporting to the SS officer on guard at the watchtower.

A quarter of an hour ago, I was sitting at the table of the central card index. It was a quiet day, no arrivals or departures expected. Not too many corpses to record, either. An average day. So I had finished entering on my cards the information provided by the daily reports from the different kommandos and from the hospital and crematorium. I was daydreaming; a sunbeam struck the window to my left.

"What are you doing?" Henk is behind me. I half turn around.

"Nothing," I tell him. "There's nothing going on today."

He motions toward the sun, outside.

"Care for a stroll?" he says. "I have to go over to the Mibau."

"I'll have to warn Seifert," I say.

He shakes his head.

"I've done it already," says Henk. "If you've nothing to do, let's go."

I tell Walter I'm going out with Spoenay. Walter works with me in filing. He motions vaguely—he couldn't care less. He's reading the *Völkische Beobachter*, the Sunday edition.

We go outside, walk around the hut, and come into the deserted *Appellplatz*. The silence is of a rare quality, at once dense and delicate. Its density is such that the slightest noise stands out sharply. The wooden huts around the square look smart in their fresh coat of bright green paint. The smoke from the crematorium is of a pale gray. There can't be much doing at the crematorium to produce such thin smoke, unless the dead are burning particularly well. Good, dry corpses can burn like brambles. Our dead pals are blowing us a final kiss of light, pale smoke. A smoke of friendship, a Sunday smoke.

"It's not real," I say.

Henk looks at me and smiles.

"No, it's not real," he says. "It's a dream."

We are walking on the *Appellplatz* in this dream.

"What?"

"What?"

His face is turned toward me as we walk.

"What's a dream?" I ask. "This? Or everything else?"

"What else?" Henk asks.

"Outside."

Henk laughs.

"What if it was all a dream?" he says. "This, outside, life?"

"That's not out of the question," I say.

He stops laughing.

"Don't worry about it," he says. "It's too tiring."

We're nearly there. The SS guard is watching us.

"Death, too, maybe."

"What?"

"A dream," I say.

"We'll know soon enough," says Henk.

But it's time to interrupt these reflections.

We are within three meters of the SS guard, the regulation distance. We salute, click our heels, raise our caps, report. Or, rather, we yell out our numbers. There's no other way of introducing ourselves.

The officer on guard has come out of the glass office by the doorway. He's holding the report book.

The SS officer knows Henk, of course. He sees him several times every day. He asks him where he's going, and comments contentedly on the fine weather. As he talks, he writes Henk's number in the report book. Then he turns to me.

"44904," he says, reading the number sewn on my chest.

Henk interrupts to say that I am working at the *Arbeitsstatistik* and that I'm going with him to the Mibau.

The SS officer is still staring at my chest, at the S inscribed in the red triangle on my chest.

"Spanish?" he says, surprised. "At the *Arbeitsstatistik*?"

He looks me up and down. He acts shocked.

"I'm Dutch," says Henk quietly.

The SS officer shrugs his shoulders. He seems to suggest that it is not at all the same thing, being Spanish or Dutch.

Henk turns to me and winks. Conspiratorially.

"The Spanish are not just anyone, you know," says Henk. "They once dominated Europe. They even occupied my country, and for a long time, too."

The SS officer looks at him, unconvinced.

"Do you know how the Dutch national anthem begins?" Henk goes on.

The SS officer obviously doesn't.

I'm still standing at attention. I'm trying not to laugh. This business of the Dutch national anthem is a joke between Henk and me.

"*Een prinsen van Oranje been ik altijd geweest / De konink van Spanje heb ik altijd geerd,*" says Henk in his best recitation voice.

It means: "A prince of Orange I have always been / The king of Spain have I always honored." Which is historically incorrect, as far as the second statement is concerned.

But it was a joke between us. I'd say to Henk that as a good Dutchman he ought to honor me, even if I wasn't the king of Spain. Henk would reply that he would quite happily shit on the House of Orange, or, for that matter, on the kings of my country.

The SS officer has no reason to be familiar with our private jokes. He looks astonished.

"There was even a Spaniard who was emperor of Germany," Hank adds quietly.

"Emperor of Germany? I don't believe that!"

The SS officer can no longer contain his indignation.

"And what about Charles the Fifth?" Henk persists.

The SS officer is not convinced. Henk changes the subject: he must not go too far.

In a neutral tone of voice, he explains to the SS officer that I am a model office worker, that I speak several languages, including German, which makes me very useful at the *Arbeitsstatistik*, where we deal with prisoners of every nationality.

The officer turns to me and asks if I really speak German.

I stand to attention and tell him, in perfect German, that I speak German perfectly.

He looks reassured. He nods and tells us to be on our way.

We go through the gate. We are now on the other side, walking along the snow-covered avenue. As far as the eye can see, there are tall granite columns crowned by Nazi eagles, or simply imperial eagles, on either side of the long, snow-covered avenue.

"He wasn't Spanish," I say.

"What?"

"Charles the Fifth," I say. "He was Flemish."

"Shit!" says Henk. "That's right!"

He laughs. We both laugh.

We are walking along the avenue. There's a nip in the air.

I came back alone. Henk stayed at the Mibau. What he had to do turned out to take longer than expected. I had to come back alone.

The avenue is deserted. I am walking slowly, looking around me.

A little while ago, on our way to the Mibau, Henk also looked around him.

"Suppose we get out?" he said.

We looked at the beech forest around us. We looked at the solidly built SS barracks, farther on, at the end of a side avenue. We looked at the snow that covered the trees and the barracks. At the whole landscape. The snow that covered Europe from the Russian plains in the East to the Ardennes in the West.

"Why not?" I said.

Henk shrugged his shoulders.

"No chance of getting out," he said.

We were outside the electrified boundary of the camp proper. But that whole collection of factories, depots, barracks, office buildings—the logistic base of the SS Totenkopf division—was surrounded by a second barrier of barbed wire. And beyond, the countryside was patrolled by troops.

I looked at the snow that covered Europe.

"The Russians manage to get out," I said.

Henk shrugged his shoulders again.

"The Russians get out in the spring," he said. "Anyway, the Russians are mad!"

It was true. The Russians did get out in the spring, and the Russians were mad.

As soon as the fine weather returned, the Russians working outdoors, repairing roads or railroad tracks, excavating or quarrying, wherever they happened to be, took off.

Spring returned; it was April.

Goethe would have ordered his barouche. He'd have taken Eckermann for a ride around the Ettersberg, among the tall beech groves. Goethe would have commented on the beauties of the landscape, the tiny events in the life of the birds; he would have interspersed these commentaries with profound or entertaining reflections, memories of Schiller or Hegel, perhaps even of Napoleon. Eckermann would have listened to it all, wide-eyed, committing it all to memory, for his only mission on earth was to write down Goethe's every word. It would be spring, in the fine forests of Thuringia!

Then, suddenly, as spring was returning, with the first swallow of that fragile spring, the Russians would take off. They had no preconceived plan, they had not thought out their escape. They just took off.

It always happened the same way. Suddenly a Russian stopped working. He leaned on his shovel or his pick, in the warm spring air with that smell of spring borne on a light breeze, like mist. It went to his head, a sort of drunkenness. A light dizziness. The Russian would straighten up, look around him. He would then drop his shovel and take off.

It was not an escape, but a compulsion. One can't resist that kind of compulsion.

There was that light, sweet-smelling mist. The Russian looked up. The woods were green over there, the copses decked out in tender shoots. The Russian could no longer stay there, shifting soil with his shovel, it was too stupid. He took off. He threw down his shovel, dashed down the slope toward the hedgerow, the copse, the green corn, the first shoots, the murmuring stream, life outside. He ran madly toward the immense, distant plains of his country, in the spring sunlight.

Sometimes the Russian got a bullet in the back of his neck before he'd gone a few steps. But death had been sweet, it had had the smell of spring about it, at that last moment when his face was buried in the ground. Sometimes the escapee was caught after a few hours of woodland freedom, and his face still wore the expression of an unbounded childish joy when he was hanged on the *Appellplatz*.

As soon as the fine weather returned, the Russians took off, it was well known.

"They're mad, the Russians!" Henk said.

No doubt they were, but that Russian madness made my heart beat faster.

Years later, I was reading Varlam Shalamov's *Kolyma Tales* when suddenly my blood seemed to ebb away. I felt like a ghost floating in someone else's memory. Or was it Shalamov floating in my memory like a ghost? It was the same memory in any case, divided into two.

On the Kolyma, too, Shalamov tells us, when spring returned the Russian peasants would take off. But, of course, they had no hope of escaping. Hundreds of kilometers of taiga to cross, with the punishment squad at their heels. They took off all the same, the Russian peasants, as soon as the transient spring of the Great

North returned. The punishment squads of the Special
Sections of the Ministry of the Interior caught them and
cut off their heads, which they brought back carefully
wrapped to prove that they really had caught the escapees
so they could claim their rewards.

The heads of the Russian peasants, Shalamov tells us,
were lined up in front of the *kommandantura* at Kolyma.
Eyes open on death. Mad eyes, pale-blue, icy-gray: tiny
lakes in which was reflected the sudden, lethal ardor of
spring. Mad eyes of the Russian peasants in Hitler's
camps and in Stalin's.

There is no such thing as an innocent memory. Not for
me any more.

I was in London, reading Varlam Shalamov's *Kolyma
Tales*. It was in the late spring of 1969. I could probably
give the exact date if it were of the slightest interest.
There are years that disappear almost entirely from the
memory—from mine, I mean—and they have to be recon-
stituted, sometimes painfully, from a few events that have
left verifiable traces, in the form of documents. But that
year has remained in my memory, in its transparent
entirety, in all its details, all its meanderings.

Anyway, I was in London in late May 1969 and I was
reading *Kolyma Tales*.

I had business appointments every morning at the
offices of a film studio on Dean Street. I walked from my
hotel, via Piccadilly Circus and Shaftesbury Avenue.
From the corner of Old Compton Street, I could follow the
thread of little Italian cafés, of which there are so many in
Soho, a district traditionally populated by immigrants,
with their perfectly drinkable espressos.

In the morning, of course, I chose to follow the Italian
cafés, which in fact were run by Spaniards of both sexes,
the Italians having already climbed a few steps on their
social ladder.

These morning visits served a double purpose. First, the imbibing of one or several cups of real coffee, an indispensable prelude to seemingly interminable discussions about a project for a film that had occupied me off and on for a year, and which was never to be made, but which brought me various incidental benefits, including a number of visits to London. The consumption of espressos was all the more necessary in that later, in the offices of my potential film producers, I would never manage to get more than a pale, warm beverage almost entirely lacking in aroma and caffeine. The other purpose or pleasure to be derived from these morning visits to the coffee bars was that I could speak Castilian with most, if not almost all, the waiters and waitresses. Communication, even in its most limited or technical form, the transmission of an order or a wish—in this case, concerning a cup of coffee—was thereby greatly facilitated. But there was more to it than that. It meant that I could savor once again Spanish words and Spanish accents, bits of anecdotes begun or guessed at, able to comment on some event in Spanish life, especially sports.

So I would be leaning on the bar of a London café, watching the precise gestures of a waiter who had not shown the slightest surprise at hearing me order a strong, black coffee in Castilian, because he probably belonged to that new generation of Spaniards who are no longer surprised by anything, having escaped forever from the provincial, antiquated horizon of everyday life in their country. Then, just as the waiter put down a cup of coffee in front of me and offered me a Spanish newspaper, the *Marca*, a sports paper, and just as I accepted the offer, I would remember the old days, in Madrid.

In the old days in Madrid, I spent hours in the cafés. It was in the early fifties. I did not yet have any real safe hideouts. I lived under pseudonyms, of course, but here or there, usually subletting a room with a small washroom or share of the bathroom, in the house of some widow, whose husband had been a civil servant or a regular army officer who had died for his country—one always dies for one's country, even if one dies in one's bed, when one is an officer in the Spanish army—who, by subletting some of the rooms in her enormous, dilapidated apartment, eked out her meager widow's pension. I had impeccable false papers and changed my name regularly whenever I moved, but I always remained a native of the province of Santander, which I knew well enough, having spent all my childhood there, or at least all those long summer vacations, to be able to answer the questions of an interested, sometimes even indiscreet, but never malicious lonely old woman, questions that it would be quite normal for a landlady to ask. So, a native of the distant Cantabrian province of Santander, I explained to all these good menopausal ladies that I was in Madrid to prepare for an examination, with a view toward getting a job as a sociology teacher. The sociology made a favorable impression on these widows of army officers or civil servants in the Ministry of Public Works. I don't know why, but I offer the information for what it's worth. The hypothetical preparation for the said examination forced me, however—or, rather, forced the character I was pretending to be, a role I had to play convincingly—to spend long hours in libraries and university seminars. There was a problem, though. Without arousing suspicion, I could hardly come back to the house several times a day, whenever I had to keep one of my many secret appointments. So I arranged these appointments, as much as possible, to coincide with the regular timetable of a future sociology teacher. But it was quite impossible to avoid completely having hours of free time, or waiting, between one appointment and another. So, as I was saying, I was forced at that time, in the early fifties, to spend long hours in Madrid cafés.

Those who did not know me then may find it difficult to believe, but the truth is that I was not in the least interested in soccer in those far-off years. In fact, I was so little interested in it that my ignorance about it never failed to arouse pained and vaguely mistrustful surprise, if not downright suspicion, in the various cafés in which I was forced to spend so much time, leaning on the bar in front of a cup of coffee. One cannot, or at least at the time I'm talking about one could not, stay in a Madrid café for more than a few minutes—unless one sat at a table ostensibly or perhaps even hostilely absorbed in solitary reading, or in the laborious writing of a begging letter to the authorities—one could not stay for long without having to confront the expansive cordiality, the innate need of the natives of Madrid to communicate with their fellow man. However, every conversation necessarily turned on the subject of soccer. It was the time when the European career of Real Madrid was beginning, a time when, every Sunday on the radio, and every Monday and Tuesday in the press, the sports journalists commented at length on the exploits of Di Stefano, the Argentine center forward nicknamed *la saeta rubia*—the blond arrow— who brought delight or despair to the frenetic Spanish supporters. (Oh, those dummy shots that got him free from the opposing players! Those unexpected dribbles that sowed panic in the enemy defense, when he didn't even have the ball at his feet! Those goals scored from some imperceptible, aerial vantage, performed with the grace of a ballet dancer!) The day when, at the bar of the Café Inglés on the Plaza San Bernardo, I was foolish enough to admit to someone next to me not only that I didn't know the results of the final day of the soccer championship, but also to confess that the name Di Stefano did not mean a great deal to me, I felt an icy silence fall around me, thickening like a mayonnaise reaching the precise point of its correct consistency. I suddenly felt like a Martian on some subversive mission on our planet whom the Earthlings had just exposed through his inadequate knowledge of some aspect of daily life. But it was very dangerous for me to seem like a Martian, for my nonconformity to be unmasked. On the contrary, I had to melt into the crowd, become anonymous, ordinary: I suddenly realized that I had to be able to discourse endlessly and brilliantly on Gento's dribbling, Di Stefano's finesses, the impeccable if uninspired technique of Luis Suarez, and so on.

Still, it was politics, as you may have guessed—paradoxical as it may seem at a time when the passion for soccer in Spain was, according to right-thinking folk, part of the demobilization, depoliticization of the masses—it was politics that drove me to take an interest in soccer. Nowadays, of course, I no longer need that pretext, perfectly respectable though it may be. My love for the game needs no justification: I love it for the pleasure of the spectacle alone.

Anyway, I was in a little café on Dean Street, or some nearby street, in London, in the late spring of 1969, and the waiter handed me *Marca*, a Spanish sports paper. He commented briefly but pertinently on the latest results of the Spanish first-division championship, in a way that clearly revealed his preferences and his origin: he was a Basque, there could be no doubt about it, and what was bothering him that morning was the recent appalling performance of Real Sociedad, the San Sebastián club.

I sipped the warm, bitter coffee, talked to the waiter, who was from Pasajes, and felt at home in that tiny male nation, temporary as it no doubt was, but full of nostalgia for those bright days in Madrid.

• • •

But I was in London, reading Varlam Shalamov's *Kolyma Tales*. At Buchenwald, too, the Russians escaped in the spring. They did not even really escape: they took off. They stopped working with shovel or pick, quite suddenly. They straightened up. Maybe there had been a slight gust of warm air, bearing all the scents from the spring vegetation, rustling the leaves nearby. Perhaps they had heard the full-throated song of the birds. In Buchenwald, within the camp boundary, even though it was surrounded by the tall dark mass of a thick beech wood, one never heard birdsong. One never saw birds. There were no birds on the Ettersberg. Perhaps the birds could not stand the smell of burning flesh, vomited over the landscape in the thick smoke from the crematorium. Perhaps they didn't like the barking of the German shepherds that always accompanied the SS detachments. But in the spring, in one of the construction kommandos, working outside the camp boundary, perhaps it was the strange, poignant nostalgia caused by the unexpected song of a bird, a triumphal shower of trills, that had made this twenty-year-old Russian straighten up. Perhaps he listened to the birdsong during a brief moment of suspended time. Perhaps he listened, a smile on his lips. And then, suddenly, he threw down his shovel or pick and ran off, with a piercing shout, the cry of a Sioux Indian on the warpath, a howl of wild joy, which was odd, because it would have been better to take off as quietly as possible.

But I'm telling you about these escapes the Russians made in the spring as if I'd witnessed one. I never did. Sebastián Manglano saw one once. He told me about it. He told it very well.

Sebastián Manglano was born in a poor working-class district of Madrid, near the Cava Baja. He had the drawling accent, swagger, the male boastfulness of the young bloods of Madrid. But he had taken part in the civil war when little more than an adolescent, in a unit of the Fifth Corps of the Republican Army, a crack corps commanded by Communists and the darling of the propaganda machine of the PCE. The mixture of these two biographical elements turned out to be a rather good one, for as his Communist education had not managed to stifle his untutored spontaneity, he had a perhaps crude, but always just perception of injustice and the abuse of power.

In short, Manglano was not a bad companion in misfortune. The only thing I can really reproach him with is that he got lice, probably at the Gustloff Works, where he had been transferred after his period of quarantine. Since we had become roommates in Block 40, we were both sent for disinfection, in accordance with the hygiene regulations—he because he had found lice in his clothes and I because I was his roommate. The mere fact that I worked at the *Arbeitsstatistik*, an obvious sign that I belonged to the ruling political bureaucracy, did not spare me this disinfection. Mind you, in Block 40, where a good proportion of the élite, the aristocracy of prisoners, were housed, we had other roommates who were not sent for the regulation disinfection; but that was because they were Germans. They did not come from those distant, dubious, unclean Mediterranean lands from which Manglano and I originated. A louse on a Spaniard is not at all the same thing, in its foreseeable consequences, as a louse on the smooth, pink, delicate, well-fed skin of a German, an Aryan prisoner. So they sent off to be disinfected only members of the inferior races, those whose blood was not pure enough to resist contamination at once. When I say "they," I don't mean the SS, of course: they didn't necessarily interfere in so banal a detail of everyday life. I mean the block leader and his assistants.

So we were sent for disinfection, Manglano and I. Once

again, we were completely shaved, as on our arrival at the camp, and plunged firmly into a vile bath of greenish cresyl by young Russians who did not conceal their delight at keeping our heads in it as long as possible.

But I don't in the least regret that episode. To begin with, it was a time when I was still curious about everything and almost insensitive to physical pain. Nothing outside myself, nothing objective, could humiliate me: those crude, stupid Russians, who were taking a petty, if understandable, revenge on us for the fate that was generally accorded their compatriots in the Nazi camps, hardly affected me, let alone humiliated me. Only one person could humiliate me, and that was myself. The only thing that could have humiliated me was the memory of some shameful act that I myself had committed. I wasn't pushing men's heads into the stinking, greenish water of the disinfectant bath. I wasn't on the side of the murderers, the haves, and profiteers.

Anyway, the disinfection building is on the western boundary of the Buchenwald camp, right against the wall of the armament factory, in more or less the same row of buildings as Block 40. It's behind the showers and the clothing stores. Manglano and I reported at the correct time and were told to wait outside the door. It was midwinter, the last winter of that bygone war. It was cold enough to freeze the blood, and it probably would have frozen ours if Manglano had not warmed us by telling, with his usual verve and imagination, stories of his youthful love life. It was while we were waiting to be disinfected that Manglano told me about the crazy escape of a young Russian which he had witnessed, the spring before, while still working on the construction kommando.

"I was in a good mood that day," Manglano told me. "The night before you came to see me in the quarantine block, do you remember? You brought me a little tobacco, from the family."

The family, of course, was the Party. *La familia.* For a number of reasons, sometimes clear enough, historically determined, and therefore easy to uncover, and sometimes much more obscure, the Spanish Communists were very reluctant to use the word "Party," to call it the Party even among themselves, in private conversations, far from any indiscreet or possibly ill-intentioned ear: the ear of the enemy. *"Es de la familia,"* or *"Es de casa,"* one would say knowingly when referring to a comrade. "He's one of the family," or, more succinctly and even more revealingly, "He's one of us." This inveterate habit must have had a historical origin. To begin with, the PCE has been underground for most of its existence. This euphemism could be seen as a conspirational precaution, and, initially, it was in a way. Later, during the civil war, the PCE played a political role out of all proportion to its real size in the country, a role that depended on a whole series of external factors, but one above all: Soviet military aid, and the hold on the state apparatus that this aid gave the Communists. At that time, the PCE was frenetically involved in the tactics of infiltration—"entryism," in short—into every organization, every institution, and above all into the army and police. The PCE carried out at a certain level the same tactics as Stalin's "special services," which, from the time of the civil war, had infiltrated a wide range of Spanish organizations—beginning with the Communist Party itself. All this reinforced the habit of a metaphorical, euphemistic reference to party membership, which could not be made public for tactical reasons.

But this love of secrecy had more to it, of course. It revealed something deeper. It stressed the relationship between the secret and the sacred. The Party was, in fact, the radiant entity whose name must not be taken in vain, or used lightly, and whose existence must on no account be revealed to the uninitiated. So, on occasions when one could hardly avoid referring to it, we had got used to doing so by means of these significant euphemisms.

But Manglano was telling me why, that day of the previous spring, he had every reason to be in a good mood. Not only because, the night before, I had brought him his tobacco ration in the spirit of Communist solidarity. It was also because that morning, when awakened in his hut in the Little Camp by the strident whistles of the guards, he had noticed with gratitude and wonder that his masculinity had not deserted him forever, as he had been fearing for several weeks.

"You see," Manglano told me, "it was ages since I had anything to put in my hand! It was as if it was dead, gone to sleep forever. Nothing when I woke up, and yet, I don't want to boast, but I used to wake up like a donkey down there. Then, for weeks and weeks, nothing. I'd tickle it, squeeze it, shake it whenever I could, but nothing doing, nothing to get hold of! Then suddenly, that morning, as I woke up, without any warning, without so much as a by-your-leave, there it was, the real thing, in all its glory!"

This is, of course, only approximately what he said. I could not adequately cover, in translation, Manglano's vivid, inventive, exuberant Castilian.

We were standing outside the door of the disinfection building, and the descriptive warmth of Manglano's story helped us to forget the freezing cold around us. About thirty or forty meters away, at the end of the esplanade that stretched in front of us, between the clothing stores and the showers, I saw Goethe's tree. Or, rather, its charred remains. For although the SS had spared it when they built Buchenwald, an American phosphorus bomb had set fire to it during a bombing raid in August 1944.

On the trunk of the tree, it was said, had once been the carved initials of Goethe and Eckermann. I can well believe it.

I was beginning to get numb in the cold of that winter's morning, and Manglano's story, the story of the crazy escape of a young twenty-year-old Russian the spring before, was growing incoherent and repetitive. For the third time already, the Russian in Manglano's story had straightened up, eyes alert, a smile on his lips—a "blissful" smile, Manglano had said for the third time—just before throwing down his pick and dashing toward a small wood, emitting a cry like a Sioux Indian on the warpath.

"Why Sioux?" I asked, with obvious bad faith.

"What?" said Manglano, interrupted in his flow.

"Why Sioux and not Navajo, or Comanche, or Apache?"

Manglano frowned.

"Why not Sioux?" he said sullenly.

"For Christ's sake!" I yelled back. "Do you know the difference between the war cries of the Sioux, Apaches, Navajos, Comanches, or God knows what?"

But we weren't able to follow up on this interesting point. The door of the disinfection building opened, and a fat, rubicund individual yelled at us to come in.

Still, despite our final, superfluous controversy, which was in any case quite absurd, as to the exact Indian origin of a war cry emitted by a young anonymous Russian as he made his unpremeditated escape, I was in possession of first-hand evidence about the spring escapes of Varlam Shalamov's compatriots at Buchenwald.

But not all the Russians escaped in the spring, on impulse, just like that. As at Kolyma, there were also in Buchenwald carefully worked-out, long-thought-out escapes.

I was in London, reading in *Kolyma Tales* the story of the escape of Lieutenant-Colonel Yanovsky and his group, and I remembered Pyotr. We called him Pedro at Buchenwald. He was Russian, of course, but he had fought in Spain in the armored corps. He spoke fluent Castilian.

Pyotr had decided that it was really too stupid to rot away in a concentration camp. Especially since, being a Russian, he could very easily be seized by some unspeakable SS warrant officer and end up in the crematorium. Now, the idea of going up in smoke when the end of the war was only a matter of months away seemed to Pyotr to be particularly stupid. So he had decided to escape from Buchenwald. I say "escape," and not "take off," any time, anyhow, at the first bittersweet whiff of spring.

A proper escape has to be planned.

The first thing to realize was that one must not try one's luck in Buchenwald itself. From inside the boundary of the camp, or from one of the kommandos working near the camp, from which the prisoners would return each evening to the camp for roll call, it was practically impossible to escape. So Pyotr had worked out an escape plan for a group of men from a kommando working some distance from the camp, combining the maximum favorable conditions.

That was why he had come to me. Through my job at the *Arbeitsstatistik*, I could help him get sent to the best possible place.

Pyotr's choice had finally lit on a mobile kommando repairing railway lines bombed by the Allies, which traveled on those rails in a special train that was both prison and workshop, an *Eisenbahnbaubrigade*. He joined it along with a group of about fifteen young Russian volunteers that he had collected. It wasn't spring. It was late autumn. The winter would soon be with us, the longest, coldest, and last winter of the war. Some weeks later, a report reached the *Arbeitsstatistik*. A collective escape had taken place in the *Baubrigade*: Pyotr and all his pals had got away. Within several days, two of them were recaptured. The SS report announced in the same sentence that the two young Russians had been recaptured and immediately freed: *entlassen*. This was the usual administrative euphemism to convey that they had been executed, freed of their heavy, miserable, earthly manifestation, and that they could be struck off the list of prisoners in Buchenwald.

As the days and weeks passed, other reports of this kind reached us. One of Pyotr's group had been recaptured here or there and immediately executed: *entlassen*. Because these reports indicated very precisely the places where the Russians had been recaptured, one could follow the progress of Pyotr's group across Europe, eastward, toward the Red Army. The last report placed the group in Slovakia, near the Hungarian border. After that, we heard nothing of them. Four or five men still remained with Pyotr, at liberty. Would they go on walking, at night, across Europe? Had they managed to reach the Red Army lines?

Later, I thought a great deal about this escape of Pyotr's and about Pyotr himself. In my personal mythology, Pyotr had become, in a way, the living embodiment of Soviet man: the new man, the true man. At certain difficult times during the cold war—class against class, science against science, their morality against ours—I would try to reassure myself, to comfort myself with Pyotr's memory. Of course, Fougeron's* paintings weren't up to much, they were even, between ourselves, pretty hideous, and I was well aware of this. I didn't believe everything I was told, but beneath it all, nevertheless, was Pyotr himself, Soviet

*Neo-Realist French painter vaunted by the Communists. —ED.

man, the true, simple man. Of course, the statement from the Cercle des Philosophes Communistes, published in the November 1950 issue of *Nouvelle Critique*, was an aberration, castigating the "return to Hegel" at length as "the last word in academic revisionism," and ending with these empty, abject words: "This Great Return to Hegel is no more than a desperate recourse against Marx, in the specific form taken by revisionism in the final crisis of imperialism: revisionism of a fascist character." In the silence of my innermost schizophrenic self, I undoubtedly regarded such a judgment as an aberration that had nothing to do with me; there was always Pyotr, the memory of Pyotr to give me hope. One wasn't fighting—at least I wasn't fighting, unhappy fool that I was—for the sake of pontificating on the relationship between Marxism and Hegel, or on the respective merits of Fougeron and Braque: one was fighting, I was fighting, so that Pyotr, with his irrepressible gaiety, his quiet courage, his sense of fraternal justice, should become the man of tomorrow.

But in London, in 1969, in the little café on Dean Street, I no longer needed that fable, those fabrications. I now knew that the myth of the new man was one of the bloodiest in the bloody history of historical myths. I had ordered another coffee. I was talking to the waiter, a Basque from Pasajes. We weren't talking about soccer any more. Our commentaries on the recent defeat of Real Sociedad, the San Sebastián team, had brought us quickly to the real subject, which was politics, of course, the history of our country. Of our countries, I should say.

I was reading *Kolyma Tales* in London, my heart in my mouth. Now I knew what had been Pyotr's fate. An exemplary fate, no doubt, but not in the sense that I had understood it, at the time when I used to recount the beautiful, moving story of Pyotr's escape, the long march of Pyotr and his pals across Europe, the nighttime of Europe, the mountains and the forests of Europe. An examplary fate because Pyotr must have ended up in one of the Gulag camps, of course. Maybe he came across Varlam Shalamov at Kolyma. All the circumstances of his life combined to make Pyotr an ideal candidate for deportation to one of Stalin's camps. Had he not fought in Spain? Had he not escaped from a Nazi prison camp? All the right circumstances, no doubt. Had he also tried, like Shalamov's Lieutenant-Colonel Yanovsky, to escape from one of the Kolyma camps? Was Pyotr that Soviet officer who had escaped from a Nazi camp and was then sent on to Kolyma, whose heroic end is described by Shalamov in "Major Pugachov's Last Struggle"? Or had he, a Communist broken by Communism, exhausted by the cold, the hunger, the inhuman labor, died without understanding why, wondering what error he had committed, when, why, where it had all gone wrong? Or—such a thing was not unthinkable, even if it was painful to think it—had he, a true specimen of the new man, a truly faithful, exemplary Communist, had he become a Stakhanovite of forced labor, a pitiless overseer, a shrieking, hate-filled robot of Correct Thought, a murderer of his fellow deportees?

Anyway, it was no longer any comfort in 1969, none at all, to remember Pyotr, whom we called Pedro because he had fought in Spain.

On the contrary, it was rather depressing.

But I was on Dean Street, at the entrance to the building where the film company that I have already mentioned had its offices. I was about to go in when I turned around to observe once more the animated movement of the street. On the building opposite, on the even-numbered side, I suddenly saw a plaque stating that Karl Marx had lived there.

And no doubt this coincidence was not without meaning.

At Buchenwald, twenty-five years earlier, I sometimes dreamed that Goethe, immortal and Olympian—Goethean, in other words—was still walking on the Ettersberg, accompanied by that distinguished fool Eckermann. Not without some degree of intellectual perversity, I was pleased to imagine Goethe's conversations with Eckermann on the subject of the Buchenwald camp. What would Goethe have said if he had noticed, as he walked along the Avenue of Eagles, one December Sunday, for instance, the wrought-iron inscription on the monumental camp gates, *Jedem das Seine*, TO EACH HIS DUE? In 1944, of course, I did not know that Varlam Shalamov would hear of that inscription, some day not too far off, somewhere in the concentration-camp zone of Kolyma. One or another of the many Russians from Buchenwald later deported to the Great North—Pyotr, who knows?—must have mentioned that inscription when he arrived at Magadan. And, as happens so often, almost inevitably, in accounts transmitted by word of mouth, the meaning of the original inscription had gradually become transformed. Thus Shalamov writes: "It is said that over the German concentration camps there appeared a quotation from Nietzsche: 'Everyone for himself.'"

And in the accounts that must have been brought back by Russians talking, in some hut at Kolyma, of their experience in Buchenwald, *Jedem das Seine* ended up as *Jeder für sich*: TO EACH HIS DUE had become EVERYONE FOR HIMSELF. Which, of course, is not at all the same thing. In fact, the only rather surprising thing in this whole business is that Shalamov should have attributed this banal expression of the immemorial self-interest that characterizes what is called the "wisdom of the nations," EVERYONE FOR HIMSELF, to Nietzsche. Why Nietzsche? I still haven't found the answer.

Anyway, in 1944, as I stood there imagining with a certain perverse pleasure what Goethe would have to say about this inscription over the Buchenwald gate, TO EACH HIS DUE—a cynically egalitarian notion—I did not know that Varlam Shalamov was to make a most valuable contribution to those imaginary dialogues on the Ettersberg. I knew nothing of Varlam Shalamov. I knew nothing of Kolyma.

Or, to be more precise, if I had known, I would not have wanted to know anything about it.

But that day in 1969, at the very moment when I discovered the commemorative plaque on the façade of a building on Dean Street, reminding us that Karl Marx had lived there—and it was from there that the jolly family group set out, on foot, noisy but well behaved, toward the green fields of Hampstead, if Liebknecht is to be believed; it was here, at 28 Dean Street, that Marx lived from 1850 to 1856, and wrote The Eighteenth Brumaire of Louis Bonaparte and hundreds of articles and political tracts—that day, I knew enough to stop wasting my time arguing with Goethe, catching—too easy an undertaking, perhaps, but always a salutary one nonetheless—bourgeois humanism in the trap of its own historical hypocrisies. That day, it was Marx I dreamed of seeing come out of his house, at No. 28, in his shabby frock coat. What would he have to say to Varlam Shalamov?

The evening before, at my hotel, I had gone back to Kolyma Tales. I was at page 87, reading a short piece entitled "How It All Began."

Suddenly the blood drained from my face, then from my hands, retreating to my heart, which was beating wildly. I had read this: In the triangular beams of the searchlights that lit the mine at night, snowflakes danced like particles of dust in a sunbeam. . . .

Snowflakes in searchlight beams!

There are still several thousand of us former deportess. (I don't much care for that term, of course, but what are we to be called? Survivors of the death camps? Aside from the pitiful grandiloquence of the term, the word "survivors" reminds me of natural disasters, earthquakes, floods. What exactly has one survived? Death? Hardly: one never survives one's own death. It is always there, lying in wait like a patient cat, biding its time. Does one survive the death of others? That won't take us very far: we don't need camps to know that it is always others who die. The experience of death is social, a revenge or a victory of the species, said—or words to that effect—Dr. Marx, whose life in London was recorded on a plaque on Dean Street.) Anyway, there are several thousand of us, men and women, in the West, several hundred thousand in the East—I'm not saying that these are the exact figures; this is just to give a rough idea—who cannot think of the swirling of snow in searchlight beams without having a sort of cardiac arrest, an arrest of the memory.

This happened to me in 1963, in April, at the Gare de Lyon.

Gare de Lyon?

I was not on my way back from some secret trip. I would probably never come back from a secret trip again. I was not on my way back from Spain, in any case: one does not come back from Spain, or leave for it, from the Gare de Lyon. Besides, since December 1962, I had no longer been working underground in Spain, or anywhere else. I had taken up my own identity again—I mean, the identity officialdom seems to attribute to me.

I was not thinking of anything in particular, as I remember, only of how I could escape being trapped in the anticipated rushing crowd of passengers and stride across to the exit. I had got off the train at the uncovered part of the platform, when suddenly I was startled by an unexpected gust of snow. A strident voice announced something over the loudspeaker, the arrival or departure of a train, no doubt, the kind of announcement that is generally made in railway stations. I looked up. My heart was pounding before I even knew why. Then I saw that whirlwind of light snow caught in the beam of search-lights, that expanse of dancing, frozen light.

I stopped stock still, transfixed, trembling.

Dancing, frozen light, dancing light, light . . .

Standing still in the coming and going, the commotion, the confusion of reunions, I stared at those light snow-flakes dancing in the beam of a searchlight. *Dancing, frozen light.* What were those words saying, inside me? Where did they come from? Who was saying them, whispering them, if not myself? Where did they come from, if not from the furthest reaches of myself?

No doubt I could have pulled myself together, given myself a quiet talking-to, said to myself that this was nothing to make such a fuss about. It was not the first time that, for no apparent reason, I had been revisited by some blinding memory of Buchenwald. The snow, the search-lights: all right, that's nothing to get so worked up about. Yes, yes, an incommunicable memory. I was used to them.

But I was not remembering Buchenwald, that day in April 1963; that is the point.

I was remembering a place where I had never been. I had seen the light snow swirling in the air, at the Gare de Lyon, and I was remembering a camp in which I had never set foot. That was why I couldn't dismiss that memory with a word or a gesture, as I had so often done before. A word or a gesture would have been enough to exorcise a memory of Buchenwald, however brutal, however painful it might have been. A word or a gesture, to put it back in its place, in the desert of a memory of inexhaustible and lethal riches, but of which one can share only a few crumbs. I was not remembering Buchenwald. I was remembering some unknown camp whose name I did not know: the special camp in which—forever, it seems to me, to the end of time perhaps—Ivan Denisovich Shukhov is a prisoner.

I had read Solzhenitsyn's account some days before and I was still living in that obsessional world. So, when I caught sight of the swirling snow in the light of the lamps at the Gare de Lyon, the snow of that sudden spring storm, I had not remembered Buchenwald, at five in the morning one winter's day, perhaps even a Sunday. I had remembered Ivan Denisovich at the beginning of *his* day, on his way to the infirmary, when "the sky was as dark as ever," while "the two searchlights were cutting broad swathes through the compound." I was not in Gérard's place in some distant memory of Buchenwald. I was in Shukhov's place, or, even more sadly, in that of Senka Klevshin, whom I may have known—in a special camp, somewhere in the USSR.

Standing motionless in the commotion, in the coming and going, I was overcome by a sensation of unreality I had experienced before.

But let me be quite clear about it. It was not the Gare de Lyon, the crowd, the swirling snow of that sudden spring storm: it was not, in short, the world around me that seemed unreal. It was I who seemed unreal. It was my memory that held me in the unreality of a dream. Life was not a dream, oh no! It was I who was. What's more, it was the dream of someone who appeared to have been dead for a long time. I have already named, despite its unnamable indecency, the sensation that has sometimes assailed me over the years. That serene, quite desperate certainty of being no more than a dream of a young man who died long ago.

That evening, at the Gare de Lyon, when the dancing, frozen light of the swirling snow in the beams of the searchlights reminded me of something that I had read recently in Solzhenitsyn, that evening I was about to take one more step that would lead me, perhaps inexorably, toward a solitary madness, toward the flickering flame of my own insanity, which, however, might be no more than a reflection of the barbaric holocaust that has consumed this century. I was about to cease being the memory of a dead man, the desperate, lucid dream of a young man who died long ago, who may very well have been me, who might have been me, under any name, even an assumed one, even that of Gérard Sorel, gardener; I was going to abandon my unreal being and begin to inhabit, or, rather, to be inhabited by, another life, occupied by another memory: that of Ivan Denisovich to begin with, then, as the years passed, with the help of other reading, that of all the zeks from the Gulag camps whose memories and names have been preserved for us in innumerable accounts; perhaps, at the very frontiers of death, or madness, I shall finally be invested by the monstrous work of some anonymous, silent memory, the flat, devastated memory, now devoid of the slightest spark of hope, of the slightest possibility of pity, the muddy, gloomy memory of some unknown zek, forgotten by all, erased from every memory in this world.

Perhaps; why not?

Surely there was a way of dealing with this pain. Surely there was a way of erasing the dream while erasing the dreamer, whoever he was. And of erasing the guilt I felt at having lived in the blessed innocence of the memory of Buchenwald, the innocent memory of having belonged to the camp of the just, without the slightest doubt, whereas the ideas for which I thought I was fighting, the justice for which I thought I was fighting, was serving at the same time to justify the most radical injustice, the most absolute evil: the camp of the just had created and was running the Kolyma camps. Of course, one could always commit suicide. Fadeev had committed suicide.* Only with blood can blood be erased.

Was there blood in my memory?

I spent the days after reading Solzhenitsyn's account exploring my memory. I went on pretending I was living normally. I answered the questions that were put to me. I may even have held doors open for old ladies in métro stations. I passed the salt and the bread, when asked for the bread or the salt, at table. I certainly must have indulged in a few witticisms, a few clever remarks on some film or book. But all that was superficial: bubbles on the surface of life. Deep down, with that obsessive meticulousness that usually characterizes moments of profound self-questioning, I continued to analyze my memory.

No, there was no blood in my memory.

Let me be quite clear: my memory was full of blood. To the extent that my memory overlapped the history of this century, it was full of blood. The century has been bespattered with blood, like every other century in history, perhaps even more so. But it was blood for which I could take responsibility, which I could also reject, refusing from now on to take part in the conflicts of this century. I don't mean *that* blood, the blood trickling from history. I mean blood that one may have in one's memory and even on one's hands, ineradicable, when one has

*Alexander Fadeev, 1901–56, secretary of the Union of Soviet Writers. —ED.

fought in the ranks of Communism during the Stalin period. And I don't mean just the Stalin period, as if there had been no blood before the Georgian and none after him. No, I mention the Stalin period in particular because it was the one during which I became a Communist, even if it was only after Stalin's death that I became a leader of the PCE.

I mean left-wing blood, all the innocent blood, whose ever it may be, that one may have shed—directly or more subtly, through the apparently logical mediations of a terrorist ideology that is convinced of its own aberrational, virtuous truth—precisely because one was a Communist leader, because one had at one's disposal a piece, if only a piece, of absolute power. The power of life or death, as it is so aptly put.

But there was no such blood in my memory.

There were a lot of unpleasant, shameful, or ridiculous things, plenty of repugnant, seeping, good-bad faith, schizoid ideology, empty terrorist single-mindedness: there was plenty to pick out patiently. I had to set fire to the dead wood of my memory, certainly, but there was no blood that had to be erased with blood.

There was nothing to be particularly proud of, either. Maybe it was a question of age. Maybe I was five or ten years too young to have blood on my hands, blood in my memory. Perhaps innocence is only a question of age.

Anyway, if only by biographical chance, there was no such blood in my memory. I could go on living the life that had been given me, which was either truly mine or that of someone else, who died at Buchenwald twenty years earlier. I could go on living the life that had been changed, invisibly but radically, by reading *A Day in the Life of Ivan Denisovich*.

That was how it all began, in April 1963, at the Gare de Lyon, as I was looking up at the snow swirling in the beams of floodlights.

• • •

But I was in London, some years later, in front of the building where Karl Marx had once lived.

In the first line of his *Eighteenth Brumaire*, certainly the most important work that he wrote at 28 Dean Street, Marx refers to Hegel. It was quite a harmless, lighthearted remark, despite its fate at the hands of generations and generations of distinguished Marxists. It was no more than a private joke between Engels and himself. Marx's famous remark that the characters and events of history are repeated twice, according to Hegel, who appears to have forgotten to add that they occurred first in the form of tragedy, and second as farce—this famous little remark was actually pinched from Engels. In a letter dated December 3, 1851, the day after Louis Bonaparte's coup d'état, Engels wrote to his friend about the event. Engels was in good form that day. His letter is sharp, brilliant, caustic. It is also quite wrong. I mean wrong on the main point: his judgment on the historical meaning of the imperial coup d'état is remarkable for its blindness. Anyway, it is in that letter that Engels formulates, with much force and sarcastic precision, the idea that history repeats itself, an idea that Marx took up word for word, softening its literary form, but at the same time giving it a general significance of which Engels had probably been quite unaware.

It is not Engels who interests me at the moment, however, but Hegel. Old Hegel, always the butt, in their private correspondence, of Marx's or Engels's brilliant jokes or subtle analyses; that "old fogey" as he was later called by the epigones—almost two hundred years ago, when he was still only a young man, he characterized in a few lines the very essence of the concentration-camp system to come.

In notes that he made at Berne and Frankfurt while reading a book by the jurist Carmer, Hegel analyzes the

Gefängniswesen, the carceral system. And he comes to the following conclusions: *"Mit kaltem Verstande die Menschen bald als arbeitende und produzierende Wesen, bald als zu bessernde Wesen zu betrachten und zu befehligen, wird die ärgste Tyrannei, weil das des Beste Ganzen als Zweck ihnen fremd ist, wenn es nicht gerecht ist."* "To consider men and to command them, according to cold reasoning, sometimes as laboring, productive beings, sometimes as beings to be improved, becomes the most terrible tyranny, for the Best of the Totality conceived as end is alien to them, when it is not based on justice."

Can one express in fewer words the common essence of the Nazi and Soviet repressive systems? To put to work and to correct, to re-educate by forced labor, is that not where the profound identity is to be found, whatever the differences due to the historical or even geographical circumstances between the two systems?

In 1934, when the Nazi Ministry of the Interior drew up the norms for administrative internment in the concentration camps, the system had already been working in the USSR for fifteen years. It was in February 1919, at the eighth meeting of the Pan-Russian Executive Central Committee, that Dzerzhinsky declared: "I propose to maintain the concentration camps in order to use the labor of the prisoners, individuals without regular occupation, all those who cannot work without a certain coercion. . . ." What a marvelous sentence! Who has ever worked without some degree of coercion? What proletarian ever went to work in a factory without some economic and extra-economic coercion forcing him to sell his labor power freely? But Dzerzhinsky's words, besides opening the way to completely arbitrary government, conceal the dialectical hypocrisy that now presides over the ideology of work. Since the victory of the

Bolshevik revolution, work has been regarded as a matter of honor for the worker, as his way of expressing his loyalty to the revolution. Any reluctance to work, therefore, may be regarded as an offense, or at least as a lack of good will. Half a century later, in Cuba, Fidel Castro's law against idleness reproduces exactly the same ideological structure. Marx's son-in-law, Paul Lafargue, born in Cuba and author of a disrespectful pamphlet entitled *The Right to Idleness*, must have turned over in his grave. And Dzerzhinsky continues: "If we consider the various branches of the administration, this measure"—that is, the maintenance of the camps—"would punish lack of zeal, latecoming, etc. It would allow us to bring our bureaucrats to heel. So we propose to set up a school of labor."

That's it! School—the word is out! So old Hegel was perfectly right: it was through pedagogical terror, which he had already denounced at the end of the eighteenth century and which consists, basically, in regarding men *bald als arbeitende und produzierende Wesen, bald als zu bessernde Wesen*, it was through forced labor, productive and re-educational, that Lenin and Dzerzhinsky intended to correct, on a massive scale, all the parasites, idlers, vermin—and the hysterics, too. There was a word constantly falling from Lenin's lips or pen in referring to his political opponents: they were sick, and so they had to be treated, and his successors certainly did just that— because the opponents were an encumbrance to the new Soviet society being born.

In 1934, then, when the Nazi Minister of the Interior declared that administrative detention was the exclusive affair of the Gestapo (*"Zur Anordnung der Schutzhaft ist ausschliesslich das Geheime Staatspolizeiamt zuständig"*)—reproducing almost word for word a sentence of Dzerzhinsky's from the speech already quoted,

"The right of internment in the concentration camps has fallen to the Cheka"—in 1934 it was already some years since Gorky, a violent opponent of the Bolshevik revolution in its early days and often a lucid critic of its dictatorial aspects—had sung the praises of the new repressive system: "It seems to me that the conclusion is obvious: camps such as the Solovki are indispensable," he declared in 1929. And, repeating without knowing it what Dzerzhinsky said, Gorky adds that the Solovki camps must be regarded "as a preparatory school." I need hardly add that Varlam Shalamov, who knew the Solovki before knowing the Kolyma, did not share that opinion. But Shalamov is not a Socialist Realist writer. He is not an engineer of souls. Perhaps the Solovki should be regarded as a "preparatory school" for the hell of Kolyma? A rough school in which many were called but few chosen.

Anyway, in 1937, when the first prisoners, who had come from other camps in Germany, began building Buchenwald, on the heights of the Ettersberg, the concentration-camp system of the Gulag had reached its peak.

But am I right to use the word Gulag? Certain Marxists, including the stupidest, most hypocritical, and most sinister Marxists, those of the French Party—would like to forbid us to use the word Gulag. They produced a pitiful lampoon, *The USSR and Us,* which the leaders of the French Party did their utmost to promote at a time when it was fashionable to keep one's distance from "real socialism," which has since become "globally positive" once again. In this book, then, intellectuals whose names I would prefer to forget wrote the following paragraph: "The use of the word Gulag gives rise to thoughts of the same kind"—they have just said why they refuse to use the term "Stalinist"—"this word is an acronym. It is formed from the Russian initials of the words 'Chief Administration of Corrective Labor Camps,' "—bravo, again, old Hegel!—"which up to 1956 designated the administration of the camps. *Solzhenitsyn realized the emotional charge that these two strange, disturbing sylla-bles might carry; the mass media have organized around them a colossal and obsessive orchestration.* The word then came between the average Westerner"—What is this new species? What new hybrid is being referred to?—"and any rational, differentiated view of the social-ist world, of its evolution and its reality."

My italics, of course.

How can one describe, dispassionately and accurately, intellectuals—for they are intellectuals, I repeat—capable of producing such a statement? Are they cynics, madmen, or fools? Or, rather, do they take us for fools, madmen, or cynics? The word Gulag is indeed an acro-nym. It has always been one. And the "emotional charge" that these two syllables may carry does not fall from some metaphysical heaven, is not semantically inevitable. For those two syllables not to be "strange" and "disturbing," all that is needed is for the camps never to have existed in the USSR; it's as simple as that! The "emotional charge," then, derives from the fact that we now know what Gulag means. Not only thanks to Solzhenitsyn, though his contribution has been crucial, and qualitatively new. And before he "realized" the "emotional charge" that these two syllables contain—as the intellectuals of the French Party declare with abject hypocrisy—Solzhenitsyn was subjected to it. He was subjected to the "emotional charge" of the Gulag for eight years. Varlam Shalamov was subjected to that "emotional charge" for twenty years. So if the two syllables of the word Gulag are significant, it is because they refer more or less clearly to a historical experience. It is not on the level of phonetics that the problem arises. We now know, more or less, what the content of that experience is. And if the mass media have contributed to spreading this knowledge, then long live the mass media! In my opinion, the knowledge is still fragile, far from being sufficiently established, sufficiently widespread. On the contrary, it has a tendency to grow blurred, to become too banal (perhaps because of the same mass media—in which case, down with the mass media! I know how to be dialectical, don't worry), for the sociological and political roots of Western deafness to the realities in the East are always very strong.

What would those intellectuals of the French Party have said when *Holocaust* was being shown on European television screens—or average Western ones—if someone had published something like the following: "In view of the emotional charge that may be carried by the words *gas chamber* and *crematorium oven*, the Jews—read: the Zionists—have organized through the mass media a colossal and obsessive orchestration of those words"? They would no doubt have declared it a scandal. (Or at least I hope they would have!) Yet they are doing exactly the same thing. Their action is identical in its ignomony.

So these historians, economists, critics—they are all that, alas!—of the French Party would like to stop us from using the word Gulag. In any case, they stop themselves from using it. Perhaps they think they can suppress the thing, the reality of the camps, or at least the effects of that reality, by suppressing the word that designates it. For Marxists-and-proud-of-it this would be a singular proof of idealism. Anyway, their argument is that the word Gulag serves as a screen "between the average Westerner and any rational, differentiated view of the socialist world." It strikes me that they have forgotten one rather useful adjective: "dialectical." A rational, differentiated, and dialectical view: that's what we need! In any case, let us deduce from this learned formula that for our intellectual watchdogs there really is a "socialist world."

And this time that world, that fine world, is not even qualified. It is not qualified as "real," or "primitive," or "unfinished." That world is socialist, no more and no less. Well, if that's the way it is, I don't belong to that world.

In 1937, when the first German prisoners were assembled on the Ettersberg to cut down the beech forest, the system of the corrective labor camps, the Gulag, in other words, the great hurricane of that terrible year, was about to be unleashed on the USSR.

There have been different stages of the terror in the USSR. Certain thresholds were crossed before the terror reached its height under Stalin. The year 1937 is undoubtedly one of those thresholds.

Shalamov's book, which I was reading yesterday—I mean, the day before the day that I am now reconstituting through writing, that day in 1969, in London, when I suddenly found myself opposite a building where Karl Marx had once lived, which gave rise to this apparent digression—the chapter in *Kolyma Tales* that I was reading yesterday, and whose title was "How It All Began," deals specifically with the threshold crossed in 1937 in the historical world of the terror, in the very history of the Gulag.

"In the whole of 1937," Varlam Shalamov writes, "two men, out of an official work force of two to three thousand, one prisoner and one free man, met their deaths in the *Partisan* mine [one of the mines in the Kolyma zone]. They were buried side by side, under a tumulus. Two vague obelisks—a slightly smaller one for the prisoner—were erected over their graves. . . . In 1938, an entire brigade worked permanently digging graves." For the whirlwind struck the Kolyma camps, and the whole of Soviet society, at the end of 1937. On orders from Colonel

Garanin, who was eventually shot as a "Japanese spy," just as his master, Yezhov, who replaced Yagoda (also shot) as head of the NKVD, was eventually to be shot, and replaced by Beria, who, in turn . . . Colonel Garanin, as I was saying, unleashed over the Dalstroy, the concentration-camp zone of Kolyma, the insane whirlwind of 1937.

On orders from Colonel Garanin, the prisoners in the camps of the Great North were shot in their thousands. They were shot for "counterrevolutionary agitation." And what exactly does counterrevolutionary agitation consist of in a Gulag camp? Varlam Shalamov tells us: "To say aloud that the work was hard, to murmur the most innocent remark about Stalin, to remain silent when the crowd of prisoners bawled out: 'Long live Stalin!' . . . shot! Silence is agitation." One was shot "for committing an outrage against a member of the guard." One was shot "for refusing to work." One was shot "for stealing metal." But, says Shalamov, "the ultimate offense, the one for which prisoners were shot in waves, was for not meeting the norms. This crime took entire brigades into a common grave. The authorities provided the theoretical basis for this strict regime: throughout the country the five-year plan was broken down into precise figures for every factory, for every work team. At Kolyma, requirements were drawn up for each placer, each barrow, each pick. The five-year plan was law! Not to carry out the plan was a counterrevolutionary crime! Those who failed to carry out the plan were soon got rid of!"

The Plan, then, the tangible proof, it was said, of the superiority of Soviet society, the Plan that made it possible to avoid the crises and anarchy of capitalist production, the Plan, then, an almost mystical notion, responsible not only in civil society, so to speak, but also in that quite uncivil case of a despotism of unremitting labor—

because it bound the worker to his place of work, whether this was a factory or a penal colony—the Plan was simultaneously the cause of a refined doubling of terror within the Gulag camps themselves. The Plan was as lethal as Colonel Garanin. In fact, you couldn't have one without the other.

But, Shalamov tells us, "the eternally frozen stone and soil of the *merzlota* rejects corpses. The rock has to be dynamited, hacked away. Digging graves and digging for gold required the same techniques, the same tools, the same equipment, the same workers. An entire brigade would devote its days to cutting out graves, or rather ditches, where the anonymous corpses would be thrown fraternally together. . . . The corpses were piled up, completely stripped, after their gold teeth had been broken off and recorded on the burial document. Bodies and stone, mixed together, were poured into the ditch, but the earth refused the dead, incorruptible and condemned to eternity in the perpetually frozen earth of the Great North. . . ."

Yesterday, when I read those lines—that is, not yesterday, but the day before that spring day ten years ago in London—when I read those lines yesterday, that image burned itself into my eyes: the image of those thousands of stripped corpses, intact, trapped in the ice of eternity in the mass graves of the Great North. Graves that were the construction sites of the new man, let us not forget!

In Moscow, in the mausoleum at Red Square, incredible, credulous crowds continue to file past the incorruptible corpse of Lenin. I even visited the mausoleum myself once, in 1958. At that time, Stalin's mummy kept Vladimir Ilyich company. Two years before, during a secret session of the Twentieth Congress of the Soviet Party, Nikita Sergeevich Khrushchev set fire to the idol, which, like all his peers, he had worshiped and venerated. And in 1960, in Bucharest, Khrushchev suggested to Peng

Chen that Stalin's bloody mummy be taken to China. It was finally removed from the mausoleum after the Twenty-second Congress of the Soviet Party. But in the summer of 1958, Stalin was still in his red marble tomb beside Lenin. I can testify to that. I saw them both. At peace, intact, incorruptible: all they lacked was the power of speech. But, fortunately, they did not have the power of speech. They just lay there, the two of them, silent, lit up like fish in an aquarium, protected by members of the Guards, standing motionless like bronze statues.

Ten years later, in London, after reading that passage in Varlam Shalamov's book, I remembered the tomb in Red Square. It occurred to me that the true mausoleum of the revolution was to be found in the Great North, in Kolyma. Galleries might be dug through the charnel houses—the construction sites—of socialism. People would file past the thousands of naked, incorruptible corpses of prisoners frozen in the ice of eternal death. There would be no guards; those dead would not need guards. There would be no music, either, no solemn funeral marches playing in the background. There would be nothing but silence. At the end of the labyrinth of galleries, in a subterranean amphitheater dug out of the ice of a common ditch, surrounded on all sides by the blind gaze of the victims, learned meetings might be organized to discuss the consequences of the "Stalinist deviation," with a representative sprinkling of distinguished Western Marxists in attendance.

And yet the Russian camps are not *Marxist*, in the sense that the German camps were *Nazi*. There is a historical immediacy, a total transparency between Nazi theory and its repressive practice. Indeed, Hitler seized power through ideological mobilization of the masses and thanks to universal suffrage, in the name of a theory about which no one could be in any doubt. He himself put his ideas into practice, reconstructing German reality in accordance with them. The situation of Karl Marx vis-à-vis the history of the twentieth century, even that made in his name, is radically different. That is obvious enough. In fact, a large segment of the opponents of the Bolsheviks, at the time of the October Revolution, claimed allegiance to Marx no less than did the Bolsheviks themselves: it was in the name of Marxism that not only the Mensheviks, but also the theoreticians of the German ultra-left criticized the authoritarianism and terror, the ideological monolithism and social inequality that spread over the USSR after the October victory.

The Russian camps are not, therefore, in an immediate, unequivocal way, *Marxist* camps. Nor are they simply *Stalinist*. They are *Bolshevik* camps. The Gulag is the direct, unequivocal product of Bolshevism.

However, one can go on a little further and locate in Marxist theory the crack through which the barbaric excesses of Correct Thought—which produces the corrective-labor camps—were to flood, the madness of the One, the lethal, frozen dialectic of the Great Helmsmen.

On March 5, 1852, Karl Marx wrote to Joseph Weydemeyer, who published in New York *Die Revolution*, a periodical of uncertain frequency, because of financial difficulties, like most of the socialist journals of the time. It was for Weydemeyer's journal that Marx was finishing, in those rainy days at the end of the London winter, his articles on the *Eighteenth Brumaire*, which were finally to appear in an issue of *Die Revolution* under the title slightly altered by Weydemeyer—*Der 18te Brumaire des Louis Napoleon*, instead of *Bonaparte*—published at the Deutsche Vereins-Buchhandlung von Schmidt und Helmich, at 191 William Street.

So, on that March day in 1852, Karl Marx was writing

to Weydemeyer. Two days before, he had received five pounds sent him by Frederick Engels, from Manchester. The Marx family must have eaten more or less their fill that week, after paying off their most pressing debts to the grocer and doctor. Now Karl Marx glanced out of the window of his flat. He looked absent-mindedly over at the narrow doorway of the building across the street. He saw nothing of particular interest. Indeed, there wasn't anything of particular interest at that time: the film company had not yet moved in. He went to sit down at his desk. In his almost indecipherable writing, he wrote the date at the top right-hand corner of the sheet of paper. Under the date, he added his address, 28 Dean Street, Soho, London.

It was in this letter to Joseph Weydemeyer that Marx explained his own contribution to the theory of classes and of the class struggle. After admitting that bourgeois historians had already described the historical development of this class struggle, and bourgeois economists the economic anatomy of classes, Marx went on to explain what was new in his contribution: *was ich neu tat*. "What I did that was new was to prove: 1) that the *existence of classes* is only bound up with particular *historical phases in the development of production,* 2) that the class struggle necessarily leads to the *dictatorship of the proletariat,* 3) that this dictatorship itself only constitutes the transition to the *abolition of all classes* and to a *classless society.*"

This is an extremely well-known passage, one that has been interpreted this way and that, which generations of learned commentators have dissected, which brilliant polemicists have thrown in one another's faces for over a century. And yet one can still come back to it. It still provides matter for reflection. One can still find something new in it: *etwas Neues*.

What, then, is the contribution that Marx declares he

has made in his theory, at the concrete level of history and of the class struggles that make history? It is to have shown (or demonstrated: Marx uses the verb *nachweisen*, which may be interpreted in both senses; but in both senses it is used wrongly by Marx, who never showed or demonstrated what he advanced, as we shall see) a certain number of points.

Let us leave to one side the first, that concerning the historicity of the very existence of classes. This question belongs to a philosophy of history with which I am not concerned for the moment. The idea that mankind, in order to pass from a classless society, that of primitive Communism, to another society of the same kind, but in a developed form, swimming in the butter of abundance, is destined to go through a long historical purgatory of ruthless, indecisive class struggles—always producing, moreover, real effects different from those that Marxist theoreticians, beginning in this case with Marx himself, had foreseen—such an idea leaves me completely cold. It no longer excites anybody, the idea that there was once, and that therefore there will be again, in the depths of history, ideal, idyllic societies, communities without states. I am well aware that to set this idea, expressed concisely enough in Marx's first point, to one side is somewhat arbitrary. I am well aware that the sub-Hegelian philosophy of history that underlies the idea contained in Marx's first point also underlies the other two points. But one may, nevertheless, for purely methodological reasons, exclude this first point from our present analysis, temporarily bracket it out.

Whatever one may think, therefore, of the question of the historicity, of the relativity, of classes, it is easy to see that the next two points listed by Marx do not belong to historical science—if science it be—but to prediction. Or even to prophetic preaching. That the class struggle should necessarily lead to the dictatorship of the proletariat is no more than a hypothesis, perhaps a pious wish. But neither the hypothesis nor the pious wish has been verified or fulfilled anywhere by real history. The dictatorship of the proletariat, in the Marxist sense, has never existed anywhere. A century after Marx's letter to Weydemeyer, it still hasn't come about.

At this point, of course, I can hear the indignant cries from the distinguished Marxists at the back of the hall. (There are only two or three fools in the whole world who haven't realized that when one writes, one always puts oneself on public display, whether one likes it or not. And if one is putting oneself on public display, one can imagine the hall in which it takes place.)

The Marxists all squawk at once.

"What about the Paris Commune?" someone yells out. I was waiting for that one. In a tone suggesting that nothing more is to be said on the matter, someone quotes Frederick Engels: "Well, gentlemen, do you want to know what this dictatorship is like? Look at the Paris Commune. That was the dictatorship of the proletariat." Well, gentlemen, look at the Paris Commune, but look at it carefully. You will see some very fascinating, very instructive things, but you will never see the dictatorship of the proletariat. Forget Engels and the high-flown words with which, twenty years after the events, he ends his introduction to Marx's *The Class Struggles in France*, forget Engels's literary fabulations, come back to the harsh truths of history, and you will not find the dictatorship of the proletariat. Read the writings of the period, beginning, of course, with the contemporary accounts of the sessions of the Commune itself, and you will see that the attempted coup of the Paris Communards, at once grandiose and pitiful, heroic and petty, steeped in a just vision of society and shot through with the most confused ideologies, has got nothing to do with the dictatorship of the proletariat.

But I am not allowed to continue my demonstration (*Nachweisung*, Marx would say: yet I have the advantage over him of speaking with my back to history, of trying to explain it; I have no need to fantasize, and can therefore demonstrate, or show, what history has demonstrated). I am interrupted: voices rise up on all sides.

Very well, I shall continue at another time, perhaps in another place. But above the din of Marxist voices, I shall say just a few words, even if I have to raise my voice, on Marx's third point, namely, that the dictatorship of the proletariat is a mere transition—a state that would be already an antistate—toward a classless society, toward the suppression of all classes.

Here, too, we are confronted with a mere postulate: a *petitio principii*. Real history has demonstrated—*nachgewiesen*—quite the contrary. It has shown the continual, implacable reinforcement of the state, the brutal exacerbation of the struggle between the classes, which not only have not been suppressed, but, on the contrary, have crystallized still further in their polarization. Beside the veritable civil war unleashed against the peasantry in the USSR in the early 1930s, the class struggles in the West are gala dinners. Compared with the stratification of social privileges in the USSR—functional privileges, certainly, bound up with the status and not, or not necessarily, with the individual—real social inequality, that is to say, relative to the national product and to its distribution, is in the West nothing but a fairy tale.

In brief, what Marx claims is new in his contribution to the theory of classes and of the struggle between them has nothing theoretical about it, nothing that throws light on reality and enables one to act on it. It is no more than prediction, preaching, wishful thinking, an expression that must have been used quite often at 28 Dean Street.

And it is here, on this precise point of the Marxist theory of the dictatorship of the proletariat as an inevitable transition toward classless society, that the lethal madness of Bolshevism took root and nourished the terror. It was in accordance with these few points dryly listed by Marx one day in March 1852—listed, moreover, as if they were self-evident—that all the Great Helmsmen have begun to think—and, worse still, to dream at night —as if inside the heads of the proletarians. It was in the name of this historic mission of the proletariat that they have crushed, deported, dispersed, through labor—free or forced, but always corrective—millions of proletarians.

An idea underlies these points—these theoretical novelties—which Marx pedantically enumerates: the idea of the existence of a universal class that will be the dissolution of all classes; a class that cannot be emancipated without emancipating itself from all the other classes of society and without, consequently, emancipating them all. One might have recognized the trembling voice of the young Marx announcing, in 1843, in an essay that he wrote, not on Dean Street, but on the Rue Vaneau in Paris, "Contribution to the Critique of Hegel's *Philosophy of Right*: Introduction"; the epiphany of the proletariat. But this universal class does not exist. The lesson of the hundred years that separate us from Marx is, if nothing else, that the modern proletariat is not this class. To continue to maintain this theoretical fiction has enormous practical consequences, for it paves the way for the parties *of* the proletariat, the leaders *of* the proletariat, the corrective labor camps *of* the proletariat: that is to say, it paves the way for those who, in the silence of the gagged proletariat, speak in its name, in the name of its supposed universal mission, and speak loud and clear (to say the least!).

So the first task of a new revolutionary party that would not speak in the name of the proletariat, but would regard itself only as a temporary structure, constantly disintegrating and being reconstructed, as a focus of receptivity and awareness which would give organic weight, material strength, to the voice of the proletariat—its first task would be that of re-establishing the theoretical truth, with all the consequences that this involves, about the nonexistence of a universal class.

But this blind spot in Marx's theory, through which it is linked to the aberrational realities of the twentieth century, is also its blinding spot: the focal point at which the entire grandiose illusion of the revolution shines. Without this false notion of a universal class, Marxism would not have become the material force that it has been, that it still partly is, profoundly transforming the world, if only to make it even more intolerable. Without this blinding, we would not have become Marxists. We would not have become Marxists simply to demonstrate the mechanisms of the production of surplus value, or to reveal the fetishisms of mercantile society, an area in which Marxism is irreplaceable. We would have become teachers. It was the deep-seated madness of Marxism, conceived as a theory for universal revolutionary practice, that gave meaning to our lives. To mine, in any case. As a result, there is no longer any meaning in my life. I live without meaning.

But this is no doubt normal enough. In any case, isn't it dialectical?

The dialectic "is the art of always falling on your feet!" Fernand Barizon said at Nantua, nine years earlier, looking me in the eyes and raising his brandy glass.

That was it! It was the dialectic that reminded me of Barizon, that day in London.

Of course, I had thought of Fernand several times during the preceding days, those days toward the end of spring 1969 when I was reading *Kolyma Tales*. That is understandable enough. But the recollections of Barizon had remained vague, in the background of my memory. In the foreground there had always been snow. The snow on the Ettersberg on those Sundays, the snow at Magadan or Kargopol.

But this time, because of the dialectic, the memory of Barizon was more specific. Very specific.

I remembered the trip with Fernand in 1960, from Paris to Prague—that is, I, not Barizon, went to Prague—with our stop-overs at Nantua and Geneva. At Zurich, too, but we haven't got there yet. We will soon enough.

Anyway, we were in Geneva, in the buffet of the Gare de Cornavin. We'd stopped talking. We were about to say good-bye. A loudspeaker had just announced that passengers for the Zurich express could proceed to Platform 2, and Barizon remained silent.

"You know, old boy!" he said suddenly.

I looked at him.

"What would you say if I went with you to Zurich?" he asked.

"To Zurich?" I said, rather startled. "You want to get on the train with me?"

He shrugged his shoulders.

"The train? What's the good of the train? We could keep on in the car. You didn't tell me your plane left tomorrow afternoon. We have plenty of time."

Yes, we had plenty of time.

Disconcerted, I looked at Barizon. I like to travel alone. Or, rather, I like to go by train or plane alone. I find it relaxing. It gets me thinking, too. My brain works well in the temporary unfamiliarity of solitary travel. But I was not averse to the idea of continuing the conversation with him, either.

There are traveling companions, on that kind of trip, with whom one has no desire to speak. Indeed, one has nothing to say to them. Two weeks before, I had made a short trip to San Sebastián and Vitoria with a French Party member from Bayonne or Saint-Jean-de-Luz, I don't remember which. It was quite impossible to talk to him about anything. He was cantankerous and sententious. What's more, he was a vegetarian. He never stopped complaining about the food, though Basque cooking, for heaven's sake, is unbeatable! On the way back, when we were settling up, he asked me to reimburse him for the gas, which was natural enough and quite normal, but he also wanted so many centimes per kilometer for the depreciation of his car. I made a gesture of exasperation, but he wasn't joking. He explained that, for all the similar journeys he made for us, for the underground apparatus of the PCE, he had always calculated so many centimes per kilometer, to make up for the depreciation of his small, private car. I then understood and secretly approved of his wife for leaving him two or three months before. He had told me about this at Vitoria, one evening when he was complaining about the price of olive oil in particular and the indecent behavior of women in general.

But with Barizon it wasn't like that.

"Yes, all right," I said, "we have plenty of time. Let's go to Zurich by car, if you like."

He did like. He nodded, apparently pleased.

"The only thing is," I said, "I'll have to get out my French identity card before leaving."

He looked at me quizzically.

"Don't you see?" I said. "You noticed it yourself, just now. Salagnac and Barizon together, two Frenchmen, no problem. But a Uruguayan and a Frenchman together, that might intrigue some clever devil if the slightest thing goes wrong. At the hotel in Zurich, for example. It's not much of a risk, but why take it, if there's an alternative?"

He looked at me and whistled between his teeth.

"You think of everything, Gérard!" he said, with a touch of sarcasm. "I know now why you're a big shot!"

I shook my head.

"No," I said. "You understand why I'm not in the clink after so many years."

Fernand looked at me.

"Keep it up, old boy!" he said gravely.

I took a swig of beer and raised my glass.

"Don't worry! I'm immortal!"

Next day, we were on the deck of one of the steamers that go around Lake Zurich. It was a bright, sunny autumn day. We were looking at the landscape: the blue water of the lake flecked with white foam, the green meadows, the scorched mountain in the autumn light.

These trips around the lake, before catching the plane for Prague, were almost a tradition. Sometimes I did them alone, sometimes with my traveling companions, when I had traveling companions.

That day I was making the trip around the lake with Fernand Barizon, but another time I did it with Carrillo. I once traveled with him to the East, via Zurich. It wasn't Fernand who drove the car then, but René. Anyway, we had already been around the lake, Carrillo and I. He was relaxed when traveling. He took to remembering the past, important episodes in his life as general secretary of the clandestine Spanish Party or in the history of the Communist movement. Was it there, on the deck of a boat going around Lake Zurich, that he told me how Khrushchev and other members of the Praesidium of the Soviet Party had liquidated Beria, shortly after Stalin's death? I'm not sure. At any rate, we were traveling somewhere when he told me. Travel broadens the mind, as we know, and sometimes it loosens the tongues. I don't know why that is so, but it is. Traveling even seems to loosen the tongues of old Communists. To some extent, anyway. Which is no small achievement.

Khrushchev had invited to dinner, in one of the state reception rooms at the Kremlin, a number of delegates to the Congress of Communist parties held at Moscow in 1957. Carrillo was one of them. During dessert, Khrushchev told them how Beria had died. He told all those European Communists, who sat there as if hypnotized, how they had managed to get rid of Beria during one of the sessions of the Praesidium after Stalin's death. It wasn't easy, for all the members of the Praesidium were searched by KGB men before going into the meeting, in accordance with the practice established during Stalin's lifetime. In theory, it was impossible to get arms into the room where the Praesidium meetings took place. They got around all the same: since army generals were not searched on entering the private area of the Kremlin. Bulganin, who had the rank of a marshal, was able to get a few automatic pistols in, with the complicity of another senior officer. A segment from the highest echelons in the army was, in fact, involved in the plot against Beria, and certain military units were standing by, in case they were needed afterward. So it was Bulganin who got a few small arms into the Kremlin hall where the Praesidium meetings of Stalin's heirs usually took place. No sooner had the meeting begun than the plotters grabbed the weapons and killed Beria point-blank. Beria's corpse was then rolled in a carpet so they could get it out of the Kremlin without anyone's suspecting what had occurred. Then, given the green light by a telephone call, certain crack army units arrested Beria's principal collaborators and the commanders of the special troops of the Ministry of the Interior who were presumed to be loyal to Stalin's last chief of police.

In that state reception room at the Kremlin, all gilt and chandeliers, where the banquet given for the fraternal delegates took place, Khrushchev finished his account, with his usual verve, of how they managed to get rid of Lavrenti Beria. He may have embroidered the story a little. It may, in fact, have been more complicated, and more sordid, too. But a heavy, icy silence fell on the guests. A deathly silence. The fraternal delegates didn't even dare to look at one another. Then old Gollan, the general secretary of the Communist Party of Great Britain, leaned toward his neighbors and murmured: "A gentlemen's affair, indeed!"

It was Carrillo who recounted this incident to me; he had been sitting quite near Gollan on that occasion. And I'm fairly sure that Carrillo recounted the incident to me at Zurich on one of the steamers that travel around the lake.

This time, however, I was not going around Lake Zurich with Santiago Carrillo. This time I was with Fernand Barizon.

We were on the blue lake in the autumn sunlight, opposite the village of Wädenswil.

"Did you notice the guy on the quay just as we were leaving?" I said to Barizon.

"What guy?" he asked.

"A short, thickset fellow with a goatee and a bowler."

The detail of the bowler seemed to stir something in his memory.

"A bowler? Yes, I remember a bowler hat," Barizon exclaimed, "but not the guy who was under the bowler."

"It was Lenin," I said.

Barizon nearly choked on his cigarette. He coughed and spluttered.

I hit him on the back a few times, but the pure air of German-speaking Switzerland soon brought Barizon's normal breathing back.

"And I'm Napoleon," he said, as soon as he had recovered his breath.

"Ah, yes!" I said. "What a historic meeting that would've been! What would I give to have been there. A discussion between Lenin and Napoleon on strategy. 'You go in, then you wait and see what happens.' We have seen in both cases what happened. We certainly have."

But Barizon listened to my lucubrations with detached mistrust.

"Did he really look like Lenin, that guy?" he asked. "I didn't even notice."

I nodded.

"It was Lenin, I tell you. Anyway, it's not surprising if he comes back to haunt the places where he spent his happiest days."

Barizon turned around and looked at the old city of Zurich laid out on the hillside, in the distance.

"Lenin was happy in Zurich?" he asked.

I nodded. "Of course," I replied. "There was Inessa. And he spent all his time in libraries, reading books on philosophy and political economy. Those are the best times for revolutionaries, the ones they spend in libraries."

Barizon turned toward me, obviously displeased.

"No, no!" he said. "The best times for revolutionaries are when they're making the revolution!"

"Oh, yes!" I said, sarcastically. "Though you have to admit that those moments are rather rare. Then it all starts to go wrong. In any case, it doesn't turn out as you expect."

Barizon contemplated the lakeside. He turned to me and said: "Hey, Gérard, now you're a big shot and you travel around all over the place, you may be able to tell me something. What are they like, the Russians?"

• • •

"The Russians are mad!" Henk Spoenay had said, sixteen years before.

We were talking in the snow, on the Avenue of Eagles. We had been talking about the Russians, their escapes or escapades in the spring. Without realizing, I had stopped in my tracks. I was looking at the snow-covered landscape, scarcely seeing it.

I was daydreaming.

Anyway, it wasn't spring. We were in December. That's right. Late December, one Sunday in 1944.

I'd been thinking of Pyotr, whom we called Pedro. He was still on his long march across Europe, eastward, toward the Red Army. There was another Pedro among us at Buchenwald, and he wasn't a Spaniard, either. He was a Slovak. Both Pedros had fought in Spain, the Slovak in the International Brigades and the Russian in the armored division, with the Soviet military specialists. They both spoke fluent Castilian.

I have forgotten Pyotr's surname and patronymic, if I ever knew them. On the other hand, I remember very well the name of the other Pedro, the Slovak: Kaliarik. He was actually named neither Pedro nor Kaliarik. He was named Ladislav Holdos. But I learned that only twenty years later. In April 1945, when I left Pedro the Slovak, or Kaliarik, I did not know that he was going to become Holdos once more. We said good-bye briefly, "*Salud, suerte, hasta la vista,*" without knowing that it would be twenty years before we met again. We didn't exchange names and addresses. What was the point? To begin with, neither of us had an address. All we exchanged were our boots, I remember.

We had been together on April 11, 1945, and during the days that followed, in the combat groups of the underground resistance in Buchenwald. Kaliarik, of course, was higher placed than I in the underground military apparatus. He was older than I, by at least ten years, and he had that experience of war that forms the common background, the unquestionable acquisition of so many generations of Communists. In the twentieth century, in fact, if you think about it, it's on the terrain of war, civil or otherwise, that the Communists have been most effective. On occasion, they have even been brilliant. As if the military spirit were consubstantial with twentieth-century Communism. So much so that it is through war, and the military—all too soon militaristic—spirit, that movements which were originally very far removed from Marxism, and even violently opposed to it, such as Castroism and all its Latin-American derivatives, ended up in the bosom of the Communist Holy Church, in the martial ranks of the heirs of the dead Marshal Stalin. Twentieth-century Communism has ruined all the revolutions that it has inspired or taken over after they have taken place, but it has made a brilliant success of several decisive wars. And it isn't over yet: this prediction will be confirmed in the not too distant future. A transparent enough present for whoever has eyes to see confirms it day after day. It's understandable: the failure of the revolution, that is to say, failure in the domain of social reconstruction, leads inevitably to armed expansion, if only through Afro-Cuban, Arab, or Asiatic soldiers.

Anyway, Kaliarik commanded one of the shock groups, armed with automatic rifles stolen part by part from the Gustloff Works, which occupied the Buchenwald watchtower on April 11, 1945, just as the SS were pulling out. "The first attack wave was launched against the celebrated tower, on the orders of a Czech known as Pedro," says Olga Wormser-Migot in her book *When the Allies Opened the Gates** . . . Except that he was a Slovak, a fact that weighed heavily on his life later, this was my Pedro; my pal Kaliarik. I belonged only to the second wave, to the

*Quand les Alliés ouvraient les portes. —ED.

reserve that was armed at the camp gates with submachine guns, *Panzerfaust*, and other weapons seized in the SS guard posts. So we met up, Kaliarik and I, on the Weimar road, in the beech forest so dear to Goethe, on that celebrated night of April 11. A lot of Castilian was spoken that night in the undergrowth around Weimar.

But we did not indulge in long leavetakings some days later. Nor did we exchange addresses. We exchanged only our boots. It so happened that the leather boots I had found in the clothing stores of the SS barracks fitted him better than me, and vice versa. We made that important discovery one day in mid-April, sitting in the sun outside of Block 40, a few days after the end of that war. So, of course, we changed boots, and on May 1, 1945, when I arrived in Paris just in time to take part in the May Day march, I was wearing Kaliarik's boots. I thought of him, too. Not only because of those supple boots that he had exchanged for mine, but also because of the sudden snowstorm that fell on Paris that day, on that May 1, just as the May Day march was breaking up at the Place de la Nation. I looked at the swirls of light snow and I thought of my pals.

But it was only twenty years later, in 1964, that I saw Kaliarik again and learned that his real name was Ladislav Holdos.

I was going to see some friends who lived on the Boulevard Voltaire, to meet the Londons,* whom I did not

*Artur London, deputy minister of foreign affairs in Czechoslovakia, was involved in the show trial known as the Slansky trial, which took place in November 1952. Rudolf Slansky, the general secretary of the Czechoslovakian Communist Party, together with ten party members in key positions, among them Josef Frank, the deputy general secretary of the Party, were sentenced to death and executed; three of the accused, one of them Artur London, were given life sentences and were later amnestied. London escaped to England, where he published *The Confession*, an account of the methods by which the accused were brought to confess the most improbable crimes against the state. —ED.

know, though in 1945, on my return from Buchenwald, I had once bumped into Artur London coming out of a public meeting in Paris. I was with Michel Herr at the time, but I can't remember whether he introduced us or whether he just told me that the tall, thin guy over there, who had come back from Mauthausen, was the legendary leader of the M.O.I.* It doesn't matter whether we were actually introduced: it was over in a few seconds.

In 1964, when we met properly, at friends', on the Boulevard Voltaire, London recounted to us, as we sat breathless for hours, with ever-increasing hatred and anxiety, all the adventures of his arrest, trial, and imprisonment in Czechoslovakia. Certainly that account, at least as it's engraved on my memory, was more implacable, more devoid of any desire for autobiographical justification, than the transcription of the same events that London produced later in The Confession. But this is not the time to speak of The Confession. I must respect chronological order, don't forget. In fact, despite the sinuous, crafty detours of my memory, which look like "flash forwards" because of the lost and rediscovered traces of Kaliarik, whose real name was Holdos—despite all this apparent coming and going, then, we are still reliving a Sunday in December 1944, in Buchenwald. The Confession does not yet belong to this relived experience. What interests me at the moment, on this autumn night of 1964, on the Boulevard Voltaire, is not Artur London's account, which, some years later, was to provide the raw material of The Confession, but the presence of Pedro Kaliarik. It was he who had shared with me the Sunday in question, and many other Sundays in Buchenwald.

One evening, I entered Jean Pronteau's apartment on the Boulevard Voltaire. The Londons were there, and

*Main d'Oeuvre immigrée, an organization for foreign workers, very active in the French resistance. —ED.

there was this other man, whom I recognized at once, Pedro, my Slovak pal from Buchenwald.

It might have been a great celebration, that reunion with Kaliarik. Why wasn't it? Twenty years later, quite unexpectedly, one meets up with an old pal. One has so many things to say to him, so many memories. We might have started with the pair of boots we exchanged: Do you remember the boots we took from the SS stores? I could have told Pedro what happened to those boots. Then we could have recalled those April days after the liberation of the camp. Do you remember, Pedro, the night on the Weimar road, that family of Nazis caught by one of our patrols? Pedro would have remembered it. And we could have remembered many other things that lay dormant in our memories, but were ready to be brought back to life. We might have laughed and laughed, uncontrollably, as all those memories flooded back. There would, of course, have been the shadow of the pals who went up in smoke. It would have passed over us, for a single, light, fraternal moment. There would, of course, have been the crematorium chimney in our memories of that far-off sunny April day. But we would surely have laughed, despite the shadow of death, despite the smoke from the crematorium.

Is it really too much to expect of life that one should feel such joy at meeting a long-lost pal like Pedro, twenty years later, by chance, and remembering with him the radiant innocence of the past?

But it wasn't possible. We were unable to remember the past together. Or, rather, we did remember the past, but it was not the past of Buchenwald. It was the past of innocence. In 1945, Kaliarik had gone back home. He had become Holdos again, Ladislav Holdos. Under this name, his real name, he had become a member of the Praesidium and secretariat of the Slovak Communist Party, and then a member of Parliament, and vice-chairman of the

National Slovak Council. But early in 1951, Holdos was arrested. He was accused of belonging to a Slovak bourgeois-nationalist group in the circle around Clementis. On February 21, 1951, the Central Committee of the Czechslovak Party heard a report on "The Discovery of the Work of Espionage and Sabotage Carried out by Clementis and the Fractional Anti-Party Group of Bourgeois-Nationalists in the Slovak CP." Months passed. The scenario of the trials changed. In the end Clementis was no longer to be the principal protagonist, the star of a show trial in which the horrors of Slovak nationalism would be unmasked before the appalled collective gaze of the people. Clementis was to be switched, after all, to a subsidiary role, in the Slansky trial. He was to be condemned to death with Slansky, in 1952. He was to be executed, and his ashes thrown to the wind on an icy road on the outskirts of Prague. The ashes of Clementis and of Josef Frank, mixed together, were to be disposed of in the same way, at the same time, on a snow-covered road in Bohemia.

Clementis's codefendants, who included (in addition to Holdos) Novomesky, Okali, Horvath, and Husak—yes, Husak! who came out of Stalin's prisons in order to carry out, implacably, the repressive policy of Stalin's heirs after August 1968—still had to wait years for those at the top to work out the scenario of their trial, for the meticulously elaborate protocol of their deviation to be laid bare, and the scripts of their confessions to be written. Their trial finally took place between April 21 and April 24, 1954, at Bratislava.

As I listened to Pedro, ten years later, in Paris, on the Boulevard Voltaire, I was seized by a desperate anger. It was no doubt the same anger that made Pedro's voice tremble.

Some weeks before, Nikita Sergeevich Khrushchev had been overthrown. A page in history had been turned. The one and only chance that history had offered Communism of reforming its political system—without the bloody confrontations of a general, and necessarily chaotic, revolt, without the massive destruction involved in an external military conflict—was to be thrown away, after all. No other historic chance of this kind would occur. Of course, Nikita Sergeevich had been the victim, above all, of his own contradictions, of his strategy, which, to say the least, was not noted for its coherence. He had surely succumbed to the historically determined limitations of his undertaking, which could have succeeded—as a reformist strategy—only by releasing a mass democratic movement, which would have brought with it, of course, the seeds of a supersession of that very undertaking. We have seen it clearly enough in Poland and in Hungary, and we are beginning to see it in China. But Nikita Sergeevich had not only been sacrificed by his peers, who would re-establish the absolute power of the new ruling class, reassured by Khrushchev's liquidation of the terror, at least as far as that class was concerned; he had also succumbed to the incomprehension, the attacks, the evasions, and the undermining of most of the international Communist movement. Once again, and with obscure and unavowed—unavowable—consequences worthy of a detailed analysis that cannot even be sketched out here, the Communist movement as a whole, despite a few occasionally interesting exceptions, had played the pernicious role for which it had really been created, whatever one may pretend to think. In the 1930s it had facilitated, through its abject, unconditional submission, the definitive Stalinization of the system. Twenty years later, in the 1950s, the international Communist movement was to prevent the propagation of the shock wave caused by the Twentieth Congress of the Soviet Party. Under the impetus of the French Party in the West and the Chinese in the

East, it was to freeze the situation at a level that the national apparatuses could tolerate.

But, that autumn of 1964, I was not going to express regret for the disappearance of Nikita Sergeevich, in that apartment on the Boulevard Voltaire where I met up with Ladislav Holdos. At that time I had nothing left to regret—and nothing to hope for, either. I was moving to the end of my personal battle within the leadership of the PCE. Shortly before, on September 3, 1964, I had been summoned by a delegation from the Executive Committee. The meeting had been set for two o'clock in the afternoon, in front of the town hall of Aubervilliers. I knew all the apartments and houses in that suburb, where for years we had held secret meetings of the PCE leadership, well enough to know where this particular meeting would take place. They could even have skipped the useless detours and said exactly where and when the meeting would take place. But no. The secrecy that is second nature in all Communist parties, and which is justified on the hypocritical grounds of "revolutionary vigilance," had been at work. On September 3, 1964, at two o'clock in the afternoon, before that meeting to which I had been summoned, I was still a part of the leadership of the PCE: a member of the Central Committee of the Party, temporarily suspended from the Executive Committee, while my political deviations were being examined. But I was already being treated as an enemy, as a potential traitor. So not only was I not told to go straight to the apartment in which we would unquestionably end up, but, what is more, the car that came to collect me in front of the Aubervilliers town hall made a number of detours, as if it were necessary to throw some pursuer off the scent or even to make me lose my sense of direction. What annoyed me most in this sinister comedy was that the pal who accompanied the driver of the car and who

was entrusted with the task of bringing me to the meeting
had worked with me underground in Madrid. "Bernardo," indeed, was showing increasing nervousness. So,
to make it still more uncomfortable for him, I showered
him with sarcasm. I told him that the comrades were
inconsistent, that they had shown once again to what
extent they were incapable of serious work. They could-
n't have it both ways: either I was an enemy or I was not.
The way they were treating me suggested that they
regarded me as an enemy, perhaps even as a police agent.
If so, they were really too stupid. For if I were a police
agent, I would have to have been one for a long time. I
hadn't joined the police that morning while brushing my
teeth. So I could already have given the address of the
apartment to which they were unquestionably taking me,
despite the comedy of their detours. I could have given
the police many other addresses, too. "Bernardo," I said
to him, "do you know how many secret addresses I know,
here and throughout Spain? Do you have any idea of the
secrets that I could hand over, and which you couldn't
protect, whatever you did? You see, you don't even know
them yourself. Do you want me to give you the addresses
and passwords for our underground printing presses in
Madrid?" "Bernardo" was getting more and more anxious. So, too, was the driver. He began to drive quite
wildly, and I didn't fail to point this out. "I don't suppose
you know Carrillo's secret address? There aren't many of
us who do, I can tell you! Would you like his telephone
number, too?" But the terrified "Bernardo" begged me to
stop talking. And why should I stop talking, Bernardo?
You haven't gagged me or blindfolded me. Actually, you
should have, to be consistent. What's the point of asking
me to stop talking when no one will ever silence me
again. In fact, that's what's bothering you, isn't it?

Anyway, on September 3, 1964, a delegation from the

PCE informed me that the Central Committee had ratified my exclusion from the Executive Committee and that they expected me to rectify my erroneous opinions. But I refrained once again—for the last time—from practicing the deliciously masochistic and comforting exercise of Stalinist self-criticism and, after a few verbal thrusts, things quieted down. We already knew where we stood.

And so, that autumn night of 1964, when I met up once again with Pedro, I was already on the other side. I no longer regretted anything, or hoped for anything. And yet a dark, useless anger—useless because quite desperate, quite incapable of being expressed in any kind of action —welled up within me as I listened to Pedro's account.

In April 1954, Pedro had appeared before a court at Bratislava. The trial followed the scenario drawn up by the secretariat of the Central Committee of the Czechoslovak Party. Pedro—that is, Ladislav Holdos—had been condemned to thirty years' imprisonment.

The trial had begun on April 22, 1954. Nine years earlier to the day, Pedro and I had exchanged our boots in Buchenwald. It might be considered surprising that I should remember such a detail, or that this really was too much of a coincidence. But there were simple enough reasons for me to remember it: it so happened that Kaliarik and I exchanged our fine, supple leather boots the day before I left Buchenwald, in a truck belonging to the Abbé Rodhain's repatriation mission. And since I left Buchenwald on April 23—a date I remember quite easily because it is Saint George's day and because it amused me to leave Buchenwald on the feast day of Saint George, the patron saint of the cavalry of the same name, and even more venerated as the patron saint of Catalonia—it is therefore quite simple to deduce that we exchanged our boots on the 22nd. And nine years later to the day, the trial of Ladislav Holdos began at Bratislava.

I was thinking of all this as I listened to Pedro's account almost twenty years after we had said good-bye in Buchenwald. I was thinking, too, that Pedro's trial had actually taken place over a year after Stalin's death, that Stalin had gone on killing, imprisoning, calumniating, destroying lives, even after his death. I was thinking that in 1945 the deportees were still dying in Buchenwald, even after the liberation. The Jewish survivors of Auschwitz went on dying, in the Little Camp at Buchenwald. I was thinking that Stalin himself had been like an immense concentration camp, like an ideological gas chamber, like a crematorium of Correct Thought: he went on killing even after he had disappeared. I was thinking, above all, that Stalin had destroyed any possibility that our memories could be innocent. For we might have been able to hug each other, Pedro and I, that evening on the Boulevard Voltaire, at Jean Pronteau's—hug an old pal, without giving it a thought, without stirring up memories one preferred to forget. We might have talked about that pair of boots we had exchanged, about the good old days at Buchenwald: good because we managed to endure, just endure, freely, accepting the risks and the moments of anxiety, and also the tiny bursts of hope and joy, to endure in the struggle for a just cause. But it was no longer possible, now. We hugged each other, certainly, but not in remembrance of those supple leather boots we'd exchanged: we were talking about the trial that had opened in Bratislava nine years later, to the day. We hugged each other and a dark anger, both futile and guilty, welled up inside us both. Futile because there was nothing to be hoped for any more, whatever one may have occasionally pretended, in the sluggishness of an ideological movement that by its nature cannot conceive of struggle without hope, or of perseverance in the struggle without success. And guilty because Pedro surely remembered the confessions that had been extracted from him, and because I remembered my former comfortable silences and my servile, willing deafness to the cries of some of those victims who had been my comrades.

Our memories were no longer innocent for us.

But I'm in Buchenwald, in December 1944, late December, a Sunday. I left the camp with Henk Spoenay. I'm coming back from the Mibau: Henk had to stay on. A little while ago, an eternity ago, on the way out, before all these detours into the future of my memory, Henk and I were talking about the Russians.

"The Russians are mad!" he said.

I hadn't yet heard of Kolyma.

At the end of the long snow-covered avenue stood the monumental gates of the camp, surmounted by the watchtower.

I'm walking in the sun, slowly.

"It's a dream," Henk said, a little while ago, on the *Appellplatz*.

But what is a dream? Is this landscape a dream, with its blue-white snow, its pale sunlight, the gently rising smoke over there? Or am I a dream dreamed by this landscape, like a coil of smoke hardly more substantial than the one over there?

Am I only a dream of future smoke, a dreamy premonition, as it were, of that smoky inconsistency that is death? Life? Or is all this, this world of the camp, and the pals, and Fernand Barizon and Henk, and the Jehovah's Witness, and Jiri Zak's orchestra, all this swarming life, is it only a dream in which I am one of the characters and from which someone, someday, perhaps the dreamer, will be able to awaken? And even the rest, outside, everything that took place before, everything that will take place after, is that, too, only a dream?

I feel a sort of dizziness in the pale sunlight of this winter dream. It is not disturbing. It is not even unpleasant. It is simply that there is no longer any criterion for reality. I am not stupid enough to pinch myself, to hope to verify my waking state by means of the sharp, brief, precise pain caused by pinching. That wouldn't prove anything.

There is no longer any criterion for reality; everything is possible. I take a few more steps, then stop.

Goethe might appear at the end of the avenue, with his faithful friend Eckermann, the ever-faithful fool. Wasn't this their favorite walk? Goethe and Eckermann, on the avenue bordered with granite columns crowned by heraldic, hieratic eagles.

They might appear between the trees, on the Falkenhof side.

"Today," Eckermann might write later, "despite the cold, Goethe expressed a wish to walk on the Ettersberg.

" 'This morning,' Goethe said to me, 'I was thinking that my memory of these beautiful woods is imbued with the declining, wild dampness of autumn, or with the ardent upsurge of the spring, whose virile verdure can now be glimpsed. My memory of the Ettersberg seems to be associated with the colors of September and May, with the smells of those two seasons. And yet I'm sure that I went among those fine trees in midwinter, on pleasant sleigh rides, sometimes at night, by the gay light of torches. That memory has faded. As I get older,' Goethe added, 'I seem to take refuge in the mist of a more self-indulgent memory.'

"I could not prevent a smile, hearing Goethe speak of old age. There is such vivacity, such youth of soul on that majestic brow! How could one believe that this admirable man, this Goethean genius, will soon be two hundred years old?

"On this matter, I could not avoid a rather melancholy thought. I only hope that this unfortunate war will be over in five years, in 1949, so that the two hundredth centenary of my master's birth may be properly celebrated by all the European peoples, at peace, reconciled on the occasion of this very commemoration! How unfortunate it would be if this could not take place, and what a loss for mankind!

"Indeed, who better than Goethe himself might receive at Weimar the great ones of this world on the occasion of that Congress of Universal Peace which will bring to an end—nay, an apotheosis—the festivities marking the bicentenary of his birth? After the inevitable but now imminent defeat of the Reich—a defeat from which, Goethe predicts, the German nation will draw strength for a revival—which German politician, indeed, could represent German history and wisdom better than Goethe? Who better than Goethe could plead with President Roosevelt, Marshal Stalin, Prime Minister Churchill, and General de Gaulle the cause of German participation in the reconstruction of Europe?

"Anyway, that morning, Goethe was in a very restless, rather nervous mood when I entered his study. He was looking vaguely at some Russian icons, which had been sent to him kindly by Colonel von Sch., who is fighting on the Eastern Front, and with whom Goethe keeps up a most interesting correspondence. I began to give him a summary of the Sunday newspapers, but he soon interrupted my irksome reading with an impatient gesture.

" 'Let us cease for a moment,' he said to me, 'this preoccupation with the affairs of the world! What is new, in fact, under the sun, my good Eckermann, my dear friend, for someone like myself who was at Valmy, who watched the flood tide of the French Revolution roll in, who witnessed the glory of Napoleon rise and fall? No, truly, history is sadly repetitive. On this point, how right my old friend Professor G. W. F. Hegel was! You met Professor Hegel in October 1827, when he came to Weimar and I gave a tea in his honor. At the time I'm thinking about, the time in Jena, you hadn't yet come to work with me, my dear Eckermann! Jena! It was the center of the civilized world, my friend! I can still remember that splendid time, and not only, as some wicked tongues would have it, on account of little Minna Herzleib, my Minchen! Not at all! At that time Jena, with its university, for which I was responsible through my post with the Grand Duke, was the place where some of the greatest German minds of this century lived and worked—I mean, of the last century! Schiller and Fichte, Schelling and Hegel, and Humboldt, and the Schlegel brothers, Brentano and Tieck and Voss, and many more! All those great minds were working in conditions of poverty, for in Germany the wealth of the mind has often flowered in the nourishing soil of material penury! I remember once I had to give ten thalers to Hegel through a mutual friend, the professor was in such desperate straits!'

"But, dismissing with a gesture these sublime if melancholy memories, Goethe cried: 'Today I want to take you on the Ettersberg. The observation of nature in winter will surely provide us with many a subject of conversation.'

"While agreeing with what he had said, I wondered if it was the real reason for Goethe's impatience. I suspected that this was not so, I don't know why. Without further delay I ordered the sleigh, and we soon set out, smothered in a mountain of furs, to the trot of two sturdy, plumed horses, up the Ettersberg, that fine hill, unfortunately so spoiled by the building of a corrective-labor camp, *Umschulungslager,* in which criminals of several nationalities are confined."

A noise on my left interrupts my daydream.

A sheaf of snow sparkles in the sunlight, behind a

curtain of trees, over by the barracks. An army truck, no doubt, whose wheels have skidded over the fresh snow. It only lasted a second. A bright crunching sound, muffled.

It's over. Silence has returned.

While I'm about it, I might as well imagine that Goethe's sleigh has arrived over there, suddenly, in a cascade of snow. Perhaps Goethe has expressed a desire to visit the Falkenhof.

I stand there, motionless in the cold sunlight of this December Sunday, dreaming that Goethe and Eckermann have appeared at the end of the avenue flanked by Nazi eagles.

I move slightly. I tap the compact snow with my feet. I blow on my fingers. The avenue remains deserted.

I can imagine anything on a December Sunday in that historic landscape, on the Ettersberg. The Grand Duke Charles Augustus organized a hunting party here in honor of Napoleon, after the talks at Erfurt. I could equally well imagine Napoleon emerging from some path, wearing the uniform of the Imperial Guard that he wore on the day that he received Goethe at Erfurt. *"Voilà un homme!"* he is supposed to have said of Goethe, which, after all, is not a very original thing to say. Then, at Weimar, during the magnificent reception in which all the ambitious, servile German nobility crowded in under Talleyrand's sarcastic gaze, he is supposed to have addressed to Goethe those famous words which some ignoramuses think were invented by Malraux: "Destiny is politics!"

Suddenly I see the tree.

On my left, in the middle of the slope, a solitary tree, standing out from the snowy mass of trees that hide the forest from me. A beech, probably. I cross the avenue and walk up the slope in the soft, fresh, immaculate snow. I am quite close to the tree, close enough to touch it. This tree is not a hallucination.

I stand there in the sunlight, contemplating this tree, transfixed with wonder. I want to laugh. I laugh. It lasts for centuries, a fraction of a second. I let myself become suffused with the beauty of this tree. Its snowy beauty, today. But also the certainty of its inevitable verdant beauty, which will outlive my death. It is happiness, a sharp, violent happiness.

But the noise I hear is not hallucination. Nor is the harsh voice demanding:

"Was machst du hier?"

I turn around.

An SS warrant officer has his 9-mm automatic pistol trained on me. The noise I heard is easy to make out, retrospectively. The officer has just inserted a bullet into the barrel of his weapon. What I heard was the metallic click of the breech.

How can I answer him? He's asking me what I'm doing here. What *am* I doing here?

An explicit, detailed answer would take us too far. I would have to tell the SS warrant officer about Hans, Michel Herr, the things we read, the Boulevard du Port-Royal. I'd have to talk to him about Hegel. We knew the passage by heart: *Die Knospe verschwindet in dem Hervorbrechen der Blüte*—"The bud disappears in the bursting-forth of the flower." But that would take us too far. The SS warrant officer would probably not hear me out, especially since a detailed account would involve a number of incidents, digressions, and sidetracks. He wouldn't hear me out. He'd put a bullet in my head before the end.

That would be a pity.

So I opt for a more precise answer. I tell him it is because of the beech. This wonderful tree.

"Das Baum," I say to him, *"so ein wunderschönes Baum!"*

But perhaps that's too laconic. He looks at me as if I've gone out of my mind.

Finally, he turns around for a moment. He walks over to the beech, examines it, tries to understand what it's all about. He makes a visible effort, but obviously without success. He comes back to me. He points the automatic revolver at my chest again. He's going to shoot.

But I have just realized that nothing can happen to me. My time has not yet come.

The face of the SS warrant officer may be twisted into a hateful grimace as he threatens me with his weapon, he may yell at me, but I don't see the premonitory signs of death anywhere. The officer may have been following me as I wandered off the authorized paths, he may suspect that I am trying to escape, he may have the right, perhaps even the duty, to kill me there and then, but I can't see the light, luminous shadow of death anywhere.

The insatiable, porous, familiar shadow of death is so absent at that moment that the SS officer, his hate, his weapon, his right to kill me, become of no account whatsoever. He is quite simply pitiful, this SS officer, as he tries to turn this incident into a tragedy, tries to look like the impalpable, voracious shadow of destiny.

Death does not look like this SS warrant officer, not at all.

It was from Giraudoux that I learned to recognize death. In fact, at the time, when I was in my twenties, I learned everything I knew from Giraudoux. Everything that mattered, I mean. How to recognize death, yes, but also how to recognize life, landscapes, the line of the horizon, the song of the nightingale, the tremulous tenderness of a young woman, the meaning of a word, the rich savor of an evening of solitude, the nocturnal rustling of a row of poplars, the misty shadow of death: I always come back to Giraudoux. In 1943, in the farmhouses of the Othe, I, a stranger, who had always been a city dweller, knew how to talk to the peasants who opened their doors to us, offered us food and shelter, despite the risk of Nazi reprisals. I talked to them in the words of Giraudoux and they understood me. That language, for me the quintessence of literature, seemed quite natural to them. I was no longer a stranger, an exile from the landscapes and words of my childhood. The words of Giraudoux gave me access to the memories of those French peasants and winegrowers. I could talk to them about bread, salt, and the seasons with Giraudoux's words. Then, most likely to show me that they accepted me into their community, they called me a "patriot." I was a "patriot," and I was fighting for the future of their memories, for the future of their vines and their wheatfields. I ate their thick, richly flavored soup by lamplight, in the farmhouses of the Othe, of the Châtillonnais, of Auxois, and I nodded when the head of the family congratulated me on being a "patriot." I thought of Giraudoux. We were happy together.

So that day in 1944, in the December sunlight, near that great snow-covered tree, off the avenue flanked with tall columns, everything that I have learned from Giraudoux confirms that my time has not yet come. Not yet.

Curiously enough, it is often in peaceful, pleasant places that I have recognized death: in working-class dance halls, along the riverbanks, in woodland clearings in autumn. Death did not notice me, of course: otherwise I would not be here to tell this story. All my efforts to attract its attention were in vain, presumptuous. It had not come for me. Death was a young woman who did not notice me; that annoyed me.

Gradually, over the years, I learned to detect its presence, even when it abandoned its earthly appearance, when it hid itself in a gust of wind, the sound of oars on transparent water, or the beating of horses' hoofs, or the leafy trembling of a poplar, the undulation of ripe corn. Even when it became, in some stupid fashion, a landscape, a traffic light blinking at the crossroads, an inert cup on a table, I recognized it.

I recognized it in Paris, in the autumn of 1975.

You see how complicated it is, chronological order. I was taking you with me, in December 1944, along the avenue of imperial eagles that led to the monumental gates of the Buchenwald camp. And then, suddenly, because of Varlam Shalamov and his *Kolyma Tales*, I was forced to make a detour via London, in the spring of 1969, and here we are four years ago now, in Paris, because of Giraudoux this time, rather than Shalamov. It is 1975, four years from now, going back. And therefore thirty-one years after December 1944. It's crazy how the memory goes back and forth.

In 1975, in Paris, in the autumn, death appeared to me in a *brasserie* in the sixteenth arrondissement. The setting may seem incongruous, but the time was right: midnight.

There were four of us. We'd been to the theater. At a nearby table, a noisy group was enjoying a champagne supper. Men and women, waving their arms around, shouting and laughing, as if to prove to themselves that they existed. As if they feared that at the slightest silence, at the first angel to pass overhead, they would disintegrate and vanish. What would become of them if they fell head first into some gap in the conversation? Perhaps shapeless piles of rotting meat, heaps of vegetable leavings, garbage, would have to be removed, and the ground hosed down. They would become what they actually were: characters from a Bacon painting.

Meanwhile they sat up straight, nervous, in cigar smoke, in a delirium of chatter, making a desperate effort to prove to themselves that they enjoyed life, that it was worth living, but, no doubt, without quite managing to convince themselves. For the shimmering phosphorescence that surrounded them—it did not emanate from them, it hung over them only as the Pentecostal reflection of an already dead star, far away, in the depths of the centuries—that flickering light was merely a firefly. There was a stink of corpses at the next table.

I might have known it was then that she would appear.

Crossing the *brasserie*, with its smell of food, its commotion, a young woman came and sat down at the next table, greeted by cries of surprise and delight. "Daisy, there you are! How wonderful!"

So death was called Daisy that night. What could I do about it?

The death that was called Daisy sat down at the next table, in a whirlwind of floating black-and-white silk. She had long legs, hips whose delicate, voluptuous bone structure could be surmised from the clinging fabric. Her face was made up very white, with blood-red lips and bluish eyelids.

I shut my eyes, then opened them again.

She was still there; she was even talking. She was telling some story that made the diners at the next table laugh till the tears rolled down their cheeks. I had no desire to laugh. I didn't find it at all amusing that death should be endowed with the power of speech. In fact, I found it rather terrifying that the death called Daisy should speak, that night, with such self-assurance.

I tried not to hear what death was saying, but she spoke loud and clear, in a deep contralto voice. She was telling a story in a mixture of languages, in a French sprinkled with English terms, curt and crude, almost vulgar. This bitch of a death liked to talk dirty. What's more, she was a polyglot: that was all we needed.

I looked at Daisy's long legs, trying to forget her words. I imagined the movement of their slender curves under the black-and-white silk, right up to the estuary of the vagina, accessible and close, navigable. A poor attempt, no doubt, to try to reverse roles. For it was I who was open, gaping, and death had penetrated me.

At that moment, she suddenly turned toward me. She stared at me, and I held her gaze. Then she hid her eyes behind dark glasses with large tortoise-shell frames. Daisy had put on her mask.

That night, in a *brasserie* in the sixteenth arrondissement, death spoke to me for the first time. It was only indirectly. But perhaps it was quite simply that I had reached the age when one hears the voice of death. A voice inside oneself, no doubt.

I listened to Daisy's voice, to her contralto modulations, moving back and forth within me, digging its groove. It left me trembling, breathless. Yes, for the first time it made me tremble.

The next day, the telephone rang in my apartment at an unusual time. A far-off, tired-sounding voice, hoarse with pain, told me that Domingo "Dominguin" had been shot in the head, at Guayaquil. Domingo, my best friend from the Madrid underground. Domingo, my brother. That bitch of a death had won this time.

But thirty-one years before, in 1944, in the December sunlight, in the snowy forest where Goethe and Eckermann were fond of walking, there is not the slightest sign to suggest the presence of death.

I look at the SS officer who is training his automatic revolver on me, his finger on the trigger. He is going to shout, but nowhere do I see the shadow of death. I think even Giraudoux would be quite certain on that score. The color of the sky is still the same: not a wrinkle has appeared on the face of the landscape, no tinkle of ghostly sleighbells reaches my ear.

I look at the SS officer and I see around him nothing but images of life. It seems to me that the beech has cast off its shroud of snow, that the spring brooks have begun to whisper in that ice-locked hill. I can almost hear the buzzing of insects in the summer air.

I look at the SS officer and I see the ruddy faces, the laughing eyes of the fair-haired children that he will have. I see the outline of the woman, with her firm legs, her matriarchal hips, her steady gaze, who will give him these children. I even hear piano music, in the distance: a sonatina.

I look at the SS officer. I want to laugh. I want to call over to him: "Drop your gun, old pal! You're too light-weight for the part! You don't even have the weight of the thin smoke of death. Today is not the day. My time has not yet come!"

Then, to put an end to a situation that is beginning to get ridiculous, with that lout of an SS officer seeming to think that he is destiny, though he is really a respectable family man, I stand to attention, yell out my number, present myself, looking into space, into the blind empti-ness of the pale sky where I see not the slightest sign of approaching death.

I mean *my* death. Smoke is still rising gently from the crematorium chimney.

Four

"You wanted to see me, old pal?"

I'm talking to Daniel in the office of the *Arbeitsstatistik*. He turns around, smiling.

Daniel often smiles. In fact, whenever I've seen him, he's been smiling. But, then, I suppose there must be times when he isn't smiling. Every now and then. So, out of concern for the truth, I don't say that he is always smiling, just that he is often smiling: don't worry, I'm a realistic novelist.

"Oh, there you are! So you got out!" says Daniel.

Yes, I got out with Henk Spoenay.

In the end, the SS officer who had caught me near the beech tree decided to bring me back to the camp gates, the barrel of his Mauser stuck in my back. In this *opera buffa*, the role of angel of death had not been given to him. He must have realized this at the last minute.

He got me back to the camp gates, and the officer on guard, the same one who had let Henk and me pass an hour before, leapt out of his office. They pushed me into a windowless room, on the ground floor of the watchtower. They yelled at each other, stared at the report book, got angrier and angrier.

They were going to rough me up, no doubt about it.

But just then Hauptsturmführer Schwartz arrived and took matters in hand.

I reported to him, again, as soon as he entered the room. Stiff, head erect, yelling my number, the name of my kommando, why I had been outside the camp bounds. It was an impeccable report, no doubt about it. I was getting very good at this little game.

Hauptsturmführer Schwartz resumed my interrogation in an unemotional voice. I answered with an equal lack of emotion. Soldiers the world over like conciseness, but the SS were fanatically concise.

Schwartz checked that Henk Spoenay and I had reported, an hour earlier, to the officer on guard. He checked that our numbers and the reason for our sortie outside camp bounds had been entered in the report book. He asked why I had come back alone. I replied that Spoenay had been kept longer than expected at the Mibau and had sent me back to the camp to carry on with my work at the *Arbeitsstatistik*.

He nodded; everything was in order.

He then touched on the most delicate aspect of the interrogation. I was ready for it.

"Why did you leave the road?" he asks.

I look him straight in the eye. It's important that he see the innocence in my face.

"Because of the tree, Hauptsturmführer!" I say.

I know that's a good point for me, too, that I should get his rank in the SS hierarchy exactly right. The SS don't like to get tangled up in complications about their rank.

"The tree?" he says.

"There was a tree, by itself, a beech, a very fine tree. As

soon as I saw it, I thought it might be Goethe's tree, so I went up to it."

He looks very interested.

"Goethe!" he exclaims. "So you know the works of Goethe?" A distinct change of tone. *Kultur* has its uses.

I nod modestly.

"And you speak German very well," says Hauptsturm-führer Schwartz. "Where did you learn it?"

I seem to have lived through this moment before, had to answer the same question before.

Yes, that's it, about a year and a half earlier, in a train bound for Les Laumes. I was with Julien. The Germans were checking papers, and the officer, after examining them all, glanced up at the luggage.

"*A qui appartient cette valise?*" he asked in hesitant French.

I looked up and saw that he was pointing at my case, the case I was taking to Semur, filled with Sten guns that had been taken apart, and loaded magazines. Julien had one, too, on the luggage rack above his head.

I avoided looking at Julien. I knew that, like me, he had a Smith and Wesson 11.43 in his belt.

I turned to the *Wehrmacht* officer.

"*Das gehört mir!*" I said. I told him it was mine.

"*Ach so!*" he said, radiant. "*Sie sprechen Deutsch!*"

He was obviously delighted that I spoke German.

"*Also, bitte schön,*" said the officer politely, "*was haben Sie in diesem Handkoffer?*" He wanted to know what I was carrying in that case. It was the least one could expect.

I stared into space, as if trying to remember.

"*Zwei oder drei Hemde,*" I said, "*ein Paar braune Halbschuhe, ein grauer Anzug, und so weiter. Nur persönliche Sachen!*" I listed all the personal effects that I was supposed to be carrying in my case.

The officer shook his head, radiant:

"*Sie sprechen ganz nett Deutsch,*" he said. "*Wo haben Sie's gelernt?*" He wanted to know where I had learned such good German.

"*Bei uns zu Hause haben wir immer ein deutsches Fräulein gehabt!*" I replied, in a rather superior tone of voice.

The officer smiled approvingly, almost with complicity.

"*Danke schön,*" he said, bowing.

It seemed to flatter his national pride that there had always been German governesses in my family. It seemed to reassure him completely as to my character. Suddenly he was no longer concerned with the contents of that case. To open it would have been a superfluous formality: as if a young man who had been brought up by German governesses could be carrying in his case anything that was forbidden!

The officer gave me an enthusiastic salute and left the compartment.

I then noticed that all the other passengers were looking at me suspiciously.

Julien was also looking at me, not suspiciously, but flabbergasted.

"Just like that, you speak Boche?" he said, leaning toward me.

"What can I do about it? That's life!"

"But what was that you were telling him?"

"The truth, just the truth," I said. Julien spluttered with amusement.

"Such as?"

"I told him what was in my case. That's what he wanted to know!"

Julien leaned even closer to me. He couldn't help laughing.

"And what is in your damned case?"

"Nothing much," I said, "two or three shirts, a gray suit, a pair of shoes, various personal articles."

By that time Julien was on the point of choking. He slapped his thighs. He couldn't take any more.

The other passengers were now looking at us with alarm.

But that was just over a year earlier, in the train that was taking Julien and me from Joigny to Les Laumes.

And Hauptsturmführer Schwartz is now asking me the same question, where I learned German. I give him the same answer:

"Bei uns zu Hause haben wir immer ein deutsches Fräulein gehabt!"

I explain to the *Hauptsturmführer* that we have always had German governesses in our family, in Spain, that I learned German from a very early age and have kept it up since. Yes, I know the works of Goethe.

Schwartz looks at me, frowning. He seems to have a problem.

"German governesses?" he cries. "You must be from a good family! What are you doing here?"

That's Schwartz's problem. He wonders how I managed, with such an excellent background, to get myself mixed up with all these hooligans and terrorists. In short, how I could be on the wrong side of the barrier.

I must say, I'm getting rather sick of my social background, or, rather, of the way it is used against me, the way it is thrown in my face. Today it's Hauptsturmführer Schwartz who can't understand why, in view of my background, I'm here, in a corrective-labor camp. He can't understand how I can be interested in Goethe. It doesn't go with his idea of a Spanish Red arrested for resistance work. Schwartz frowns, perplexed. It seems suspicious to him.

The other day it was Seifert, explaining in his mealy-mouthed way how generous he was being in letting me work in the *Arbeitsstatistik*, in spite of my background. A philosophy student from a bourgeois family—good heavens, it was the first time he had seen that in his office! I got the impression that I was there as an experiment. If I made one false step, I'd be sent back to burn for all eternity in hell, in the stockpot of my class origins.

Later, throughout my political life, it was the same. My class origins were there crouching in the darkness, ready to leap out at me at the slightest unorthodox thought. I spent my time remonstrating with my background. I talked to it as one talks to a pet dog: "Down, down! Don't bother the guests!"

But let me be fair. Sometimes my social background was seen as a good thing, even a very good thing, as when the comrades felt the need to emphasize the Party's radiating influence and its broad appeal. Look how broad-minded our party is! Not at all sectarian, you see! This is our Comrade Sanchez; he comes from a family of the *haute bourgeoisie*, closely linked with the aristocracy: some of his cousins are dukes and duchesses! Comrade Sanchez is an intellectual, isn't he? And yet he has attained the highest responsibilities in our great Communist Party!

I would assume a well-behaved, modest air, as if for a birthday photograph or an award ceremony. I could hear, hovering around me, the little chubby angels, broadcasting my background on their tiny trumpets. It was just like a Murillo painting!

All right, that period of euphoria could not last forever. In this life everything comes to an end. My social background returned, like the witches in *Macbeth*, decked out in the blackest rags. Once again, when all was said and done, I was an intellectual of bourgeois origin, subject by my very nature to doubt, vacillations, negative attitudes, *anarchisme de grand seigneur*. The worm was in the fruit after all!

I listened to what my comrades had to say as they sat on either side of the long table, like a court deciding my fate, in March 1964, in a former castle of the kings of Bohemia. I didn't feel in the least guilty. I looked at them, these new puritans who were descended from the working class, in much the same way as the best Boston families descended from the *Mayflower* voyagers, or the monkey descends from the tree. I could have laughed in their faces—and wept, too, it's true.

I knew very well what had become of those sons of the people, or most of them, anyway: timorous, devious functionaries, attentive to the slightest wind that blew through the corridors, antechambers, and seraglios of the apparatus. I wanted to tell them what they could do with their leaders from the working class, the Thorezes, the Rakosis, the Ulbrichts, the Gottwalds, etc., etc. But it would have been quite pointless. They sat there, on either side of the long table, deciding my fate like the apostles, severe but just; a tiny tongue of fire hovered over their heads, the Holy Spirit had descended on their bald pates, because they were of working-class origin. All I could do was go back to my hell.

But we haven't got that far yet. Today it isn't Seifert or Carrillo reminding me of my social background. It's Hauptsturmführer Schwartz. He is surprised that, with such a background, I should be in Buchenwald, on the wrong side of the barrier.

I shall always be suspect, then, whichever side I'm on, for inversely identical reasons. One day I shall have to explain to them, all of them, what a Communist intellectual is. Before this book comes to an end, I must explain to them in greater detail that it is precisely my suspect side that is of most value, that is my raison d'être. If I were not suspect, I would not be a Communist intellectual *from* the bourgeoisie, but an intellectual *of* the bourgeoisie. If I am suspect, it is because I have betrayed my class. I am a traitor to my class because I have had the vocation, the will, the capacity—the luck, too—to betray with my own all classes, class society as a whole, because my role (and I'm speaking here in the first person only metaphorically, out of convenience, of course: I am speaking not about myself, but about the Communist intellectual, generically) is precisely that of negating classes as such, class society in whatever form it presents itself, even at the risk of forging ahead and ignoring the meanderings of realpolitik, which is a term that denotes the reality of politics and the politics of reality. It denotes, that is, any conservative politics, since revolutionary politics is essentially a negation of reality, a creative, disordered overthrow of the legitimate order, the natural order of history. Hence its improbable nature. If I am not suspect, and therefore a hell hound of the spirit of negation, a permanent critic of all social relations, I am nothing. Neither an intellectual nor a Communist nor myself.

But it would be rather difficult to explain all this to Hauptsturmführer Schwartz, at least in such terms. So I avoid answering his question.

"I thought it was Goethe's tree, Hauptsturmführer," I tell him. "I couldn't resist the temptation of taking a closer look."

Schwartz nods, understanding.

"You're quite wrong," he says. "Goethe's tree, the one on which he carved his initials, is inside the camp, on the esplanade between the kitchens and the clothing stores! And anyway, it's not a beech, but an oak!"

I know this already, of course, but I put on a show of great interest, as if delighted at acquiring a new piece of information.

"Oh, that's the one!"

"Yes," says Schwartz. "We spared it when the hill was cleared of trees, in memory of Goethe!"

And he embarks on a long speech about the respect shown by the National Socialists for good German cultural tradition. I am still looking him in the eye, still standing to attention, as is the custom, but I am no longer listening. I am thinking that Goethe and Eckermann would be very pleased if they heard him. I am thinking of the sumptuous beauty of the beech on the Avenue of Eagles. I'm thinking that Daniel had something to tell me, just now, and that I left with Henk without speaking to him. I am thinking that it's Sunday, that Hauptsturmführer Schwartz is a sinister idiot, that the British troops have crushed the ELAS partisans in Athens. I'm thinking that I'd like to get out. Now.

Just then, someone knocks on the door, and an image bursts. The door would open and Johann Wolfgang von Goethe would make his entrance, and stand there, majestic. The door does in fact open, but it's not Goethe who comes in, but my pal Henk Spoenay.

"So you got out!" Daniel says to me.

We're in the office of the *Arbeitsstatistik*.

Daniel's smile is sweet, gentle, almost ecstatic. Such smiles are usually stupid, but Daniel's is one of the most intelligent smiles I know. That's because above that sweet, gentle, almost ecstatic smile are two of the liveliest eyes I know. That must be why.

"Yes, I got out," I say to Daniel. "I had an appointment with Eckermann and Goethe."

"Well?" says Daniel. "What's so extraordinary about a meeting with Goethe and Eckermann? Everybody knows they go for walks on the Ettersberg!"

I try not to admit that I'm bested.

"Maybe you know what we talked about as well?"

Daniel looks at me and nods.

"What else would one talk about with Goethe except Goethe himself?" he says, as if pointing out the self-evident.

Then we look at each other and burst out laughing. It's Sunday.

Daniel is a tailor. He used to make made-to-measure suits, near the Rue Saint-Denis. It's a well-known fact that tailors, like typographers, are thoughtful guys. The rhythm of their work gives them time to read and to think. It's no accident that these two guilds provided the workers' movement with hundreds of activists throughout the nineteenth century. Usually, of course, the tradition that they represented was revolutionary syndicalism. But it's hardly the fault of the tailors and typographers if Marxism—or what passes for it—has never really taken root in the French working class. There must be another reason.

Daniel is a tailor. He's a Jew, too. But he isn't here because he's a Jew. He doesn't wear a yellow triangle, sewn upside down under the red triangle to form the star of David, as do the few German Jews who are still alive to recount the death of all the German Jews who died here. He's here because he's a Communist.

Anyway, all the conditions required for a sense of humor are fulfilled in Daniel, because he's a Jew and a tailor.

"You win!" I say to Daniel.

I sit down next to him, in the *Arbeit* hut.

He looks at me and takes out of his pocket a tiny scrap of paper, folded in four. He puts the paper in my hand.

"Three pals from the *maquis*," Daniel says. "They're coming from a camp in Poland. The Party will raise the question of what work they are to do as soon as they come out of quarantine. In the meantime, they mustn't get themselves sent out of the camp. The Party wants them to stay inside. See what you can do."

I nod, I tell him I will, I get up.

At the long table of the central card index, Walter is still deeply engrossed in his *Völkische Beobachter*, the Sunday edition. Unless he's dreaming with the newspaper open in front of him, which is quite possible.

Walter is one of the few old German Communists in the *Arbeit* who aren't mad. I mean, who aren't mad in an aggressive way. He must have his share of madness, I'm sure, but it's a gentle madness. Walter is affable. You might even say that he is sometimes aware that there are people living around him, sometimes he even speaks to us, asks us questions. Most of the other old German Communists don't even see us.

When I say "us," that isn't quite right. There are subtle distinctions to be made. There is a sort of hierarchy at work. The most invisible of us are really us: those of us who came to Buchenwald from the occupied countries of Western Europe. We have been here since 1943, approximately. So we're ten years behind them and we always will be: it's not something you catch up on. In 1943, they had already been in the camps and prisons ten years. What could we know of their lives, their obsessions? How could we understand what had driven them mad? We were outside, drinking beer: they were inside. We were outside, walking in the Parc Montsouris: they were inside. We were outside, stroking young women's hips, shoulders, eyelids: they were inside.

Ten years behind. It's too much. It makes us transparent. They look at us, they don't see us, they've nothing to say to us.

Slightly less invisible, bearers of a minimum of real existence, are the deportees from Czechoslovakia. Or, rather, from the Protectorate of Bohemia-Moravia. Not only do they come from an imperial, partly Germanized

Europe, but also they have been here since 1939. That's quite a time: they knew the end of the old days, when the camp hadn't yet been turned into a sanatorium.

Then there are the others: Poles, Russians, other Eastern Europeans. They're in a class of their own. They constitute the plebs of the camps.

But Walter is affable. He talks with all of us. Even with the Belgians. Even with the Hungarians, on occasion.

August, too, I must admit. But August is not an old German Communist. Or, rather, he's a real old Communist and a real German, but he had emigrated to Argentina well before the Nazis came to power. He came back to fight in Spain, in the Brigades. He was interned in the camp at Le Vernet in 1939. It was there, at Le Vernet, that the Vichy police handed him over to the Gestapo.

August, then, was a bit cosmopolitan, if you see what I mean. Anyway, though he wore the red triangle without any black letter of national identification imprinted on it, like the Germans, August was considered administratively by the SS as a foreigner, as a Spanish Red, a *Rotspanier*. Like me, in fact, like the other Spanish Reds. It didn't bother him in the least, I must say, being cut off, administratively speaking, from the German national community.

August was rather proud of being a Spanish Red. He was short, round as a ball, irrepressible, with bright green eyes behind his glasses, and he spoke Spanish fluently. Castilian, I mean—or, rather, Argentine.

That was really worth seeing: August standing on a chair in the *Arbeit* office, to get closer to one of the loudspeakers, listening to the official communiqués of the *Wehrmacht* announcing in funereal tones the progress of the Russian tanks through Poland. "*Macanudo,*" he cried, "*macanudo!*" But that won't make you laugh, probably. You have to understand Spanish—or, rather, Argentine—to appreciate the odd charm of that word in the mouth of an old German Communist in Buchenwald. And the Russian tanks moved through Poland. Anyway, August was affable, like Walter. There are always exceptions to the rule.

You must be mixing up dates, memories, different journeys. It wasn't that time you saw August again in East Berlin. It was another time, earlier. You were traveling normally, with a real passport and an officially recognized, verifiable identity. Friends of the DEFA* were making a film about the life of Goya, and they'd brought you over to discuss the scenario with you, to ask your advice.

Anyway, you kept some proof of that journey. Since you have been able to, since your life has become public, since you have had nothing (almost nothing) to hide from the police of various countries, you have kept with cranky avidity the tiniest proof of your existence, as if you needed to reassure yourself on the matter, make up for lost time. As if your memory couldn't function without old theater stubs, postcards, fading photographs, from years, countries, travels long ago.

All you have to do is open a drawer and take out a yellowing envelope.

Nr. 17/5/7657

EINREISE—und *WIEDERAUSREISE VISUM*
zur einmaligen Einreise nach
und Wiederausreise aus der
Deutschen Demokratischen Republik
über die Grenzstellen

zur Einreise	:	*Schönefeld*
und Ausreise	:	*Schönefeld*
Gültig vom		6 Dez. 1965
bis zum	:	21 Dez. 1965
Reisezweck	:	*Berlin u. Babelsberg*
Berlin, den	:	6 Dez. 1965

*State Film Corporation of East Germany. —ED.

You look at that one-way visa, valid for either entry into or exit from the German Democratic Republic. You look at the stamps on this visa. Two red rectangular stamps, those of the border police at Schönefeld Airport. The black circular stamp of the Foreign Ministry, with a fiscal stamp, free of charge: *Gebührenfrei*. But the important thing is the date: December 1965. Actually, you didn't stay until December 21. You left East Berlin on the 11th. You have a very precise reason to remember that fact so precisely. The day before, December 10, was your birthday.

But that wasn't the time you saw August again; it was another time, years before.

The material traces of that last visit, in December 1965, are in the yellowing envelope. You examine them. A credit card from the Magistrat von Gross-Berlin, enabling you to make purchases worth up to two hundred marks. You never used it; the card was not stamped. You must still have two hundred marks in your account in East Berlin. Theater programs. *Die Tragödie des Coriolan* and *Der aufhaltsame Aufstieg des Arturo Ui*, at the Berliner Ensemble—Brecht. Memories flood back, images. *Der Drache* by Yevgeni Schwarz, directed by Benno Besson, at the Deutsches Theater. You look through the programs. You saw Schwarz's *The Dragon* on December 10, the evening before your departure. Your last evening in East Berlin. You'll never go back. Three bank notes, too. A five-mark note, with the picture of Alexander von Humboldt on one side. You smile, thinking of Malcolm Lowry! Calle Humboldt at Cuernavaca; you laugh to yourself. Two twenty-mark notes. Looking at them, you laugh even more. You must admit you didn't expect that! Twenty-mark notes bearing the portrait of Johann Wolfgang von Goethe on one side and, on the verso, the façade of the National Theater at Weimar. Chance has arranged matters very well, you must admit! Goethe, with his broad, high-domed, Goethean brow. He has the look of a man who has seen everything: human, understanding, Goethean. There's a man! Napoleon exclaimed. No doubt, yes, a man. More than that, even, a humanist: a man professing humanity, a cross between man and official-dom. It wearies you just to think about it. You pick up the twenty-mark note and hold it against the light. On the left-hand side of the note there is a blank space with the serial number at the top: CF 378575. Below, in the watermark, against the light, Johann Wolfgang von Goethe appears again. You watch his face appear against the light. A puff of smoke, a mist, an incorporeal dream: the ghost in the watermark of bourgeois humanism. It is that ghost that guarantees the authenticity of this democratic currency. It wearies you just to think about it. You put the twenty-mark note back into the yellow envelope with the other mementos of that last trip to East Berlin, in 1965.

But that wasn't the time you saw August again; it was another time, years before.

It was in the lounge of the hotel reserved for guests of the Socialist Unity Party (the East German Communist Party). The party functionary had told you that Seifert and Weidlich were not in Berlin, that you couldn't meet them. He asked you if there wasn't any other German comrade from Buchenwald you would like to see. You thought of August, and mentioned his name. They traced him very quickly. Yes, he was living in Berlin. Yes, you could see him.

An hour later, a black Russian limousine—curtains of thick tulle over the rear windows—took you through East Berlin to the place where August worked. It was hot and humid. You looked out at the city living limply under that humid heat.

August worked in some institution connected with the Ministry of Foreign Trade. It couldn't have been very important work; the building was rather dilapidated, and some distance from the main administrative centers. You mounted the steps leading up to that once private town-house. You were shown into an antechamber, where you waited for a few minutes, then into August's office. He hadn't been told you were coming. It was a surprise, in a way. August looked up and saw that unexpected, perhaps inopportune visitor come in. August hadn't changed much, at first sight. Then, thinking you were being funny—though it may have been because of the emotion you felt, to hide your emotion—you said to him in Spanish, trying hard to put on an Argentine accent: *"Macanudo, viejo, no habés cambiado nada!"* That's wonderful, my old friend, you haven't changed at all! But he moved his head from side to side, confused, and cried out: *"Was? Was?"* Confused, not understanding. Then you moved forward a couple of steps and you saw that he had changed. In fact, despite your first impression, he was not at all the same man. Something in the eyes, that was it, an internal wearing away.

August saw you approach. He obviously hadn't recognized you. Well, there was nothing surprising in that. You had changed, too. You told him you were the Spaniard from the *Arbeitsstatistik*, and you reminded him of your name. He repeated what you said to him, nodding. He was trying to match a face with your face, that was obvious. Your twenty-year-old face on your thirty-five-year-old face. He said, "Oh, yes, yes, the Spaniard from the *Arbeitsstatistik!*" But one could see that the certainty he was expressing was abstract. He knew that there had been a Spaniard in the *Arbeitsstatistik*, rather as one knows that Napoleon lost the battle of Waterloo. No image came to mind, none at all.

You stood before him, disconcerted, as if you'd lost your shadow. You had lost your twenty-year-old image in August's memory, and it was a kind of little death. Pained, you talked of this and that very rapidly. Certain episodes, shared, perhaps even derisory, memories, to try to conjure up your twenty-year-old image in August's memory. A light morning mist would lift over the landscape of his memory, and you would appear with the brightness, at once blinding and blurred, of images from the past when they reappear. But August did not remember; or, rather, he knew that there had been a Spaniard at the *Arbeitsstatistik,* but it was not a memory. He was talking to you, pleasantly, as one might speak to the corporeal, crude, unexpected form of an abstract certainty. You were no more than an idea, you had not managed to become flesh and blood. And yet, you'd been twenty, damn it! Despite appearances to the contrary, despite August's failure to remember you, you had been twenty years old at Buchenwald. But the ghost of your twenty-year-old self certainly did not arise in August's memory, and the absence of that ghost made you feel light, ghostlike. Trying to resign yourself to the inevitable, you stared uncertainly at Ulbricht's portrait hanging on the wall behind August's desk. You told yourself that perhaps you had never been twenty years old, who knows? Perhaps you'd dreamed it all. Perhaps you had not yet come into the world.

Then, pretending that you really had recognized each other, you talked of this and that. August asked you what had become of you. You told him, without going into details. It was difficult, especially without going into details, to tell this man who had aged so much, whose memory and life had undergone some strange erosion, what had become of you. Anyway, had you become anything? That day, trying to sum up your life since Buchenwald for August, it seemed to you that you hadn't become anything at all, that you had simply gone on being the same as you were at twenty, which was scandalously undialectical.

Willi Seifert had become something. He had become a major-general in the *Volkspolizei*. He would have had no trouble at all telling you what he had become if you'd asked him. "What's become of you, Seifert?" "I've become a major-general in the *Volkspolizei*," he would have answered, without a second's hesitation. But August nodded as he listened to you telling him in brief what you thought had become of you. You couldn't have been very convincing. August nodded, absent-mindedly, as one might when listening to a stranger in a train recounting some stupid, interminable incident he had had with the ticket collector.

Then there was a moment's silence. August was no longer trying to remember your twenty-year-old face, that was obvious. He nodded mechanically, and you felt like an intruder, not only in his memory, but also in his everyday life. Yet before getting up to go, you had reciprocated his politeness: "And what about you, August, what's become of you?" you asked him. He stared back at you, or through you, for a long time, it seemed. "Oh, life, you know," he said, "it comes and goes. One has one's ups and downs." He wasn't very explicit, but at the time you didn't really want to know more. Ups and downs, of course. Suddenly, August leapt forward and said, in a changed voice: "You know, for those of us who were in Spain, there have been some very tough times here!" You felt that he was trying once again to match a face from the past with this face from the present. He looked at you anxiously. You felt that he would say more if your image

from the past, your twenty-year-old image from Buchenwald, came back to him. You thought, at that moment,
that he would confide in you if your image from the past
managed to take shape. You held your breath. You waited.
But nothing must have happened, nothing at all, no click;
your image remained in the shade. You had been thrown
far away from each other—you in your little death, he in
his loneliness.

August apologized for not being able to spend more
time with you. He had work to finish, he explained. It was
the day of some official commemoration, and the party
staff committee had asked him to make a speech for the
occasion during the solemn meeting that would take
place, at the end of the day's work, with all the employ-
ees. August showed you the typed pages that he was still
correcting. "It's a great honor, you see, that I should be
entrusted with this task, after all the political difficulties
I've had!" And suddenly, in a monotonous voice, he read
you a passage from this speech that he had been asked to
give, a passage dealing with the great virtues of Comrade
Walter Ulbricht. He then looked up at you briefly, and he
seemed to have recaptured the vivacity of fifteen years
ago, though imprinted now with a desperate irony.

But the light went out of August's eyes. You might as
well leave.

You were in the corridor, you descended the steps, you
were once more in the humid heat of the street, it was
unbearable. No, you would not go to Weimar and visit the
Buchenwald memorial. You had nothing to do with the
Buchenwald memorial. You had seen photographs of it,
and you had nothing to do with it. So much the worse for
Bertolt Brecht if the idea of that appalling memorial had
been his. That great ugly tower, surmounted by a gigantic
bell, the *Glockenturm*, you knew where they could stuff
that ignoble phallus erected on the Ettersberg. Along with

the group sculpture by Professor Fritz Cremer, eminent artist of the people, that stands in front of the *Glockenturm.*

You wouldn't go to Buchenwald, ever. Your pals wouldn't be there any more, anyway. You would not find Josef Frank there, for example. He had been hanged, in Prague, in his own country, by his own people, and his ashes thrown to the winds. You would find only Willi Seifert or Herbert Weidlich. They were still alive. But that didn't interest you now. They were no longer your pals from Buchenwald; they had become policemen. You weren't interested in policemen.

You hadn't found August, either.

He used to be quite round, rosy-cheeked, indestructible. His eyes threw lightning flashes from behind his gold-rimmed spectacles. He listened to the communiqués of the *Wehrmacht* announcing in funereal tones the progress of Stalin's tanks across the plains of Poland, and he cried, *"Macanudo, viejo, macanudo!"* He had fought in Spain, he had been in the French camps, he had been handed over by the Vichy regime to the Gestapo. Deprived of his German nationality, he became nothing but a Spanish Red at Buchenwald: he was indestructible. But you did not find August. The power of his own people— your people—the power of Seifert's police had worn him down, making of him what no other power had managed to make of him: a broken, disillusioned old man, cynically, desperately preparing a speech in praise of Walter Ulbricht.

You looked at the black limousine parked on the road, at the foot of the steps. You told the chauffeur that you wanted to go for a walk, that he could go. But the chauffeur would have none of it. He had instructions, he told you. He had to take you back to the party hotel. You tried to reassure him, you told him that you would come back to the party hotel, but you wanted to walk. You didn't give him time to argue. You set off on foot in the direction of the hotel. You walked slowly in the humid Berlin heat. After a while, you turned around. The black limousine was following you at a distance of ten meters. Looking at the black limousine, you suddenly felt a sort of sickening illumination. You recognized the implacable sign. The black limousine was the shadow of death following your footsteps. It was as if you were walking in front of your own hearse. For the first time the shadow of death seemed to be following you, showing interest in you. Under the leaden sky, in the humid heat of Berlin, the black limousine, which seemed, grotesquely, to embody the power of your people, was nothing but the shadow of death.

And yet it would seem that death has still not won the game. The very day you are correcting these pages, you have received a Christmas card. *Frohe Weihnachtstage und GLÜCK im neuen Jahr* was printed on the first page of this card. The word *GLÜCK*, happiness, was written in gold capital letters, just the one word! So someone was wishing you "A Merry Christmas and HAPPINESS for the New Year." Then, on the second page, in firm handwriting, were these words: *wünscht seinem jungen Kameraden Jorge in dauernder Verbundenheit, der alte Freund, August G.*

So you stood there, trembling, staring at the Christmas card from the German Democratic Republic, staring at August's signature, his address. August, "the old friend," wishing a Merry Christmas and all possible HAPPINESS to "his young comrade Jorge." You were no longer so young, you thought! But it was your youth of long ago, at Buchenwald, that August was addressing, of course. So you began to hope, hope against hope, that death would not win the game hands down. You said to yourself that, finally, some glimmer of light had stirred in August's memory, that, finally, he had rediscovered, perhaps in the book that you had written, the image of your twentieth year. Through what comrade in East Berlin had August found your address in Paris? Through W., through K., through J., through C., through S.? You told yourself that it didn't matter, the important thing was that he had recovered his memory. You looked at August's Christmas card, wondering whether there would still be enough Communists throughout Europe to take up the struggle once more, to attack death, the organized, institutionalized state amnesia, to take on the black limousines, the blue, green, or red stripes on the helmets of the People's Police, the infallible dialecticians, the Great Helmsmen of all kinds.

Hoping against hope, you began to hope that death would not win the game hands down.

I am back at my seat at the big table of the central card index.

Walter looks up from his newspaper.

"Oh, you're back," he says.

He merely observes the fact. I say nothing; one does not comment on an observation.

"Oh, this is for you," says Walter.

He hands me a few typewritten pages from one of the shelves on which the long filing boxes are placed. We used to have books, large hard-bound registers, to record the numbers of living and dead, who was doing what work, who had left the camp with the various work parties. But Seifert got us to make a card index. It's more practical, apparently.

I get up to take the pages that Walter is holding out to me. They are daily reports of the different kommandos, indicating changes in their composition. Absences, departures, arrivals, and so on. There are also reports from the *Revier*, the camp hospital, and those from the crematorium.

Ordnung muss sein.

It's certainly a quiet Sunday, without much to do. I have just twenty or thirty cards to bring up to date in the numerical sections that I'm responsible for. Each of us is responsible for a few thousand numbers. Of course, the Germans who work at the card index have kept for themselves the lowest numbers, those of the prisoners who have been there the longest. For those numbers, there's very little to report. They don't change kommando or go out on work parties, the old-timers. Curiously enough, they're very seldom ill, either. Nor do they seem to die any more. In short, they don't cause much work.

As luck would have it, I've been given the numbers between 40000 and 70000. And there's a lot going on for those numbers. It's a real pleasure to work on them! They come and go and die with disconcerting rapidity.

So I start handling the filing boxes, erasing on each card out-of-date information, adding in pencil the new information provided by the various daily reports.

I use this opportunity to deal with the French pals whose names and numbers Daniel has given me. I take out the scrap of paper, unfold it, stick it under my left hand, after making sure that no one is watching. It's like copying at school. I assume a detached, self-confident air, as if I were trying to fool the attentive eyes of the supervisor.

The three numbers of the pals whom Daniel has asked me to deal with are consecutive. It's easy to see why. When the transport was organized in the Polish camp from which they were transferred, the three must have arranged to travel together in the same compartment. On arrival at Buchenwald, they stayed together during the formalities of disinfection and dressing. They were probably together in the same resistance group. They must have been arrested together and have sworn to stay together when their deportation was ordered. And they've managed to stay together; their numbers are consecutive. And they'll stay together here, too.

On the first two cards, I write DIKAL and today's date. On the third card, to change things a bit, I write DAKAK and yesterday's date. DIKAL means: *Darf in kein anderes Lager*, "not to be transferred to any other camp," and DAKAK, *Darf auf kein Aussenkommando*, "not to be sent on any outside kommando."

Of course, I have absolutely no right to write these things on the cards. It is the *Politische Abteilung*, the section of the Gestapo that supervises the camp, which decides which prisoners are DIKAL and DAKAK, on information coming from Berlin. When the Gestapo want to keep certain prisoners close by, they send us orders to put the prisoners on the DIKAL or DAKAK lists. Generally speaking, it's not a good sign when the Gestapo want to keep you close by. It means that your case has not been finally settled, that the Gestapo may at any moment take you back for further information, as they say. On the other hand, the prisoners belonging to one of these lists, DIKAL or DIKAK, are sure of staying in the main camp at Buchenwald.

In this way, I use the fearsome authority of the Gestapo to protect those pals. Daniel and I often have a good laugh at the way the Gestapo's authority is being diverted.

If Seifert or Weidlich realized what I was doing, I'd be kicked out of the *Arbeitsstatistik* at once. I might even get sent on some particularly harsh outside kommando, unless the PCE managed to get me kept on inside Buchenwald. But it would have to pull out all the stops, and even

then, nothing could stop me from getting several months'
hard labor. In the quarries, for instance.

What I'm doing by falsifying the cards is regarded as
sabotage by the SS. If the SS themselves discover what
I'm doing, the penalty will be hanging on the *Appellplatz*, in front of the assembled prisoners.

But is the risk of being discovered by the SS real or only
hypothetical? I've examined the question from all angles,
as objectively as possible.

This month, December 1944, the strategy of the SS
officers in charge of the Buchenwald camp is fairly easy
to guess. They want at all costs to avoid being sent to
the front. They want to go on living at home, in the comfort of their sinecures. So at all costs we must avoid any
incident that might attract the attention of Berlin to the
running of Buchenwald and thus lead to disciplinary
measures.

But how can incidents be avoided? The best solution is
to leave the management of the camp's internal affairs to
the German Communists, who have occupied the key
posts in the internal administration for years, ever since,
after a ruthless and bloody struggle, they eliminated the
common-law prisoners. To run things, and enable the SS
officers, lazy and corrupt as they are, to get on with their
large-scale dealings and private junketings, the German
Communist prisoners have to enjoy a certain autonomy.

The German Communists who occupy the key posts in
the administration of the camp—seniors, kapos, block
leaders, foremen, *Stubendienst*, *Lagerschutz*—are in fact
extremely capable, hard-working men with a remarkable
sense of organization. They can be depended on to keep
the wheels turning.

But all these qualities, indispensable to the smooth
running of the camp, with its factories, its outside kom-

mandos, its tens of thousands of prisoners, most of them working for the Nazi war machine, all these qualities of the German Communists also lead to a gradual erosion of the real authority of the SS, and an almost imperceptible but nonetheless effective extension of the underground counterpower of the international Communist organization in Buchenwald.

The German Communists who occupy the key administrative posts represent the visible summit, the official hierarchy of this underground organization. But Communists of other nationalities, especially the Czechs, the French, and the Spanish, also play a part in it. (The deportees from the East are a different problem altogether: there are very few Communists among the Russians, almost none among the Poles; and there are very few Yugoslavs in Buchenwald at all, perhaps because very few members of the Yugoslav resistance are deported, or because the Nazis tend to shoot them on the spot.) And this rule is tending to increase, even visibly, in the official administration. Every opportunity is being used to impose on the SS a wider participation of foreigners in the administration of the camp. Thus, after the United States Air Force bombed the Buchenwald factories, in August 1944, the foreign prisoners avoided any panic, came rapidly to the aid of the wounded, and helped to put out the fires that broke out as a result of the American phosphorus bombs in the camp proper. Using all this as an argument, the German Communist leaders in Buchenwald had persuaded the SS to open up the ranks of the *Lagerschutz*—internal camp police force made up entirely of prisoners—to the foreigners. Not to all foreigners, of course—there was no question of having Russians in the *Lagerschutz*, for example—but to the Czechs and the French, those belonging to truly European countries, even in the eyes of the SS.

This steady, patient, molelike reinforcement of the counterpower of the political elements in Buchenwald—which made this camp quite unique in the Nazi concentration-camp system—this reinforcement doesn't stop with the Communist organizations. It constantly goes beyond them. Applying, in effect, the strategy laid down by the Komintern in the 1943 document by which it actually dissolved itself, the different parties practice the policy of the antifascist united fronts. In this way, with variants proper to the particular composition of each national community, resistance elements drawn from the Christian Democrats, agrarians, socialists—Gaullists, in the case of France—have come together in the many underground networks that maintain the cohesion of the prisoners and provide them with daily information, material and moral support, under the direction of the different national committees, at the head of which is the international committee.

But this steady increase of the counterpower of the political elements, indispensable on the one hand to the smooth running of the camp, causes, on the other hand, a slowing down in the rhythm of work in the camp factories, a constant, inexorable slowdown of production, by means of systematically organized sabotage. Hence, of course, the risk attached to any conflict between the SS command at Buchenwald and Himmler's headquarters in Berlin.

So the SS officers find themselves in a situation of objectively contradictory requirements. If the administration of the camp, with its labor force and its factories, is to function properly, they have to leave us alone. In order for the headquarters in Berlin not to get alarmed, not to intervene, the production of the armament factories has to be maintained at a reasonable level. They cannot, therefore, allow us to do exactly as we please.

The *Arbeitsstatistik*, insofar as the organization of work and the distribution of the labor force are in its hands, is at the very center of this contradiction. Hence the almost daily conflicts between Willi Seifert and Hauptsturmführer Schwartz. We are forced to adopt a policy of wearing down the SS command by alternating periods of calm and periods of sudden tension.

Some weeks ago, for example, Schwartz called us together and delivered a threatening speech. We were standing at attention, in the *Arbeit* hall, and Schwartz threatened us with the worst reprisals. He knew perfectly well, he yelled, what we were trying to do at the *Arbeit*, what category of political prisoner we were protecting! He was going to see to it himself that all this changed, he yelled. But he did not see to it for long, as it turned out. He soon got tired of inspecting our work every day. Life resumed its normal course.

All things considered, the risk of having the SS catch you falsifying cards in order to prevent certain comrades from being sent away on one of the transports is pretty much hypothetical. Anyway, the occasional interventions on the part of Hauptsturmführer Schwartz are not a real danger. If we were to be detected, there would have to be a complete, systematic checking of the whole filing system. That would take weeks, even months. Furthermore, it's practically impossible for the Gestapo to initiate an operation of this kind at Buchenwald without our getting advance warning. The German comrades have placed a network of informers in the key posts at the SS administration. Hairdressers working for the senior officers, domestics working in the SS villas, electricians or plumbers working in the same villas or in the offices: a whole network of prisoners, recruited mainly from the *Bibelforscher*—conscientious objectors or Jehovah's Witnesses—collect and transmit information about the

intentions or state of mind of the SS. Even direct telephone calls to Berlin are regularly intercepted.

So it's not from the side of the SS but, paradoxically,
from that of the German Communists that I am in danger
of being discovered. Again, one should not exaggerate the
risks, however. I would have to be caught in the act, in the
process of falsifying a card, for the scandal to break out
with all its predictable consequences. The German pals
have such a respect for established norms, for the conven-
tions that govern our activity—according to which it is
the international underground organization that makes
up the lists for work parties and nomination to privileged
posts—that the idea that you could falsify cards, do what
Daniel and I call underground work, or the protection of
individuals, would never even occur to them. If Seifert or
Weidlich happens to come across cards marked DIKAL or
DAKAK, he won't check in the files that a note from the
Gestapo requesting that such-and-such prisoner be
placed in a particular category has in fact been received.
No, they respect bureaucratic order, and they think that
we all share that respect. They don't know that underground work is often the only thing that gives a bit of
spice to life.

All in all, I'm not being particularly daring. I've
done much more difficult things in my time. Much more
difficult.

Years later, in the smoky atmosphere of cafés, I sometimes took part in discussions that had some bearing,
abstractly, on these questions, the same questions that
preoccupied Fernand Barizon that Sunday in Buchenwald in December 1944.

I remember one evening, among others.

It was at the Méphisto, a café with a cellar for music
and dancing, which used to be at the corner of the Rue de

Seine and the Boulevard Saint-Germain. Today there is probably a boutique in its place. Everywhere in this district, boutiques have taken over for the cafés and bookshops that were once its most charming feature.

Anyway, it was in the Méphisto, late one night.

We were sitting in the cellar, but we weren't dancing. We were listening to a Louis Armstrong record. Anyway, at the moment at which that scene, that event long ago, begins to re-emerge in my memory—like those photographic images that develop before your eyes, whose vague colors and indistinct outlines become sharper—at that moment, we were listening to one of Armstrong's records. I'd swear to it. It may even be mainly because of Armstrong that that night, or, rather, that early morning, is stamped on my memory, among so many other nights, so many other, similar, early mornings.

So I was listening with one ear—my better ear—to Armstrong's trumpet playing and with my other, less attentive, ear to the discussion taking place around the table.

That discussion was of concern to me, perhaps not of greater concern than Armstrong's music, but it was at least of equal concern to me. But there is an obscure relationship between the lucid, raucous despair of Armstrong's music and the subject that we were discussing so learnedly at my table.

At my table were Pierre Courtade and Maurice Merleau-Ponty.* There were many others, of course, as well as some good-looking women around. But Pierre Courtade and Maurice Merleau-Ponty stand out from the rest in my memory because they were doing most of the talking.

They were discussing the relationship between moral-

*French philosopher, phenomenologist. —ED.

ity and politics. On the one hand, neither the time nor the place seems appropriate for such a vast subject. On the other hand, why not? Why shouldn't one talk about morality and politics at half past three in the morning, in the Méphisto, with the rumble of Armstrong's trumpet in the background? In fact, it's a very good time and place to do so. An excellent atmosphere. Especially if you were in the year of grace 1948. The cold war was beginning to produce its most pernicious effects. The elective affinities, the political alliances, the cultural convergences of the resistance were being shattered under the pressure of an aberrational polarization. Camp against camp, class against class, morality against morality: *their morality and our morality*. But this last formula came from neither Courtade nor Merleau-Ponty. It was much older: it emanated from Trotsky.

Anyway, we'd got to talking about morality and politics that night. We had most likely talked about a great many other things beforehand, but we came around once again to the relationship between morality and politics.

Someone, I don't know who, had taken as a literal or a metaphorical example in his argument the situation of the resistance in the Nazi camps. It wasn't because of Barizon, certainly. None of my companions had even heard of Barizon or of his problems. But Courtade didn't yet know that he would, twelve years later, in 1960, be indirectly linked with Fernand Barizon, in my imagination at least, on account of that stop at Nantua. No, whoever it was—maybe Merleau-Ponty himself—used as an example in his argument certain books by David Rousset. It was Rousset who first broached the question, not Barizon, in his *L'Univers concentrationnaire* and in his novel, *Les Jours de notre mort*. In these writings on the Nazi camps, Rousset was the first to go beyond the threshold of mere reportage and to attempt an overall view, an overall analysis. It was this that enabled him, shortly after that evening at the Méphisto when we had been discussing his books, to pose the problem of the Russian camps, the problem of the Gulag.

But there was no question of the Gulag, at least directly, that night at the Méphisto. We were talking about the Nazi camps.

Was it necessary to occupy certain positions of power in the internal administration of the camps, in order to use this partial power to the benefit of the resistance? Did one have the right to remove certain prisoners, for political reasons, from the transport lists in order to ensure their survival? By saving some, was one not condemning to death others, who would inevitably take the place of the prisoners removed from the lists?

Such were the questions being discussed at that table, if only abstractly. I did not, at least in the beginning, have the impression that we were talking about something I had lived through. It was as if, in a way, they were talking about the problem of hostages during the Paris Commune in 1871, for instance. Or about the themes touched on by Trotsky in *The Defense of Terrorism*: or perhaps Simone de Beauvoir's play, *Les Bouches inutiles*.

It concerned me no more than that, at least to begin with.

I have to admit that happened quite often during those years: I would hear people talking about the Nazi camps, even about Buchenwald itself, without intervening, as if I hadn't been there myself. I had managed to forget. Or, rather, I had managed to push the memory of it far back in my mind. So I sat in my corner, in my silence, listening to people perorate on the camps, very interested in what they were saying. I really was interested. I was a pretty good listener.

Then something somebody said would suddenly release my memory. Often it wasn't enough to say something myself, to intervene as a witness or as a survivor. I wasn't even sure of ever having been there. Generally I just got up and left. I left those good folk perorating on the Nazi horrors, on the ideological custard pie of the executioner-victim relationship.

Sometimes, too, but not very often, I did speak.

That night at the Méphisto, I was listening to a learned discussion of the question of resistance in the Nazi camps. I remained outside the debate. I judged the arguments on each side from the outside, without saying a word. It was interesting, abstract. And then, suddenly, my memory flooded back to me. Its muddy waters came flooding out as though a dam had burst open.

It was Armstrong's trumpet playing that started it.

Suddenly the record, which I was still listening to with my good ear, brought down the walls of Jericho. I was in Buchenwald again, one Sunday afternoon, and Jiri Zak, a young Czech Communist in the *Schreibstube*, asked me to go with him to a rehearsal of the jazz group he had helped to form in the camp. I was listening to Armstrong in the Méphisto, and I heard at the same time the Dane that Zak had discovered playing "Star Dust" that Sunday during a rehearsal. There was Markovich, too, on the sax. And Yves Darriet, who was working out the arrangements.

"You're all talking rubbish!" I said suddenly.

They looked at me, rather surprised. Then Courtade exclaimed: "Christ, that's right! You were there!"

That was it, I had been there. Not only had I been there, but I was still there.

"Why don't you start from a concrete situation," I said, "instead of broad principles?"

They all nodded. They seemed to like the idea of a concrete situation. They weren't against it, at any rate.

"Right, the concrete situation is simple," I went on.

"One day, the SS administration gives orders for a transport of three thousand prisoners to leave for Dora, an outside kommando, the following Thursday at eight in the morning. This is just an example, of course. But you may be sure that the following Thursday at eight o'clock, three thousand guys will leave for Dora. Dora is a very bad camp! It's a construction site where tunnels are being dug for an underground factory that will make V-1s and V-2s—the so-called German reprisal rockets, V for *Vergeltung*, Retribution, which are being used to bomb England. Dora is hell. The last circle of hell, if you like. But the alternatives are not whether to leave for Dora or to stay behind. There is no choice, make no mistake! Whatever happens, three thousand guys will leave for Dora, on the right day, at the right time. And if the internal administration, which at Buchenwald is largely in the hands of German political prisoners—for each camp is a case apart, and I'm only talking about Buchenwald—refuses to get this transport ready (this is a hypothesis one can make here, three years later, sitting quietly, discussing broad principles!), if the German political prisoners refuse to get this transport ready, then the SS command will take away internal administrative power from the political prisoners and perhaps give it back to the common-law prisoners. Or the SS will prepare this transport, and all the others thereafter, itself. Therefore, three thousand prisoners will set out for Dora on the following Thursday at eight o'clock. The only choice available is the following: does one let chance take its course, or does one intervene to alter, in some minimal way, the workings of chance? It may not be chance, but destiny. Or God. Whatever you like. But there is no other choice: either we let God, fate, or chance take its course, or we intervene with the forces we have, with the power at our disposal. How, in fact, is a transport list made up? First, one draws on the prisoners in quarantine, in the Little Camp, prisoners who haven't yet been given definite assignments in the camp. It's there, in the Little Camp, that the reserve army of the sort of proletariat that we have become is to be found. Let's suppose that three thousand prisoners aren't available in the Little Camp. The list for Dora will then be made up with prisoners from the Big Camp who haven't been given work directly related to war production. A steelworker working at the Gustloff, for example, the automatic-rifle factory, has practically no chance—or, rather, runs no risk—of being sent to Dora. The first transport list for Dora is drawn up, then, on the basis of the available-labor situation. Blindly, in fact. Only then does the activity of the underground leadership come into play. Each national committee, which coordinates the various resistance organizations, presents a list of those it would like to see exempt from the transport. Actually, when I say each national committee, that's not quite true. The Germans aren't sent on transports. Or, rather, they go out only as kapos, bosses, to keep the ordinary prisoners in line. Two possibilities are open to the Germans: either they are sent voluntarily on transport by the underground leadership, in order to keep the new kommandos in line; or they are Greens (common-law prisoners) or SS informers, who are sent out of Buchenwald for security reasons. The Czechs aren't sent out on transports, either, unless they go in the same capacities as the Germans. The Spanish don't go at all. The Spanish community is quite small at Buchenwald: no more than a hundred and fifty prisoners. By a decision of the underground leadership, this community is entirely exempt from transport. In memory of the civil war, that's the reason. For there are quite a few former members of the International Brigades among the Communist leadership at Buchenwald. And Spain is the sweet paradise of their antifascist memories. So let's say that, generally speaking, it's the Russians and the French, the largest national groups, that make up the bulk of the transports. But where was I? Oh, yes, the underground committees present a list of those they want to keep in the camp. Sometimes keeping someone in the camp means keeping him alive. If one is sent to Dora, for instance, one's chances of staying alive are considerably reduced. When they draw up these protective lists, the committees include only members of the resistance, of course. From a metaphysical point of view, I know, all men are worth the same. From the point of view of God, from the point of view of human nature, every man is the equal of every other. Each man is a generic being, each man is Mankind, in a sense. God would no doubt refuse to select the three thousand prisoners to go to Dora. When the Day of Judgment comes, if it comes, God won't judge men or souls on the basis of their role in the resistance, their attitude in the camps, their death at Dora, or their survival at Buchenwald. God will keep out of this: it's not his problem. It isn't by saving two or three maquisards that God will act on the course of things, on the history of the world. That's obvious. But we aren't God—and even if we proclaim the metaphysical equality of all men, we are forced to judge, if we wish to act in any way on the course of things. In Buchenwald, all men were not of equal value. A maquisard was not of the same value as a guy who had been picked up by chance in a blocked-off district after an assassination attempt, or who had been arrested for black-marketeering. They might be equal before God, they certainly carried the same red triangle which the SS gave to all Frenchmen, political prisoners or not, but they weren't of equal value in Buchenwald, from the point of view of a resistance strategy. In six months, perhaps, they might be of equal value—if we were free in six months, if we were still alive."

I'm free, I'm alive. I gulp down some beer to get my breath back. I'm not going to try here to reproduce in detail the discussion we had that night at the Méphisto. I couldn't anyway.

Besides, I'm not recounting a night at the Méphisto in 1948, however interesting such an account might be, but a day in Buchenwald, a Sunday to be precise, some years before. Four years before.

Yet at the Méphisto, on that far-off night (far off in every sense: from today, from the moment I'm writing these lines, thirty years after the night in question at the Méphisto; far off, too, though in a different way, from the Sunday in Buchenwald; less so, no doubt, in terms of actual time, since only four years separate Buchenwald from the Méphisto, but very far off indeed in historical time, since in 1948 we were reaching the climax of what has come to be called the cold war, the noisy climax, with all flags unfurled, of the Stalinist schism, or schism that was not only epistemological—not only Marx against Hegel, proletarian science against bourgeois science, Lysenko against Mendel, Fougeron and those of us who were told to consider painting as a weapon, against painting considered as one of the fine arts—but also political and moral, and cultural), on that far-off night at the Méphisto, a number of points of agreement were worked out between us.

One had to resist; that was the first point. In order to do so, one had to use every opportunity, however small, offered by the order imposed by the SS themselves; that was the second point. Therefore, the German Communists in Buchenwald were right, historically, to wrest scraps of power in the internal administration of the camp.

To question that, said one of us, I don't know who, would be as childish as to declare, for instance, that any discussion by the trade unions of a collective agreement with the bosses—even if the bosses in question were of the most ruthless kind—because the discussion that would necessarily take place within the legal system established by the bourgeois state, and might even reinforce these norms—must necessarily be a betrayal, an abandonment of class positions.

In short, one had to dare to struggle, and to know how to struggle by every means at one's disposal, including legal.

That night at the Méphisto, none of us had heard of Alexander Solzhenitsyn, of course. At the time Solzhenitsyn was still only an anonymous zek. He was beginning the third year of his tour of the islands of the Archipelago. He was still in the first circle of hell. But today, as I am describing that far-off episode, so strangely precise in my memory in certain of its details, quite vague in others, today I cannot help thinking of what Solzhenitsyn says about resistance in the third world of *The Gulag Archipelago*.

Today, I would very much like to bring Solzhenitsyn into that discussion at the Méphisto.

"Now," I would say, using Solzhenitsyn's words, borrowing those words that sound so right and proud, "now, as I write this chapter, rows of humane books frown down at me from the walls, the tarnished gilt on their well-worn spines glinting reproachfully like stars through cloud. Nothing in the world should be sought through violence! By taking up the sword, the knife, the rifle, we quickly put ourselves on the level of our tormentors and persecutors. And there will be no end to it. . . . Here, at my desk, in a warm place, I agree completely. If you ever get twenty-five years for nothing, if you find yourself wearing four number patches on your clothes, holding your hands permanently behind your back, submitting to searches morning and evening, working until you are utterly exhausted, dragged into the cooler whenever someone denounces you, trodden deeper and deeper into the ground—from the hole you're in, the fine words of the great humanists will sound like the chatter of the well-fed and free."

Yes, from a certain point of view, our discussions at the Méphisto were the chatter of the well-fed and free.

Alexander Solzhenitsyn makes this pertinent observation about a crucial problem in the life of the camps, the elimination of informers. Indeed, it was with this that all resistance began, whether in the Russian camps or in the German camps. On which link must one exert pressure in order to snap the chain of servitude? Solzhenitsyn asks himself, and he replies: "Kill the stoolie! That was it, the vital link! Make knives and cut stoolies' throats—that was it!"

One may be delighted—at least I am—with the way Solzhenitsyn inverts the well-known Leninist thesis of the "weakest link." It's not the only time, indeed, throughout his long life and work as a writer, that Solzhenitsyn reverses certain of the principles or formulas of Leninism, which are quite brilliant on the tactical level, to the advantage of a strategy of denunciation and awareness of the despotic realities of the new society of exploitation that has sprung from Leninism.

But the resemblance between the conditions of the resistance in the Nazi camps and in the Bolshevik camps stops there, at that crucial and in a sense original point, concerning the need to eliminate informers. In every other way, the situation is radically different.

Though it is not my purpose, for the moment, to list the differences between the German and Russian camps, let alone embark on a lengthy analysis of them, I would just like to make one point.

In the Nazi camps, the situation of the political prisoners (leaving aside the question of the Greens, who are irrelevant to the discussion) was quite clear: the SS were our enemies, we abhorred their ideology, and we knew very well, therefore, why we were in Buchenwald. We were there because we wanted to destroy the SS order, because we had taken risks and made decisions, quite freely, which had brought us where we were. In a way, it was nothing out of the ordinary for us to be there. It was normal that, having taken up arms against Nazism, we should, if caught, be deported. Indeed, we might have been shot, and we would have found that equally normal. It was only because things were beginning to go the wrong way for Nazi Germany on the fronts of that world war, because the needs of war production demanded an increase in forced labor—in which the productive aspect was now more important than the corrective one, to continue to use the terms bequeathed us by old Hegel—that we had not been shot.

But if they had come to fetch us at dawn one autumn day, in the prison at Auxerre, and stuck us up against a wall, there would have been nothing abnormal in that. Only fools could have been surprised by it. Or the innocent, the unaware, who had joined the resistance believing it to be some kind of exciting adventure. They might have thought, suddenly, with their backs to the wall, about to be shot, that the game wasn't worth the candle. But for us Communists, no surprise would have been justifiable.

In Buchenwald, then, we had, besides the temporary satisfaction of being alive at all—I'm speaking, of course, for myself, and for those of us who were still alive; nothing will ever give me the right to speak for the dead, and the very idea of assuming such a role fills me with horror; that's why I'm not a "survivor," why I will never speak as someone who has survived the death of his comrades; I'm only someone who is alive, that's all, which is probably less impressive, but more true, and easier to live with, too—we knew very clearly why we were there. The camps were clearly marked out, as it were. It was a question of them and us. The SS and us, death and life, oppression and resistance, their morality and our morality.

But in the Russian camps, on the precise point that concerns me here, the situation was quite different. Who were the political prisoners in the Gulag camps, by virtue of the notorious Article 58? The overwhelming mass of political prisoners were innocent people who had never had the slightest intention of overthrowing, or even of changing in any way whatsoever, the Soviet regime. They were there, in their hundreds of thousands, millions even, because their fathers had been comfortably well-off peasants, at a time, actually, when the peasants were being encouraged to make life comfortable for themselves; because one of their brothers had once, by chance or out of mere curiosity, taken part in a meeting of the left-wing opposition; because they were inhabitants of Leningrad and the population of that city had been decimated by massive deportations after the provocative assassination of S. M. Kirov; because in private—but there was no longer any privacy, Lenin had explained this quite categorically in his letter to People's Commissar of Justice Kursky in 1922—they had made some favorable comment on a Russian novel published abroad; because they had declared that it was wrong that they should have to line up so long for a bar of soap. All that was counterrevolutionary agitation! Five, ten, fifteen, or twenty years of corrective forced labor in a camp, according to the terms of Article 58! "And following Russian custom," Varlam Shalamov comments with icy irony in his *Kolyma Tales*, "the features of the Russian character, the imprudent individual who gets five years congratulates himself on not getting ten, the foolish individual who gets ten years congratulates himself on not being sent down for twenty-five, and the idiot whom the judges condemn to twenty-five years is pleased that he has escaped the scaffold."

Side by side with this mass of innocents—in both senses of the term, innocent of the crime they were accused of and innocent by nature—there were members of the Communist Party. But they were not equipped, either morally or ideologically, to resist the regime of the camps. The political system outside, whose security organs had arrested, interrogated, often tortured, and deported them—was it not, despite possible Stalinist deviations, an object of interminable, whispered debates, more or less their own work? Was not the state, despite its bureaucratic distortions, a workers' state, their state?

They could not easily, as we could, say "them and us," distinguish between "them and us." They were "us" themselves, small screws in the same apparatus, small cogs in the same state, "us" confronting the class enemy, the imperialists, the fainthearted: "us" deported and "us" slavemasters. And it is probably no accident that Zamyatin's prophetic novel is called *We*. Nor that Elisabeth Poretski's book is called *Our Own People*. "We" and "Our"—key words in the wooden language with which the scaffolding of the guillotines were built.

In the PCE, it just occurs to me, the word "we" and its derivative "our" spread like a cancer through our official language. The theoretical journal of the Spanish Party was called—and still is called, in 1979—*Nuestra Bandera* (Our Flag), the publishing house of the PCE was called *Nuestro Pueblo* (Our People), and the cultural journal, which I myself edited, was called *Nuestras Ideas* (Our Ideas)! And it is certainly Solzhenitsyn who, with the dose of vengeful sarcasm that is still required, has most lucidly brought out and diverted this inveterate habit of the Communist "we" and "our," which has for so long disarmed resistance to oppression and which continues to disarm it.

So, in order to make a valid comparison of the situation of the political prisoners in the Nazi camps and in the Stalinist camps, one would have to assume that the first had been filled mainly with Nazis. Filled, for example, with former members of Röhm's SA. If the purge in the ranks of the SA undertaken by Hitler in 1934, during the "night of the long knives," had not ended up with some hundreds of assassinations and summary executions, but had sent to the concentration camps thousands or tens of thousands of members of the SA, potential plebeian and extremist opponents of Hitler's new conservative policies, then a comparison between Hitler's camps and Stalin's camps would have been possible, at least from the point of view of the political prisoners.

If this had been the case, the SS would have hated and fearfully despised the SA prisoners, just as the NKVD officers hated and despised, with a touch of fearful horror, those who were prisoners under Article 58. And the SA officer, picked on and beaten by his former SS comrade, his companion in the struggle for the National Socialist revolution, would have understood no more than the wretched member of the Soviet Party understood what was happening to him. Like the Russian zek, he would have worked zealously to fulfill the norms of the production plan. The SA prisoner, too, would have built the Buchenwald crematorium in record time. And sometimes, in the evening, after the interminable roll call, with an empty belly, he might have reflected that Hitler could not possibly be aware of all these ignominies, that if only Hitler had known. . . !

Anyway, to return to that evening at the Méphisto, it would have been interesting to hear what Solzhenitsyn would have had to say. But we would probably not have listened to him. I, at least, would not have heard his voice. I was deaf at the time.

And so, on that far-off night at the Méphisto, when we seemed to have reached agreement on a number of precise conclusions, Merleau-Ponty quietly reminded us that these particular points belonged to the domain of strategy.

"But I wasn't talking only about strategy," he said. "I was talking about morality."

"In the case we're talking about," I retorted, "morality meant having a correct strategy!"

Merleau-Ponty smiled. He knew my weakness for pungent formulas.

"Formula for formula," said Merleau-Ponty. "I offer you another: there are just wars, there are no just armies!"

"Innocent!" I said, irritated. "No innocent armies!"

Merleau-Ponty frowned.

"Are you sure?" he asked.

I was sure, but I was wrong. It was Merleau who had correctly quoted that well-known sentence. Too bad, I prefer my version. There are just wars, there are no innocent armies!

But Pierre Courtade intervened, pursing his lips in his usual ironic way:

"Come on, Merleau! You're not going to tell us that's from Lenin! You quoting Lenin, that's all we need!"

We laughed, but it wasn't a quotation from Lenin.

Suddenly I was reminded of something from the past. I had an acute impression of having experienced this before.

• • •

"What, what?" Barizon had asked, one Sunday long ago, in Buchenwald.

I repeat the sentence I've just quoted: "There are just wars, there are no innocent armies!"

He looks at me suspiciously.

"You're going to tell me that's from Lenin!" he says.

I shake my head.

"No, it's García."

"Who's he?"

Barizon is on his guard. His thick black eyebrows arrange themselves in a scowl.

"What? You've never heard of García?"

I pretend to be deeply indignant.

"García, one of our classics? Marx, Engels, Lenin, and García!"

He is ready to explode with anger.

"You're pulling my leg, Gérard!" he yells.

Gérard laughs and puts a hand on Fernand's shoulder, to calm him down.

The sun is shining, but there's a nip in the air.

Half an hour before, just after the roll call, they'd been together in the Block 40 mess.

"Don't go away after the soup!" Barizon had said. "I want to talk to you. There's something I want you to explain."

Half an hour before, Gérard whistled between his teeth.

"Shit! The working class is asking the petit-bourgeois intellectual for explanations! That's something."

But Fernand Barizon is used to it. He shrugs, not in the least put out.

"The working class shits on you, but it'll forgive you, because it's Sunday."

His thick eyebrows arrange themselves in a scowl.

"Petit-bourgeois?" he says. "And what's this sudden

and quite unexpected modesty? If I understand correctly what you told me about your childhood, you're a fucking son of a fucking *big* bourgeois, no?"

We both laugh.

"You're telling me!" says Gérard. "There are plenty of dukes and duchesses among my cousins."

Barizon, of course, doesn't believe a word of this. The Spaniard is always spinning yarns about something or other.

"You don't have to exaggerate, old boy," says Barizon. "Your background is bad enough as it is!"

They both laugh.

"What's your problem, then?" Gérard asks.

Barizon waves his hand in a negative gesture.

"Wait a second!" he says. "First let's eat our goddamn awful soup. Then we'll talk."

They are sitting in the mess of C Wing, on the second floor of Block 40. They're waiting for that goddamn awful soup. Though on Sundays that goddamn awful soup is a bit less goddamn awful than on other days. It's almost decent. It almost gives you a taste for living. A goddamn awful soup for a goddamn awful Sunday.

And what was behind it all? An ineradicable whiff of Judeo-Christian humanism, cleverly stuck at the very heart of the Nazi system? Because Sunday, it's said, is the Lord's day? Or, quite simply, the demands of production? A cleverly objective calculation of the time required for the labor force to recover its strength? Is that why we get this break on Sundays? Was the workers' Sunday invented by God or by the immemorial and ever-resourceful despotism of work itself?

Anyway, on Sundays in Buchenwald, the soup is thicker than on other days. It's no great achievement, I suppose, but it's almost a real soup. With real bits of real vegetables: real swede, real chunks of cabbage. Strands of meat visible to the naked eye, if one isn't too hungry, or if, though hungry, one nevertheless takes the time to look at what one is eating in the hope of making it last longer. And, above all, real noodles. Large white noodles, if a bit overcooked.

Yes, Fernand's right, the Sunday noodle soup is a serious business. It should be eaten seriously. No question of chatting at the same time. Conversation is distracting. That's a rich man's pleasure, conversation at table: one plays delicately with a piece of food on one's plate while improvising some brilliant cultural digression. When you're really hungry, when you're poor, when you're a zek (shit! I mean *Kazettler!*), eating isn't a pleasure, it's a need.

And because it's a need, it can become a ritual.

At Marseille, in a house in the working-class district of La Cabucelle, they'd have had no difficulty understanding what Gérard is thinking at this moment, in my head. At La Cabucelle, at the Livis', it was the father who set his hand to the pasta on Sundays: *la pasta della domenica.* Sunday was the day for white shirts. The day of the pasta cooked by the father, who officiated in the kitchen with a touch of Latin gravity. It's what his own father and his father's father had always done, at Monsumano, before Fascism, before exile. On Sunday, with white shirts for the men, and the women in their Sunday best, sitting with their hands on their knees as in old sepia family photographs, awaiting the pasta cooked by the father; it was a feast day at La Cabucelle, at the Livis'.

But in Buchenwald, in December 1944, neither Gérard nor Barizon has ever heard of the Livi family. They cannot know that one of the boys is becoming Yves Montand. That story of Sunday pasta, however, with its rituals and its seriousness, with its laughter and its snatches of operatic arias, suddenly launched and as suddenly broken off, is a story that they could tell each other later, if an occasion arises that brings them together. The story of exile, no doubt.

It was in the mess of C Wing of Block 40, immediately after the Sunday roll call. A Sunday in Buchenwald, and not at La Cabucelle. Gérard and Fernand Barizon were waiting for the Sunday noodle soup to arrive.

Now they have eaten that goddamn awful soup in silence, seriously. (I won't try to say how it really was, eating the Sunday soup, for I've forgotten. I wouldn't be able to reconstitute the truth of that long-ago moment; I would have to make it up. Or I would remember that hunger from long ago through the accounts of Shalamov, or Solzhenitsyn, or Herling-Grudzinski, or Robert Antelme; with their help I would surely rediscover the right words, the words that would sound right; but I myself have forgotten them. In *The Long Voyage*, I wrote: "A single real meal, and hunger has become something abstract. It is no more than a concept, an abstract idea. And yet, thousands of men have died around me because of this abstract idea. I am content with my body, I find that it's a prodigious machine. A single dinner was enough to efface in it that now useless, now abstract, thing, that hunger from which we might have died. . . ." I wrote those words because they were true, or true for me: that's what passed through my head, through my guts. But I received several indignant letters from readers; not any readers, but former deportees, who were wounded that I should speak this way about hunger. For two pins, they would have questioned whether I myself had ever actually been deported, if they'd dared call me a liar; one of them, who was particularly indignant, told me that I must have gone mad. He himself, he told me, for months on end, had been unable to resist grabbing leftovers, peelings, food that had been thrown away, and to devour it like an animal. All right, perhaps I was mad; it's quite possible.) But now that they have eaten their Sunday noodle soup, Barizon and Gérard are walking in the December sunlight.

The loudspeakers are broadcasting music all over the Ettersberg, and Gérard has put his hand on Barizon's shoulder, to calm him down.

Behind his pal, in the middle of the esplanade, he sees a group of Frenchmen from Block 34. He thinks he recognizes Boris, who stands a good head above those around him.

"Don't get steamed up, Fernand!" says Gérard. "García is one of Malraux's characters in *Man's Hope*."

Barizon relaxes.

"Oh!" he says. "That's better!"

"Malraux's better than Lenin?"

"Don't start again, Gérard, do you mind? I know Malraux, that's what I mean."

Barizon remembers Malraux very well.

In November 1936, at Albacete, when his company was going to join the Fourteenth International Brigade on the Madrid front after a brief period of instruction, the political commissar had asked all aircraft mechanics to come forward. Fernand did so, because he had worked for almost two years at Bloch's, after his escapade in Brittany with Juliette. But he didn't like what followed at all. Instead of sending him into battle with his pals, they claimed they were keeping him to repair the engine for Malraux's flight. Barizon didn't mince his words. He hadn't come to Spain to repair fucking aircraft engines! The company political commisssar would hear nothing of his objections. He was simply implementing orders. That was all. Orders are orders! He had been asked to find aircraft mechanics and he didn't want to let Barizon go.

The streets of Albacete were not exactly filled with skilled aircraft mechanics.

In the end, Barizon had managed to meet the famous Malraux.

The year before, he had seen him from a distance at a big public meeting at the Mutualité, in the midst of all the smoke and commotion. He couldn't hear very well what Malraux was saying, but the man had presence. At Albacete, Malraux had smoked cigarette after cigarette and listened to him attentively. In the end, Barizon won the day. They let him set out with his company for the Madrid front.

" 'Comrade,' I told him," Barizon says, " 'the Brigades aren't an employment agency. I'm not looking for work, I want to fight. Duconneau, the political commissar, explains to me that anybody can hold a rifle, that skilled workers are needed for an aircraft engine. Well, comrade, I'm through with skilled work! Here I'm not a steelworker, but an infantryman. My only skill is in killing Fascists. If I have to dirty my hands, it won't be with grease, but with blood. There must be plenty of mechanics in Spain. Mobilize them, requisition them, give them productivity bonuses, overtime pay, paid vacations, family allowances; it's got nothing to do with me! You must respect the reasons I came to Spain!' And Malraux agreed with me."

"What did you think of him?" Gérard asks.

"I thought he was a scream," says Barizon.

They are now walking back the way they came, along the avenue that separates the row of wooden huts from the row of two-story cement-block houses.

"Well?" Barizon asks. "What did García say?"

"There are just wars, there are no innocent armies."

Barizon thinks about it for a few seconds.

"That's not bad," he says. "Only I'm not talking about morality, I'm talking about strategy."

Barizon is not indifferent to morality, far from it. On the contrary, he has a very acute sense of justice and injustice: "You don't do that" is one of the key sentences in Barizon's language. And his sense of justice and injustice is not like common sense according to Descartes: it isn't the most fairly distributed thing in the world. So Barizon constantly makes a moral choice in his everyday behavior, in the Gustloff Works, in his relationships with the people around him. But in the case of the question that concerns him today, which he wanted to discuss with the Spaniard, that of a strategy of resistance in the camps, Barizon doesn't think that he is posing a moral problem to himself.

In other words, it is just to resist: that's a question of morality. But what is the best way of resisting: that's a question of strategy.

"All the same," says Gérard, "it's not so simple."

They have turned left, down a side path that rises up the hill. They are now between Blocks 10 and 11, almost on the edge of the *Appellplatz*.

Barizon looks at the tower, then turns to Gérard.

"With you it's never simple," he says.

"The pro and the con, the more and the less, the flower and the fruit: it's dialectics, Fernand, that aren't simple!"

Barizon looks at the tower again. A little to the left, he looks at the crematorium chimney, topped by thick smoke. He then looks at the snow covering the forest. He smiles at Gérard.

"And the crematorium, is that dialectical, too?" he adds sarcastically.

But Gérard can't be thrown by a question like that.

"Of course," he says.

"How do you explain that?" Barizon asks, frowning.

"The crematorium is death, isn't it? The solid sign of death. But death is not beyond life, outside life, after life. Death is in life, it is life. Similarly, the crematorium is in the camp. It's much more than a symbol; it's the death that is at the heart of our life, that is our life. The crematorium is the sign of death, but it is also the sign of the life left to us to live, our most probable future."

Barizon looks at the crematorium chimney and whistles through his teeth.

"My word," he says, "you ought to be a schoolteacher! Or a preacher!"

And then, with an air of finality, he says:

"The crematorium is shit!"

Gérard pokes a finger at Barizon's chest.

"Shit is dialectical, too."

But Barizon makes a gesture to interrupt him.

"OK! Spare me your demonstration!"

They both laugh.

They look at the crematorium chimney, the tower, the solid walls of the bunker built onto the guardhouse. They look at the snow, that white shroud from which, one day or another, the renewal of spring, the new life of nature, will emerge. But they may not be there to see it.

"Before you interrupted me," says Gérard, "I was having the pleasure of telling you that it's not so simple: one cannot separate morality and strategy in an absolute way."

They have started walking again. They are moving away from the *Appellplatz*, along the path by the huts that house the Soviet prisoners of war.

Will Pyotr get through to the Red Army?

"You know it yourself," says Gérard. "Didn't you say just now that the fact of being privileged, because you're a Communist in a Nazi camp, presented certain problems for you?"

Barizon nodded.

It's true that it's not a simple matter.

"Well, what of it?" says Barizon.

"So I come back to García's formula, which explains everything: there are just wars, there are no innocent armies. We are waging a just war, in difficult conditions, among the most difficult one can imagine, at the very heart of the Nazi system. But we are not innocent for all that, not inevitably so, anyway, since this just war brings us privileges, cushy jobs, power that we can abuse. We see that every day, don't we?"

Barizon nods.

"Well, what of it?" he repeats.

"Well," says Gérard, "in these circumstances, each individual reacts in his own way. It's a question for the individual. To have or not to have. To have a morality, to have courage. Anyway, most of the time, morality is a question of balls. If you don't want to go on running risks, you stop behaving in a moral way. If you've got two, you've got one—two balls, one morality."

Gérard can think of plenty of examples. Fritz and Daniel, for instance. They are about the same age. They are both Communists. Fritz has probably been a prisoner longer than Daniel, by a few years. You should probably bear that in mind. It may explain certain things, but it doesn't justify anything. Fritz applies the regulations, exercises the partial power that has come to him—which is small enough, from the point of view of the life of the camp in general, but sometimes decisive for the life of a particular prisoner—in the internal administration of the camp, as if that power and the regulations were neutral: neither good nor bad in themselves. As if it were simply a matter of keeping the wheels of the bureaucratic machine turning in the best possible conditions of rationality and profitability.

Daniel, on the other hand, exercises this power and applies those regulations by constantly turning them against the aims for which they were drawn up: trying to reduce to a minimum their profitability and rationality, since both were conceived for the benefit of the Nazi war machine, to the detriment of the deported work force. And this attitude, of course, drives him constantly to take more risks than that bastard Fritz.

So it's a question for the individual.

For a strategy to become a morality, it isn't enough that it be just in principle. The men who put it into practice must also be just, uncorrupted by the power they have won in order to deploy this strategy, and because they have deployed it. For power snowballs, as we know.

But Barizon is still laughing at the business of the balls.

"That's not bad!" he exclaims. "When you've got two, you've got one! Mind you, your fine formula can be turned around, old boy! One morality and two balls: and it's the morality that makes them swell!"

"There you are," says Gérard. "It can be turned around because it's a truly dialectical formula."

It can be turned around, but not canceled, *aufgehoben*, thinks Gérard. It's the damned *Aufhebung* that explodes the Hegelian dialectic, makes it unreal because of its striving after perfection. But he keeps this thought to himself: there's no point in provoking Barizon.

Barizon has stopped walking and is looking at him.

"You know something? You're a pain in the ass!"

"I know," says Gérard.

At the Méphisto, four years later, the discussion became confused. In my memory, at least, it's become confused. But one thing has remained in my memory with heart-rending clarity—Armstrong's trumpet playing.

"And what about you?" Pierre Courtade asked me at some point during those early morning hours. "Haven't you written anything about the camps?"

I shook my head.

"No," I replied, "it's too soon."

Courtade gave a short sarcastic laugh.

"What are you waiting for?" he said. "For it to be too late? For everyone to have forgotten?"

I shook my head; I just didn't want to talk about it.

But when the time to write finally did come, I would not write the account I described to Fernand Barizon, in 1960, in Geneva. I would write another—the same, that is, but in a different way.

In 1960, Barizon asked me: "How would you tell it?" "I would tell about a Sunday," I replied. In fact, I hadn't answered his question, as you may have noticed. I didn't tell him how I would tell it, but what I would tell, which is not the same thing. But we won't get bogged down in that. Anyway, Barizon didn't. He accepted my answer without complaint.

Curiously enough, it seemed to me that the idea I'd just had, in Geneva, of recounting a Sunday in Buchenwald, which just seemed to cross my mind—Do ideas cross one's mind the way pedestrians cross roads? Do ideas also obey the highway code and cross at the traffic lights, at the right moment?—I had the curious impression that this idea was not new, whatever I might think. It reminded me vaguely of something, this idea of telling about a Sunday in Buchenwald.

Two days later, I was in Prague.

I no longer know why I was in Prague, what the exact reason was. But I was in Prague, and this urgent reason must have left me a certain amount of leisure, for I was examining a Renoir painting in the Prague National Gallery, a voluptuous, joyful painting of a voluptuous, joyful young woman in a sun-drenched landscape. I don't know why this young woman of Renoir's reminded me of the Sundays in Buchenwald, but that's where I thought of it, in front of her.

Perhaps it was just the contrast.

I'm sometimes very sensitive to contrasts. I'm stirred deep down by them, I mean. Almost wounded by them. It happened to me in those years. The contrast, for instance, between some acute, perhaps furtive or transient, but truly poignant happiness, and the memory that would suddenly come back—because of that happiness?—of a moment in the camp. A moment of anxiety, in the noisy, restless, hostile, closely packed crowd of the dormitory at night. A moment of madness, looking out across the landscape of the Thuringian plain in its banal beauty. A moment of appalling hunger, when one would have sold one's soul for a bowl of noodle soup. But there was no devil in Buchenwald to sell one's soul to. There were only men; too bad. Anyway, contrasts like that, between present if transient happiness and those days long ago. I don't say anything, of course, when it happens. I just let those disconcerting moments pass. I don't reveal anything to anybody ever; what would be the point? I let people think that that sigh was a sigh of satisfaction, a sigh of happiness, perhaps even of pleasure. If I spent my time listing the moments when my life is somewhere else, I wouldn't be very good company. So I say nothing.

In any case, I was looking at this painting by Renoir in the Prague National Gallery, and I remembered the Sundays in Buchenwald.

I remembered that I had already written something, long before, about the Sundays in Buchenwald. Two days earlier, then, in Geneva, talking with Barizon, I hadn't just invented this idea. I had already begun writing a play about Sundays in Buchenwald ten years before. It was called *Les Beaux Dimanches*. I never finished that play.

Anyway, I can see myself again coming back from UNESCO, whose offices were on the Avenue Kléber at the time. I was on my way back to the furnished apartment I rented on the Rue Félix-Ziem, behind the Montmartre cemetery, to work on this play. I can't pretend that I went back every evening to work on it. No, I would often spend the evening, and even a good part of the night, between the Montana and the Méphisto, for example, in Saint-Germain-des-Prés. I must say that the male companions of those interminable nocturnal wanderings and discussions were fascinating. So, too, sometimes, more rarely, were the female companions.

Well, if I was writing that play, *Les Beaux Dimanches*, on the Rue Félix-Ziem, I can figure out the precise date for that period of writing.

It was 1950.

I was living on the Rue Félix-Ziem, in fact, in September 1950, when the French government banned the PCE's press and legal activities in France. You may remember that at the time a hundred or so activists and middle cadres of the PCE were arrested during a police raid. Some were confined to residence in Corsica, others were expelled to Eastern Europe. But word of this raid and its exact date were known in advance to the leadership of the PCE, which also had its offices on the Avenue Kléber, almost opposite UNESCO, which was very handy for me. State secrets are not always well guarded in a liberal state, even in authoritarian and restrictive periods, which crop up every so often in the history of liberal states. I'm not complaining, of course, about the porosity of the machinery of the liberal states—or democratic states, if you prefer, those in which the domination of the dominant minority is carried out in a mediate, and often even benign, way, through the system of parliamentary majority—I'm not complaining. On the contrary, I wish that all oppositions, in every country, whatever the regime to which they are opposed, could partake of such a porosity in the state machinery.

So, on the Avenue Kléber—across from UNESCO, in

the offices of the PCE—we got several days' advance notice of this imminent police raid. Someone had crossed the avenue and asked to see me.

At the time I was assistant head of the Spanish-translation section. I received this emissary in my office, on the top floor of the UNESCO building. This noble institution occupied the premises of the former Hôtel Majestic, which had served as headquarters, during the occupation, of a number of branches of the Nazi police. My office was a former room of this former hotel. In the former bathroom next door, from which the sanitary fixtures had been removed, there were various storage and filing cabinets. I was sitting at my desk and listening to the emissary from the PCE, who had crossed the Avenue Kléber to speak to me. I could see part of the bathroom next door—the door had been taken off. I could see the filing cabinets, but also the faucets. They were quite useless, since the bathtub itself had been taken out. They were even rather odd, those elaborately decorated faucets of a former bathroom in the Majestic, left fixed to the wall.

Sometimes the mere sight of them, as I looked up from some papers in front of me, disturbed me. Sometimes those rococo faucets fixed on the wall, over a phantom bathtub, made me feel vaguely uncomfortable. A sort of shiver ran down my spine. It was easy to understand why. The faucets reminded me of the absent bathtub, and the bathtub, even absent, reminded me of the Gestapo, who had occupied these premises some years earlier. It so happens that the bathtub was my worst memory of the Gestapo. I'd had no dealings with the Gestapo from the Majestic, I suppose, but the Gestapo at Auxerre also knew how to use the bathtub. And when I looked up from my work, thinking about some linguistic problem, I'd see the faucets of the phantom bathtub.

The night before, a commission had met: should *droits de l'homme* be translated as *derechos del hombre* or *derechos humanos?* I was in favor of *derechos del hombre,* which seemed to me closer to the French origin of the notion and to a certain established tradition. And traditions are not to be ignored when one is dealing with language, which is the vehicle of a cultural history and a collective memory. But the Latin Americans held firmly to *derechos humanos.* That's what they called them and, anyway, in English it was "human rights"; and, as we know, the official, diplomatic, and commercial language of South America was already tending more and more to be English.

Some years later, after the Twentieth Congress of the Soviet Party, I remembered those violent linguistic disputes. I had left UNESCO in 1952 to become a permanent official of the PCE, but I remembered those interminable discussions long ago, in the ad hoc commissions of UNESCO whose task it was to unify official language. But we also had interminable discussions in the editorial commissions of the Central Committee of the PCE, after the Twentieth Congress of the Russian Party. How should we define the celebrated "cult of personality"? Invariably, when I belonged to such an editorial commission set up to comment on the political resolution of a plenary session of the Central Committee—and I often did take part in such commissions—I described as "cancerous" the notorious "cult of personality." I always wrote "the cancer of the cult of personality" in the draft submitted for its final revision to the highest authorities of the PCE, of which I was also a part. And the word "cancer" always provoked a discussion. No, it was impossible to use the word "cancer," I was told. First, the word "cancer" had too pejorative, too pernicious a connotation. So what? Wasn't the "cult of personality" pernicious? Yes, of course it was pernicious, but the word "cancer" usually suggested a fatal illness, whereas the cult of personality, I was told, had not been fatal for socialist society. Had not socialism found within itself the organic resources that had made it possible to eliminate the cult? But I have no desire to reproduce in detail the casuistical meanderings of such a discussion. Let's say that I settled for the term "tumor." But "tumor" was also rejected, after the usual thorough examination. For there are malignant tumors, as we know. Anyway, in most cases, the term "tumor" is merely a temporary euphemism for "cancer," I was told. Eventually we settled for the term that had been laid down in advance, the consecrated term that I had done my best to avoid: "excrescence." The cult of personality had been only an unhealthy and temporary excrescence on the healthy, vigorous organism of socialism, which had found in itself the strength necessary to overcome that excrescence and to cauterize the wound. There, that settled it!

But we mustn't get off the point.

I'm in my office at UNESCO, in September 1950, and I'm not thinking at all of the cult of personality. How could I, given what I was and when it was? I'm thinking of the discussion the day before on *derechos del hombre* and *derechos humanos*. That is to say, *droits de l'homme* and human rights. I'm thinking of an Argentine functionary on the ad hoc commission with whom I had words. "*Droits de l'homme*," he said, "and what about *droits de la femme*?" I retorted that the *homme*, or *hombre*, who had, in this expression, the right to certain inalienable rights, was a generic, bisexual, perhaps even pansexual being: the man of the rights of man was just as much woman and child, and since I knew that this Argentine was something of a pedant, as well as being very left-wing, I amused myself by making Marxist allusions, hints at Marx's *Gattungswesen*, allusions that irritated him all the more, I don't know why. Perhaps because he detected in me smugness rather than complicity.

So I am thinking about *droits de l'homme*—and the rights of women, too, of course: don't try, like the Argentine, to persuade me that I was a misogynist—and I notice the rococo faucets of the Gestapo's bathtub. They bring back unpleasant memories. The most unpleasant of all possible memories. Meanwhile, the emissary from the PCE is telling me, under the seal of secrecy, that the French police are planning a raid on the Spanish Party and that it was thought that my apartment would be a sufficiently safe refuge in which to hide an important comrade.

I look at the elaborate faucets of the former Hôtel Majestic and nod. Certainly, that apartment on the Rue Félix-Ziem, which the UNESCO accommodation service got for me, is a safe enough refuge.

So it was that Victor Velasco and his wife came to take shelter in the apartment where I was writing, from time to time, a play called *Les Beaux Dimanches*, which remained unfinished. Velasco was one of Carrillo's assistants on the commission that ran the Party's underground work in Spain. At the time I did not know Carrillo. I met him three years later

A few days after Velasco moved in, the French police raid took place, as expected, and, also as expected, the leadership of the PCE apparatus went underground and escaped.

So the premises on the Avenue Kléber—those of the PCE, not those of UNESCO—were abandoned. This complicated my life somewhat. Hitherto I had only to cross the avenue, and, vice versa, the emissaries of the PCE had only to cross the avenue when they needed me.

But I'm in Prague, in the National Gallery of the

Sternberg Palace, looking at a Renoir painting, in the autumn of 1960.

I've just remembered that I was writing *Les Beaux Dimanches* ten years before, on the Rue Félix-Ziem. It was a story that took place in Buchenwald, on a Sunday, as its title suggests. It was the story of an informer, or a stool pigeon, if you prefer; the story of his discovery and liquidation. The action of the play took place one Sunday afternoon, in one place—the *Arbeitsstatistik* hut—and it concerned the physical elimination of the SS stool pigeon. The rule of the three unities was scrupulously observed, you may be sure. And one of the characters in the play was called Gérard, of course.

I'm remembering all this as I stand in front of the portrait of an appealing young woman, whose love of life—and Renoir's, by the same token—spills over into a sun-drenched landscape, where there isn't the slightest trace, not even the most distant possibility, of crematorium smoke. So, two days before, when I was telling Fernand Barizon that I would recount a Sunday in Buchenwald, I wasn't improvising on the spur of the moment. Without knowing it, I was rediscovering an old obsession.

But I'm in Buchenwald, sixteen years earlier, one Sunday, and I've finished doctoring the cards of the three French pals whose names and numbers Daniel gave me. Now they have become untouchable. They will be protected by the Gestapo itself and there will be no sudden instructions to send them out of the camp.

I put into my mouth the scrap of paper that Daniel gave me. I chew it slowly and swallow it.

The sunlight strikes the windows on my right.

"Do you want the paper?"

Walter is talking to me, holding out the *Völkische Beobachter*.

I say yes, I'd like the paper. He hands it to me over the card index.

"This Greek business," says Walter, "what a terrible thing!"

At first we refused to believe what was happening to Greece: it had to be Nazi propaganda. Then, when the evidence became too overwhelming, the question we asked ourselves was not so much why the British had decided to crush ELAS—that was understandable enough—as why Moscow was being silent about it. Why did the Russians let it happen? Or, if the Russians had decided to avoid any confrontation with the British, in the interests of the anti-Nazi alliance—that, too, was understandable—why did they allow the Greek Communists to engage in a confused, and therefore demoralizing, strategy, swinging between uprisings and the most shameful compromises?

At the *Arbeitsstatistik*, we, a small group of Communists of various nationalities, passionately discussed the affair. Morning and evening, as we waited for the roll call, a circle would form. There were Germans: Walter and August. Sometimes, too, Georg Glucker, trenchant and apocalyptic, as at the time, I imagine, of his youth and of the slogan CLASS AGAINST CLASS. Sometimes there was Jupp, the German from Silesia who spoke Polish like a Pole, and Jan, the Pole from Silesia who spoke German like a German. There was a Czech, Josef Frank. A Belgian, Jean Blume. And Daniel A., the French comrade. Seifert and Weidlich occasionally dropped in on our discussions, but not very often. Anyway, when they were present they didn't say much. They didn't seem to have an opinion of their own.

The passionate discussions on strategy—which concerned not only Greece but also Western Europe in general and France in particular, from which fragments of news reached us about the disarmament of the patriotic militias—had revealed two currents of opinion among us.

For some, the important thing was to maintain the

anti-Nazi alliance on the international plane, the united front of the resistance at the national level. The maintenance of autonomous armed forces under a Communist leadership would have provoked the intervention of American and British troops, which would have been disastrous in the context of the existing balance of power. Who knows, they said, whether the Anglo-Americans might not even take advantage of incidents of this kind to sign a separate peace treaty with the German High Command, thus closing the circle around the USSR?

For others—including myself, of course: I had neither the age nor the experience necessary to put me among the "realists," those who had already guessed, or sniffed, Stalin's intentions, with the flair peculiar to old-timers—for us, then, the balance of power in Europe was not intangible. It could be altered if the strategy of the Western workers' movement were oriented toward the transformation of society; a strategy based, certainly, on very broad alliances, but guaranteed by an autonomy, preferably armed, of working-class and revolutionary forces.

But for some days now, in late December 1944, we had reached the beatific stage of theory. The confused, sometimes violent arguments about strategy now calmed down in the reassuring, syrupy warmth of a vaguely Hegelian dialectic. As if the movement of our thoughts had obeyed an identical gravitational force, we were all basing our justification of the course of things on the same mystificatory reasoning. The dialectic of the general and the particular—that's what we had to think about. The problems of the revolution in Greece were merely one particular aspect of a general question: that of the antifascist war. Everything else must be based on the correct solution. Secondary contradictions between ELAS and Churchill, painful as the consequences might be, ought not to take

precedence over the principal contradictions between the
Nazi camp and the antifascist camp. The particular Greek
problem had to be sacrificed, if necessary, painful as it
might be, on the altar of the general cause of antifascism.

We mumbled on in such pseudo-dialectics, like prayer
machines, and the crushing of ELAS was transformed
into a vagary of history whose general course was—O
wonder of dialecto-tautology!—precisely in the direction
of History. The crushing of ELAS entered the luminous
field of theory. Theorized, it became bearable.

"This Greek business, what a terrible thing!" Walter
had said, handing me the *Völkische Beobachter.*

I nodded.

Yes, it was a terrible business, in spite of all our fine
dialectical exercises.

Five

The smell of baked potatoes fills my nostrils. It's gradually overcoming me. It's making my mouth water. The smell of baked potatoes is making my pulse beat faster. I'm going to faint.

Meiners is baking potatoes.

Before the smell of baked potatoes, with which a new chapter of this Sunday begins, I was dozing. I was in the mess of the *Arbeitsstatistik*, my forehead resting on my folded arms on the table. I had lost all consciousness of what was happening around me. I heard the door to the *Arbeit* office open and shut: I didn't doubt the reality of this noise of a door opening and shutting. I heard steps on the wooden floor: I didn't doubt the reality of this noise. Part of me went on living in a state of confused wakefulness, while another part was lost in glowing dreams.

Earlier, I'd been in the *Arbeit* office, in front of the rows of the central card index. The sunlight was striking the windows, the smoke from the crematorium rose in the sky, someone coughed, the British tanks had crushed the forces of ELAS, the name of the newspaper open in front of me, *Völkische Beobachter*, was printed in modern Gothic characters underlined in red, the Marne was beautiful in the spring, I'd had enough.

I got up, looked around me.

The stove was roaring, everything was in its place, it was unbearable. Daniel was in his place, beside old Fritz, the old devil. Daniel had his back to me; he couldn't see the wildness in my eyes. I took a couple of steps and staggered, seized by a sudden desire to get out, an irresistible need to bury myself in the fresh sheets of a real bed for a long, dreamless sleep. I looked across the room. At the back, I saw August. He was in his place, between the Polish pal from Silesia who spoke German perfectly, and the German pal from Silesia who spoke Polish perfectly.

I would go over to August. He would look up.

"*Que pasa, viejo?*" he would ask me, in his Argentine accent.

"*Domingos de la gran puta!*" I would have answered, to express the visible disarray in my eyes.

Yes, it was a bitch of a Sunday, that's what it was. A real shitty Sunday. A bitchy, shitty Sunday, that's what it was.

August wouldn't have played the old veteran: it wasn't his style. He wouldn't have thrown a fit, explaining that Buchenwald was a sanatorium these days compared with what it used to be, that in the good old days Sundays really were bitches of Sundays, with roll calls often lasting seven or eight hours. August wouldn't have enumerated all the bitches of Sundays that I hadn't known and thrown them in my face, to shame me, to weigh me down with the weight of all those Sundays at Buchenwald that I hadn't known.

August would have shrugged his shoulders and smiled.

"*Asi es la vida, viejo!*" he would have said.

Yes, of course, that was life. And there was no truly

imperative reason why it should be otherwise, that was what was so goddamn awful about it. That life should be like that—period—that's what was so goddamn awful about it.

But I hadn't come to chat with August. I walked over to the common room at the back of the *Arbeit* hut, next to Seifert's office.

The common room was empty.

I warmed up a cup of the black liquid they gave us in the morning and of which there was always a big urnful in the common room; I plugged in one of the electric heaters that had been made here, and which were totally forbidden by the SS, and drank a cup of the reheated liquid.

Then I smoked a cigarette.

It didn't take much time to drink the reheated liquid and to smoke a cigarette. Soon I fell back into the physical exhaustion of a moment earlier. It reminded me of something, feelings and words from long ago. Perhaps I was doomed to this sort of anxiety. Perhaps the present circumstances had nothing to do with it. Perhaps I would have experienced, and would experience again, an identical anxiety wherever I happened to be. Perhaps it was the mere fact of living that brought on such an anxiety, even if there had been no icy silence on the Ettersberg, no smoke from the crematorium, no brutal uncertainty of that Sunday at Buchenwald. Perhaps life itself brought on this *Angst*, anywhere, in whatever circumstances.

I was in the center of the Place de la Contrescarpe in 1942, in the spring, standing quite still. You, standing still? Still, in the spring? Still, you, in the spring? Centrifugal, spinning immobilities. Tiny vegetal fragments floated in the air. Standing quite still in the middle of the square, driven by an internal movement, imperceptible but febrile, I would let myself be covered with tiny vegetal fragments. One day soon, bird droppings would complete this work of immobility. A statue in the middle of the square, friable, soon eroded by the elements, I would replace for a while the bronze statues that had disappeared from the city's squares and gardens. Standing still in the middle of the Contrescarpe, for how long now? I tried to put some order into my mind—that empty cupboard, that cesspit, that public toilet—to break free of my immobility by putting order into those dark places.

You, I said to myself, you got up this morning at the usual hour. Underline that adjective several times: the usual, even when it is no longer reassuring, even when, by some cunning reversal, it becomes the very essence of the unspeakable, even in this case, the usual provides an anchor, stops you from floating off forever. You, I said to myself, got up, then, at the usual hour. The windows of your room overlook an interior garden. Underline that reality of the interior garden several times, dwell on it, even: an enclosed place, but open to the sky, sometimes in flower, in leaf, filled with uncitylike sounds, its center adorned by a decapitated gray stone statue of a woman. The stone breasts are lit from one side by the morning sunlight, sometimes, on mornings when there is sunlight. So you, I said to myself, live in a room with two windows overlooking an interior garden, and you woke up in that room this morning.

Not bad, waking up: a sort of beginning. Let's begin at the beginning. And yet, this morning, I told myself, you had no sense at all, even for a futile moment, of a beginning. Nothing in that room with its two windows overlooking an interior garden had any of the brightness of the new. Nor did anything have the tender, reassuring patina of the old. The objects, the furniture, the light, the books, the contours: everything seemed to be there for the first time, but everything was already dilapidated, eroded by an irremediable, timeless process. You, I said to myself, you, as you woke up, were contaminated, you were convinced, from the moment you opened your eyes on that tiny universe of the room with two windows overlooking an interior garden, of being there not only by chance, by accident; not only there for the first time, without links, but also convinced that you had been there forever: a motionless, senseless eternity. You, I said to myself, you knew at once that nothing would begin today: or, rather, that nothing would begin again.

In the middle of the Contrescarpe, in the spring of 1942, I tried to put some order—chronological order, if possible —into my mind. I was standing there, motionless in the middle of the square, incapable for some indefinite time of moving, of deciding to move, of choosing a direction, a purpose for my later movements. There was no question of it. It was absolutely unthinkable.

You, I said to myself, you are living in a room with two windows that overlook an interior garden. There's a chest of drawers between the two windows. A table and shelves for your books against one of the two walls perpendicular to the wall with the two windows. There is a bed against the second perpendicular wall. A washroom behind the fourth wall, the one parallel to the wall pierced by the two windows. This washroom may be entered through an open door in the parallel wall on the right, at the corner of the perpendicular wall against which the bed stands, and also through a second door, leading directly to the hall of the apartment, a door that also offers direct access to your room, which provides a number of possibilities for exits and entrances, through the washrooms, or avoiding it, possibilities which, on days like this, take into account the risks of becoming trapped, endlessly turning around and around in a labyrinth.

I, you said to yourself, I live in a room with two windows, a washroom without running water, at 350 francs a month, payable in advance. I, you said to yourself, I rent this room in a house on the Rue Blainville from an ordinary couple, neutral not only because they are of Swiss nationality, but also, in some sense, ontologically neutral: a man, a woman, a couple. An ordinary, hardworking family: the husband works in a factory in the suburbs, as an engineer, he claims, a job which the modesty of his life style, his wife's iron control over every centime of household expenditure, and the very fact that they rent the finest room in their apartment, would lead one to suppose was somewhat less important than he claims, or merely the mythological attribute of a social status that he, the Swiss, would like to be higher.

I, you said to yourself, I don't care whether he's an engineer or a window cleaner, that Swiss, that ordinary, hard-working individual who mixes up my name and that of the village near Paris where my family is living, calling me, on the few opportunities that present themselves for calling me anything, Monsieur de Saint-Prix. His wife, and the mother of his children, blond and bovine, a strict housekeeper, is also hard-working, endlessly turning over mattresses, quietly polishing, suddenly overcome with a feverish haste which one guesses to be obstinate, implacable, on gala days when it is announced that certain tickets in one's ration book make one eligible for handouts of rice, split peas, or any other kind of dried vegetables, on gala days when, untidy-looking, sometimes even disheveled, this matron with her firm legs, her well-upholstered, monumental behind, which was nevertheless in proportion to her height, comes into my room to persuade me to hand over any of said tickets that I would not myself use, or to exchange them for a number of breakfasts. The children, too, are hard-working: an older daughter, two boys in their respective schools, well behaved, hard-working, neutral.

I, you said to yourself, I live in a room chosen for its two windows overlooking the interior garden, a garden with trees and with birds in those trees, for the pale sun that shines from the rectangle of sky, for the mutilated statue of a woman, her stone breasts still intact, for its closeness to the Lycée Henri IV, and, more specifically, for its proximity to the lamppost on the Rue Thouin, which helped us, in those far-off days, to climb the wall of the Lycée Henri IV, which is not only the place where I began that year, and left after a term, but also, not so long ago, the sacrificial place, that of the second severing of my umbilical cord: a huge, dark decrepit place, labyrinthine, with courtyards, staircases, corridors, latrines, dormitories, cloakrooms, classrooms, study rooms; a cave on entering which one caught glimpses of the shades of knowledge, or of that knowledge that was imparted to us in the small, unleavened, charismatic slices of lessons, apparently disarticulated, dislocated by the timetable that split up into random pieces the radiant, mystical body of Napoleonic secondary education; an initiatory asylum in which the boarders, the prisoners, were cured, through bloody amputation and mutilation, of the disturbing ills of adolescence, of its violent, cunning madness, where we were prepared by cultural training for the sweet, resigned madness of manhood; Henri IV, a hatchet to cut the umbilical cord of childhood, the roots of the mother tongue, the colors of the childhood sky, the vegetal filaments of verbs and figures, of that disturbing postwar, inter-war time of my childhood. I, you were saying to yourself, I live in that habitable room, an enclosed place of exile in the endless deserts of exile, where the trees of the interior garden deposit the moving shadows of their leaves, their rustle of crumpled paper.

You, you were saying to yourself, you are motionless in the center of the Place de la Contrescarpe, at the very watershed, at the summit of the slopes that might lead you, through the gentle inertia of a mechanical, dreamlike walk, to surprising activities, you, so incapable of deciding between one thing and another, in the grip of *an overwhelming, central fatigue, a fatigue that sucks you in,* then saying, aloud—at the risk of scaring the birds or, on the contrary, of attracting the attention of some smooth-faced woman, who suddenly turns to you, disheveled and already possessive, her feverishly greedy eyes hearing you pronounce aloud those words that Artaud had written, years before, solely with the intention, unnamed and no doubt for him obscure, of describing his physical state (your physical state, none other but yours)—the words from *Description of a Physical State* which were, in that spring of 1942, the incantatory refrain of your life, a refrain that was not to be without its consequences: *The movements to be recomposed, a kind of deathly fatigue,* you were saying to yourself, aloud, in order to have done with that *fatigue of beginning the world, the sensation of one's body to be carried, a feeling of incredible fragility, which becomes a searing pain,* you were saying, to yourself and then more loudly in *a moving vertigo, a kind of oblique dazzling that accompanies all effort, a coagulation of heat that tightens over the whole extent of the cranium or breaks up into pieces on it,* you were rediscovering, having spoken those words, having spoken them in a sufficiently clear and loud voice to scare the birds in this empty, theatrical place, you were rediscovering the strength to move—O miracle!—first a finger, then a hand, an arm, the right shoulder, the muscles tensed along the spine, one leg, then the other, the whole body, in a movement comparable, you were saying to yourself, to that of a birth, or the bursting-forth of a plant, which temporarily becomes arrested, no doubt because you named it, exposed it, endured it to the end of endurance, that naked anguish just now, *of the muscles twisted alive, the feeling of being made of glass and brittle, a fear, a retraction before movement and noise,* and you'll let this burgeoning movement spread, snatch you from the maternal, moist immobility of a moment ago, you let yourself be carried forward, in the dazzling certainty that this physical state would recur, that this kind of deathly fatigue would be the salt of your life.

But I'm in Buchenwald, two years later.

Today it isn't the memory of some lines from Artaud recited aloud that helps me emerge from the depths of anguish precisely because he names it, describes it, catches it in the trap of words; today it's the smell of baked potatoes that has drawn me from a nightmarish somnolence.

I had heard the door open and shut, the sound of utensils being handled. I'd opened one eye and glimpsed the tall, thickset outline of Meiners. He's doing something near a hot plate.

I emerged from my somnolence with a start.

Meiners has turned his back to me. He's busy with a pan in which he is roasting potatoes.

The common room where we now are is equipped for this very purpose. There's a long table, chairs, cupboards, a few electric hot plates. The cupboards are meant to provide space for our spare provisions. Each of us has a locker of his own. I, too, have a locker, but it's always empty. I have no spare provisions. How could I have spare provisions, for God's sake! Daniel doesn't have any, either. Nor Lebrun, whose name isn't really Lebrun. He's an Austrian comrade, a Jew, who was arrested in France under the name of Lebrun and who has managed to maintain this fiction for the Gestapo. Anyway, Lebrun, since Lebrun it is, has no spare provisions, either. Nor Jean Blume, our Belgian pal.

It's the Germans, the Czechs, and the Poles—the old-timers, in short, the veterans, those who were there before the camp was turned into a sanatorium—who have spare provisions. Piles of provisions. Margarine, black bread (and even white bread), potatoes, cans of condensed milk, cans of meat, and God knows what else!

When we go to the canteen, Daniel and I, during the midday break, it's to chat, smoke a cigarette, perhaps daydream. We heat a cup of the blackish liquid, of which there is always a great pot available. And we are well aware that this is an exorbitant privilege compared with the way other prisoners live. A cup of blackish liquid, silence, no SS officers in view, the possibility of snatching a bit of sleep, a shared cigarette: it's paradise! We know very well that it's paradise. If, on top of everything else, we also manage to eat something together, in the *Arbeit* canteen, it's something we've saved from our daily rations. When we manage to overcome our hunger, not to swallow in one gulp the ration of black bread and margarine that's handed out at half past four, at reveille, with the morning liquid, then we eat the rest of the bread and margarine during the midday break, in the *Arbeit* canteen.

Germans, Czechs, and Poles eat during the midday break. They eat at all hours. They roast potatoes, cut thick slices of bread which they spread with thick layers of margarine. They eat sausage and canned meat. They simmer sweet desserts which they make with egg powder, skimmed milk, and flour. They sit at the long table and eat. Each one for himself. Each eats in his own corner, in solitude. We've never seen them eat a meal together, organize a feast. The haves don't even share with the haves. The only shared meal I ever took part in was one to which Willi Seifert invited us. We all ate together: even us, French, Belgian, Spanish, Austrian Jew. It was a dog stew. But let's not anticipate events, as they say in popular novels. Let's not anticipate: it's a bit later, in the evening of that December Sunday in 1944, that we are to be invited by Seifert to a feast of dog stew. I shall come back to it in due course. We must not disturb chronological order.

Anyway, the old-timers are eating.

Their pals are dead, gone up in smoke. They, too, might have died. They built the camp, the crematorium, the *Totenkopf* barracks, the first factories. They worked under the sun, under the snow, under blows, harassed by dogs and the SS. They saw their comrades killed by a bullet in the back of the neck because they were no longer capable of keeping up with the column transporting stone. They saw the SS explode in laughter as they threw a comrade's beret over the line that he was forbidden to cross. If the comrade did not go and fetch his beret, the SS killed him for breaking the dress regulations, which required the wearing of the beret; and if the comrade went to get his beret, the SS shot him for crossing the forbidden line. The old-timers waged a cunning, unremitting war, for years on end, on the common-law kapos, those who wore green identification triangles, in order to survive in the jungle of the camps. They saw the green kapos plunge the heads of their best comrades into the ditch of the latrines in the Little Camp until they suffocated. They murdered the green kapos, in the silence and darkness of the night, with knives or iron bars. Their way to power was strewn with corpses, enemies and friends. They proved themselves to be better administrators than the green kapos, they proved to the SS that the camp, with its factories, its outside kommandos spread over the whole of central Germany, could not function without them, and the SS agreed to give them some power, in the interests of order, in the interests of the smooth functioning of the Nazi war machine. They have come out of the cold, out of death, out of the smoke, out of madness. Now they eat. They have won this right, they think, this privilege accorded to veterans. They have their share of power, their share of the trafficking and deals in the camp. They eat the crumbs that this trafficking and power bring them.

Sometimes Daniel and I watch them eat. None of them ever shares the smallest piece of bread, the smallest spoonful of soup, the smallest slice of sausage. I wonder if they see that we have only our daily rations to live on. Sometimes, during the day, when the common room is empty, I open the cupboards and look at the provisions accumulated by the veterans. I gaze at the cans of food, the bottles of beer, the hunks of bread. In certain lockers, the bread has sometimes gone moldy. I look at the greenish patches of mold on their white bread. I'm overcome with hate. And I have a sudden, overwhelming desire to kill someone.

Meiners has turned around. He is coming over to the table I am leaning on, carrying the pan in which his roasted potatoes are sizzling.

Meiners wears a black triangle. That means that he is an "asocial." He must have been deported for illegal trafficking of some kind. It was almost certainly some big black-market affair. There's nothing shabby-looking about Meiners. He's a handsome fellow, with the presence of a German film actor of the 1930s, a musical-comedy actor of the UFA. I gather that Meiners was placed in the

Arbeitsstatistik by the SS, some years ago, in an attempt to counterbalance the preponderant influence of the German Communists. But Meiners realized soon enough that he had bitten off more than he could chew, that it was in his interests to remain neutral in the secret battle between the Communists of the *Arbeitsstatistik* and the SS of the *Arbeitseinsatz*. He managed to get forgotten by both, and in the end to get really forgotten, occupying a subordinate post, preoccupied solely with the problems of his own survival. All the same, he was the best fellow in the world: always courteous, always even-tempered.

Meiners has sat down at the table. He has arranged his cutlery on a small checked tablecloth. He also has a white napkin. He has placed the roasted potatoes on his plate. He has opened a can of pâté and a bottle of beer. He has cut several slices of thick white bread. He begins to chew slowly, staring into space.

I'm at the other end of the long table, staring at him.

What is Meiners dreaming about as he chews his bread, his pâté, his roasted potatoes? I'm not impartial, of course. My hate for Meiners at that precise moment, my hate for his pâté, his roasted potatoes, his bread smeared with thick layers of margarine, certainly prevents me from being objective. I have an irrepressible tendency to imagine that Meiners's head is filled with the stupidest, most contemptible daydreams. Whereas, for all I know, he may be dreaming of the most delicate things: a wife whom he loves and who is waiting for him, a piece of music by Mozart, a page of Goethe.

I look at Meiners, fascinated.

Suddenly I sense that he has become aware of my presence, and that this presence disturbs him. Or, rather, that the fixity of my stare disturbs him. I watch the embarrassment settle in, gradually overcome him, making his gestures jerkier. His quickly averted glances in my direction are imbued with a silent, anxious questioning. It's as if he is now hurrying to finish off his meal. He puts twice as much in his mouth each time. He no longer wipes his lips after each bite or before each swig of beer. He is beginning to eat coarsely, like a glutton.

"Have you finished yet?"

He looks at me, astonished.

"What?" he says.

"I asked you if you'd finished," I say to him.

He looks at his plate, then at me.

"Almost, yes. Why?"

"Because it stinks, what you're eating!"

He looks at me, surprised. He bends down over his plate and sniffs.

"Isn't it rotten, that shitty pâté you've got there?" I persist.

He looks up, displeased. He waves his fork in the air.

"That pâté comes from the SS canteen!" he declares, as if that were irrefutable proof of its excellence.

"It smells of shit, your pâté," I say. "What do the SS put in their pâté? The shit from the latrines of the Little Camp? The corpses of the Jews that recently arrived from Poland?"

He almost chokes in disgust, dabs his lips with his white napkin.

"But it's excellent pâté!"

He's practically shouting.

"It stinks, your pâté," I say. "I wouldn't touch it with a ten-foot pole. You'll get the runs soon enough, you'll see."

His eyes roll wildly in their sockets.

He's beginning to have doubts about his pâté. He sniffs it again.

"Can't you smell anything?" I say. "It's making me sick."

He holds out the can of pâté.

"Put it away," I say. "We're not in the latrines!"

His hand is trembling convulsively.

"What's more," I say, "it's Sunday. You've probably got a ticket for the brothel this afternoon. What if you suddenly want to shit when you're about to mount the girl!"

He looks at me with wild and staring eyes. He doesn't like the prospect at all.

I think he is about to scream.

But the canteen door opens and Daniel comes in. If it had been a German, I'm sure Meiners would have asked him to be a witness to my aggressive behavior. Meiners is very particular about questions of protocol. He carries respect for the social and national hierarchies of our world to the ultimate, proof of a good bourgeois education. For him, there are first of all the Germans. But one must be more specific. By Germans one means Germans from the Reich, *Reichsdeutsche*. The other Germans, those of the German national minorities in the countries bordering the Reich, Sudeten, Silesian, Baltic Germans, for example, in short, the *Volksdeutsche*, are regarded less highly by him. By the SS administration, too, it should be said. Only *Reichsdeutsche* have a right to brothel tickets. No foreigners, not even *Volksdeutsche*, have a right to brothel tickets. One does not shoot one's load officially when one is not a German from the Reich.

So if a German, a real German, had appeared at the door at that precise moment, Meiners would certainly have asked him to be a witness to my upsetting aggressiveness. But it's a Frenchman, and a Jew to boot. Meiners can stand no more. He gets up, puts away his things, and rushes out.

"What's the matter with *him*?" Daniel asks.

"You scared him off," I say hypocritically. "He probably doesn't like Jews!"

Daniel laughs.

"Why should he like Jews? Do you know anyone who likes Jews? Does Fritz like Jews? And he's an old Communist. What about you, are you sure *you* like Jews?"

"You're a pain in the ass," I say kindly.

But he isn't to be put off.

"I'm not even sure *I* like Jews all the time," he says.

I look at him: I know what he's thinking. He looks at me: he knows that I know what he's thinking. We're thinking the same thing.

There were several hundred of them on the esplanade that extends behind the *Arbeitsstatistik* hut. They were standing close together. Perhaps out of habit, perhaps to keep standing. They had been packed tightly together for weeks, in the trains that had brought them from the camps in Poland.

They stood close together in the falling rain, in the freezing mist of that day. Not a sound rose from the tottering mass. Not a single human sound, at any rate. Not a voice, not a murmur, not even a pained whisper. They were frozen in silence under the falling rain, in the grim damp of that day. Sometimes one heard what sounded like a herd of cattle—the noise of their wooden clogs striking the stones in the sodden, muddy ground. A herd of cattle standing in some market place, some cattle fair, striking the paving stones with their hoofs. No other sound.

Seeing them like that, huddled together in the fine, steady rain, one could imagine their infinite patience, the resigned expectation of catastrophes that life had so ferociously taught them. That's all they were: infinite patience, resignation that nothing could touch any more. Their life force was no more than that fatal weakness of cattle in their pens. They had asked no questions, not why they had been put there, or what was going to happen to them. They'd been assembled just now in front of the hut of the quarantine camp. All those who were still capable of walking, of putting one foot in front of another, had been brought here. They'd put one foot in front of another, painfully, as if each time might have been the last time. They were there now, and they asked no questions, they did not even murmur to one another, they just waited. They'd been lined up and handled, the way one lines up and handles bags of cement, tree trunks, stones. A hundred per row, six rows deep. There were six hundred of them huddled together, waiting.

They could see the rear of the *Arbeit* hut, but they didn't know that it was the *Arbeit* hut. All they saw was a hut. Through the windows of that hut, they could see tables, card indexes, a stove that must be lit since they saw men in shirt sleeves moving around it, warm and dry. Us, warm and dry. They certainly weren't surprised. There were always those who were warm and dry while they were outside digging the ground, or the snow, or the mud, or burying their pals' corpses.

If they'd turned their heads, they would have seen the crematorium building, with its massive chimney, from which the bitter, icy wind occasionally blew down smoke. But they didn't turn their heads; it wasn't their habit. They waited, just waited, making that intermittent sound, of a herd of cattle in a pen at a fair, with their wooden clogs on the sharp gravel of the esplanade soaked by the snow and rain of winter.

We looked out, Daniel and I.

Whole trainloads of them had arrived from Poland during the last few weeks. Rokossovski's offensive had stopped short at the gates of Warsaw in September, thus allowing the Germans to crush Bor-Komorowski's uprising. The Polish Front was not moving at the moment. It was in Hungary, around Budapest, that the Soviet thrust was developing.

Yet just as the light from a dead star still comes to you through space, through the galaxies, through light-years, the migrations from the Polish camps caused by Rokossovski's offensive during the summer and autumn were still having their effect on us. Like the light from a dead star, whole trainloads of deportees from the camps of Poland had been wandering across Europe for weeks. Sometimes, having no survivors to transport, the trains had been abandoned on sidelines, or out in the countryside. Sometimes the trains reached the special station at Buchenwald, in the center of the Ettersberg forest, and the column of survivors would stagger along the avenue of imperial eagles, toward the camp gates.

We watched the survivors of *those* survivors, Daniel and I.

They had to be arranged in groups of fifteen in the annex that had been built some months before onto the back of the *Arbeit* hut. That was the domain of Fritz, that senile, chauvinistic, malicious old Communist. It was there that he gathered, every evening after roll call, those inmates who had been reported as legitimately absent in the various kommandos or exempt from work for reasons of health, in order to check that everything was in order, that they had the correct notes from the camp doctors. He took his job seriously, Fritz, the old bastard. He tracked down any inmates who weren't following the regulations, who were trying to shirk their duties. In the complexity of the life and organization of work in Buchenwald, there was always, for the cleverest, the bravest—or the most desperate—the possibility of shirking, of taking an irregular day off from time to time. Irregular according to the norms established by the SS, that is. But Fritz had made those norms his own. With the quiet conscience of a bureaucrat, he embodied the punctilious respect for established order, the respect for work as such. He was a real bastard, that guy, and, what's more, he tried to teach us how things should be run, old Communist, old proletarian, old son of an old bitch that he was. Daniel was his assistant in this checking work, and disagreements between them were inevitable, almost every day. For Daniel did exactly the opposite of Fritz. He gathered the inmates exempt from work, or reported as legitimately absent from their kommandos, and if he found that their papers were not in order, he did his best to cover up for them, by fiddling with the index cards and reports as much as he could. This caused arguments, sometimes violent arguments, between them.

That day, Seifert had appointed us—Daniel, me, Fritz, and another German comrade, Georg Glucker—to sort through the six hundred survivors from the Polish camps. It was just a question of determining which among them were skilled workers, *Facharbeiter*. In principle, according to the directives of the SS command, the survivors of the Polish camps were immediately sent to the outside work parties, sometimes within four or five days of their arrival in Buchenwald. The SS command in Buchenwald quite clearly didn't want Jews in their camp.

On the other hand, in order to try to save at least some of the Jewish survivors by keeping them in the camp—where the conditions of life, or survival, or even death, were better than in the outside work parties to which they were usually sent—the international underground organization had decided to draw up a list of skilled workers who we would then claim were necessary to productive activity in Buchenwald. The SS command could usually be won over on the grounds of productivity: they had already agreed that certain prisoners from the Polish camps should remain in Buchenwald as skilled workers.

We were sitting behind the long table in the annex that was Fritz's domain. The old bastard himself was there, and Daniel and I, and Georg Glucker. Glucker was one of the maddest of the old German Communists who had gone mad in Buchenwald. He was given to sudden, apparently unpredictable fits of anger. Recently, as Christmas approached, the object of his anger had been the Czech pals who had been secretly bringing back fir branches from the forest, in order to make imitation Christmas trees to decorate their rooms. Glucker insulted them, frothing at the mouth, calling them *Christbaumsozialisten*, "Christmas-tree socialists," which seemed to him to be the ultimate insult, and of which he was excessively proud, as if the Czech pals could be intimidated by being called Christmas-tree socialists by this Glucker, whom we all knew to be quite mad.

So we were sitting behind the long table and were about to bring in the first group of survivors from the Polish camps.

The annex door opened, and the first fifteen survivors —living corpses—came in. With them came the icy December cold, and that bastard Fritz started yelling and shouting at them to shut the door, shit, quickly, assholes!

"*Türe zu, Scheisse, schnell, Scheisskerle!*"

They shut the door, those assholes.

Then, in the tumult, in the noise of wooden clogs on the annex floor, the fifteen survivors from the Polish camps lined up in front of us, trying to stand to attention and click their heels, and, all together, with the same rhythmic gesture, they gave the Nazi salute.

Then there was silence.

I didn't dare look at Daniel and Daniel didn't dare look at me. We looked at the fifteen Jewish survivors from the Polish camps giving the Nazi salute.

Standing to attention stiffly, mechanically, frozen in the pitiful stiffness of a gesture that, it seemed, would go on forever. Frozen, heels together, standing like corpses in the shadow of the trains, of the gas chambers, trembling from the superhuman effort they were making to hold their right arms in the Nazi salute.

I didn't have to shut my eyes. I didn't shut my eyes.

They stood there in front of us like ghosts, the fifteen survivors from the Polish camps, in the steam that the stove drew out of their soaking clothes, as stiff as posts in that last, pitiful effort to give the Nazi salute.

Then that bastard Fritz broke the silence:

"Aber Juden, nur Juden, das sind sie nur!"

Jews, nothing but Jews, that's what they are, said Fritz. And then he burst into that neighing laugh of his.

The Jews from the Polish camps, stock still, their arms still raised in the Nazi salute, did not react. They had been called Jews. There was nothing new in that. They were used to it. They stood stock still, waiting for someone to give them an order, to tell them what they had to do.

Gaining momentum, Fritz began to insult them. And it was then that Georg Glucker intervened.

He stood up, his face white, his hands trembling. He shut Fritz up with a few cutting words. Then, stressing each syllable in an effort to calm himself, he explained to the Jews from Poland that they were making a mistake, that they were not dealing with the SS or the servants of the SS, that we were prisoners like themselves, that we were simply luckier than they because we weren't Jews, that we were nevertheless Communists, and the Communists were the determined enemies of anti-Semitism— and he turned to Fritz as he said that—and he was standing and stressing each word, each syllable, like a schoolmaster, as he had probably done fifteen years before, facing the factory workers of Essen or Wuppertal, for he was from the Rhineland, standing now and speaking to the Jews who had come from Poland, and I looked at Glucker's face, drained of blood. I saw his mad, pale-blue eyes, shining implacably with all the madness of those years, against which his words were trying to erect a barrage made up of old certainties, and Glucker stopped speaking, as he stood there opposite the fifteen ghosts of Jews from the Polish camps giving us the Nazi salute.

They began to lower their arms, to relax. They looked at one another, whispered, tried to figure out this novel situation. At last they filed out. We'd drawn up the list of those who were to stay in the camp as skilled workers.

I had still not looked at Daniel, who was sitting directly to my right. And he had not looked at me. I just heard his quick breathing.

The first two Jews from the Polish camps whose cards I had to fill out were Hungarians. I didn't put them on the list of skilled workers. To begin with, they were both furriers. And anyway, they had no chance of surviving, even if they'd stayed in the camp. They stayed upright as if by a miracle, by a last stubborn, desperate effort of their exhausted bodies, of their shaky minds. The adhesive shadow of death was already visible in their staring eyes.

The third to pass before me was Polish. He was much younger than the other two; that is, if one looked at him closely, with a good deal of imagination, one could deduce that he was a young man. Probably five or six years older than I, which meant twenty-five or twenty-six. Not yet entirely indifferent to everything around him, he wanted to know where he was. He asked me a few rapid questions, in German. I told him again what Glucker had just told them all. He nodded, trying to assimilate this new reality. He was trying to understand how it was possible that we should be there, snug and warm, in shirt sleeves, like bosses, without being the zealous servants of the SS.

Then I, too, asked a few questions.

I asked him why they had given the Nazi salute. But he didn't understand this question; it seemed absurd to him. They just did, that was all. It's what they were used to, it was the rule, nothing else. He shrugged his shoulders. My question seemed absurd to him, and it was.

Then, changing the subject, I asked him where they had come from. He told me that they had been traveling for some months, stopping off at all sorts of places. They had set out from Poland, he told me, a long time ago. They had been in a small camp near Czestochowa. One day they heard the rumble of cannon, the noise of approaching battle. And then, one morning at dawn, the Germans left. They were alone, with no Germans to guard them. No guards on the watchtowers. They called a meeting, and the old-timers decided that it was suspicious, a trap, without question. Then, led by the old-timers, they formed into groups, left the camp that had been abandoned by the Germans, and walked to the nearest town, in ordered ranks. No one left the column. In the town there was a railway station. German convoys were moving westward. They went up to the Germans and said: Here we are, we've been left behind. They had to argue with the Germans. The Germans didn't want them. Eventually the Germans put them on a train. They went out west, with the Germans.

"But why?" I asked, puzzled.

He looked at me as if I was stupid.

"The Germans were leaving," he explained.

"So?"

He shook his head, confused by my failure to understand. He said quietly: "If the Germans were leaving, it was because the Russians were coming."

That seemed irrefutable. I nodded.

"Yes," I said to him, "so what?"

He leaned toward me, irritated, suddenly angry. He was almost shouting.

"Don't you know," he shouted at me, "that the Russians hate Jews?"

I looked at him.

He moved back, hoping that I had understood now.

I think I *had* understood, in fact. With some effort, I asked him what his occupation was.

"Worker in furs," he said.

I looked at him, I looked at his number. I put him down as *Facharbeiter*, skilled worker. I put him down as an electrician. It was the first trade that came into my head.

You will never forget the Jews from Czestochowa.

You will grow old, the dark veil of regressive amnesia, perhaps of imbecility, will stretch over part of your inner landscape. You will no longer know anything of the violent tenderness of the hands, mouths, eyelids of women. You will lose the Ariadne's thread of your own labyrinth. You will wander blinded through the dazzling light of imminent death. You will look at T., the child that you have loved above all else in the world, and you may have nothing to say to the man that he will have become, who will regard you with a mixture of pitying affection and restrained impatience.

You will soon be dead, old chum.

You will not have gone up in smoke, in a light cloud over the Ettersberg, floating around for a last farewell to your pals before being dispersed by the wind over the plain of Thuringia. You will soon rot, underground, anywhere: one piece of ground is as good as any other to rot in.

But you will never have forgotten, never. You will always remember, to your dying breath, the Jews from

Czestochowa, standing there frozen, making a superhuman effort to stretch their right arms in the Nazi salute. Having truly become Jews—that is to say, on the contrary, having become the true negation of the Jew, conforming to the image that a certain history has given the Jews. An overtly anti-Semitic history that puts up with Jews only when they are wretched and submissive, so as to be able to despise them while exterminating them. Or another, more cunning, history, which doesn't always know that it's anti-Semitic, which even pretends that it isn't, but which puts up with Jews only when they are oppressed, victims, in order to be able to feel sorry for them, to lament, if necessary, their extermination.

You remembered the Jews from Czestochowa again, today, May 1, 1979.

You were sitting at your desk, with all the uneasiness a writer feels when his work is unfinished. For several weeks now, you had been working on this manuscript with an eye toward having done with it, you told yourself. It wasn't the first time you had claimed to be finishing it and not done so. Perhaps, quite simply, you really didn't want to have done with it. Perhaps it was simply that this unfinished manuscript, forever taken up again, rewritten, forgotten, rediscovered, proliferating through the years with a dangerously autonomous life which you no longer seemed capable of mastering, perhaps this manuscript was quite simply your life. And you certainly weren't going to put an end to your life! You certainly weren't going to put an end to your memory of the camps. Perhaps you weren't managing to finish this story because it was, by definition, interminable. Because the word "end," even if one day you managed to write it, would be but a pitiful acknowledgment of the temporary interruption of a piece of writing—of memory—on which the work, overt or subterranean, explicit or hidden, would immediately resume.

Anyway, you were sitting at your desk, in the grip of that vague, lonely uneasiness that comes when you are unable to pick up the thread again, the meaning, the necessity, of a piece of writing, when suddenly it seemed that the light was changing outside. You looked outside and saw the trees in the garden beyond your window, which spring had covered with green shoots; the light had indeed changed. A little while ago it was a spring light, transparent and deep. But it had suddenly become gray, thick, though suffused by a glowing iridescence.

On this May 1, 1979, a sudden snowstorm swirled down on Paris, before your eyes, over the trees of the small square on the Boulevard Saint-Germain. Then you understood, with beating heart, that this snow was both a reminder and a portent.

Thirty-four years earlier, on May 1, 1945, you had just arrived in Paris. You could still remember a snowstorm that descended on the May Day marches. Snowflakes whitened the shoulders and hair of the demonstrators, fell on the red May Day flags. As if that last ephemeral snow—the last snow of that winter, that war, that past—had suddenly fallen, only to emphasize the passing of that past, of that war, of that winter. As if all the snow that had for so long covered the beeches of the forest around Buchenwald had just melted, shaken by the spring breeze that stirred the red flags, unfurled them, suddenly covered them with bands of material that were not mourning bands, but brilliant bands of hope.

But this snow, today, May 1, 1979, was not only a reminder. It was also a portent. Some hours earlier, a friendly voice had told you on the telephone that Edward Kuznetsov had just been freed from Brezhnev's Gulag. He had arrived in New York and intended, it seemed, to get to Israel as soon as possible.

Then you remembered the Jews from Czestochowa.

Some months before, in late January 1979, you had

taken part in a meeting organized by the International Committee for the Liberation of Edward Kuznetsov. To all the political, public reasons for your being there, beside the men and women who had fought for Kuznetsov's liberation, reasons so obvious that it would be pointless to recall them here, were added some private reasons. The first was undoubtedly that Kuznetsov did not submit to his condition as a Jew, that he had chosen it. He had chosen that connection even if it contradicted the strict terms of Judaic law, which established that descent must be exclusively maternal, visceral, physical. Perhaps he contradicted the terms of the law because this connection that he had desired was ideal, even symbolic, because it was a choice, because it had consequently to be put into practice against all laws.

But through his determination to be a Jew, Edward Kuznetsov placed himself at the antipodes of the Jews from Czestochowa. He submitted to nothing, he accepted nothing, he subjected himself to nothing: he was a Jew, freely, irrevocably. He was a Jew against the whole world: against himself, or a considerable part of himself, anyway.

There were other private reasons why you were so concerned with Edward Kuznetsov.

Some time before, you had had the opportunity of reading a letter written by Kuznetsov in the special camp in which he was serving his sentence, and published in a Parisian weekly. And you had been particularly struck by these lines:

"Experience overlays imagination. Dream slips into dream. The bewildered memory scratches its head and stammers. And that is not so much the result of time gone by: everything that exists on the other side of the watch-towers belongs to another planet. . . . But sometimes I catch myself red-handed in subtly schizophrenic attempts to elucidate some frightful doubt that seems to me like an illumination: the camp and everything that proceeds from it is the only reality, the rest being nothing more than a mirage, a mirage stemming from the hallucinatory action of the watery soup. Or I suddenly take it into my head that on that very special New Year's Eve of 1971, when I was taken out to the firing squad, I really was shot. But, perforated with bullets like a colander in the real world, I would continue to function mechanically in an illusory dimension, the fruit of my insistent prayers at the moment the shots were fired."

So it seems that you were not the only one to have that dream, that dream of living in a dream, of dreaming that you were the dream of someone who died long ago. Those lines of Kuznetsov, written a quarter of a century after you left Buchenwald, express word for word feelings that were yours, that belonged to you alone. Those lines unveiled, with a touch of irony, which is needed to compensate for the strangeness of that sensation, the *subtly schizophrenic attempts* with which you had managed to surprise, and even to enjoy, yourself. It certainly seemed, then, that your case was not a desperate one, since it was not unique. A sickness of the soul that seemed to have attacked you and you alone would certainly have been incurable: there is no therapy for the extreme singularity, for the unique case. Science is not interested in it. But if your case was not unique, if Kuznetsov had felt—and the fragment of his letter that you have just quoted proves beyond any doubt that he had—the same symptoms as you, at least you might one day talk about it together.

Provided that he is eventually freed, of course.

So you were on the platform at a meeting, at the Jewish Cultural Center on the Boulevard de Port-Royal, on January 29, 1979. You were listening to Jean-Pierre Vernant, who had just begun talking, after Andrei Sinyavsky. You were listening to him attentively because Vernant, whatever biographical differences there are between you, comes from the same past as you, from the same cultural horizon of Communism. And you listened to him all the more attentively because you had just read or reread, some weeks before, most of his work on Greek mythology and thought. That was because, some weeks before, you had become particularly interested in the myth of Persephone, in the disturbing story, so full of hidden meanings, of her stay in hell.

But it was about another journey that Jean-Pierre Vernant was speaking that January day. You were listening to him speak about the condition of the Jews in the USSR. Vernant was saying more or less that the national status of the Jew in the USSR "consists in depriving you of everything positive that the notion of nationality may have: you are a Jew, therefore you are not a Russian, therefore you are not a Ukrainian, and you do not have the rights that they have, but at the same time you are denied, because you are a Jew, the positive rights that form part of nationality. You have no autonomous culture. Your language is not recognized. Your religion cannot express itself, and in this sense, in a way, you are not Russian and you are not anything else. You are 'nothing,' or, to be more precise, you have the means of becoming something only by creating for yourself a nation, that is to say, by being a Zionist. And so much is this the case that for the overwhelming mass of the people, to be a Jew and to be a Zionist are one and the same thing."

You were listening to what Jean-Pierre Vernant was saying, thinking that he was right, overwhelmingly right, that Zionism is indeed one of the ways—probably the major way during periods of massive dereliction, of planetary persecution, of genocide—of affirming Jewish identity, of projecting it into the future, of rooting it in the blood of the future, which is not that of the Promised Land, of course, but simply that of *a* land, a motherland—or, in the case of Kuznetsov, who had voluntarily chosen another Jewish connection, that of a father-motherland—of a homeland, in any case. And Zionism has played and is still playing that immense role, even if it carries within itself its own contradiction, the seeds of its ideal destruction, since it leads the Jewish people to become a people like any other, a state like any other. A state, undoubtedly, that is absolutely necessary on the historical plane, to be defended absolutely against all attacks, one of the few places in the world where no compromise is acceptable, the existence of Israel being a touchstone of the inhumanity or humanity of the species, being also the condition, whatever the dusky obscurity within which this aspect of the question may now lie, for the possible emergence of an Arab Palestine that is more than a matter of high stakes in oil, of a strategic territory, of an exchange currency between the great powers, that is, therefore, a Palestinian fatherland, a homeland for the Palestinian Arabs, the inversion of Zionism, its significant inversion. But though this need of the Jews for a state like any other state is true on the historical plane, it is, at the same time, a fatal danger for them on the metaphysical plane. For the Jewish people, it seems to you, are caught up in a contradiction that is their essence and their greatness, which makes them, if not a chosen people, which is unthinkable, at least a reading people: the people of the Book. This contradiction is expressed in the Jews' inalienable right to be a people, like other peoples, with a land and a state like any other people, even if that right—you choose the words carefully—even if that right, having become a concrete reality, has gravely prejudiced the latent Arab rights that have been aroused by the Zionist right itself, but which are equally indisputable, to the land of Palestine. Palestine was not, as the founding fathers dreamed, *a land without a people for a people without a land*, but a populated land. So the obverse of the Jews' inalienable right is the metaphysical impossibility of being a people like any other people, the metaphysical need to be the people of Pierre Goldman and not only that of Menachem Begin. A need that is expressed in the impossibility, not only material but also spiritual, which the state of Israel experiences, of absorbing all the Jewish people, of reabsorbing the Diaspora, for the Diaspora carries as much evidence of Jewish national identity as the Jewish state itself.

But you were listening to Jean-Pierre Vernant, and you suddenly thought of the Jews from Czestochowa. You thought of that Polish Jew who was only five or six years older than yourself but looked like an old man, and whom you had put on the list of the *Facharbeiter*, the skilled workers. Did he survive Buchenwald? Suddenly you began to hope wildly that he had survived it. Perhaps you had saved him by putting him on the list of skilled workers, you began to hope madly. Perhaps he had followed, after the Nazi defeat, one of the Zionist channels that brought the Jewish volunteers from the refugee camps scattered across Europe to Palestine, then under the British mandate. Perhaps he had fought in the ranks of the Haganah. Perhaps he had rediscovered his status as a Jew, his stature as a Jew, in the ranks of the Haganah. Perhaps he had found himself among the hundreds of Jewish volunteers who had landed a few days before from a secret ship that the Haganah had launched for an assault on the fortified positions of Glubb Pasha's Arab Legion, around Latrun, the Trappist monastery of Our Lady of Latrun, which is not a place name, but the deformation of a Latin word, for there was once on the hill where the

Trappist monastery was built a castle erected by the Templars known at the end of the twelfth century as the Castel du Bon Larron (*Castellum Boni Latronis*). And you had visited the Trappist monastery of Latrun, in the autumn of 1972. You had looked down from the hill, among the ruins of the Christian fortress in which the Arab Legion had set up its cannon, across that Biblical plain where the Jewish volunteers of the Haganah had assembled at night. And perhaps he was among them, that Polish Jew from the camp at Czestochowa, who had been so indignant because you didn't seem to understand that he had fled from the arrival of Russian troops, who had in his twenty-year-old eyes twenty centuries of death and resignation, but who had perhaps discovered a combative and human eye for the twenty—what are you saying?—for all the centuries to come till the end of centuries. Perhaps the Jew that you had saved at Buchenwald was repeating to himself, as hundreds of Jews around him were doing at the same time, the few Hebrew words that he had just learned, words of command that he had to know at all cost, in order to understand the orders from his superiors, so he whispered these words so as not to forget them, for his life might depend on them, and the victory of his people might depend on them, and he was obscurely moved when saying these words of Hebrew that he had learned that day, and which did not speak of obedience or resignation, but were words to fight with, words to kill with: Forward! Fire! Deploy for action! Attack! Fire at will! Fix bayonets! March! Sinister, cutting words, lacerating, violent words, ignoble words that expressed, that night on the Biblical plain that faces the site of Latrun, dignity regained, possible identity, fatherland, motherland, the land flowing with milk and honey, as the Book puts it, rediscovered at last. And the multiplied whispering of all those Hebrew words of command rumbled in the night like a tragic, mysterious chorus, reaching the ears of the guards of the Arab Legion, who understood none of it, or who understood perhaps that something strange and great, something huge was beginning to move in the world, like a living body moving in a mother's womb: the living body of the persecuted, oppressed, humiliated Jew, having apparently abdicated his essence, but rediscovering it suddenly, placing himself in the world once again, in the Biblical, terrifying night in which the survivors of Auschwitz and Birkenau, Buchenwald and Dachau were to mount their assault on the heavens, on that celestial, star-filled immensity over the land of Judea, were to come to life in blood and tears.

But you were supposed to be on the platform of the Jewish Cultural Center, on the Boulevard de Port-Royal in Paris, on January 29, 1979. You were supposed to be listening to speeches made by men and women about Edward Kuznetsov. You were now listening to Marthe Robert, but part of yourself was far away. Part of yourself was wandering vaguely in the memory of the Jews from Czestochowa, a memory that had kept coming back to you, insistently, as you traveled through Israel in the autumn of 1972. Perhaps that part of yourself that seemed to be far removed from Marthe Robert's words was, on the contrary, coming back to them, perhaps the memory of the Jews from Czestochowa was bringing you back to what Marthe Robert was saying.

You were remembering the Jews from Czestochowa who had entered the annex of the *Arbeitsstatistik* hut one winter day long ago, in a group of fifteen, the first fifteen Jews from Czestochowa, making a superhuman but pitiful effort to stand to attention, their right arms stretched in the Nazi salute. And Fritz had not been wrong about it. That old bastard Fritz, old Communist, old shit. He had insulted them at once, yelled at them, on the verge of hysteria. All too happy, that bastard Fritz, to find Jews apparently so like the image that he himself had of them, he the old Communist, the anti-Semite.

You remembered the Jews from Czestochowa years later, in Israel. You remembered them as you stood on the hill of Latrun. You remembered them on the site of Solomon's Pools, a human landscape—humanized by thousands of years of man's labor, thousands of years of Jewish labor, which was rooted in the soil and the springs before being dispersed throughout the world and forbidden land, before it was forbidden to Jewish labor to devote itself to the land, to turn it, to plow it, to possess it—an incredible human landscape of ancestral beauty around Solomon's Pools, cut out of the living rock to collect the living water.

But suddenly you hear your name, or, rather, the name that you have gone by for some time. You hear the voice of Hélène Parmelin announcing that you will speak next.

You can't help thinking, with a brief inward smile, that the women of that family are certainly authoritarian. They certainly have authority. For you had no intention of speaking, that evening in January 1979. You had just passed a note across to Hélène Parmelin telling her of your intention not to speak. You don't particularly like talking in public, especially when circumstances hoist you up onto a platform. The public platform, it seems to you, is certainly one of the most impossible places. Besides, your whole training is, rather, of underground speech, of short, private meetings. But that's not the main reason. The main reason was that you had wanted, that evening, to speak only about the Jews from Czestochowa, which was impossible. It seemed to you impossible to speak in public, just like that, of this personal memory that had suddenly come back to you. It seemed indecent. No doubt you might have spoken about it individually with most of the people who were there that evening. But to speak about it to a gathering of those people, delivered over to the massiveness of their presence, seemed to you impossible. Or indecent. You could have talked about Edward Kuznetsov, of course. But Kuznetsov was not there, he was in one of Brezhnev's special Gulag camps. So you no longer had any desire to speak at all.

But the voice of Hélène Parmelin urges you on, makes you speak. This reminds you of an episode long ago, when it wasn't the voice of Hélène that snatched you from silence, but that of her sister, Olga Wormser. You were at the House of Youth and Culture, at Sarcelles, years before. Anna Langfus* had asked you to go. She was organizing a public debate there on the experience of the concentration camps, and it was Olga Wormser, the historian of that experience, who was to take the chair that evening. You had published *The Long Voyage* a couple of years earlier, and you seemed just the person to take part in such a shindig. You didn't dare refuse, because it was Anna Langfus who had asked you. So you found yourself once again behind a table, at the House of Youth and Culture in Sarcelles, with men and women who had been deported. They recounted their experiences, in turn. The whole thing was perfect; you were fascinated. It was fresh as springwater; it was handmade. They were all perfectly at ease in their role as witnesses. You are saying that not with any pejorative or contemptuous intent whatever, but with astonished admiration. For all those former deportees from the resistance were worthy, highly worthy individuals. There were even what are called heroes among them. But you listened to them, fascinated by the ease with which they spoke, by their flow of words, by the assurance of their testimony, by the certainty they dis-

*Polish writer who survived the concentration camps. —ED.

played of being alive. The more ardently and precisely they spoke, the more you felt yourself sink into a confused nothingness, the less you knew what you could say to those worthy inhabitants of Sarcelles who had come with the highly respectable, perhaps even praiseworthy, intention of hearing those survivors convey to them an experience, without knowing that it was incommunicable. The incommunicable on order, or at least at a particular time, arranged in advance, at the sound of a gong, at the third stroke! And now it was your turn to speak, and Olga Wormser had finished introducing you. You no longer know what you were able to say. You remember only that after one or two minutes you suddenly stopped, as though you had lost the thread of what you were saying. An ordinary enough situation in which the narrator, after some incident or digression, turns to the public, and to himself, temporarily disoriented, with the question: Where was I? Where were you, indeed? You had lost not only the thread of what you were saying, apparently, but also the thread of your life. You no longer knew where you were in general, or why, or how. The truth was, you were no longer anywhere. How could you go on with what you were saying if you no longer knew where the speaker was, or even who he was? What experience could you tell them about, since you had no other experience to convey to them except that of death—the one thing that, by definition, you couldn't have experienced, that only someone else could have experienced? But who, then? Why was he not here in your place, that someone else who might have been able to live through, and therefore convey, the experience of your death? Then, in despair, you turned to Olga Wormser on your right, who was chairing that pleasant meeting, and you whispered to her: "I wonder what I'm doing here, where I am!" And she looked into your eyes, and in a gentle but firm voice repeated the last sentence that you had spoken before you had sunk into that anguished silence. Then you turned to the inhabitants of Sarcelles, who were sitting, row upon row, in front of you, and mechanically you resumed your speech at the point at which you'd left off. There was nothing else to be done. You could only resume your role of survivor, after that sudden lapse of memory that had made you lose the thread of what you were saying. You could only resume your role as witness. You weren't there for anything else. You were there to play that role, to perform it. You had forgotten your lines, you had fallen forever into that dark pit that is the stuff of nightmares, but you had been prompted, and the show could go on. You were there as surviving witnesses, all those heroes and yourself, and the role of a witness is to witness, nothing else. A witness does not disappear down a trap door, like a character in some melodrama. A witness has always had a speaking role. You couldn't remain silent. So you talked at Sarcelles, you recounted your life as a survivor. You might have recounted your death, but one mustn't expect too much of listeners at that type of public meeting. They'd come to hear an account of your life, or of your survival, and it would be indelicate to burden them with an account of your death.

But now you looked up and stared out at the crowd sitting before you, row upon row, in that hall of the Jewish Cultural Center on the Boulevard de Port-Royal. You spoke, of course. Hélène Parmelin was right. You hadn't come there to sink back into an abyss of private thoughts. You had come to talk about Kuznetsov, to help him, as far as possible, through what you said. So you spoke.

Some months later, on May 1, 1979, you remembered it all again. You remembered Edward Kuznetsov and those words that he had written in a letter. Now that he was free, you might one day talk to him of that impression you shared: of living the life of someone else. And you remembered the Jews from Czestochowa. Perhaps one day you might talk to Kuznetsov about them. And you remembered the snow, the immemorial shroud of the camps, stretching from central Germany to the Soviet Great North. You remembered whirlwinds of light snow, in spring, during a May Day procession, thirty-four years before, the space of a lifetime, as you looked at the spring whirlwinds of that sudden snowstorm on May 1, 1979.

Thirty-four years before, you had just returned from Buchenwald. You looked at the May Day red flags, festooned with ephemeral fringes of snow. At the same moment, Stalin's Gulag camps were beginning to see the arrival of the Russian survivors from the Nazi camps. The day before May Day, they took away the camouflage curtains from the windows of the prison cells of the Lubyanka, in Moscow. "The war was visibly coming to an end," Alexander Solzhenitsyn was later to write.

At the very moment when you were treading the soil of liberty, in the shining innocence of that victory over fascism, Alexander Solzhenitsyn was beginning to tread the paths of hell. On May 1, 1945, at the Lubyanka, the silence was deeper than ever. And then, on May 2, the prisoners of the Lubyanka heard a salvo of thirty cannon shots, "which meant that the Germans had just abandoned another European capital. Only two remained to be taken, Prague and Berlin; we had to guess which of the two it was," says Alexander Solzhenitsyn. But even if they had not guessed which it was on that day, the question was settled on May 9, by a new salvo of thirty shots: the other, Prague or Berlin, had just fallen. The last European capital had been taken by the Red Army. But, Solzhenitsyn adds, "it was not for us, that victory, not for us that spring."

And today, on May 1, 1979, you were thinking, as that

sudden snowstorm seemed to announce the freeing of Edward Kuznetsov, for whom is this spring? Today, as people are getting ready to celebrate the thirty-fifth anniversary of the Allied victory, of the end of Nazism, of the end of the German camps, what do the thousands of prisoners who remain in Brezhnev's Gulag camps think of this spring, after the freeing of Edward Kuznetsov?

And again you remembered the Jews from Czestochowa. You thought that we had to go on fighting for them.

"And Blum, did you meet him, too?" Daniel asks.

"Blume? No," I say. "I only went with Spoenay. Jean Blume stayed here, you must have seen him."

Daniel shook his head.

"Not Jean. Léon! Léon Blum, I mean."

I look at him, puzzled.

Since Meiners left the canteen, since Daniel's and my silent evocation of the Jews from Czestochowa, which took only a second, just enough time to look and turn away, we had both stayed in the back room of the *Arbeit*, chatting until the midday roll call.

Sunday morning is drawing to its end, all the same.

Sunday mornings don't last any longer than other mornings, but they seem interminable. Sunday mornings last for seven hours, like all other mornings. From about five o'clock, give or take a few minutes, depending on the duration of the morning roll call, to noon. At noon there's a break. It's the same every day, the same timetable. But Sunday morning seems longer than the others, perhaps because one is in a hurry to get to Sunday afternoon, to those few hours of free time. You are beginning to understand me at last.

However, this particular Sunday morning is coming to an end.

"Not Jean," Daniel has said. "Léon! Léon Blum, I mean."

I look at him; I don't understand at first.

I've just been telling him about my walk that morning, the incident with the SS officer near the big tree, the conversation with Hauptsturmführer Schwartz about Goethe's tree. I told him of my daydream about Goethe and Eckermann taking a walk. If I get out of here alive, I told Daniel, I'll write a book one day and call it *Conversations on the Ettersberg*. In it Goethe and Eckermann will talk, one December day in 1944, as they walk around the Buchenwald camp. And they will talk to all kinds of surprising people, you will see, I told him.

But why is he talking to me about Blum?

"Blum? What's Léon Blum got to do with this story?"

"Well," says Daniel calmly, "if it's true that he's a prisoner in a villa in the SS quarters, he's a good character for your book. Don't you like the idea of imagining what Blum and Goethe would say to each other?"

In August of that year 1944, after the bombing of the Buchenwald factories by the American air force, the rumor had spread among us that Léon Blum was being interned in an isolated villa behind the Falkenhof. French or Belgian deportees who had worked on repairing the damage caused by the phosphorus bombs had recognized him, it was said. It was even said that someone had spoken to him, through the bars of a window. There had been no confirmation of this rumor, but word had spread.

"Blum? Even if he is at the Falkenhof, I don't want him in my book!" I say.

"You've got to put him in," Daniel says, obstinately.

"I've got nothing to do with your Blum!"

But Daniel won't give in.

"To begin with, he's not my Blum," he says, quietly as ever. "Second, if the story of the Ettersberg amuses you, Blum is part of it. He's a character in your story, just as Goethe, Eckermann, and Napoleon are. Third, how can someone who wrote *Nouvelles Conversations de Goethe avec Eckermann* not turn up in your book? You pinch his idea of making Goethe immortal, then you don't want anything to do with him! You've got to put Blum in! It's the least you can do!''

He's right. I sit there, amazed.

I'd forgotten Blum's book, yet I had read it. We'd even talked about it, on the Boulevard de Port-Royal. And it was, no doubt, when all is said and done, the unconscious memory of that reading that had planted within me my literary daydream about Goethe on the Ettersberg, walking with his familiar, one day in December 1944.

No. 39 Boulevard de Port-Royal was where Lucien Herr* had lived, at the end of his life.

You entered the solid-looking middle-class apartment building at No. 39. You went through the porch, crossed a courtyard that was like any apartment-building courtyard. Beyond, when you had gone through the second building, you found yourself in a strange place: a green space, with trees and flower beds—at least when gardens were in flower—a piece of countryside in which a few chalets and small houses were scattered, apparently spared by the construction projects on the Boulevard Port-Royal.

One of those small houses belonged to Lucien Herr's family.

I used to go there often in 1941 and 1942. Straight-backed, dressed in black, tireless, her gray hair sticking up in untamable locks, Mme Lucien Herr brewed strange, aromatic herb teas for us. In the library on the ground floor, with its dark wood paneling, we would talk and talk. Mme Lucien Herr came and went, a tall figure, at once warm and distracted, lost, it seemed, in some

*French socialist publicist. —ED.

private dream. Sometimes she stayed with us, attentive, looking at those young men who surrounded her son Michel, constantly straightening her hair with a sudden movement of the hand, listening as we put the world to rights and settled its accounts with our philosophical consciences, watching how we threw Hegel in Kant's face, or vice versa. Sometimes, too, she intervened in our discussions, briefly, in a way that was at once precise and allegorical, disturbing at first sight, but always significant, with some reference to her husband, Lucien Herr, or to the men she had known around her husband, who had been his friends, or sometimes his disciples: the finest brains of French socialism.

On certain afternoons—and if it was spring, the gardens all around were filled with the cheepings of birds—on certain afternoons, then—and if it was autumn, the gardens splashed us with their abundant, ever-shifting light—on certain afternoons, anyway, in the middle of some very learned (and no doubt very impertinent: we were only about eighteen or twenty) discussion about Hegel, or the *Critique of the Gotha Program*, or Sextus Empiricus, or Korsch, or Kant, or Lukács, we sometimes heard the doorbell.

Mme Lucien Herr would go to the door and return accompanied by some man or woman, an unexpected visitor, always carrying a heavy, battered leather briefcase or a small, threadbare suitcase held together with string. Mme Lucien Herr would introduce us briefly: a friend of friends. The man or woman nodded, smiled at everybody, put the battered briefcase or threadbare suitcase beside his or her chair, within reach, and joined, quite naturally, in the tasting of incongruous but heavy-scented herb teas, and in the delectation of abstract ideas.

We asked no questions; we knew very well who these visitors were. The house of Mme Lucien Herr was an asylum, we knew. It was a family tradition. In September 1897, Lucien Herr had got on his bicycle—and it was the same one, or its younger sister, an antiquated piece of machinery in any case, that Madame Herr still used to do her shopping during the period I am talking about—and went off in search of Léon Blum, who spent his vacations in the country, near Paris. Herr said to Blum, point-blank, "Are you aware Dreyfus is innocent?" And Lucien Herr became the soul, the indomitable organizer, of the campaign for the truth in the Dreyfus affair. Today, half a century later, the house in which Lucien Herr had spent the last years of his life was still an asylum for the persecuted.

They were men or women whose papers, for one reason or another, were not in order, most of them foreigners, refugees from Central Europe, involved in underground work and often Communists. Those utopian fellow travelers, anonymous functionaries of the universal, came in, put their briefcases or suitcases beside their chairs, and tasted Mme Lucien Herr's surprising herb tea. They listened to us discussing the future of the world and the reformation of philosophy. And, after a brief attentive silence, they, too, took part in our discussions. They often had pertinent things to say about the future of the world and about the reformation of philosophy.

Thus, as the months passed, some of these nameless travelers had become familiar to us. Their tastes, their passions, their obsessions had sometimes sprung out into the open as they commented on some book or event. Fragments of their past, too: a Viennese landscape, a certain light over Prague, an evening in Bavaria, under the Republic of the Councils, exploded like feverish bubbles on the smooth surface of their underground lives.

And then, one day, Mme Lucien Herr would come into the library—perhaps it was in the evening, perhaps the lamps had been lit over our anxious readings—and she would announce to us in a toneless voice, putting her hair in order: So-and-so has been shot, or So-and-so has been arrested by the Gestapo.

We learned the real names of these travelers only at the last moment, as if they had rediscovered their identity, the roots of their uprooted being, only for this last journey. We sat motionless, looking at Michel's mother, trying to remember exactly what So-and-so had said, some time before, when he gave us a copy of Korsch's *Marxismus und Philosophie*. We looked at Michel's mother, her tall, fragile, yet indefatigable figure, and we remembered what So-and-so had told us about the extermination of the Polish Communist Party by Stalin. They were messages from beyond the grave, which spoke to us of a confused, bloody, sometimes sordid history, but one in which the utopia of the universal still functioned symbolically. Pitifully.

It was in 1941 or 1942, on the Boulevard de Port-Royal, in Lucien Herr's house.

And it was there, too, that I read Léon Blum's book, *Nouvelles Conversations de Goethe avec Eckermann*. It was a copy signed by the author, of course. I also think it was the last book in Lucien Herr's library that I read. After that, Michel Herr and I, having temporarily settled our accounts with our philosophical consciences, had thrown ourselves into underground work. Then there had been the night trains, the suitcases filled with weapons, the parachute drops, the *maquis* in the forest of Othe, the fine Smith and Wessons with their long barrels and thin coats of paint, those superb 11.43's, which we always carried with us, slipped into our belts between our legs, as an additional sign of our virility.

But I look at Daniel.

"You're right," I say. "I must put Blum into my book."

Six

Léon Blum walks over to the window. He parts the curtain.

Soon it will be noon. Any moment now, Joachim will be here, with the German and French newspapers.

Léon Blum parts the curtain and looks out.

It's a beautiful day, this Sunday morning. The very pale blue, almost transparent sky is like a piece of stained glass set in the black and white ribs of the forest.

Blum adjusts his spectacles, with a short, precise gesture.

There is hardly anything but sky, and treetops that offer a pleasant enough view. Otherwise, the horizon is blocked by the high fence around the villa, and the thick curtain of trees beyond that fence. There is hardly any other solution but to look up at the sky, when the sky is clear, as it is today. A very pale blue over all this snow in which are reflected the infinite subtleties of white—from the blue-tinted white of the patches of shade under the trees to the immaculate, blinding white, iridescent in the sunlight—and then there are the black branches of the tallest trees.

Those are all the colors of nature.

Léon Blum suddenly remembers another Sunday, long ago. The gentleness of the russet-tinged September spread over the countryside around Toulouse. It was 6:00 A.M. on Sunday, September 15, 1940, when police inspectors from the Vichy government arrived in great numbers and surrounded the country house L'Armurier. "At 6:00 A.M., the legal time, the police banged on the door. This respect for the legal time is quite marvelous," Léon Blum had thought. That same evening, he found himself confined in the Château Chazeron, in the Auvergne mountains, above Châtel-Guyon.

Since then, and until early April 1943, when he arrived at this villa lost in the middle of the forest of the Ettersberg, he will have known nothing but prisons, Chazeron, Bourrassol, the fortress at Portalet. "Prison was no doubt a gap in my experience of life. Any experience must benefit man. Let's try it." Léon Blum is looking down at the gloomy fence surrounding the villa on the Ettersberg. He remembers writing that sentence in the *Memoirs* that he had begun to write immediately after his arrest at L'Armurier.

Léon Blum is looking at the fence that blocks the horizon, reduces it to this enclosure constantly surveyed by guards making rounds. Here they are again, in fact. A sudden weakness overcomes him, his eyes mist over, he takes off his spectacles.

For some time now, the guards who regularly cross and recross the enclosure along the tall fence, holding German shepherds on leashes, have been Russian volunteers from Vlasov's army. Men who move quietly, rather heavily, like peasants, wearing long black greatcoats, walk around and around, tirelessly, holding their dogs on leashes. The dogs pull on the leashes, panting. The Russian soldiers, dressed in black, cross the visible space with their heavy peasant tread.

It seems to Léon Blum that the disturbing black outlines of Vlasov's Russians give still greater emphasis to the secret presence of death. When will it make itself known, that inexorable death? He had thought, in July of that same year, 1944, that the moment had come. The German French-language newspapers had announced the execution of Philippe Henriot* by a resistance group. Léon Blum had discussed it with Georges Mandel, while they were imprisoned together in that villa on the Ettersberg. They agreed that they would have to expect reprisals, "that victims would be offered by Darnand† and his militia to Henriot's shade." Which of them would it be? Léon Blum? Georges Mandel? Or both?

"The unfortunate Georges Mandel set off alone. We helped him get his luggage ready and nervously pack his blankets for the air journey that he was told he would take. We accompanied him to the gate in the barbed-wire fence that separated us from the rest of the world. He had no illusions as to the fate that awaited him, and the most attentive observer would not have detected the slightest alteration in the movements of his hands, in his walk, in his language, in the intonations of his voice. Never had we seen him so calm, so poised, so lucid. From our window we watched him leave in the car that was to take him to the airport, filled with the same sinister foreboding, and thinking that one day or another, soon perhaps, we would follow the same path."

Léon Blum wipes his glasses, which have misted over in this sudden burst of emotion.

Vlasov's Russians in their long black greatcoats have just disappeared from the visible space when he puts on

*Nazi propagandist for Radio Paris. —ED.
†Pro-Nazi founder of a military organization. —ED.

his spectacles again. Léon Blum looks at the very pale blue, almost transparent sky.

He looks at the sky for a long, long time.

In summer—he has already known two summers in this place—if one chose a certain angle of vision, one could perceive, through a gap in the trees, an open place nearby: a clearing in the forest. Léon Blum discovered this view quite by chance, but since discovering it, he often came, in summer—in autumn the view was blurred by the falling leaves and the glowing russet of the landscape; in winter, by the uniform whiteness that altered the volumes and contours, flattening them; it had to be the height of summer, when the trees were at their greenest, for that open space of the clearing to be glimpsed between them—he often came, in summer, feeling, strangely, that he was being indiscreet, as if he were observing some private scene through a keyhole in contemplating the tiny, luminous landscape of that clearing. He asked Janotte to share the joy of this vision, which yielded a soothing happiness like that provided by the contemplation of certain Renaissance paintings, depicting some Biblical or warlike scene, but in the depths of which the landscape inscribes the meticulous purity of a humanized nature.

Together, then, Janotte and he had often contemplated that clearing, so close but so far away.

Sometimes they thought they could see people there. One day, one could imagine a group of men and women sitting at the foot of a tree, around the bright patch of a white tablecloth spread on the grass as if for a picnic. Another day, a woman on horseback, sitting very upright in the saddle, motionless, her long fair hair falling over her shoulders, obviously keeping her horse reined in. The poignant charm of these visions—life outside—had imperceptibly driven Léon Blum to come, on certain summer afternoons, and give himself up to daydreams, stimulated by the shapes he saw there, but conquered by his own imagination, before that window that opened, it seemed, not only on the mysterious clearing, but also on the depths of his own inner life. So, inscribing the figures of his imagination on that luminous screen cut out of the leafy verdure of the forest, Léon Blum had sometimes amused himself by dreaming of the appearance of Goethe and Eckermann in the distant clearing. By thus making a link with one of the literary fantasies of his youth, he made a link, nostalgically, with that youth itself.

On the road that led to the barracks of the SS, Goethe suddenly ordered the sleigh to stop. The coachman, surprised, pulled so strongly on the reins while applying the brake that the back of the sleigh skidded into the soft snow of the roadside, raising a powdery, iridescent foam.

"Excuse me," Goethe said to the coachman, who had turned toward us, with the politeness which it was his custom to employ with inferiors, "excuse me, my good fellow! But we are going to get down and continue on foot. Please come back in an hour and wait for us on the grand avenue."

The coachman nodded.

"Very well, Excellency, in an hour, on the Avenue of Eagles."

So we got down from the coach.

I was intrigued, wondering what sudden inspiration had driven Goethe to this change of program. But I was not to be left in the dark for long.

"Do you know the Falkenhof, my dear Eckermann?" he asked me, as soon as we had set foot on the compacted snow of the path.

I admitted my ignorance.

"I have never visited it myself," Goethe continued. "But a Bavarian officer of the *Totenkopf* who some time ago loaned me his diary of the Russian campaign described it for me in great detail. We shall go and see it!"

As he spoke, Goethe moved toward a clearing in the forest where a few small wooden houses could be seen. Hunting lodges, to judge by their architecture.

As we walked, I learned—and I could not prevent myself from admiring the fine bearing of my master and friend, in his long gray greatcoat with its officer's collar— that the Falkenhof had been built on the express instructions of SS-Reichsführer Himmler, to house falcons, eagles, and other birds of prey trained for the very Teutonic practice of hunting, exercise, and pleasure that not so long ago gathered together, here, around this falconry, the élite of the officers of the army and the SS.

The houses, which we examined in detail, were magnificently built of oak trunks of the finest quality. The central building comprised a large hall in the Gothic style, with antique furniture of great beauty, and an enormous fireplace. A little farther on, we walked by the installations of a small zoological garden, where there were deer and does, elks and wild boar, wild sheep, foxes, and pheasants. There were also, in the perfectly arranged cages, four brown bears and five monkeys of a fairly rare species.

"You will have noticed," Goethe said to me after the visit, "the excellent condition of all those animals. One can see at a glance that they are well fed and cared for. It was precisely this that I wanted to check, for this fact, it seems to me, reveals a specifically German characteristic. Indeed, I was told that all those animals are given top-quality meat every day. Moreover, the bears eat honey and jam. The monkeys, cakes and porridge, oats with milk. At a difficult time like ours, this respect for animal life, for the requirements of nature, seems to me to be specifically German. The French would have eaten those animals, of course, as soon as food became short. The English would probably have done the same, knowing full well, however, that this would unleash a fierce press campaign, with masses of letters arriving by mail at *The Times* protesting this massacre. There might even have been questions in the Commons. That's typical of the English system: a democracy *post festum*. As far as we are concerned, this characteristic—which certain individuals will not fail to attribute to what they call 'German excess'—seems to me, on the contrary, inherent in a view of the world in which harmony between man and nature plays a determining role."

We had left the Falkenhof.

I was reflecting on the insight revealed in these words, spoken with such simplicity, promising myself that I would note them down faithfully as soon as we were back in Weimar, when Goethe grabbed my arm, an unusual gesture on his part, even at moments of great emotion. He suddenly spoke to me in a low voice, almost whispering in my ear, but with a strangely nervous edge to it:

"I would like to tell you something in confidence," he said, "for the sincerity of our conversations, my dear Eckermann, is more important to me than anything."

I stood stock still, rooted to the ground by the solemnity of Goethe's intonation.

"Yes," he added, "the real reason for my curiosity about the Falkenhof is something quite different. You can imagine that I was not going to put myself out in such weather just to see a few eagles in a cage! I am told—but I am under an obligation to remain silent, even to you, my dear friend, as to the source of this information; don't be too hard on me, it's a state secret—I am told that one of the houses on the Falkenhof has been equipped to take in prisoners of the highest rank and that at this very moment there are a number of French politicians and an Italian princess of the blood royal there. That is what I wanted to check, Eckermann!"

I was dumfounded.

With a gentle, irresistible squeeze of my arm, Goethe got me to resume my interrupted walk. I then remembered that one of the houses in the Falkenhof, situated a little to one side, was surrounded by railings, which made it inaccessible. I also remembered that Goethe had looked at it attentively for some time, and I now knew why.

"And do you know, Excellency," I asked him, without being able to control my excitement, "which French politicians are being held there?"

Goethe nodded.

"There are several of them," he replied, "but the one that interests me above all, you will easily understand why, is the former Prime Minister, Monsieur Léon Blum!"

Again I stood stock still.

It was incredible: Blum at the Falkenhof! Of course I now understood why Goethe had been so nervous, so agitated that morning. Had not Léon Blum written the *Nouvelles Conversations de Goethe avec Eckermann*? When the book appeared, anonymously at first in 1901, published in the *Revue Blanche*, Goethe had been particularly struck, not only by the quality of the style, which revealed, he said, a true writer, but also by the content of certain of the reflections, which, though improperly attributed to my master, revealed a perfect knowledge of his work and a most unusual subtlety of analysis. I would like to point out that it is Goethe's opinion that I am conveying here, in a spirit of fidelity. I myself was much less indulgent toward this enterprise of literary piracy. Thus, some years later, when the name of the author became known, I asked Goethe for permission to bring an action in the courts for plagiary of title and undue appropriation of literary material. Were not the conversa-

tions with Goethe my domain, my specialty, my preroga-
tive? Should I not protect my rights?

The legal action, however, was never pursued, for
Goethe kept dissuading me from it. I would even go so far
as to say that he prevented me from doing it. By that
point, it is true, the news of his death had been widespread for so long that the public could not now be
disabused. Goethe had done nothing to deny it, or to
challenge the touching legend that surrounded his last
moments of life, believing that his creative work might
continue more easily in the dazzling shadow of that
apocryphal death, which, with every year, enhances the
prestige, now of mythical proportions, of the Goethean
figure. Thus, despite my irritation, Goethe had refused, at
the beginning of this century, to embroil himself in the
petty annoyances of the civil service that both the trial for
usurpation of literary property and the return to public
life would have entailed. He enjoyed the irony of this
situation, and I could only respect his attitude, despite
the anger aroused in me by all these literary parasites who
dress themselves in borrowed robes and try to aggrandize
themselves at the expense of the real grandeur of my
master. So we abandoned any attempt to silence Léon
Blum, whose good faith, according to Goethe, was not in
question. Personally, I was not so sure. After all, wasn't
Blum a Jew? One knows only too well the underhanded,
cunning mentality of that race.

It wasn't until much later, on April 30, 1932, when Paul
Valéry delivered his celebrated "Discours en l'honneur de
Goethe" in the Sorbonne, on the occasion of the centenary of the presumed death of my master, that the great man
decided to break his silence. He wrote his extraordinarily
moving "Discours d'outre-tombe," address from beyond
the grave. But times had changed. When this text was
finished, radiating—I can confirm, I who am to this day

its only reader—all the wisdom that the Goethean synthesis of the classical spirit and Faustian demonism can produce, Herr Adolf Hitler had just had his investiture as chancellor confirmed by the Reichstag. Goethe had decided to adopt toward the new regime an attitude of understanding neutrality, an attitude quite consistent with the conduct of his whole life, when all is said and done. But a writer so close to Goethean thought as Thomas Mann soon broke with the new revolutionary regime and chose exile. This profoundly disturbed my revered master and friend, all the more so as the philosopher Martin Heidegger, on the other hand, so far removed from Goethean humanism, and whose persistence in speaking of Hölderlin to the detriment of my master's work had not failed to irritate Goethe—Heidegger, then, adopted an attitude of sympathetic understanding toward National Socialism.

In the circumstances, Goethe wondered whether the French intellectuals, to whom the "Discours d'outre-tombe" had been particularly addressed, would not question the authenticity of his text, whether they would not go so far as to believe that the news of the resurrection of my master was merely a propaganda maneuver on the part of Dr. Goebbels. This possibility deeply worried Goethe, who decided in the end not to publish his "Discours" and to remain in the anonymity of a presumed death. While inclining to his wishes, I did not approve of his decision, for I was aware of the effect such a publication might have had in Europe, despite the misunderstandings and blindnesses of partisan passions.

But I was drawn into this whirlwind of memories by the pressure of Goethe's hand on my arm, urging me once again to walk.

"Excellency!" I exclaimed, looking at him, without knowing how to express the contrary feelings that swarmed in my mind.

Goethe nodded.

"You now understand, my dear Eckermann," he said, "both my curiosity and the excitement I felt this morning. Monsieur Blum at the Falkenhof! What an opportunity to elucidate, man to man, the problems raised by his interpretation of my thought! And yet I fear that this opportunity will be missed. All the efforts that I have made so far, in confidential representations to highly placed acquaintances, have, I do assure you, been in vain. It seems that I shall not, after all, get permission to visit Léon Blum!"

We were walking slowly along the paths of that snow-covered forest of the Ettersberg. Goethe gripped my arm affectionately.

"I regret it for you, too, my dear friend," he said. "A book by Eckermann, *Goethe's Conversations with Léon Blum*, would not fail to have a certain influence over postwar Europe, while at the same time enjoying an assured and well-deserved success in the bookshops!"

We were walking slowly, and I seemed to be living through one of those privileged moments when Goethe's thought reached the summit of its power of penetration and expression.

"In fact, my good friend," Goethe added, "the theme that I would have liked to discuss with Monsieur Blum is that of the relations between the intellectual, as one says nowadays, and politics. You know my ideas on that subject. I believe that the intellectual cannot be uninterested in politics, in men of power, that he should give these men the benefit of his advice and thought—on condition, however, that he refrain from the direct exercise of power. For intelligence and power are essentially different things. That is why true intellectuals invariably fail when they allow themselves to be perverted to the extent of accepting the direct exercise of power. When they do so, either they try to organize the contradictions of social reality in terms of their own intellectual vision, which is essentially evolutive and comprehensive—in which case the power of reality and the reality of power exhaust them, reject them, and condemn them—or, on the contrary, they bend themselves to the contradictions of reality, to the tactical requirements of the present; they glorify them, deify them under the charismatic species of Virtue, Utopia, or the motive forces of History, as you wish, and then the intellectuals become the theoreticians of despotism, of absolute, arbitrary power, which in the end devours them. Monsieur Blum belongs to the first category, of course, and his experience, on which he must have reflected at the Falkenhof, would no doubt have been of great value to me. I would very much like to have discussed these matters with the former Prime Minister, but, alas, I despair of getting permission to see him."

As we walked, we had left the forest paths and now found ourselves on the esplanade in front of the gates of the re-education camp built on the north side of the Ettersberg some years before. Goethe looked at the gates, in the center of which was an inscription in wrought iron, perfectly legible from where we stood: *Jedem das Seine*.

He nodded, sadly.

"Did you know," he said, "that the tree in whose shade we were so fond of resting is still inside the camp? That, again, is a typically German gesture, and one that I appreciate! Despite the terrible demands of war, that tree—which the officers and soldiers of this garrison continue to call 'Goethe's tree,' which, no doubt, will not fail to raise the spirits of the wretches imprisoned here for various reasons—that tree has not been cut down. It was still standing proud and majestic, somewhere between the kitchens and clothing stores, some months ago. Yes, I appreciate that gesture of respect toward the memory of our history. Even in 1937, when the construction of this

re-education camp was begun, I was profoundly touched
by the representations made by the National Socialist
Cultural Association of Weimar, demanding that the
camp should not bear the name K. L. Ettersberg, out of
respect for the imperishable links between that place and
my life and work. I can tell you, Eckermann, I was
profoundly touched at the time by those representations
and by the decision finally made—in the highest places, I
understand from a reliable source—to call this camp K. L.
Buchenwald!"

I thought I could detect the damp brightness of a tear in
Goethe's eye at that moment, and I turned away, trembling with emotion myself.

But Goethe went on at once.

"Who knows?" he said. "Perhaps these unfortunate
individuals, this mixture of nationalities of all kinds, will
contribute to forging a common soul for Europe. Many are
the cunning byways of history, as you are well aware, my
dear Eckermann!"

Then Goethe took me again by the arm and guided me a
few steps toward the camp gate.

"You see that inscription?" he asked. *Jedem das Seine.* I
don't know who wrote it, or who decided to put it up. But
I find it most significant and most encouraging that such
an inscription should decorate the gates of a place where
freedom has been withdrawn, a place of re-education
through forced labor. For, after all, what does it mean, "to
each his due"? Is it not an excellent motto for a society
organized to defend the freedom of all, of the whole of
society, to the detriment, if necessary, of an excessive,
harmful individual freedom? I already told you, over a
century ago, and you noted it down in your *Conversations,* under Monday, July the ninth, 1827. Do you remember? We were talking about the political situation in
France, about the new press law, with the Chancellor—

Herr Chancellor Meyer, of course, not Herr Hitler, for we've known a number of chancellors, haven't we? I was saying to you that day: 'The law restraining the press can have only a beneficial effect, especially as its limitations concern nothing essential, but are only against personalities. An opposition which has no bounds is a flat affair, while limits sharpen its wits and this is a great advantage. This necessity exites my mind and for the same reason, as I have said, I like some restraint upon the press.' "

Goethe had said all that without pausing, and I couldn't help admiring his memory: I was quite sure that it was, indeed, to be found, word for word, in my *Conversations*. The cunning look in his eye proved to me that he himself was equally sure.

"I'm struck, Excellency," I said to Goethe, "by the continuity and firmness of your thoughts on this matter. But I think, if you'll allow me, in turn to offer you proof of the excellence of my memory—stimulated, no doubt, by the nobility of your words—I think the most precise and pertinent formulation of your conception of liberty was made on Thursday, January the eighteenth, 1827, as I noted it in my *Conversations*: 'Freedom is an odd thing!' you said to me on that day. 'And every man has enough of it, if he can only satisfy himself. What avails a superfluity of freedom which we cannot use? If a man has freedom enough to live healthy, and work at his craft, he has enough; and so much all can easily obtain. Then all of us are only free under certain conditions, which we must fulfil. The citizen is as free as the nobleman, when he restrains himself within the limits which God appointed by placing him in that rank. The nobleman is as free as the prince; for, if he will but observe a few ceremonies at court, he may feel himself his equal. Freedom consists not in refusing to recognize anything above us, but in respecting something which is above us; for by respecting it, we raise ourselves to it, and by our very acknowledgement, make manifest that we bear within ourselves what is higher, and are worthy to be on a level with it.' "

Goethe had listened to this reminder of his own thought, nodding with visible satisfaction.

"You see, my good fellow," he said. "I'd quite forgotten those remarks. But I still hold to them, and that is why I cannot help thinking, whoever the author of that inscription *Jedem das Seine* over the gates of the re-education camp may be, I cannot help thinking that I had something to do with it, that the breath of my inspiration is to be found in it. To each his due, indeed, to each the place that is due to him, through birth or talent, in the hierarchy of individual freedom and constraints that make up the liberty of us all."

As we talked, we had turned our backs on the camp gates and were walking again in the forest paths, toward that clearing of the Falkenhof, which seemed to obsess Goethe's thoughts on that day and irresistibly draw his steps.

But Léon Blum lets the curtain fall, gives up dreaming about that clearing peopled with apparitions.

He comes back to his desk.

He puts aside Emile Faguet's book, which he has been reading the last few days, and in which he has just annotated a passage before going over to the window. Actually, it isn't a passage by Emile Faguet that he has just annotated, but an extract from Plato's *Laws*, which Faguet quoted in his essay, and which he pretended not to understand, whereas, for Blum, Plato's text was of luminous precision. Léon Blum puts aside Faguet's book and begins looking among his papers for a note he wrote some months ago which he would like to pick up again and develop. He finds it easily enough; his papers are always in order.

On April 22, 1943, some days after his arrival in this villa on the Ettersberg, Léon Blum had jotted down an idea that had come to him for a work on liberty. "My starting point is that the idea of liberty, in the political sense, is as complex a reality as the concept of freedom in the philosophical sense," he had written. "When one examines the philosophical concept of freedom," Blum added, "one is led to break it down, or, rather, to rearrange it in layers, for there is a pragmatic, psychological conception of freedom, which crowns a moral conception, itself surmounted by a metaphysical conception, that of Kant, Schopenhauer, and, closer to our own time, of Bergson. What I find tempting is to discover whether the same does not go for political liberty."

But it is not this question, on which his reflection has so much matured of late, that interests Léon Blum today. He has remembered a note concerning the form to be given to his work. He finds it, at the end of the page that he has just reread: "The subject is so vast that, simply to indicate its developments, and to anticipate all kinds of ambiguities, one would need the sinuous flexibility and variety of the Platonic dialogue."

A Platonic dialogue; that was it.

Standing in the middle of the room with that page from April 22, 1943, in hand, Léon Blum wonders whether, in line with his first inspiration, the best form to give this essay on liberty for which he is constantly taking notes may not be that of a dialogue. Just now, looking out at the December sky of so pale a blue, over all the whiteness of the forest, remembering the apparitions of Goethe and Eckermann in the clearing, Léon Blum told himself that it might be enough to give these dialogues the form of a sequel to the *Nouvelles Conversations*. But that seemed a bit too facile, when he thought about it.

To confront this problem of freedom in all its depth and complexity, what one needs is a true dialogue, that is, a plural, multivocal discourse, a dialectical confrontation. Now, Eckermann is not the man for this kind of discourse. He is, when all is said and done, too gray, too dull, too preoccupied also with not losing a single crumb of his master's reflections in order to transcribe them faithfully, to serve as the vehicle of a true supersession of the structure of the alternate monologue that belongs as much to Eckermann's *Conversations* as to his own *Nouvelles Conversations*.

No, a true Platonic dialogue, that's what's needed. So, to begin with, one would have to increase the number of participants in those *Conversations on the Ettersberg*, enlarge the circle. He himself, for example, ought to take part in it, expounding his own ideas, without having to use the trick of an imaginary Goethe and a hypothetical Eckermann. "I could myself intervene as a third person," Léon Blum thinks. "Four years of prison qualify me to speak of freedom in the political sense as well as the metaphysical!"

Léon Blum smiles.

He's still standing in the middle of the room, holding the page that he wrote over a year before. He wonders what other characters he might summon to this new version of the *Conversations*. Of course, it would be amusing to summon living characters in imagination. Paul Valéry, for instance. Not only because, on April 30, 1932, at the Sorbonne, he delivered a famous speech to commemorate the centenary of Goethe's death, or even because Valéry strove so hard, throughout his life, to be regarded as a thinker that it would perhaps be only fair to give him an opportunity to prove it; but above all because his aphoristic style of intellectual reflection accords perfectly with the form of the Platonic dialogue.

But it's not possible, Léon Blum thinks, to include living people in this book. Neither Valéry nor even the Spanish philosopher Ortega y Gasset, a distinguished Germanist, the author of several remarkable articles on Goethe, and especially an essay, *The Revolt of the Masses*, among other thought-provoking historical works, an excellent contributor to any debate on the question of freedom in the twentieth century. But no, no living people. Publication of such a book would lead to too many disagreements, polemics, corrigenda, feuds between clans and coteries. "I must resign myself to including in this new version of the *Conversations* only individuals who have disappeared from the stage of history. It would be a dialogue of the dead, a dialogue in Hades, or in the Elysian Fields, or in Plato's cave. Why not? That, after all, is what it's really about. Am I myself not, in a sense, dead?" thinks Blum. "Have I not already one foot in the grave? Am I not wraithlike enough to mingle among the illustrious shades that I am trying to raise?"

An idea suddenly occurs to him.

He would have to put Herr, Lucien Herr, in these *Conversations on the Ettersberg*. But of course; why didn't he think of it before? It's obvious! Herr, the author of an admirable preface to the correspondence between Goethe and Schiller, Lucien Herr, the best specialist on Hegel's philosophy in France, the irreplaceable maieutician of the Rue d'Ulm! A strange intellectual excitement comes over Léon Blum, an excitement so vivid that it becomes physically perceptible, like an exaltation of the senses, a visceral heat, when he imagines Lucien Herr taking part in these *Conversations*.

They are not just a daydream, these *Conversations*: they are a project.

Léon Blum goes back to his desk and sits down.

That morning he read a passage from Plato quoted by Emile Faguet in his essay *Pour qu'on lise Platon*. A passage from the *Laws*, which Faguet pretended not to understand, in which he claimed to see nothing but obscurity.

Léon Blum rereads the notes he wrote that morning.

"It is neither obscure, nor contradictory, whatever Faguet says. Rather than obscurity, I see in it a sort of flashing of light (the cause of which I believe I can discern, and will note down in due course). Plato distinguishes between two very different notions of equality. On the one hand, equality-equivalence, the equality that is expressed in arithmetical identity, and which consists in *weight, number,* and *measurement*. In this first sense, equality ignores, denies, or tends to eliminate the diversity, the variety, of individuals, that is to say, natural inequalities; it subjects them all, for good or for ill, to the same rules of measurement, number, and weight. On the other hand, equality-equity, which accepts the human 'raw material' as it is, which recognizes as a premise the diversity, variety, and consequently intrinsic inequality of the human givens, and which is expressed, not in numerical uniformity, but in the maintenance of a just proportion between the unequal human givens. It is this intrinsic inequality that gives more to the great, and less to the lesser. Justice, Plato concludes, is simply the equality established between unequal things, in accordance with their nature. And this definition seems to me to be admirable. Justice and equality consist in maintaining due proportion between nature and society and, consequently, in tolerating in society other inequalities than those that are the expression of natural inequalities. Nothing could be clearer than that! I often came close to that same idea, first in Eckermann"—Here we are again!

thinks Blum, interrupting his reading for a moment, this
theme of the *Conversations* is certainly getting obsessive!
—"a long time afterward in *Pour être socialiste*. I have
always considered that equality was the scrupulous respect of variety and, consequently, of natural inequality.
The formulas of equality, consequently, are, not THE SAME
STANDARD FOR ALL, but EACH HAS HIS PLACE and TO EACH
HIS DUE."

Léon Blum has finished rereading the thoughts he
jotted down that Sunday morning.

He picks up his pen.

"This concept of equality is fully revolutionary," he
begins to write.

But at that very moment, snatches of distant music
reach him through the trees. Snatches of lively music.
Léon Blum interrupts his work again, suddenly nervous.
He throws down his pen, gets up, walks over to the
window, which he opens slightly.

Yes, music, in martial snatches, in the distance. Military music, circus music, polyphonic, with a lot of brass
and drums.

Léon Blum listens to this pom-pomming with anxious
curiosity.

Until August 1944—for over a year, that is—Léon
Blum had no definite idea as to where he was being kept
prisoner. He knew that this villa, isolated from the
outside world, was situated somewhere in the forest of
the Ettersberg. But he did not know that there was a
concentration camp nearby. He himself was to say, later,
after his return from Buchenwald: "It was also the strict-
ness of that confinement that explains a fact incompre-
hensible at first sight, I mean our ignorance for so long of
the unspeakable horrors that were being perpetrated a
few hundred meters away. The first clue was the strange
smell that often reached us in the evening through the

open windows, and which obsessed us throughout the night when the wind continued to blow in the same direction: it was the smell from the crematorium ovens."

The smell in the evening, above all in the spring and the summer, reached the prisoners of the villa of the Falkenhof through the open windows. A strange, insipid smell, vaguely sickening, sweetly nauseous and unidentified at the moment by Blum and his companions in detention, yet disturbing, carried by the wind over the forest of the Ettersberg. A smell that had become for us, who knew what it meant, familiar during the months and years. A smell that no longer made us turn our heads, a smell we were used to, as one got used to the promiscuity of the latrines, the piling up in the bunks—five or six deportees, depending on the huts, in a space hardly sufficient for two—to the yelling of the kapos, to reveille at four in the morning, to permanent hunger and fatigue, which nothing could appease for long—we never caught up with our hunger or lack of sleep; to the interminable roll calls on evenings of collective victimization, to the impossibility of a moment of solitude; just as one gets used to the deaths of one's pals, who go up in smoke, thus causing that strange and familiar smell that mingles, in the memories of those who still have occasion to remember it, with the bitter smell of the makhorka and that of the shit in the latrines of the Little Camp, to make up that strange and familiar smell of death at Buchenwald, revived in the spring and summer, and penetrating like an obscure message through the open windows of Blum's villa on the Falkenhof, through the open windows for miles around: those of the Thuringian farmhouses, those of the country residences of the burghers of Weimar, those of the churches and chapels of every Christian denomination, in which one would pray to God on Sundays in the obsessive smell from the crematorium.

But Léon Blum is by the window. He is listening to the pom-pomming of the military music, the only clue, besides that strange smell carried on the wind, of the disturbing reality of the world around him.

However, that music and that smell were contradictory clues. The martial music was gay, full of life, while the strange, insipid, penetrating smell suggested something quite different, other realities. Often, at the beginning of his confinement at the Falkenhof, or at midday on certain Sundays, Léon Blum had tried, near the open window at night in the anxiety aroused by these distant signs, these obscure messages, to pierce the mystery of that insipid smell, of that apparently lively music.

Later, after the bombing of the factories and barracks at Buchenwald by the American airforce, on August 24, 1944, part of that mystery had been cleared up. Deportees had been given the urgent task of repairing the *Totenkopf* barracks inside the camp itself. Léon Blum had caught glimpses of them moving around the barbed-wire fence outside. Some of them had even got into the enclosure itself, and had been able to exchange, despite the surveillance of the SS, a few quick words with Belgian and French prisoners in the house. That was how the first news of the existence of the camp had reached him.

By the half-open window, today, on this December Sunday, Léon Blum listens anxiously to the distant pom-pomming of the military marches. Shuddering, he shuts the window. He goes back to his desk. He takes up again the abandoned sentence, he takes up again his thoughts on Plato's view of equality, on the formulation of that equality as TO EACH HIS DUE.

In German one would have said *Jedem das Seine*.

That is exactly the formula that is written, in wrought-iron letters, on the monumental gates of Buchenwald. It is true that Léon Blum did not see those gates. He does not, like Goethe, enjoy the privilege of immortality, or the gift of ubiquity. It is also true that he might not have understood that inscription even if he had seen it, for he doesn't speak German. Léon Blum has never had a gift for foreign languages. He said so himself: it's rather curious for a Jew.

A Jew; an exceptional prisoner at the Falkenhof!

I couldn't get that idea out of my head as I walked beside Goethe.

We had turned away from the great gates of the corrective-labor camp and were walking slowly on the great avenue bordered with columns crowned by imperial Teutonic eagles. It was still quite cold, but the sun was shining in an utterly clear, translucent blue sky, against which, on our left, stood out the light, pale-gray smoke from the chimney.

"Do you think, Eckermann," my master and friend suddenly said, "that a politician like Prime Minister Léon Blum could still play a role in postwar Europe?"

"I was just asking myself the same question, Excellency," I said, "though I have not come up with an answer."

Goethe gave me an affectionate, cunning smile.

"I think I have already told you, my dear Eckermann, what conditions are required to make an epoch in the world!"

"Yes, Excellency!" I replied. "You expressed your opinion on this matter on May the second, 1824, a Sunday, like today."

"In 1824? That's such a long time ago. What did I say on that day, my good friend?"

"You said, Excellency: 'To make an epoch in the world, two conditions are notoriously essential—a good head, and a great inheritance. Napoleon inherited the French Revolution; Frederick the Great, the Silesian War; Luther, the obscurantism of the clergy.'"

"That's enough, Eckermann, that's enough!" said Goethe, interrupting with a gesture my reminiscence of his thoughts from long ago. "No one can deny that Monsieur Blum has a good head, even if he has fallen into the snares of exercising power. But what is his inheritance? The social achievements of his government in 1936? That isn't an inheritance that he and his friends can claim for themselves alone. It's a legacy from French society as a whole, and that society will finally incorporate those reforms into its inheritance, whatever the political system to come or the future balance of power in the Parliament. Paid vacations are hardly something to make an epoch in the world, my good fellow! Given that, what might be Monsieur Blum's inheritance? Socialist humanism? That isn't a great inheritance, either; or, rather, yes, it is a great inheritance, but its putative heirs are so numerous, and would wish to take advantage of it for such discordant ends, that none of them will be able to make it really fruitful. Socialist humanism is a little like Monsieur Descartes's good sense: the thing in the world that is most widely distributed. Things that are too widely distributed lack internal dynamism, my dear Eckermann. Have you ever seen a people of smallholders making an epoch in the world, overthrowing the order of states and empires? It's unthinkable! No, Monsieur Blum has a good head and I expect much from his reflections on history over these last few years, about which he has no doubt thought a good deal during his retreat at the Falkenhof; but he has no great inheritance, he will not make an epoch in the postwar world!"

Goethe fell silent and I did not try to urge him ahead. I knew well enough that he would continue in his own good time.

"You see," he went on, as expected, after a few minutes' meditative silence, "the great inheritance of the postwar period to come is nationalism. It is easy to see that we have not yet emerged from the period inaugurated by the French Revolution, by the Jacobin view of "Nation and Politics." Of course, it is easy enough for me, who lived through that period of the revolution and its aftermath, to understand this essential fact. It's no small matter, living through almost two centuries of the world's history! It's nothing I can take credit for, of course, it's a gift from heaven, but I'm free to benefit from it. That's an aspect that Paul Valéry was able to detect in his 'Discours en l'honneur de Goethe,' in which his perspicacity on a number of points must be recognized. Monsieur Valéry said, you will remember: 'What I find more striking than anything else about Goethe is his very long life'—and he had no idea how long!—and he added later: 'the period of time that went into the making of Goethe was filled with events of the first magnitude, and during his prolonged presence in the world, it offered for his contemplation, his meditation, his acceptance, and sometimes for his rejection, a great number of important happenings, among them a general catastrophe, the end of an age, and the beginning of another.' Well, this age whose beginnings I witnessed, and which the French Revolution inaugurated, is the age of nationalism. I know very well to what extent this statement is paradoxical. To all appearances, at least. Is not the period that we have just lived through, to all appearances, the period of the Internationals? We have known four. The first, however, died its beautiful death with neither flowers nor crowns. The second did not resist the confrontation of the nations during the world war of 1914–18. The third was dissolved, because it was no longer anything more than a fiction, an embarrassment to the national policies of Russia, by Marshal Stalin himself, hardly a year ago. And the fourth has been nothing but the romantic adventure of

that great writer led astray into politics—another one!—
Herr Trotsky. So, the age of the Internationals has not yet
come! It must be recognized that the idea to be found at
the source of this inspiration is simple and strong. I
would even say that it has the breadth of the great
self-evident truths, but history has proved over and over
again that strong ideas, the great self-evident truths,
always emerge prematurely, in the shining form of utopias. I don't know what will become of the utopian
thought of Dr. Marx—another German! we are to be found
everywhere, Eckermann, and it is this that allows us to
face the future with confidence!—but it is significant that
as soon as his disciples and sectaries have tried to apply
Dr. Marx's theory to the concrete, complicated realities of
history, it has always come up against the national
question (the peasant question, too, but that is a particular aspect of the national question). In fact, what is the
revolution of the Soviets? Nothing more than a confused,
violent parenthesis, after which the history of nations
will resume its course. What are we faced with today, on
the plains of the East? The army of the Soviets or that of
Russia? But there is no room for hesitation, my good
friend! The army of the Soviets was defeated, dispersed at
the first whiff of war. Indeed, Marshal Stalin himself gave
a helping hand to it, with his great purges of officers,
before Chancellor Hitler finished the job. What now rises
before us is the ghost of Suvorov, who is subjecting our
armies to the fate meted out to Napoleon's! Remember,
Eckermann, with what calm, what detachment of spirit—
I was working at the time on a new version of my *Theory
of Colors*—I witnessed all the ups and downs of the
ephemeral Republics of the Councils in Saxony and
Bavaria, in the 1920s. Others were terrified, thinking that
it was already the end of our civilization. They were
wrong! The great problem of the time, despite the cries of

the ideologues, was not the international organization of the Councils, but the German nation, humiliated, dismantled, disoriented by defeat. It was the German nation that imposed its solutions, and both attempts—those of the victors of Versailles and of the Bolshevik revolutionaries —on the German nation came to nothing. It is to this certainty that I would attribute my detachment from the age. You have to admit that I was not wrong, Eckermann. Today, we see that the Bolsheviks are the first to brandish the national flag, to try to monopolize the spirit of patriotism! Not only has Marshal Stalin dissolved the Third International of his own accord, but—and consider this, my dear friend, as a prediction—will not Communism have marked this age only insofar as it will have served the affirmation of nationhood? Communism is surviving only because it has turned its back on the idea of the universal Republic of the Soviets. Thanks in particular to the realism of Marshal Stalin, it has become a crystallizing element around which the old nations of Russia have grouped themselves and the new nations, hitherto subjected or colonized, will unfailingly group themselves. It is a paradox, is it not, that Communism is playing a historical role only insofar as it is abandoning its original, revolutionary aspirations and taking up the cause of the nation, the cause of a new Jacobin bourgeoisie! History is full of similar paradoxes, it's true. And it's also true, or at least probable, that it's the idea of the nation that will split open the Communist empire, which is essentially multinational!''

I had listened to Goethe's words astonished by the whirlwind of powerful ideas and rich thoughts that they conveyed to me. I remained silent when he paused in his discourse, trying to engrave on my memory everything that he had just said. Once again, I blessed the fate that had sent me as a companion so great a man!

"No, my dear friend," Goethe added, seeing that I was

waiting impatiently for the rest of his thoughts, "Dr. Marx's most powerful insight, his true inspiration, which his sectaries have been forced to betray in order to ensure the survival of their own power, is not to be found on the side of the nation. On that side, the Bolsheviks not only remain in the thrall of the Jacobin tradition, which is by definition bourgeois, but they also allow themselves to be pulled along by their adversaries, whatever temporary successes their present enthusiasm for national independence and greatness may bring them. The nation is not the affair of the workers, that is obvious. Dr. Marx's thought strove to draw from this evident truth positive consequences. Personally I see it only as proof of objective—and no doubt also cultural—limitations, which will prevent for some time to come the lower classes' playing a determining historical role. Dr. Marx's powerful insight was the critique of civil society and its anatomy, political economy. He was inspired in this research by the work undertaken by my old friend Professor G. W. F. Hegel. But, unfortunately, he was also inspired by the professor's dialectics. Remind me, my dear Eckermann, to complete that project, so long postponed, of a short essay that I have been thinking of writing for years now on the misdeeds of the dialectic. . . ."

But we were suddenly interrupted by an outburst of martial music, which announced, as we knew, the Sunday break granted to all the internees who benefited from the strict but just living conditions of the corrective-labor camp, toward whose gates we were now walking again, and whose motto, *Jedem das Seine*, had so moved Goethe a little while before.

Here is Fernand Barizon.

At the precise moment when Léon Blum returned to his work, rereading the sentence that he had just written when the pom-pomming of distant music interrupted him, "This concept of equality is fully revolutionary"; at the moment when Goethe and Eckermann, having emerged from the nebulous imagination of the Narrator, are vanishing once more, making room for the all-too-real cohorts of outside kommandos returning to the electrified barbed-wire boundary of the camp itself; at that moment, at noon, when the music of the *Lagerkapelle*, the camp orchestra, is displaying all the pomp and circumstance of its sounding brass and gleaming uniforms at the gates; at noon, when the returning columns move with rhythmic step along the Avenue of Eagles, toward that inscription, *Jedem das Seine*, which awaits them at the camp gates, and which no one notices any more, since it expresses only the banal equality before death that is their most probable destiny, and which no longer surprises anyone, here is Fernand Barizon.

He arrives with the tightly packed column from the Gustloff Works, with rhythmic steps over the snow, observing with attentive eyes under dark eyebrows that bastard of an *SS-Untersturmführer* standing a short distance away at his usual Sunday place, and whom everyone knows because he has a ready hand with the truncheon.

Do you think Fernand concerns himself with that pitiful, shitty inscription, TO EACH HIS DUE, displayed on the gates of Buchenwald? Slogans are nothing new to Barizon. He grew up in a country in which the inscription *Liberté, Egalité, Fraternité* was insolently displayed on the pediments of all public buildings (with the exception, however, of the public conveniences; one wonders why), which isn't bad, either, in its own way. Barizon, then, took absolutely no notice of *Jedem das Seine*.

To be sure, if Barizon had had the benefit of the reflections that Léon Blum had jotted down on Plato's notion of equality, he would have found something in them to criticize. First, one must always find something to criticize in the reflections of a Social Democrat: that was an old principle from which Barizon was not to be deflected easily. And besides, even if he had not had a previous discussion with the Spaniard, Barizon would not read certain of Blum's sentences without reacting. This one, for example: "Justice and equality consist in maintaining due proportion between nature and society and, consequently, in tolerating in society other inequalities than those that are the expression of natural inequalities." Fernand would find all that very suspect indeed! To begin with, Barizon is not at all sure what "natural" inequalities mean. Of course, in nature there are the deaf and the dumb, and even deaf-mutes, and those who are neither. But there is a whole pile of other inequalities that are regarded as natural, which have become natural, but whose origin is nevertheless social. At the same age, in the same class, the son of a prole has more difficulty following certain lessons than the son of a doctor or a lawyer. Natural inequality, or acquired inequality produced by the difference of social environment? Come on, Léon, come on! You have to be joking! Anyway, who will establish the due proportion of natural inequalities that should be maintained in society? And according to what criteria? Who will hold the power of decision?

But Barizon knows nothing of Léon Blum's delicate, Platonic, patrician reflections. He would have nothing to do with them anyway. He knows only that he must try to get past that bastard of an *Untersturmführer*, who stands every Sunday on the same spot and lashes out at any prisoner he doesn't happen to like the look of. The best way of avoiding the SS officer is to be in the middle of the column, which marches along the Avenue of Eagles five deep. But today he was thinking of something else when the column formed in the factory yard, and found himself pushed to the edge as the column marched out of the Gustloff Works. So he'll pass within a few inches of the SS warrant officer.

Barizon has already noticed that this guy is sadistic in a peculiar way. He doesn't attack the weakest, the stragglers, the most down and out. On the contrary, he prefers to pick on the healthier-looking, those with cushy jobs, the confident. Barizon has also noticed that this officer seems quite uninterested in the Russians. Usually, it's the young Russians that the SS attack when they feel the need to attack someone. But not this one. This one, standing every Sunday noon at the same place, having probably come out of one of the office buildings of the SS garrison that flank the avenue, isn't at all interested in the Russians. He lets them go by unharmed. His attacks are reserved almost exclusively for the Westerners.

This is Fernand Barizon's problem at the precise moment when Léon Blum is writing with such facility that he finds the Platonic concept of equality revolutionary: how can he get past without being picked on, when he corresponds more or less to the criteria required to produce the sudden, cold, brutal anger of that particular SS officer. Should he make himself as small as possible, bend his back, look away? Should he look as natural as he can, as if he had been doing this his whole life: working in the Gustloff like a convict and walking by guys in uniform who have the right of life or death over him? Should he walk by unconcerned, as if he were whistling to himself on his way home from work, as if the SS officer were nothing more than some kind of traffic cop planted on the Avenue of Eagles, as he might have been at the Quatre-Routes crossroads at La Courneuve? Or should he, on the contrary, draw himself up to his full height and walk past the SS officer like a statue on roller skates?

This is Barizon's problem, and he is annoyed with himself for forgetting to get into the middle of the column, as he usually does with consummate art, at the moment when the kommando forms five deep in the Gustloff yard.

But his mind was elsewhere today. He was dreaming about Juliette, about his escapade in Brittany with Juliette ten years before. Why had they gone to Brittany, anyway? They'd decided to get away together for a few days, on the spur of the moment. Just like that. Yes, but why Brittany?

At Beaumont-du-Gâtinais, in the farmhouse of his maternal grandparents, there were collections of illustrated magazines that he had spent a lot of time leafing through one summer. He was eight then. He can't remember why he spent all summer at his maternal grandparents' that year. But he would leaf through the magazines, alone, in a dark, cool room behind the large farmhouse kitchen. One day, under a pile of *Petit Echo de la Mode*, a periodical that he went through meticulously in the hope of discovering some more or less naked female shapes, he found a small green volume that must have been left there by mistake. It was a *Guide Joanne de la Bretagne*, quite old, from 1894. But little Fernand plunged into reading this guide with delight. Soon he knew whole pages by heart. He knew everything, not only about Brittany at the end of the last century, but also recommended itineraries and the towns to be visited en route. Years later, he still remembered it.

So young Fernand, during that distant summer in the Gâtinais, had plunged into the delights of imaginary travel. In the end he knew all there was to know about Brittany, at least about Brittany at the end of the nineteenth century. But this anachronistic knowledge did cause him a few problems in 1934. At Le Pouliguen, when he stayed with Juliette at the Hôtel des Etrangers—chosen because a particular sentence in the *Guide Joanne*, engraved in his memory, declared that the said establishment had "an electric bell in every room"—Barizon had caused something of a stir among the staff when he had asked, in an offhand manner, after the widowed Mme Le Breton, who had run the hotel in 1894, according to the little green volume. It certainly seemed, or at least that was the conclusion that Fernand and Juliette had drawn from the alarmed mutterings that the innocent question had prompted, that the name of this widow was associated with certain disturbing, albeit distant and confused, events. Anyway, during the twenty-four hours that Fernand and Juliette spent in that hotel, they were treated with a somewhat mistrustful, perhaps even fearful respect. After this experience, Juliette decided that it would not be a very good idea to quote the names mentioned in the *Guide Joanne*.

In the Gustloff yard, that morning, Fernand Barizon had remembered the *Guide Joanne*. He had remembered that fit of giggles that the episode of the widowed Mme Le Breton had inspired in Juliette, giggles that he had taken full advantage of, for Juliette was never so free and abandoned in the games and delights of love as when she was at her most lighthearted. He had thought that he ought to tell the Spaniard about the incident of the *Guide Joanne*. The Spaniard knew almost all there was to know about Juliette, but he knew nothing as yet about the *Guide Joanne*. That was a story he had not yet told the Spaniard, and Barizon was sure that it would amuse him.

Anyway, distracted by all these memories, Fernand Barizon had let himself be pushed just now into the outer row of the kommando column. When he realized what had happened, it was too late to change his place. That was why, now, on the Avenue of Eagles, Barizon is wondering what attitude to adopt as he walks past the SS warrant officer, in order to try to avoid the blows that this particular individual delivers every Sunday, according to criteria that are peculiar to himself.

However, it didn't prevent the memory of the *Guide Joanne* from bringing a smile to his lips today. He really must talk to the Spaniard about it, after the soup.

But it wasn't that day, that Sunday, that Barizon spoke to the Spaniard about the *Guide Joanne de la Bretagne*. It was much later, twenty years later. It wasn't even in 1960, during the journey (which we will return to) with its stop-overs at Nantua, Geneva, Zurich, and several imaginary places: places in the memory. Perhaps they had talked about her again at Geneva and at Zurich; it's quite possible. On Lake Zurich, they talked about a lot of things, in the disorderly, rather breathless fashion of getting something off one's chest or settling some important point. On the steamer sailing around Lake Zurich, they had talked about the Russians, among other things. Not only, or even mostly, about the Russians in Buchenwald; no, about the Russians in the USSR.

"They are the last Christian people in the world," the Spaniard had said to Barizon. "A people of infinite, unfathomable resignation, interrupted by sudden blind revolts. Fewer and fewer revolts, mind you. And don't forget, Fernand, that 'Christian' and 'peasant' have the same root in Russian. Haven't you ever been to Russia? Well, everything we've been saying for decades now about the five-year plans, about industrialization, is untrue! At least it's partly untrue. Above all, it's window dressing. Socialism, said Lenin, is the workers' councils plus electrification. There are no workers' councils left, and there is hardly any electrification, at least if you take the term as a symbol of true modernity. In the USSR, modernity is superficial, it's to be found only in certain sectors, connected basically with space research and the war industries. At bottom, Stalinism was the liquidation of the workers' councils and the capitulation before the old, ancestral values of the peasantry. You'll say that this is just another of my brilliant, well-polished paradoxes. OK, Stalinism was first of all the extermination of the peasants, but it was precisely the extermination of the modern, dynamic, capitalist—in the historical sense of the term—fraction of the peasantry. In the countryside, it's the collective farm that represents backwardness, not the capitalistic agricultural enterprise. But there's another problem! The Russians, Fernand, are the last Christians. But no, not even that! They aren't even a Christian people; they're a Christianized people. Do you see what I mean?"

Barizon saw all too well. He saw that the Spaniard had gone off, once again, into one of his asides. It was odd how that guy had changed so little despite the passing years, white hair, and experience. So Barizon let the storm blow over and then asked a few concrete questions.

In 1960, anyway, the Spaniard had talked to Barizon about a great many things on the steamer as they went around Lake Zurich.

He had talked to him about the chance meeting with Vyacheslav Mikhailovich Molotov in the corridors of the Kremlin polyclinic. That was in 1958, in the summer. The Spaniard was there with his wife. They had to have a compulsory medical examination before going on vacation to Sochi. Suddenly, as they were waiting for the result of some analysis or X-ray, there was some sort of disturbance. Doors banged, offices emptied onto the central corridor of this polyclinic reserved for the higher reaches of the Soviet political bureaucracy and their noble foreign guests. Doctors and nurses dashed toward the entrance of this corridor in a mad stampede. In that corridor, where the Spaniard and his wife were sitting on a bench and waiting quietly, the cause of all this disturbance appeared: a small man with a graying mustache, steel-rimmed spectacles, and an incredibly dull, gray complexion. Immediately they recognized Molotov. The doctors and nurses rushed up to him to shake his hand, to touch his clothes, to call him by his first name and patronymic. Vyacheslav Mikhailovich! Hardly two years had passed since the Twentieth Congress of the Soviet Party. A year since Khrushchev had removed Molotov from power with the gang of four—Malenkov, Kaganovich, and Voroshilov—to which was added Shepilov, according to the sacred formula. Everyone knew that in this struggle for supreme power, Molotov represented the most retrograde elements of the Soviet bureaucracy, that he was the symbol of the survival of Stalinism in other forms. Yet doctors and nurses in that Kremlin clinic, on the staff of which one of Stalin's last acts of terror had fallen, the "doctors' plot," rushed up to Vyacheslav Mikhailovich to congratulate him, to touch his hand, with sincere and monstrous fervor—monstrous because quite obviously sincere. The little man with the gray face, the gray mustache, the gray eyes, the gray suit, the little bureaucrat of death, had walked past the Spaniard and his wife, who had frozen in an identical feeling of horrified incredulity of which they spoke later, between themselves, realizing once again that they had reacted in unison. Vyacheslav Mikhailovich, the gloomy functionary of terror, compared with whom the Nazi war criminals, most of them at least, were mere apprentices, and even sorcerers' apprentices, since they had gone down on the side of the losers, on the wrong side of history, had walked past them, smiling to left and to right, deigning to be won over by this servile, wretched fervor. And he had cast a brief, piercing look, an icy look, in the direction of the couple sitting on the bench, those strangers who weren't there in his day. Then, in a sort of sickened vertigo, the Spaniard, I, had dreamed that Stalin himself might one day reappear, in the corridors of the Kremlin, walking with his slow, heavy step, his hand slipped between the buttons of his military jacket, walking toward his office to bring everything back under his control.

Anyway, I had talked about a lot of things with Barizon, on Lake Zurich. About my chance encounter with Molotov two years before, and of the not at all chance encounter with Suslov in that very year, 1960. But Barizon had said nothing, that time, about the *Guide Joanne de la Bretagne*. It was not until four years later, in 1964, on leaving the Mutualité, the last time we saw each other, that Fernand Barizon talked to me about that guidebook from which he could still recite whole pages. One day, long after all those journeys, after all that memory, a day in June of vivid, deep luminosity in the main square at Fouesnant, I remembered Barizon's voice talking to me in a café near the Mutualité. He was telling me this story of the *Guide Joanne* and he repeated a sentence by heart. Why *that* sentence? For no particular reason; it was just taken at random. This is how it ran: "On the left is the road to Fouesnant, principal town of the district, 2,776 inhabitants—thirteenth-century church—famous throughout Finistère for the beauty and coquetry of its women. . . ." I was standing in the town square of Fouesnant, in front of the thirteenth-century church, and I remembered Fernand Barizon. As it turned out, Juliette and he never went to Fouesnant. Not because of the young woman's hypothetical fit of jealousy after reading that sentence about the supposed beauty and coquetry of the women of Fouesnant, but quite simply because they ran out of money and had to go back to Paris. So I was at Fouesnant, and I repeated to myself that sentence from the *Guide Joanne*, whose authenticity, of course, I cannot guarantee; I can only guarantee that Fernand repeated it to me in that form.

But it is twenty years earlier, one Sunday in Buchenwald.

I'm in the office of the *Arbeitsstatistik*. The noon roll call has started. We are following its progress over the loudspeaker. One of our privileges—and it is no small matter—is to be allowed to remain at our place of work. The SS warrant officer has already been here; he has counted us, the numbers tally, he has gone off again to give the *Rapportführer* the total number of prisoners allowed, like us, to remain at their places of work. We have only to wait for the general roll call to end before rushing off to get our Sunday noodle soup. Or, rather, those who, like Daniel and me, have only their ordinary, everyday ration to subsist on will rush out for our soup. The others, the truly privileged, the *Prominente*, have no need to rush. Either the block leader will keep their soup ration for them, or they will not even bother to get it, and will give it to other privileged individuals who are slightly less privileged than themselves.

I'm sitting at my place before the rows of card indexes. I'm doing nothing, thinking about nothing in particular. I'm not even reading the weekly *Das Reich*, which someone has just passed me. I'm simply waiting for the voice of the *Rapportführer* to yell down the loudspeaker that the roll call is finished. I'm looking absent-mindedly at the crematorium chimney. I notice that the light gray smoke of early morning has thickened.

At that moment I see Jiri Zak. He must have come to talk to his pal Josef Frank. Jiri Zak is a young Czech Communist working at the *Schreibstube*. He's a quiet, thoughtful individual, who never speaks one word louder than another. His eyes twinkle behind his steel-rimmed spectacles. Yes, he has sat down beside Frank, just in front of me, on the other side of the work-force file. He sees me, and signals with his hand. Frank turns around. He, too, gives a little sign of complicity in my direction.

The midday sun touches the windows, on the other side of the hut, on the side of the *Appellplatz* and the crematorium.

Years later, I was in Prague, in the National Gallery, in front of a Renoir painting. It was in 1960. The day before I had been sailing around Lake Zurich with Fernand Barizon.

Curiously enough, Renoir's young woman and my long, meditative contemplation of her are the only memories I have of that trip to Prague. I have forgotten why I was in Prague, what the reason was for that urgent visit. I no longer remember whether I had to stay in Prague or whether Prague was merely on the way to somewhere else. Anyway, I'm sure I was not going to Moscow on that particular trip. I have only been to Moscow three times in my whole life: in 1958, for summer vacation; in 1959, again in the summer, for talks that lasted a week, just outside Moscow at Uspenskoye; and, finally, again in summer, again for vacation, in 1960, some months before my trip with Barizon.

Perhaps I was on my way to East Berlin, or to Bucharest?

Anyway, that image stands out, surrounded by night, by an indistinct nothingness: I am standing in front of a Renoir painting in the National Gallery, in one of the halls of the Sternberg Palace, inside the walls of Prague Castle.

I have always stayed at the same places in Prague, so it won't be difficult for me to imagine my itineraries to and from the Sternberg Palace.

If I had stayed, that time, in one of the villas of the modern residential quarter, to the south of the Hradčany —and perhaps even, as I had done several times, in the Villa Cepiska, named after a son-in-law of Gottwald, whose splendid residence it had been before his fall from grace, a villa that was placed, once he had been got rid of (and perhaps in order to efface, by means of this similacrum of internationalism, the sin of its previous use), at the disposal of the leaders of the fraternal parties—I would have arrived inside the Hradčany walls by way of the bridge that leads directly to that courtyard where the Spanish Room is situated.

But I'm sure there was no meeting of the PCE leadership in Prague in the autumn of 1960, which would have justified my staying at the Villa Cepiska—of that I am quite certain.

So I must have been staying quite simply at the hotel reserved for guests of the Czech Party, the former Hotel Steiner, in the center of the city, not far from the Powder Tower. But the name of the hotel, Grand Hotel Steiner, was no longer to be seen. It was a hotel without a name. Among ourselves, we called it the Praga Hotel, to facilitate communication, but this name might well have puzzled those who were not in the know, for there was indeed another hotel in the city with the same name. The establishment that was really called the Praga Hotel, which openly and officially bore that name, was merely a false scent that must have misled the uninitiated, the mere tourists. Indeed, one had only to say to a representative of the forces of order that one was staying at the Praga Hotel, or at least one had only to say so in a certain way, for this functionary to understand at once that one meant the true Praga Hotel, that one that had no name, and whose unreal, or secret, existence was protected by the true existence of the false Praga Hotel, the one that anyone might have stayed at.

Anyway, I would have had to cross the Old Town and the Charles Bridge in order to reach the sloping streets of the Malá Strana that lead to the terraces of the Hradčany, if I had left the former Hotel Steiner.

But I remember nothing.

I remember only the Renoir painting, the sheer *joie de vivre* of that laughing, slightly chubby young woman. And I remember the smell of polish in the National Gallery, I remember a creaking in the parquet floor, probably caused by a visitor whose stealthy movements behind me I was dimly aware of. I remember the bare branch of a tree framed by a window. I remember my nostalgic emotions before that laughing, sun-drenched young woman painted by Renoir. And I remember the movement of her neck, the fold of fabric over her shoulder, the hint of whiteness of the shoulder, the firm roundness of the breast beneath that fabric. I remember, with a quickening of the pulse and moistening of the palm, the idea that suddenly came to me, standing in front of that Renoir painting, that Milena, too, must have stood in front of her. I remember the memory of Milena Jesenska which suddenly came back to me that day in 1960. I remember the trembling that overcame me at the idea that Milena must have stood at this same place many times, looking at this Renoir painting. I remember a glittering memory of snow swirling in the beams of searchlights, a poignant memory that had just burst inside me like frozen fire, the memory of Milena herself: Milena Jesenska, who died in a concentration camp at Ravensbrück. I remember that memory of snow falling on the ashes of Milena Jesenska, as I stood in front of a painting by Renoir. I remember the beauty of Milena Jesenska, cast to the wind in the smoke from the crematorium. I remember the vivacious gaze of that young woman painted by Renoir, which had observed, thirty years before, the gaze of Milena, observing her. I remember the gaze of that eternally living woman, observing the face of that young woman soon to die, Milena Jesenska, young and proud, looking at Renoir's picture, long ago, and becoming, without knowing it, before the living eye of the painted, unreal woman, light as the smoke from the crematorium chimney, in the desolate landscape dotted with camp huts. I remember the memory of Milena's face going up in smoke, blurring in the wind. I remember the memory of a Sunday in Buchenwald, which rose up within the memory of Milena, in front of a Renoir painting. I remember an evanescent memory of myself, in the memory of Milena, as if it were she who dreamed, one Sunday in Ravensbrück, of the visit that I would make twenty years later to the Sternberg Palace, in order to look at that Renoir painting, which she must have known. I remember a dream of Milena dreaming my existence. I remember that I had remembered Sundays in Buchenwald and the face of Josef Frank turned toward me, briefly haloed in a flash of sunlight from the windows on the other side of the hut, the crematorium side.

The day before, I had been sailing around Lake Zurich with Fernand Barizon.

"Gérard, the secret report everyone's talking about: is it true or isn't it?"

We were facing the village of Wädenswil when Barizon suddenly asked me that question.

"You mean," I said, "the report 'attributed to Khrushchev'?"

But Fernand was in no mood for joking.

"Is it true or isn't it, Gérard?" he asked sharply.

I nodded.

I was on the Plaza de la Cybele, in Madrid, four years before, in June 1956.

It was five o'clock in the morning.

I had asked the taxi driver to drop me off at the Plaza de la Cybele, in front of the general post office. I paid and waited for the taxi to drive away. The June sun was rising over Madrid. I began to walk. I got back to my lodgings —it wasn't nearby, but I had got into this habit, three years earlier, of stopping taxis at some distance from my secret hideouts. I would finish the journey on foot, making various detours, sometimes stopping off at a café-bar, to make sure that I wasn't being followed. I no longer gave it any thought. I did it quite mechanically.

There was nobody else in that urban landscape; the square was deserted. I was alone with the goddess Cybele. She was seated on her chariot, in the middle of the square, surrounded by a pool with spurting fountains.

Suddenly, in the silence of that June dawn, I seemed to hear the noise of water. The noise of the water from the fountains around the statue of Cybele. I stopped, my heart pounding. A memory had come back to me concerning the square, that fountain, my life. I had already heard that murmur of falling water, long ago. Long, long ago.

It was a childhood memory.

There had been silence, like today. Not a June dawn, though, but an October afternoon in 1934. It was not the silence of the early hours of the morning that had enabled me, then, to hear the murmur of the fountains. It was a heavier silence. A deathly silence—as one says, and for once it was literally true. It was a deathly silence, long ago, after the din of automatic weapons. A corpse had remained on the square. A man in blue overalls, mowed down by gunfire from the Civil Guard. One of his espradrilles had rolled away from the spot where he had fallen.

In that deathly silence, in October 1934, I had already heard the murmur of the fountains surrounding the chariot of the goddess Cybele in Madrid.

But I'm not going to recount this childhood memory in detail.

Twenty-two years later, in June 1956, the memory slipped like a light cloud into the June sky. I did not hold on to it. I let it vanish, an evanescent memory that presented no problem. The good were on the right side, the evil on the wrong, in that memory. On the one hand, the butchers; on the other, the victims. On the one side, the police; on the other, the workers. Let it vanish again, since it presents no problems. Asks no questions. It's a silent memory; leave it to its silence. It will be ready, if need be.

Twenty-two years later, when I watched the taxi drive off, on the Plaza de la Cybele, it was two days since *Le Monde* had finished publishing the text of Khrushchev's secret report to the Twentieth Congress of the Soviet Party. Evening after evening in Madrid, at the house of a comrade who subscribed to the Paris daily, I had read that report, become totally absorbed in it. Not for a second did I doubt its veracity. Not for a second did I try to conceal from the cadres of the PCE who surrounded me in our underground work the barbaric truth that was emerging.

Today it is considered the correct thing to do—even in the Communist parties who fearfully denied, at the time, the existence of this report "attributed to Khrushchev" by the forces of imperialism, by the class enemy, by God knows who—to emphasize its all-too-evident inadequacies. From a Marxist point of view, our learned commentators tell us, it is clear that Khrushchev's secret report was quite inadequate. Thus, this damned report has gone from being nonexistent to being non-Marxist. Which is one of the most cunning categories of nonbeing, at least of theoretical nonbeing.

But why was Khrushchev's secret report under any obligation to be Marxist? What is Marxism? If the writings that claim to be Marxist today are to be believed, whatever the contradictions between the various interpretations of the doctrine, Marxism—that of Brezhnev as well as that of Linhart, that of Deng Zhiaoping as well as that of Althusser, that of Lecourt as well as that of Marchais— seems to be an ideological activity whose essential function is to produce concepts capable of obscuring reality, of mystifying history, of concealing the crude impact of historical facts. Marxism seems reduced to being no more than the art of justifying the way things turn out.

The only countries in which Marxism is still an instrument of research and theoretical learning are those in which there is no Communist Party, or at least no important one. As if Marxist theory were henceforth incompatible with the requirements of mass Communist practice, which is the very negation of the original Marxian project. In short, it seems that Marxism exists as a theory only where it inspires no active practice on the social and political plane. Marxism is no longer possible except in the negation of the presuppositions of Marxism.

One may, then, take up again the question already posed: if Marxism is the academic cesspit that we know, that wretched den of ideological opium, that carnival of concepts, why should Khrushchev's secret report have been Marxist? Was it not enough that it should be true?

Not for a second had I doubted the veracity of that report.

It was June; the sun was rising over Madrid. In the middle of the square, over a pool, surrounded by the murmuring water of the fountains, the goddess Cybele was seated on a chariot drawn by two lions.

There are moments in life when truth seizes you roughly, in a collapse of received ideas and established feelings. A flash of lightning illuminates your inner landscape, your mental world: everything is changed. It's a sort of bolt from the blue, like love at first sight. But there are also moments of plenitude, in which truth is not revealed in a clap of thunder and a flash of lightning, but unfolds like the light of dawn, which was already there before, in the night. It unfolds like a flower, it matures like a fruit, which was already there before, the flower in the bud—*die Knospe!*—the fruit in the flower.

That June down in 1956, on the Plaza de la Cybele in Madrid, was one of the latter moments.

To be sure, the sorcery of the place was not unconnected with that feeling of plenitude. I was in a landscape of my childhood.

Twenty-two years before, in the declining sun of an October afternoon, a man had tried to run across that square. One couldn't hear the sound of his footsteps because he was wearing espadrilles. A man in blue overalls was trying to run away. Was it because of the autumn sun gilding the old stone? Or because of the disciplined, slightly baroque beauty of that square? The fact is that the scene had nothing tragic about it at first sight. A small man wearing blue overalls was running across the Plaza de la Cybele, with short rapid strides. Harold Lloyd or Harry Langdon would have run like that, in the jerky succession of cinematographic images. Then a Civil Guard van appeared at the end of the Calle Alcala, at the corner of the Godoy Palace. It was an open vehicle, and the guards were standing on the platform, holding on to the rails. They began to fire at the silhouette of the little man in blue running across the square. At the first burst of gunfire, all the pigeons who were usually perched on the goddess Cybele—on her hands, on the manes of her lions—flew up at once. Then the man staggered, most likely hit for the first time. He ran a few meters farther, perhaps under his own impetus, but with a curious, loose-hipped hobble, for one of his espadrilles had fallen off and rolled away. After a second burst of gunfire, the man collapsed, reduced to a small wretched pile of blue clothes in the immense space of the square.

Then silence fell again on the Plaza de la Cybele. On the goddess Cybele, on her chariot drawn by two lions surrounded by the jets of water from the fountains. With a muffled whirl of wings, pigeons returned to their usual perches.

And it was at that moment, immediately after the stirring of the translucent air by dozens of beating pigeons' wings, that one could hear the murmur of the falling water around the goddess Cybele.

Twenty-two years later, in June 1956, in the coolness of dawn, when the taxi had disappeared, I once again heard the immemorial murmur of the fountains.

I was in the center of the city of my childhood, at the center of myself. I was standing in the center of my life, it seemed.

Two days before, *Le Monde* had completed publication of that serialized novel on the truth of Stalinism known as Khrushchev's secret report. Not for a second had I doubted its veracity. Ultimately, history became rational again. I don't say reasonable, for it was not that. Why, indeed, should history be reasonable? Why should it be a slow, irresistible rise toward the Light of Reason? No, even at the worst moments of blindness, I had not believed in such a phantasmagoria. But if history was not becoming reasonable again, if it was continuing to be unreasonable, full of sound and fury, it was, on the other hand, becoming rational again: open to general understanding, if only in the long term, if only in terms of fragmentary definition, if only as a continuing process, forever to be renewed.

Stalin's crimes gave the history of Russia, the history of

the Communist movement, the possibility of coherent rationalization. What was unacceptable was not that Stalin was a tyrant, but that Trotsky could have been in the pay of the Gestapo, that Bukharin could have organized sabotage and terrorist crimes; what was unacceptable was having lived in the icy light of this schizophrenic belief, with an aberrational split that produced moral emasculation.

The secret report delivered us, gave us at least the possibility of delivering ourselves, from that madness, from that sleep of reason.

Of course, no reference was made in it to Trotsky or Bukharin, whom I cite among many other possible names because of the exemplary character of their destinies. The secret report to the Twentieth Congress confined itself to rehabilitating the upper cadres of the Soviet Party, a few Stalinist leaders. The secret report was careful to distinguish itself from the general denunciations of Stalinism made, before and since, by the liberal bourgeoisie and by the opposition of the left: it drew a sharp, clear *line of demarcation* between a good and a bad period of terror, between those who were guilty in a good way and those who were guilty in a bad way, between innocent victims and victims who got no more than they deserved. And this frontier was drawn through the mid-1930s, at the time when the Great Purge was beginning to decimate the Stalinist Party itself, the cadres and the élites of Stalinist society.

It is easy to understand this limit inherent in the secret report. Addressing the Party—that is to say, the leadership of the political bureaucracy that supervised the production of the goods, ideas, and norms of post-Stalinist society—Khrushchev had a double aim.

First, he had to break the opposition of the old Stalinists who had regrouped around Molotov and Kaganovich, fierce opponents of any reform of the system. To this end, he had to shock the Congress by dragging up events that had been more or less repressed in the delegates' memories. He had to lance that purulent wound. From this point of view, the secret report was a master stroke: practically a surreptitious coup d'état. Given the degree of moral and theoretical decline, the brutal nakedness of the relations of intrigue, corruption, and power at the summit of the political apparatus inherited from Stalinism, there was obviously no other solution. No solution, in any case, that could appeal to the initiative of the masses, to democratic discussion. No "left" solution, then, of the kind that certain individuals were happy to imagine at the time, noble spirits, most of whom finally succumbed to the deadly—not for them, of course— charms of the dialectic of the late lamented Chairman Mao, which is the height of paradox: superseding Stalinism "on the left" only to find oneself on the extreme right of bureaucratic, manipulatory thought!

In fact, since Stalin's death, everything had continued to be settled in terms of maneuvers, plots, and assassinations at the summit of power. The liquidation of Beria and of the heads of the political police illustrates these methods perfectly. Of course, I have no intention of weeping over the fate of Lavrenti Beria. It's no concern of mine that he was shot like a dog during a meeting of the Praesidium, shortly after Stalin's death, and that his corpse was rolled in a carpet in order to smuggle it out of the Kremlin. It's simply that this episode shows all too well to what degree of abjection, arbitrariness, unbridled power, the leadership of the Soviet Party had sunk, to be forced to settle the problems of Stalin's succesion in this way.

Thus Khrushchev's secret report to the Twentieth Congress belongs to a series of underhanded maneuvers and acts aimed paradoxically—perhaps even dialectically;

one would have to ask the theologians of the Holy Marxist Church—at re-establishing the functioning of government in the USSR, I will not say democratically—oh, no! that would be too absurd!—but just the regular functioning. It was aimed at making the authoritarian system of the single Party, which, until then, had been systematically violated by the leadership of the Party itself, function legally. No more than that.

But by revealing certain of Stalin's crimes to the Communist cadres of the dominant bureaucracy and to the principal leaders of the "fraternal parties," Khrushchev had just reminded them, in part anyway, of the bloody, arbitrary—in sho:t, illegitimate—origin of their own power. They were all, in fact, Stalin's heirs. They had all fawned on him. They had all been "little screws" and "little cogs" of the Great Mechanism of the State–Party. It was thanks to the terror that Khrushchev had just recalled that their own power had been built up. Now, it was very dangerous for the new master of the Soviet Party—still unsure of his position, still opposed by the powerful Molotov–Kaganovich group—to remind the bureaucratic leadership too clearly of the bloody illegitimacy of its power. So it was necessary to reassure that bureaucracy at once—that was the second of Khrushchev's aims. Hence, the clear, sharp line of demarcation, like a cut from the sacrificial knife, that Khrushchev drew between the different periods of Stalin's activities. The violence unleashed against the "enemies of the people," "counterrevolutionaries," opponents, "kulaks," and "bourgeois nationalists" was just. It became unjustified terror only when it was turned massively against the Party itself, against the bureaucratic class that had consolidated its power during the previous decades, only at the moment when it was turned against itself. That is to say, from about 1934 and the assassination of Kirov.

One can imagine the scene.

One can imagine the great hall of the Kremlin in which the Twentieth Congress is taking place. One can easily imagine the average age of the delegates, their dress. Actually, one does not have to imagine the average age of the delegates: the figures are available. We know very well that the Russian political system is a gerontocratic despotism—but this feature of the regime does not derive from the fact that Stalin or Brezhnev may have read Plato's *Republic* too assiduously—no, not at all! It derives from an internal sociological given—the figures confirm this. In February 1956, at the Twentieth Congress of the Soviet Party, according to the report presented by Aristov on behalf of the mandate commission, 79.7 percent of the delegates were over forty, 55.7 percent between forty and fifty, and 24 percent over fifty. That means that the overwhelming majority of Communists present at the Twentieth Congress were at least twenty years old in 1936, at the time when the terror began to be deployed against the Party itself, at the moment when Stalin put Yezhov at the head of the NKVD (have you ever seen a portrait of Yezhov? Have you ever examined that tormented face, that mad look in the eyes, that look of having just come out of Dostoyevsky's *The Possessed*?), with the mandate to make up for the four years' delay which, according to Stalin, the security organs had allowed to elapse in the struggle against the enemies of the people.

The terror, then, is not prehistory for those men and women of mature age, assembled in the night, for a special secret session in the great hall of the Kremlin. They must remember it. It's part of their history, of their adult experience. Especially if the figures provided by Aristov are to be believed: namely, that nearly 70 percent of them joined the Party after 1931. Most of the delegates, then, not only had reached adulthood at the time when Stalin's terror was turned against the actual institutions and élites of the new society of exploitation, but had also joined the Party at precisely the same time.

They were there, then, in the great hall of the Kremlin, silent, soon to be overwhelmed, some fainting, others weeping, as they listened to the report "attributed to Khrushchev." They were there, the men and women who had joined Stalin's Party to fill in the gaps created by Stalin with the branding iron of repression. They were there, the men and women who had helped Stalin establish his absolute power in the literal sense of the term, that is to say, detached absolutely from any determination by the economy, or by the class structures of the new Russian society. For Stalin's personal power was unquestionably one of the instruments that the new dominant class provided itself with to establish its domination—if I may be forgiven these simplistic terms in cutting through the social tissues through the great diversity of historical factors, since it is clear that "class" is a more or less operative concept, and concepts, even the most operative ones, do not "provide themselves" with instruments or establish domination except in the inevitable theoretical reconstruction that men make of their own history. With this preliminary, let me cut through it all; aware of the risks of simplification that one takes with these trenchant carvings-up of history, as if it were a leg of lamb, let me cut through it all, and let me repeat that Stalin's personal power, the instrument of the new dominant class, became, in the late 1930s, relatively independent of that class. And the most obvious sign of this independence was the capacity of that personal power, having become absolute, to unleash against the bureaucracy from which it sprang, and which it represented throughout a whole historical period, the fiercest and blindest repression.

Through the system of successive, uninterrupted waves of terror, it assured not only the blithe submission of the bureaucracy, but also social mobility within that bureaucracy, in the form of a permanent and dysfunctional destruction and reconstitution of the élites. In short, it was terror that guaranteed, from a certain point onward, the circulation of jobs, values, and social rewards within the bureaucracy. And it was the end of this period, and the end of terror as the cancerous motive force of the development of the bureaucracy, that Khrushchev announced to all those men and women on that famous February evening in 1956, in a closed session of the Twentieth Congress. Henceforth, he declared, a new rationality, which would no longer be the aberrational, unpredictable, absolute personal power of Stalin, but that of the general interests of their class (that particular word was not used, of course: one would speak only of the interests of the Russian People, the Nation, the State as a whole), would govern the distribution of privileges and rewards—in short, the establishment of power relations. This was the message of that secret report, a message perfectly comprehensible to those hundreds of delegates from the icy depths of Russian history.

One can imagine the scene.

Nikita Sergeevich was on the platform, hammering out his words. Sometimes he shouted, and his voice cracked. He hammered out the monstrous truths, one after another. But that terrifying voice, which aroused the nausea of their memories, was not, for once, the monotonous pedagogical voice of an all-powerful, distant, inaccessible Father: it was their own voice. Nikita Sergeevich was one of them, and the men and women gathered on that sinister but solemn occasion could identify with him. Like him, they had hoped to break all opposition. Like him, they had broken the Party itself. Like him, they had sung the praises of Stalin. There were many of them, no doubt, who had taken part in the Eighteenth Congress of the Party, in March 1939. Perhaps they remembered that Khrushchev had then also mounted the rostrum to speak of the success of Communism in the Ukraine. Perhaps they remembered Nikita Sergeevich's words on that distant day of March 13, 1939, at the very moment when the Spanish Civil War was ending in blood, defeat, and confusion, mainly because of Stalin's pernicious policies, blindly put into practice by the Komintern advisers and the leading group of the PCE: "This success has not been produced spontaneously," Khrushchev declared to the Eighteenth Congress. "It has been achieved in the ruthless struggle against the enemies of the working class and peasantry, against the enemies of our whole people; in the struggle against the agents of the Fascist secret services, against the Trotskyites, the Bukharinites, and the bourgeois nationalists." Perhaps they remembered, some of them at least, the conclusion of Khrushchev's speech in March 1939: "Long live the greatest genius of mankind, the Master and Leader who is guiding us victoriously toward Communism, our dear Stalin!"

They remembered dear Stalin. They still shook, with respectful, fearful horror, at the thought of him.

But I'm in Prague, in the National Gallery, in front of a Renoir painting.

Why am I in Prague?

Perhaps quite simply in order to stand in front of a Renoir painting. Perhaps I've forgotten all the other reasons and circumstances of that trip to Prague because the only important thing was the observation of a Renoir painting. Not just Renoir, of course. Perhaps a painting by Vermeer, or Velásquez, or El Greco would have done as well. The important thing was not only the painting observed, but also the fact of observing it.

But I'm in Prague, in the National Gallery of the

Sternberg Palace. I'm not in Toledo, in the Church of Santo Tomé, in front of *The Burial of the Count of Orgaz.* Nor in the Prado, in front of *Las Meninas.* Nor in the Mauritshuis, in front of the *View of Delft.* Pictures around which it might be possible to reconstruct my life.

For my life is not like a river—above all not like an ever-changing river, never the same, in which one could never bathe twice. My life is always a matter of *déjà-vu,* of *déjà-vécu,* of repetition, of sameness to the point of satiety, to the point where, by virtue of being identical, it transforms itself into something new and strange. My life is not a temporal flow, a fluid but structured duration, or, worse, a construction constructing itself. My life is constantly being undone, perpetually undoing itself, growing blurred, going up in smoke. It is a random succession of arrested moments, of snapshots, a discontinuous succession of fleeting instants, of images that flicker momentarily in an endless night. Only a superhuman effort, a quite unreasonable hope, gives cohesion, or at least a seeming cohesion, to all those scattered twigs and leaves. Life as a river, as a flow, is a fictional invention. An exorcism by means of narration, a ruse the ego adopts in trying to convince itself of its eternal, timeless existence—even if in the perverse or perverted form of time passing, lost and regained—and to achieve this conviction by becoming one's own biographer, the novelist of oneself.

My life is nothing but that Renoir painting, my eyes on that painting.

But we are no longer in 1960, in the autumn, the day after the day I talked to Fernand Barizon about the Twentieth Congress of the Soviet Communist Party. Looking quite unconcerned, as if nothing had happened, as if time had not passed, had not flowed like the waters of the river, here I am, stock still, in another contemplative immobility: the same. Another I, the same I. Another painting, the same painting. The same memory of Josef Frank, in Buchenwald, one Sunday

We are in 1969, in early April.

Yesterday I met up with Jiri Zak again.

The slanting rays of the sun were touching the room in which we were sitting, but it did not herald spring. Jan Palach had committed suicide by setting himself on fire, and a few days later Alexander Dubček would finally be divested of the little power that still remained to him. Normalization could now begin: the re-establishment of Correct Thought, of corrective labor, of bureaucratic correction. No doubt we knew that there would be no Prague spring that year, despite the slanting rays of the sun that seemed to herald finer weather.

I was looking at Jiri Zak, white-haired by now. I looked at the sixty-year-old woman who was with him, Josef Frank's widow.

I had come to Prague in the early spring of 1969, with Costa Gavras, who was still considering the possibility of making a film of The Confession on the actual locations where the events had taken place. And then, since I knew that I would never come to Prague again, I spent a long time revisiting all the privileged places of my memory there. Tomorrow, just before catching the plane, I would go up to the National Gallery to take a final look at that Renoir painting with which my life was so intimately entwined.

As I looked at Jiri Zak and Josef Frank's widow, in the silence that had fallen between us, as night falls, as arms fall, after we had once more talked about the past, exchanged photographs, I suddenly rediscovered with extraordinary precision an image from my memory: Josef Frank is turning around in the office of the *Arbeitsstatistik*, probably to see to whom Jiri has just made a friendly gesture; he sees me and makes a similar gesture in my direction, and a brief smile. Behind him, behind his face, which is half turned toward me, I see the December sun reflected on the windows on the other side of the hut. I also see the square chimney of the crematorium.

At that moment Willi Seifert comes over.

"Oh, by the way," he says, "I want you all to be here tonight at six! I've organized a dog stew; there'll be enough for everyone!"

There are murmurs of approval and pleasure.

Seifert looks at Jiri Zak.

"You're not one of us, but come anyway: you're invited!"

Jiri shakes his head.

"I don't like dog," he says.

"Have you ever tried it?" Seifert asks.

Jiri Zak shakes his head.

"I don't like the idea of dog," he says succinctly.

Zamyatin didn't like the idea of dog either. I don't mean Eugene Zamyatin, the writer who died in exile in Paris. I mean another Zamyatin, an Orthodox priest deported to Kolyma. Or, rather, Varlam Shalamov talks about him in his *Kolyma Tales*. In any case, the priest Zamyatin ate what was left of a dog stew that had been "*organisiert*" by the nonpoliticals in the hut. When he had finished, the trickster Semyon told the priest that he had eaten not mutton, as he had thought, but dog. And the priest Zamyatin vomited in the snow. He didn't like the idea of dog any more than Jiri Zak did. He had certainly liked dog meat. He had found that it tasted good, as good as mutton. It was the idea of dog that had made him vomit.

But Willi Seifert laughs.

"It's not the idea of dog that one eats, it's the meat!" he says. "And dog meat is like boiled beef!"

I must say that I would agree with Seifert more than with Semyon, the trickster of *Kolyma*. Dog meat, at least in a stew, with vegetables and a good thick sauce, as we had it that Sunday in the *Arbeitsstatistik,* was more like boiled beef than mutton.

"Too bad," Jiri Zak replies, quietly obstinate. "I don't like the idea of dog."

At that moment, of course, as the noon roll call is drawing to an end, when the musicians of the camp orchestra will soon take to their trumpets, clarinets, and tubas, I don't know that Léon Blum is writing a commentary on the Platonic idea of equality. I don't know what Blum would say about the idea of dog, or what he is saying, at that very moment, about the idea of equality. Besides, even if I did know, it wouldn't mean very much to me. In 1944, I'm not particularly interested in Plato's political utopias.

For the moment, anyway, I'm not thinking of the idea of equality. I'm thinking of the idea of dog. I like the idea of dog, I must say. I like the idea of that dog stew that Seifert has "organized" for this evening. Parodying a famous remark of Engels, I tell myself that the proof of the dog is in the eating! I want to shout out this comforting truth.

Then, as if it were necessary to emphasize this optimistic conclusion of the philosophy of praxis, the voice of the *Rapportführer* yells over the loudspeaker, ordering everyone to stand to attention. The roll call is done. *Das Ganze, Stand!* It's a Hegelian term, *das Ganze,* the All, the Totality. Perhaps it's the voice of Absolute Spirit that can be heard from all the loudspeakers in the camp. The voice of the All that is speaking to us all, totalizes us in the corpselike rigidity of standing to attention, in the totalitarian fixity of the gaze lost in the pale December sky into which the smoke from the crematorium rises. Attention, Totality! cries Absolute Spirit on the *Appellplatz.*

But you must not pay too much attention to my Sunday lucubrations. It's the idea of dog that sent me off on this train of thought: the idea of dog stew. What a day, friends! *Quel beau dimanche*, as Barizon would say! First the idea of the noodle soup that will be dished out to us in a few moments, and then, at six o'clock, the idea of dog stew. It's ideas like this that make the world go round, that's for sure.

Seven

"Admiring the view?" Jehovah asks.

Or, rather, his witness: the Jehovah's Witness.

I heard someone arrive, footsteps on the snow, in the copse on the edge of the Little Camp, between the quarantine huts and the infirmary, the *Revier*. I turned around for a second, listening to that crunching of snow. I did not fear the inopportune arrival of some SS-*Blockführer*. They aren't in the habit of venturing into the camp on Sunday afternoons. Those on duty keep to the watchtowers or guard posts, snug and warm. Those not on duty are drinking beer in the SS canteen, awaiting their turn to go on guard. Or they're chasing girls, in Weimar. But if it really wasn't an SS officer, it could be some prowler. Some young Russian might have followed me and decided to pinch the leather boots I was wearing. So I turned my head when I heard the crunching of feet on the snow behind me. I didn't want to be caught by some Russian prowler armed with a knife or a bludgeon.

But it wasn't a Russian prowler, it was Jehovah. I recognized at once his tall figure and white hair.

I think he was named Johann, but I'm not quite sure.
I've decided to call him Jehovah in this story, whenever I
have occasion to name him. Jehovah's as good as Johann. I
even think Jehovah's easier to remember. And he was a
man of God; no doubt about that.

"Admiring the view?" Jehovah asks.

He is standing next to me in the copse that stretches
beyond the quarantine camp, just before you reach the
open space, the border on which the machine guns in the
watchtowers are trained.

Yes, I'm admiring the view.

Every Sunday in Buchenwald, I came and admired that
view. Or perhaps not every one of my seventy-two Sundays in Buchenwald. No doubt there were certain Sundays when a snowstorm or a torrential rain prevented me
from walking out to the edge of the Little Camp and
admiring the view of Thuringia.

It was afternoon, of course, during the few hours of
leisure we enjoyed on Sunday afternoons. And on sunny
days, I went out at sunset, at whatever hour sunset
occurred, depending on the season. The sun set almost
opposite me, slightly to the left of the observation point
that I had chosen. I looked at the sun setting magnificently over the plain of Thuringia, on the western horizon,
behind the blue line of the Thuringian hills. In winter,
this blue line was white, and the sun pale and brittle, like
an old silver coin worn with use.

Jehovah is standing behind me, and he, too, is looking
at the winter landscape in the December sunlight, brief
and glorious, like that of Austerlitz, casting its last light.

"Admiring the view?" he had said. The question was
badly phrased. He could see very well that I was admiring
the view. There was nothing else I could be doing here
but admiring the view. It was obvious that I was looking
at the Thuringian plain, the village in the distance, the

calm gray smoke that was not smoke from the crematorium: life outside. He no doubt meant: "What do you find to admire in the view?" Or "What does that view mean to you?" "What fleeting, violent happiness, threatened by some incommunicable anguish, does this view arouse in you?" Anyway, something of the kind. But he said flatly: "Admiring the view?" Even Jehovah may have difficulty clearly formulating the right questions. Even He may get caught up in the banality of everyday language, as we know.

So I say nothing, since he hasn't really asked the right question. I wait with rather sly curiosity for him to say something else.

Usually, Jehovah begins any conversation by quoting a passage from the Bible. It's an opening that has become something of a ritual since I've known him, and since we started talking to each other. And the words from the Bible are always the right words for the occasion. It's beginning to annoy me. But today, before that view of snow on the Ettersberg and the plain of Thuringia, I wonder what quotation from the Bible he's going to come up with. There can't be many references to snow in the Bible.

So I wait, with rather sly curiosity. How's Jehovah going to get out of this one?

He turns his pale blue eyes upon me.

"God thunders wondrously with his voice; he does great things which we cannot comprehend. For to the snow he says, 'Fall on the earth'; and to the shower and the rain, 'Be strong.' He seals up the hand of every man, that all men may know his work. . . ."

He declaims these words in a loud voice. Then he smiles.

"Book of Job, 37:5!"

I nod, admiring and irritated. Then I turn back to the

snow that covers the plain of Thuringia, the snow that is now Biblical, immemorial.

I met Jehovah—or, rather, his witness—some months before.

In the Nazi camps, the Jehovah's Witnesses, or *Bibelforscher*, which was their official label, bore a violet identification triangle. They had been interned because they refused to perform military service or to take the oath of allegiance to the German flag. In Buchenwald, the Jehovah's Witnesses had been singled out for special persecution. At first, they were automatically put into the disciplinary companies. On several occasions, the SS command tried to make them abandon their principles. In September 1939, for example, shortly after the outbreak of war, they were all gathered on the *Appellplatz* to hear the SS commandant announce that if one of them, just one of them, refused to join the army, they would all be shot. Two armed SS companies surrounded the Jehovah's Witnesses, but not one of them agreed to fight for Germany. Eventually, they were beaten and deprived of their last personal belongings, but the SS command did not carry out its threat of execution.

In 1944, when I arrived in Buchenwald, the *Bibelforscher* survivors were working mainly as nurses in the camp hospitals or as servants in the SS officers' villas. Quiet, devoted, tireless, they waited patiently for the end of the apocalyptic evils that had arrived with the fall of Satan on the earth, in 1914, and for the millennium that would follow, at some not too distant but as yet indeterminate date, ushering in a New World, in which the Elect would govern the earth from their heavenly home.

Yet even at this final stage in the history of the camps, the Jehovah's Witnesses were still victims of collective beatings. In the spring of 1944, I remember, they were gathered on the *Appellplatz* and searched. Meanwhile, SS detachments ransacked their barracks and their places of work, looking, it was said, for religious tracts or pamphlets hostile to the regime.

I met Jehovah in September 1944, at the beginning of September, if I remember rightly.

Some days before, after the evening roll call, a rumor had run through the camp, whispered at first, then growing gradually louder and louder till it became an explosion of silent joy, a commotion of cries and stifled chants: Paris was free, Paris had been liberated! We ran from one block to another to find our pals, to share their joy. In Block 34, which was just opposite mine, the rejoicing knew no bounds. The block leader heard the commotion that the Frenchmen were making, and for once he didn't object. He didn't come rushing out of his hut, yelling that the French were dirty, undisciplined, lazy, shit, nur *Scheisse*, nothing but shit, and all they were good for was the crematorium!

In the Nazi camps, everyone will tell you, the French were not very popular. I don't mean popular with the SS, of course: it wouldn't mean much if the French were unpopular with them. But it was among the other deportees that the French weren't—or, rather, France wasn't—very popular. The antifascists of all the nations of Europe reproached France for, among other things, the policy of nonintervention in Spain. The Poles, antifascist or not—and most of them were not, at least in the sense that the Communist vocabulary ended up giving to the term—reproached France for abandoning them in September 1939. And everyone, Poles and Germans, Czechs and Russians, everyone criticized France for allowing itself to be so easily beaten by the German army in 1940. This bitter, widespread contempt for France and the French was really frustrated love. In 1940, people expected

France to perform some kind of miracle, to reverse the tide of war. Throughout German-occupied Europe people hoped for a miracle, a second battle of the Marne.

Anyway, the news of the liberation of Paris radically changed the attitude of most of the deportees, and especially of the kapos and German block leaders, the cadres of the kazettlerian bureaucracy, toward the French.

The day after this news reached us, a pervasive joy reigned in Buchenwald. It was as if we all felt that whatever has still to happen, nothing had been in vain, since we had lived long enough to hear of the liberation of Paris. In the indistinct light of the summer dawn, in the morning murmur from the beech forest, the French deportees marched to the roll call that day in close formation, in rhythmic steps—they who had always dragged their feet, always lacked discipline!—steps, that morning, that were not obeying SS orders, but were the proud steps of victory—we didn't have our Marne, but we had Paris!—they marched up to the *Appellplatz* as one solid mass, eyes fixed on the sun rising in the East, beyond the square chimney of the crematorium.

Gustav Herling recounts a similar episode. It, too, was connected with Paris. But it wasn't a joyful occasion, for it was connected, not with the memory of the liberation of Paris, but with that of its fall.

On a June day in 1940, in the prison of Vitebsk, the door of Gustav's cell opened and a new arrival entered that overpopulated space. The man stood stock still, with all eyes upon him, and murmured: "Paris has fallen. . . ." And in the cell of that Soviet prison at Vitebsk, in June 1940, a sigh, a murmur of distress broke out. "Paris had fallen, Paris, Paris. . . . It's incredible that even the simplest people in that cell, people who had never seen France, felt the fall of Paris like the death of their last hope, an even more irremediable defeat than the surrender of Warsaw. The night of slavery, which covered Europe, also obscured the narrow piece of sky, criss-crossed by the bars of our cell," says Gustav Herling.

But perhaps you don't know who Gustav Herling is. Neither do I, I know very little about him, in fact.

It was Josef Czapski who got me to read Herling's *A World Apart*. Published in London in 1951, it is no doubt one of the most hallucinatory accounts, in its sobriety, its restrained compassion, in the naked perfection of its narrative shape, that I have ever read of a Stalinist camp. It is, moreover, a historical document of the first order, providing a detailed description as well as a fully verified general view, of the Stalinist Gulag in the years 1940–1942.

But perhaps some distinguished Marxist will reproach me with using the term "Gulag" too unscientifically. Take Alain Lipietz: he's a distinguished Marxist. And he's an even more distinguished economist. In his latest essay, *Crise et Inflation: pourquoi?*, in a paragraph devoted to capitalist despotism in the entrepreneurial world, he makes the following imbecilic remark: "The word 'despotism' can shock only nonproletarians who have never undergone an apprenticeship in a factory, and who can see Gulag only in their neighbor's eye, when Billancourt and Javel* are under their own noses." Did I say imbecilic? Perhaps a stronger word is called for. First, one should note the crude empiricism of the sneer at "nonproletarians who have never undergone an apprenticeship in a factory." As far as I know, Lenin never underwent such an apprenticeship. I cite Lenin not out of personal reverence, but simply because Lipietz still seems to make a special case of him. Marx never underwent an apprenticeship in a factory either. His apprenticeships, and very

*Industrial centers in France. —ED.

long they were, took place in libraries, which didn't prevent him from discovering the capitalist despotism in the corporation and giving not only a concrete description of it, but also a theoretical explanation for it. On the other hand, there are millions—tens of millions—of workers who have undergone apprenticeships in factories, apprenticeships without end, apprenticeships for life, apprenticeships as convicts sentenced for life by the despotism of the entrepreneur—and who are unable to put a name to that entrepreneur, to know him and therefore to struggle effectively against him. So that phrase actually amounts to very little. What exactly is the point of it? To please two or three fellow intellectuals, to please oneself, to flatter a populist sensibility that is still prevalent among Paris intellectuals, particularly when they have a predilection for the hallucinogenic virtues of the dialectic of the late lamented Chairman Mao.

But there is worse to come. There is that other phrase, about those who "see Gulags only in their neighbor's eye, when Billancourt and Javel are under their own noses." Billancourt—how much nonsense has been said about it! The Gulags—that is, the concentration camps—have never liquidated the despotism of the entrepreneur, the despotism of social-bureaucratic capital in the USSR. The Russian worker has the sad privilege of knowing both oppressions, that of the Gulags and that of despotism of the entrepreneur, beside which that of the capitalistic system is paradise. There is no possibility of liquidating the despotism of capital at the factory towns of Billancourt and Javel if one conceals from the working class, or obfuscates with sentences like the above, the existence of the Gulags in the USSR, in China, and in every country where power is monopolized by a single party that silences the proletariat, all the better to speak in its name.

• • •

In Buchenwald, then, at the beginning of September 1944, I was in the entranceway of the camp library, which had been set up in the same hut as the *Arbeitsstatistik* and the *Schreibstube*. The entranceway of the library was a tiny space between the hallway of the hut and the library itself, in which one could see the shelves piled with books beyond the counter window. I was waiting for Anton, the librarian, to bring me the book I had asked for when the door from the hallway opened and Jehovah came in.

He was standing next to me, book in hand.

"*Mahlzeit!*" he said, by way of greeting. I turned around, intrigued.

One could not say that greetings, leavetakings, or polite expressions of any kind were a frequent occurrence in Buchenwald. There were the Austrians who would greet you with their singsong "*Servus!*" to wish you good day or good luck, but they were the exception. The language of Buchenwald was rather restrained, as far as the polite forms of social intercourse were concerned.

So I turned around to the guy who had just spoken in such a quiet but warm voice.

He was wearing the violet triangle. He had white hair over a still-young face. A face still alive, I mean. Not just a mask. His pale, transparent blue eyes looked at me with almost unbearable penetration.

"*Mahlzeit!*" I said, in turn.

At that moment, the librarian came back to the counter and put down the book that I had asked for. It was a thick, hardbound volume. Jehovah looked at its title and read it aloud, his voice trembling slightly, perhaps with surprise. Or joy. Or joyful surprise.

"*Absalom, Absalom!*" he cried out.

That was the title of the book, of course.

I looked at Jehovah, intrigued.

He was still talking calmly and clearly as he looked at me.

"Now Absalom, David's son, had a beautiful sister, whose name was Tamar; and after a time Amnon, David's son, loved her. . . ."

He stopped a raised a finger.

"Second Book of Samuel, 13!"

I nod, somewhat surprised.

I'm not a sufficiently keen reader of the Bible to remember that the story of Absalom is to be found in the Second Book of Samuel. Anyway, whether it's to be found there, or in the Book of Kings, or even in the Book of Chronicles, doesn't mean much to me. In my memory of childhood readings of Holy Scripture, the name of Absalom evokes, first and foremost, one very precise image: that of a warrior caught by his hair in the lower branches of an oak or an olive tree, who in this position is pierced by the spears and swords of attacking enemies. That is my first image of Absalom: a horseman lifted off his horse and held fast by his hair to the branches of a tree. Absalom, in short, ranked for me with Samson: both were guys who had had trouble because of their hair.

But it's not to revive those childhood recollections of the Bible that I ask the camp librarian for *Absalom, Absalom!* It's because of a young woman with blue eyes.

It was at the Sorbonne, in June 1942.

She came into the room where we were waiting our turn to be called before Professor Guillaume for the oral examination in psychology. Most of the other candidates were unknown to me. I must admit that I didn't attend many lectures, that year.

I was waiting absent-mindedly in that dusty, musty room of the Sorbonne when she came in.

Later, I sometimes wondered what it was that made that young woman beautiful. In September 1944, for example, in Buchenwald, listening to Jehovah reciting a passage from the Second Book of Samuel, I suddenly remembered her beauty with a pang. Again I was overwhelmed by its radiant mystery.

Standing by the window of the camp library, listening to Jehovah recite the beginning of the Biblical story of Absalom, I remembered the strange beauty of that young woman who had suddenly appeared before me, two years earlier, in the decrepit, suffocating examination room in the Sorbonne. I couldn't help thinking of her, of course. It was she, Jacqueline B., who had lent me *Sartoris*, my favorite Faulkner novel, some weeks after we had met. I was leaning against the window of the Buchenwald library two years later, holding the thick, hardcover volume of the German translation of *Absalom, Absalom!*, and I couldn't help remembering the young woman with whom I discussed Faulkner in the summer of 1942, dazzled by the strange light in her blue eyes.

The night before, I had found the title of this Faulkner novel in the catalogue of the camp library. I was not looking for anything in particular, vaguely wanting to borrow a work of fiction this time, rather than a volume of Hegel, Nietzsche, or Lange. Suddenly I noticed the name Faulkner and the title of that novel, *Absalom, Absalom!* It wasn't the first time I'd consulted the catalogue, but I'd never noticed that novel before, I suppose because I didn't expect to find it there. Now, when I saw the name of Faulkner and the title *Absalom, Absalom!*, the blood drained from my face. Not because of Faulkner or that novel, which I had not yet read. Not only because of Faulkner, anyway. Above all because of the memory of that young woman, Jacqueline B., which had suddenly reappeared.

And so that novel—bought, like all the other books in the library, with the money of the German internees and chosen from lists drawn up by them (the SS command, naturally enough, took part of the money collected by the *Kazettler* to buy and place in the library fifty-odd copies of Hitler's *Mein Kampf* and other works by theoreticians of the Nazi Thousand-Year Reich)—that Faulkner novel just happened to be there, by chance—if one must call "chance" some obscure, perhaps even inexorable, chain of causes and effects—in the camp library.

Who had ordered it? What memories did this book hold for the German prisoner who had put it on the list of books to be bought? Why had this book escaped the successive purges ordered by the SS command, whose object was to eliminate from the library shelves all non-German authors and all dubious, decadent works?

I would never know. But that book was there, in any case. It even seems to me that the only reason *Absalom, Absalom!* was to be found in the Buchenwald library— the only serious reason, I mean, one that cannot simply be brushed aside—was precisely the anticipation of that moment—unforeseeable from a strictly logical point of view—when my eye would catch the author and title in the library catalogue.

It was destined for me, in other words.

Whereas the Second book of Samuel has nothing to do with me. I looked at Jehovah, murmured a polite good-bye, and went off carrying Faulkner's novel, which re-minded me of a young woman with blue eyes.

Life before, life outside.

Some days later, Anton, the librarian, came over to me in the hall of the *Arbeitsstatistik*. It was evening, just before curfew. I was on the night shift, the *Nachtschicht*, and I was already at work. Though that is only a manner of speaking: one hardly worked at the *Arbeit* when one was on the night shift. One could read, think, or sleep, as one wished. That was why Seifert had invented the night shift.

I'd decided to read. Faulkner's novel was on the corner of my table, discreetly hidden by a pile of reports.

At that moment, Anton came up to me. He held out a parcel, smiling in a way that was difficult to define. There was a facetious look about it, anyway.

"This is for you," Anton said.

I must have looked surprised, for he insisted, looking more and more as if he were perpetrating some joke.

"Yes, honestly, it's for you! It's from your Jehovah's Witness!"

Actually, he didn't say "Jehovah's Witness." I'm simplifying. Nor did he use the official term in Buchenwald, *Bibelforscher*, "seekers" or "investigators of the Bible." He said—no doubt intentionally, but his intentions escaped me for the moment—*Bibelliebhaber*, "Bible lover." Bibliophile, in other words. Which was perfectly logical. How could Jehovah be anything but a Bibliophile?

I nodded, a bit surprised, and took the little parcel.

Anton looked as if he wanted to add something. But eventually he just shrugged his shoulders and went off.

At that moment, we heard the whistles from the *Lagerschutz* patrols announcing curfew throughout the camp.

I opened the parcel and found a copy of the Bible. An old silk bookmark marked the page on which was to be found chapter 13 of the Second Book of Samuel: "Amnon's incest."

"Then Amnon said to Tamar, 'Bring the food into the chamber, that I may eat from your hand.' And Tamar took the cakes she had made, and brought them into the chamber to Amnon her brother. But when she brought them near him to eat, he took hold of her, and said to her, 'Come, lie with me, my sister.' "

I read mechanically a few of the lines on the page

marked by the bookmark. Then I shut the Bible and hid it with Faulkner's novel, under the files that I had to bring up to date. I was vaguely irritated. Or distressed? A feeling of unease had come over me, anyway. What did Jehovah want with me? Why was he pursuing me? But perhaps that vague distress had nothing to do with Jehovah; perhaps it was the result of the conversation I had just had with Henri Frager. Before coming to the *Arbeit* to resume work as part of the night shift, I had looked into Block 42.

I absolutely had to see Frager.

Henri Frager had been the head of my resistance network. I don't know whether his name really was Henri Frager. I knew him under his pseudonym, "Paul," that was all. It was Michel Herr who brought me into the "Jean-Marie" network and introduced me to Paul, one summer day in 1943, on the sidewalk of the Avenue Niel, opposite the Magasins Réunis. I was going to be officially attached to the Irène group in the Yonne, with the job of receiving parachutists, sabotaging German lines of communication, and passing along orders to the resistance groups in the region. I was walking on the sidewalk of the Avenue Niel at nightfall with Henri Frager, who was called "Paul," and Michel Herr, who was called "Jacques." That meeting was to make official, in a sense, my entry into the network, in whose activity I had been taking part for some time with Michel and Irène.

I saw Paul two or three times again, in Paris. And then I was arrested by the Gestapo, in Irène's house, at Joigny. Irène didn't come back from Bergen-Belsen.

Anyway, a year after my last meeting with Paul, I was in Buchenwald, in the *Arbeit* office. I was working at the work-force files at the central card index when a report was passed to me for registration. It was a list of those who had arrived the night before, August 17, 1944. A transport of about forty men, no more. One could see at once that it was an exceptional transport. First, all the deportees were to be attached to Block 17, which was a hut of special quarantine, an isolation hut. Second, all these new arrivals had been labeled DIKAL (*Darf in kein anderes Lager*) by the Buchenwald Gestapo, on orders from Berlin. These deportees were to be kept in the camp, at the disposal of the Gestapo. Finally, checking the names—Dodkin, Peulevé, Hessel, for example—one could see that they were a mixture of French and British.

All this information suggested to me that this transport consisted of officers and important heads of information networks and resistance groups, working either for Buckmaster or for the Free French.

I began filling out cards for the new arrivals.

Suddenly I saw this name in the report from the *Schreibstube:* Frager, Henri. His occupation was listed as architect. I knew that "Paul" had been an architect. It was just about the only thing I did know about him. So, as I filled in a card for "Frager, Henri, architect," it occurred to me that this man who had just arrived in Block 17 in Buchenwald was Paul, the head of my network.

There was nothing I could do to check my intuition. I couldn't make contact with Frager as long as he was in Block 17.

Some weeks later, in early September, about fifteen members of this transport were suddenly summoned to the camp gates, to the office of the *Rapportführer* in the watchtower. Next day, an administrative form from the Buchenwald Gestapo, the *Politische Abteilung,* informed all the relevant services that these men had been released. *Entlassen,* as the Gestapo report put it. But news from the underground German organization suggested quite a different version. It appeared that these men had been taken into the crematorium cellar to be hanged.

Henri Frager was not in that group.

Some time later, the survivors of the special transport were transferred to the camp proper, to be integrated into the normal life of Buchenwald. Henri Frager was put into Block 42.

The very first evening, after the roll call, I rushed over to Block 42. I asked one of the *Stubendienst*, one of the guys in charge of the barrack rooms, to get me deportee Frager so that I could give him his number. It was a number around 70000, if I remember rightly. The *Stubendienst* was none too pleased, for he was quietly eating his soup in his own room, away from the noisy mass of deportees crowded into the mess room, but he must have been impressed by the vaguely formidable authority conferred on me by belonging to the *Arbeitsstatistik*. So the Polish *Stubendienst* went to fetch Henri Frager.

We were now face to face. It was "Paul," without any doubt.

The same calm manner, the same penetrating gaze. Visibly wary, though, since he must have been wondering what I wanted him for. Quite obviously, Frager did not recognize me.

"Don't be afraid. I'm a friend."

He probably wasn't afraid of anything, but he remained on the alert, impassive, waiting to see what would happen next.

I smiled.

"In fact," I said to him, "I've worked for you."

He stiffened; his blue eyes darkened.

"Worked? Doing what?" he asked sharply.

"You called yourself Paul, on occasion?"

He twitched; his left eyelid trembled.

"I've called myself all sorts of things, on occasion," he said.

I nodded, and smiled.

"The personal message for the parachute landings

always began this way," I said: "Paul's furniture will arrive on such a day."

He was beginning to get interested, quite obviously.

"Where did we meet?" he asked. "If indeed we ever did meet."

"The first time was on the Avenue Niel, opposite the Magasins Réunis."

He looked at me even more attentively. He poked a finger at my chest.

"You were with 'Mercier.' "

I nodded in confirmation. "Yes," I said, "Jacques Mercier."

His finger was no longer poking at my chest; his right hand was on my shoulder.

" 'Gérard'!" he exclaimed. "Isn't that what you were called?"

"Yes, yes, that's right. Gérard."

"You were arrested at Irène Chiot's, at Joigny," he said.

Chiot was Irène's maiden name. Her married name was Rossel.

So he had recognized me.

But Frager became mistrustful once again. Perhaps not exactly mistrustful; certainly preoccupied.

"How did you manage to find me and identify me?" he asked.

I told him the truth, quite simply, of the certainty that had overcome me, however unreasonably, when I saw his name in the list from the *Schreibstube*.

During that September 1944, I talked a lot to Henri Frager. We cleared up, retrospectively, a number of problems concerning the functioning of the network, in the Yonne–Côte-d'Or region. The problem of "Alain" is particular. Frager told me how Alain had ended up. I would come and collect him in Block 42, after the roll call. Or, on Sunday afternoons, he'd come and collect me at the

Arbeit. If it wasn't raining, we'd go out for a walk on the avenues and paths of the camp. During one of those walks, he introduced me to Julien Cain and Maurice Hewitt, who had also been deported to Buchenwald and had worked for the Jean-Marie network, but in a different sector.

One evening in Block 42, Frager talked to me about the aircraft manufacturer Bloch, whom he pointed out to me from a distance. He said that something should be done for him. Maurice Bloch was a genuine resister, he told me, but he wasn't in a good kommando, and there was always the risk that he might be sent off on a transport for no particular reason. Frager's word was good enough for me. I mentioned the case of Bloch—who later became Bloch-Dassault, then simply Dassault—to the comrades of the French Committee. They did what was necessary to make Maurice Dessault survive in Buchenwald. So it was thanks to Frager that Maurice Dassault had an additional chance of surviving. Perhaps any chance. It's a good thing to say it now that Frager is dead, now that he can't say it himself.

For Henri Frager died in Buchenwald. He was executed by the Gestapo. Only three men of the forty that had made up the special convoy in August survived the last executions in October. Three men whom the underground organization was able to save, by giving them the identity of three deportees who had died of typhus, and thanks in particular to the decisive intervention of the Austrian detainee Eugen Kogon. These three were the Frenchman Stéphane Hessel and the Englishmen Peulevé and Dodkin, whose real name was Yeo-Thomas.

About the middle of April 1945, some days after the liberation of Buchenwald, I was in charge of a detachment on guard around the barracks and offices of the SS

Totenkopf division. We continued to occupy the area around the Buchenwald camp until the Americans arrived to take charge.

That day, while searching through one of the buildings, I happened to find the room in which the SS administration had kept their files on the prisoners. I opened the filing cabinet, which, like all self-respecting filing systems, was arranged in alphabetical order. I found my own card. HÄFTLINGS-PERSONAL-KARTE was printed on it in capital letters. In the top right-hand corner there was a rectangle, inside which there was an isosceles triangle pointing downward; also inside the rectangle was my number, 44904. The number was written in black pencil, and the triangle had been colored in red pencil and superimposed on it was a black, typewritten S. The rest of the card contained the information one would expect on an identity card.

I was looking at this card with all the information concerning me when I noticed, circled in red, a mysterious, poetic word—a word whose exact meaning, despite its obvious meaning in the literal sense, was at first mysterious. *Meerschaum:* sea foam. I assumed that it was a code name. Later this was confirmed. The code name referred to the operation that had brought together at Compiègne, in late 1943 and early 1944, the prisoners from the French prisons who were to be deported to Germany. I learned that the operation that followed ours had the code name *Frühlingswind:* spring wind.

I was looking at this poetic name, *Meerschaum,* when the door opened. It was a British officer, who looked at me mistrustfully.

"What are you doing there?" he asked sharply.

"And what about you?" I retorted, in the same tone of voice.

His eyelids trembled; he was taken aback.

"I'm a British officer."

I interrupted him with a gesture.

"That's obvious enough, you know," I said. "You'd have difficulty persuading me to the contrary. What do you want?"

This time he looked really disconcerted.

"I should tell you that I'm in charge of this building," I said to him, "until the Allied authorities occupy it. Have you any orders to pass on?"

There is nothing funnier than catching soldiers in the trap of their own regulations. Actually, the same goes for every profession. Catching linguists in the trap of words, painters in the trap of light, Marxists in the trap of the dialectic: it's just as funny.

The British officer wasn't sure yet whether he would find it funny.

Somewhat put out, he looked at the SS index card I was holding.

I waved the card.

"Meerschaum," I said. "I've just found my own card. It's told me nothing that I didn't know already, except that I'm Meerschaum. Do you know German? It means 'sea foam.'"

He nodded, as if to indicate that he did know German.

"I thought we were the dregs of the earth, as far as the SS were concerned," I said. "But not at all! We're sea foam. It's rather comforting, isn't it?"

He came up to me and looked at the card I was holding. Then he looked at me.

"If you're in charge of this building," he said smoothly, "perhaps I may ask you for instructions? Even without any order to pass on?"

He had found once again the inimitable tone of British humor. I like soldiers with a sense of humor. Marxists, too. But Marxists with a sense of humor are even fewer than soldiers with a sense of humor. The officer slipped two fingers into the outside pocket of his tunic. He took out a piece of paper, which he unfolded.

"I'm trying to locate a number of individuals," he said.

I took the paper. It was a list of names, and the first name on it was Henri Frager. I didn't feel like joking any more.

I looked at the British officer.

"You've come too late," I told him. "Much too late."

On the last Sunday in September, some months earlier, before the last of the war that was coming to an end, I had seen Henri Frager. We were walking in the small wood between the infirmary and the quarantine camp, where the slope of the Ettersberg joins the Thuringian plain. I had told Frager something that had happened to me at the Tabou camp, a year before, or in September '43, anyway. I'd gone to the Tabou with Julien. We were taking supplies of explosives to the *maquisards* of the Tabou, for some sabotage operation or other. We were in the clearing of the Tabou as night fell. I was sitting some distance away, reading a chapter of *Man's Hope*. It was a book I always had with me in my bag. It ended up impregnated with the sickening, tenacious smell of the explosive. That evening, then, I was rereading *Man's Hope* and some young *maquisards*—that's right, I suddenly think, I too was young! I was nineteen, like most of them, but I'm writing this on the verge of old age, getting old anyway, and a strange phenomenon is occurring; whereas all the other characters in my memory have kept the age they then had, I myself have got older; in my memory, I walk around, with my gray hair, with my weariness of life, in the midst of their youth—a few *maquisards*, then, had come up and asked me what I was reading. Soon there were about a dozen of them around me and we were talking about *Man's Hope* and the Spanish war. At that point, one of the little bosses of the Tabou intervened. He wasn't at all pleased. He didn't want politics in this *maquis*, he shouted. Malraux was politics, so just to piss him off, I read a page of the book aloud, the shooting of Hernandez at the end of the Toledo episode. Silence fell on the group. The boss who didn't want politics in the Tabou said nothing.

But I'm the one who lost out in the deal. For I had to leave my copy of *Man's Hope* with the Tabou *maquisards*. They all wanted to read that book, and I couldn't say no to them. So my copy of *Man's Hope* must have gone up in flames at the Tabou when the SS annihilated the *maquis* and set fire to the huts of the camp, some weeks later.

But I'd just been telling the British officer that he'd come too late.

"Much too late," I said.

He looked at me, perturbed.

How did Henri Frager die? Was he executed with a bullet in the back of the neck, in a bunker cell? Was he hanged in the crematorium cellars? The day before, I'd been to the crematorium cellars, where they hanged my comrades.

But we haven't got there yet.

We're still in September, that evening when Anton gave me a Bible with a pale-blue silk bookmark, marking a page of the Second Book of Samuel, the page about Amnon's incest.

"It's from your Bibliophile," he said, with an inexplicably ironic smile.

And I'm going to spend my night reading both a novel by Faulkner and the Second Book of Samuel, deciphering the obscure signs of the crossed lives and deaths of Absalom and Henry Sutpen, Tamar and Judith Sutpen, Charles Bon and Amnon, for a whole night. (But it was night, too, so many years later A whole life, one might say, between those two nights That of September 1944, in Buchenwald, the day when the *Politische Abteilung*, the camp Gestapo, asked for information about a number of DIKAL prisoners But bureaucratic order must be coming unstuck in Berlin, for in that list from the *Politische Abteilung* there are names of certain deportees of the special August convoy who have already been executed—*entlassen*, "released," is the cynical term of the official report—hanged, several weeks ago, it seems, in the cellars of the crematorium There are also the names of certain survivors: that of Henri Frager, for example Why is the Gestapo asking for information on Frager? That's exactly why Gérard has gone to look for Paul, in Block 42 But Paul already knew about it Wasn't it better to try to leave the camp on some outside kommando from which one might manage to escape? But Paul intimated that he couldn't make a decision individually, that his fate was bound up with that of a group He had to go on waiting, Paul would say He was serene, Paul, not resigned, but serene "Anyway," he said with a smile, "I would have been shot at once as soon as the Gestapo got hold of me That's still a few months gained!"

but it was night, too, so many years later A whole lifetime had passed and he was no longer called Gérard He was no longer called Salagnac, either, or Artigas, or Sanchez He wasn't called anything any more Or, rather, he was just referred to by his name, but sometimes he didn't answer immediately to his name, as if it were the name of someone else whose identity he had borrowed He was no longer anything but himself, oneself "Myself," he thought, with a resigned smile, alone in a hotel room in New York, at the Algonquin, in autumn in the year of grace, or disgrace, 1970 Why did he remember Absalom and the Jehovah's Witness and Henri Frager, twenty-six years later, in that room at the Algonquin, at nightfall, at the hour when the scraps of newspaper and greasy paper fly up in the sudden gusts of wind at 42nd Street? There was a knock on his door; a young woman came in A chambermaid, in the usual uniform of a chambermaid But this one was black, with the supple, long-legged beauty of a gazelle, the predatory beauty of a lithe panther All right, stop dreaming, she had only come in to make the bed Then, when she had finished, she stood at the door, and he gave her a tip She smiled nonchalantly, dignified "My name is Clytie," she said; "if you need something, please call me!" Detached, smooth, speaking in a poised, deep voice, separating the syllables, with perfect diction But the door had already shut and he remained alone, with the sharp sound of that name stuck in his heart like a dagger Clytie! Standing motionless, shivering, in the middle of that unknown hotel room Clytie! It had all come back to him, shortly afterward, with a feeling of sickening vertigo Clytemnestra Sutpen, natural daughter of Thomas Sutpen and of a black slave woman The natural sister of Henry Sutpen, Clytie, who set fire to the old worm-eaten residence of Sutpen's Hundred, to keep them from coming and taking her white half-brother and trying him for the murder of Charles Bon It had all come back to him suddenly *Absalom, Absalom!* Everything, at this early-evening hour when the scraps of greasy paper and newspaper fly up in the sudden gusts of icy wind on 42nd Street, in the midst of the white steam from the ventilation grills and the strident clang of bells from pinball machines and electronic games It had all come back to him He knew by heart the old text, all the words, verbatim, despite the passing years, and he had said aloud the words from the old text "And you are—? Henry Sutpen And you have been here—? Four years And you came home—? To die To die? Yes, to die And you

have been here—? Four years And you are—? Henry
Sutpen." He had said Faulkner's words aloud, and then,
on a sudden impulse, he had walked over to the bedside
table and opened the drawer There was a Bible, of course
He had found the page in the Second Book of Samuel
"And Tamar took the cakes she had made, and brought
them into the chamber to Amnon her brother But when
she brought them near him to eat, he took hold of her, and
said to her, 'Come, lie with me, my sister.' " "Come, lie
with me, my sister! My sister, my gazelle, my dove Never
mind your name, Tamar, Judith, or Clytie!

It had all come back to him in New York, the whole
memory, like vertigo, so many years later)

The young woman had just left.

I had shut the door. Something moved somewhere, in
the distance, in my memory. As if my memory had been a
huge, dilapidated, or at any rate abandoned house which
one would visit in the autumn and in which the sounds of
our footsteps would awaken extinguished echoes, obscure reminiscences, as if, as I walked through that
abandoned house, the impression of already having been
there, perhaps even of having already lived there, were
gradually taking over, becoming an obsession.

Anyway, something moved, in the distance, in my
memory.

Clytie?

I knew that this name, Clytie, should remind me of
something. I also knew that it was no accident that Clytie
was black. I was standing stock still, alone, in the middle
of a hotel room. I was lighting a cigarette. There were men
riding horses in my memory. Why? What relation was
there between Clytie's name and men riding horses? Or,
rather, one man on horseback, through the streets of a
small town with wooden houses: it could be an image

from a Western. Then, suddenly, I had turned to other memories. *L'Homme à cheval,* "*The Man on Horseback,*" was the title of a novel by Drieu La Rochelle. One day Anton, the Buchenwald librarian, came to see me with a few novels he had found among the luggage of a convoy of French deportees. He wanted to read one of them, and asked my advice. I suggested he read Drieu's *L'Homme à cheval.* The rest were rubbish.

Anton!

Even as I remembered how this incident of Drieu's book had ended, I knew that it was not the ending that was important. Actually, that anecdotal memory of a novel by Drieu served as a screen for what really mattered. And what really mattered was Anton himself.

Or, rather, what mattered was that I had rediscovered, through the memory of Anton, what the name Clytie should have reminded me of. The important thing was that this apparent detour through the memory of an incident concerning a book by Drieu was taking me back to Clytemnestra Sutpen, to *Absalom, Absalom!*

Then I walked over to the bedside table. I took the Bible from the drawer. My hand was trembling slightly.

"Second Book of Samuel, 13!" Jehovah had said, twenty-six years earlier, at the window of the Buchenwald library.

Now, in New York, at the Algonquin Hotel, I took the Bible from the bedside-table drawer. *Holy Bible,* it proclaimed, in gilt letters on a black cover. Another gilt inscription read: *Kindly leave this book in view.*

But Jehovah had quoted the book of Job, that December Sunday in Buchenwald, and not Samuel. I was looking out at the snow on the plain of Thuringia and wondering how Jehovah was going to get out of this one. He got out of it very nicely, thanks to the Book of Job.

I look at him, admiring and annoyed.

"In short," I say, "for every natural or historical event there is an appropriate quotation from the Bible!"

He shrugs his shoulders.

"Does that surprise you?" says Jehovah. "You should know how it is: the same thing happens to you."

I look at him perplexed.

"Me?"

"You, the Marxists," says Jehovah.

For some time we have only touched on general questions in our conversations.

Jehovah goes on.

"Quotations," he says, "you've got one for every situation!"

I shrug my shoulders.

I must admit that Barizon criticizes me for the same thing. To be sure, Fernand's point of view isn't the same as Jehovah's. Their points of view must even be quite contrary. Yet Barizon criticizes me for always coming up with some telling quotation, and he doesn't seem to regard this as the finest flower of a well-organized dialectical demonstration. Perhaps he mistrusts dialectical demonstrations that are too well organized, or he simply mistrusts my quotations: it seems to him that I make them up as the occasion demands. He isn't always right, though.

But Jehovah and I have only talked about general ideas. And for Jehovah, of course, the most general idea is that of God. We have come around to talking about God, Jehovah and I.

Last Sunday, for example, we talked about God.

I was coming out of Block 62 and Jehovah was waiting for me on the esplanade. He'd obviously been lying in wait for me. Often, knowing that on Sundays I am in the habit of going out and admiring the view of Thuringia in the late afternoon, he would be waiting for me on the paths leading to the copse that stretched to the bottom of the quarantine camp.

Jehovah was becoming persistent; that much was obvious.

Some days before, one evening when I came to change my books, Anton had looked at me with worry rather than amusement; he appeared to be concerned for me.

"And how's your Bibliophile?" he asks.

He insists on the possessive, of course.

But he doesn't give me time to answer:

"Anyway," he says, "is he a Bibliophile or just a Hispanophile? *Aber, ist er Bibelliebhaber oder einfach Spanierliebhaber?*"

The librarian really does seem to worry about me, as if he is afraid that one of his best customers, whose literary or philosophical tastes he has often shared, might be led off the straight-and-narrow path of virtue. It's amusing how most people fear deviations from correct sexuality.

I have no desire to discuss any of that with him. I just reassure him with a word. I set his mind at rest. I won't leave the path of virtue for Jehovah. His Witness, I mean. I shall remain in the common, enforced virtue of our sexual poverty, scarcely visited by the dreams that become ever more vague and disturbing as we sink deeper into the salt deserts of motionless time and perpetual hunger. Everyone knows that physical exhaustion facilitates the exercise, even the solitary exercise, of virtue. Besides, my imagination is more concerned with Juliette than with Jehovah.

I look at Anton; I reassure him with a word.

However, I wonder if he is one of the Germans who go to the brothel. I wonder if he finds it normal and virtuous to fuck one of the girls in the brothel, with the permission and under the supervision of the SS warrant officer who is the boss and pimp of the brothel girls. I wonder if he finds it normal and virtuous to bring little presents, not only for the brothel girls but also for the SS warrant officer, little presents that are indispensable if everything is to take place as desired, presents that consist of canned food, margarine, bottles of perfume, which can be obtained only by taking part in the camp dealings: by deducting from the daily rations of the deportees a share which the privileged use to pay for their virtue, their normality.

I wonder if he has fixed habits in the camp brothel, or whether he takes any of the girls at random. Who does he fuck? Stahlheber? Or Bykowski, who is one of the most sought-after?

You are probably anxious to know whether I am making this up, or whether I really do know, if not the first names, which in fact I do not know, at least the surnames of the girls in the brothel, the *Sonderbau*, special building, as it was called in Buchenwald. But I haven't made anything up, of course. I'm giving the real names, or some of them. I could give all the real names of the girls in the Buchenwald brothel, at least those of the girls who were carrying out their normal, virtuous activities there—not corrupting male virtue, that is—in December 1944, the month to which I have returned so often in this narrative.

I'm not making anything up, in this instance.

I have, on occasion, made up other things in this narrative. One never gets to the truth without making up something, as everyone knows. If one doesn't make up the truth a bit, one passes through history, especially history that has happened to oneself, as Fabrice passes through the battle of Waterloo. History is an invention, and even a perpetual, ever-renewable reinvention, of the truth. Anyway, Fabrice himself is an invention of Stendhal's.

But in this instance I haven't made anything up. I haven't made up the names of the girls—Stahlheber and

Bykowski, the latter being one of the most sought-after by the normal, virtuous clientèle of the brothel, along with Düsedau and Mierau—who worked at the Buchenwald *Sonderbau* in December 1944. I didn't know these names, of course, at the time. I didn't know them when I looked at Anton one evening and heard him expressing such concern for me in my relations with the Bibliophile, who was perhaps just a Hispanophile. It was only much later that I learned those names.

Much later, in the spring of 1965, I was working on a series of broadcasts on *Le Monde concentrationnaire*. Alain Trutat was directing the whole series for *France Culture*. My job had been to prepare a broadcast on *The SS Economic System*, and it was then, looking through masses of documents, resuming contact with former companions from Buchenwald—whom I had not seen for twenty years—that I stumbled on a bookkeeping sheet for the Buchenwald brothel. It was dated December 17, 1944, and concerned the receipts of the night before: *Einnahme im Sonderbau am 16–12–1944*. The night before, the brothel had taken in forty-five marks, in the currency of the time. Since another column showed that there had been forty-five visits, one does not have to be an arithmetical genius to conclude that the price of a visit was one mark. In the first column of that document, the names of the girls were entered. There were thirteen, but four of them were not working on December 16. Two, Rathmann and Dryska—the document doesn't give the girls' first names—were experiencing a periodic, bloody event, the meaning and occurrence of which have not failed to disturb, to haunt even, the imagination of the species for centuries. Anyway, Rathmann and Dryska were unavailable on December 16. As for the others, Giese and Jubelt, the first worked as a supervisor (the word *Aufsicht* was written in the column, where, in the case of the others, the number of visits were entered, a number that enables me to deduc? that Düsedau, Bykowski, and Mierau were the most sought-after, since each had had six visits, whereas the other girls had had only four or five apiece) and the second girl as cashier, *Kassiererin*.

Hardly the stuff that dreams are made on.

It's an ordinary, boring bookkeeping statement of the receipts for a day's work in the brothel. It is signed by the SS commandant and by the Buchenwald administrator. The latter has stamped the flimsy piece of paper—the original must have been sent to Berlin—with the ink stamp of the *Gefangenengeldverwaltung*, the Financial Administration of the Detainees. For everything in Buchenwald is administered, classified, listed, and signed: the detainees' money, the parts manufactured in the factories, the hours of work and leisure, the living and the dead, the costs of running the crematorium, the homosexuals and the gypsies, the watches and hair of the arrivals, the occupational and university credentials of the deportees, the purchases of beer or *makhorka* in the canteen, and visits made to the brothel. Bureaucratic order reigns over the SS empire.

"Bureaucracy is a circle from which no one can escape. This hierarchy is a hierarchy of knowledge. . . . Bureaucracy holds in its possession the existence of the State, the spiritual existence of society is its private property. The general spirit of bureaucracy is secrecy, mystery. . . ." But I'm not going to recall here those sentences from Marx, which we dissected at length on the Boulevard de Port-Royal, in Lucien Herr's house. Jehovah will criticize my penchant for producing a quotation for every occasion.

Here, as it happens, is Jehovah.

It was last Sunday, the Sunday before the one that I am describing here in such detail.

Jehovah is standing on the esplanade of the Little Camp, between the last barracks huts and the latrines. The brothel isn't far away, just behind the *Kino*. (But you remembered the Buchenwald *Kino* during this stay in New York It was autumn, the sun was shining, but there was a nip in the air You remembered the Buchenwald cinema, through the memory of Gustav Herling That is to say, Gustav Herling, in his book *A World Apart*, cannot remember Buchenwald, he remembers the hut of "self-governing creative activities" in the Yershevo camp It was in that hut, too, that the library of the Stalinist camp described by Herling had been set up Of course, one wouldn't find *Mein Kampf* in the Yershevo library On the other hand, one would find dozens of copies of Stalin's *Problems of Leninism*, hundreds of copies of political propaganda pamphlets There was also a volume containing speeches by La Pasionaria And Gustav Herling recounts how he had underlined in pencil a sentence from one of Dolores Ibarruri's speeches during the defense of Madrid, in 1936, a sentence that became famous: *Better to die standing than to live on one's knees!* Now, this underlined sentence had made the book very popular among the deportees of the Stalinist camp of Yershevo, until an NKVD commission, disturbed by this sudden popularity, withdrew La Pasionaria's book from the library But you aren't going to recount Gustav Herling's book You cannot talk on his behalf You have said simply that you were reading *A World Apart* in New York, in those autumn days of 1970 when you had gone to the United States with Costa Gavras and Yves Montand for a screening of *The Confession* You were reading Herling's book, and you got to the passage where he recounts a visit to the movies at Yershevo, to see an American musical on the life of Johann Strauss, *The Great Waltz* And you then remembered the *Kino* in Buchenwald, which you didn't often remember, to tell the truth Anyway, recently you've been remembering Buchenwald only through the memories, often comparable ones, of former zeks in Stalin's camps.)

Jehovah is waiting for me.

He must have seen me go into Block 62. I'd gone to settle some problem or other with Leo, the Dutch *Stubendienst* who had fought in the Brigades in Spain. When I came out, I was planning to walk down to the copse, to admire the view of the Thuringian plain from my usual Sunday observation post.

But Jehovah is waiting for me on the esplanade.

It's irritating, of course, being watched, followed, waylaid by Jehovah. But don't misunderstand me: it isn't the hypothetically sexual aspect of this persecution that bothers me. Even if Jehovah were interested solely in the opposite sex, if he had been a determined, indefatigable lover of women, spending all his leisure hours at the *Sonderbau* with the girls Düsedau, Bykowski, and Mierau, or even with the less popular Stahlheber, Rafalska, and Heck, or the still less popular Ehlebracht, Sinzig, and Plumbaum, or—why not?—with Giese, the assistant supervisor, or Jubelt, the cashier, who had both been totally inactive on the said day, at least on a sexual plane—even if Jehovah had been nothing but a *Frauenliebhaber*, his persistence would have irritated me in the end, of course.

Besides, the only clue to the hypothetical homosexuality of Jehovah—that is to say, of his Witness—leaving aside the public rumor stemming from Anton's suggestive words, was of a literary order, and therefore quite indirect. For Jehovah never made a gesture, stammered a word, or smiled in any way that could be interpreted as equivocal, or, rather, as unequivocal. On the other hand, his interpretation of *Absalom, Absalom!*, the novel by

Faulkner that I had gone to fetch from the library on the day we met, was fairly significant. For him, in fact, the theme of incest, which forms the ancestral web of the novel, was redoubled by that of homosexual love. Jehovah maintained, in fact, that it was not only, or even especially, to prevent his half-brother Charles Bon from sleeping with his sister Judith that Henry Sutpen had killed him. He had killed him because he was, actually, unconsciously in love with him. Henry would undoubtedly have been ready to consummate the incest, even if he had killed himself afterward, but he could not bear the idea that Charles Bon—all the more attractive for having black blood in his veins—should sleep with their sister: it was the carnal act with a woman that was in itself impure, unpardonable, metaphysically evil.

But it's not *Absalom, Absalom!* that we are going to talk about today, in the latrines of the Little Camp, where we have been forced to take refuge during a sudden, violent snowstorm.

It is about God that we are going to talk, Jehovah and I.

"He seals up the hand of every man, that all may know his work. . . ."

I'm holding this Bible, years later, a whole lifetime later, in my room at the Algonquin Hotel in New York. I'm rereading the passage in the Book of Job—37:5—that Jehovah had recited before the snow-covered plain of Thuringia.

I think pretty much the opposite, of course. I don't think that God marks every man with his seal, but that man leaves his mark on everything—beginning, or ending, with God. I'm thinking that today, in New York. I thought it already in Buchenwald, on that distant Sunday, that day that man has reserved to the Lord and not the Lord to man.

We were in the latrine building, and I'd explained to Jehovah, who was rather disconcerted, what my relationship with God was. Marx's atheism, I had told him, stopped halfway. No doubt he had unmasked God's humanity, His imaginary, ideological nature. But he did not carry this to its logical conclusion. Perhaps it was impossible for a Jew—above all for a Jew who denies his Jewishness and rebels against it—to carry this idea to its logical conclusion. Anyway, if God is human, the distance between man and Himself, the gap opened up by every question that is fundamental—and therefore has no unequivocal answer—He is, for this very reason, eternal. Or immortal, at least to the extent that man is. No more, perhaps, but certainly no less than man. As long as there is a man capable of imagining God, having a vital need for that imaginary entity, and even if that man is only Paul Claudel, God will not *be*, since He *is* not a Being—for there is no such Being—but He will *exist*.

In German, of course, and in the latrine building of the Little Camp of Buchenwald, among the hundreds of ghosts who had emerged from the invalid huts to look for a bit of warmth, perhaps the butt of a *makhorka* cigarette, or at least a puff, a single one, from the butt of a *makhorka* cigarette—the ultimate pleasure!—to exchange a few words with other ghosts (and they were pushed around by the new arrivals from the quarantine huts, who would be strong and fat for a few weeks longer, but in a sense even more disturbing because the gap or contrast between their physical condition and their unmatching quarantine clothes was all the more grotesque; they were also pushed around by the young Russian *Stubendienst* of the Little Camp, for whom the latrines were a privileged meeting place, a sort of bazaar where goods and favors were exchanged: alcohol, knives, pornographic photographs, catamites, bread, smiles), among those hundreds of ghosts of all ages, crouching on the wooden beam that overhung the long common ditch through which flowed the stinking liquid of the excrement, among that confused commotion, broken sometimes by piercing cries of distress or even of terror, in that place, then, and in German, it was no doubt easier to speak of God: "*Gott ist kein Sein, nur ein Dasein!*" I'd said to Jehovah. And He will exist as long as there are men and society. He will exist in that apparently nebulous constellation, from which nevertheless the very web of history is woven, of ideology. Thus an atheism carried to its logical conclusion, which would try to go beyond Marx's Judeo-Hegelian aporias, should begin by postulating the existence of God, of His being there, His divine presence, which is merely the human turned toward its own abyss of anxiety and incomprehension.

But I'm in New York, a lifetime later, and I'm putting this Bible back into the drawer of the bedside table.

This afternoon, at Yale University, a young woman was staring at me.

Of course, she might just as easily have been looking at Yves or Costa. We were all together, Montand, Gavras, and I, for a screening of *The Confession* at Yale, and this young woman might well have been looking at one of my companions, or even at both of them. As objects for female observation, we aren't a bad sample, the three of us. An Italian, a Greek, a Spaniard, all three exiles from childhood: there was a sort of joyful complicity among us that must have communicated itself to our audience. It must have been communicated to one young woman, anyway.

After the general discussion, the audience broke up into groups, where the discussion continued.

She is standing near me, the young woman with the attentive gaze.

She's wearing jeans and a white turtleneck sweater. She's slim, fair, with short hair. There's something Slavic about her. You will say that there's nothing extraordinary about that. An American girl who doesn't look Slavic looks Scandinavian, Hungarian, or Neapolitan. She looks like her family, in other words. But that girl didn't just look Slavic. She had to be Polish. I was sure of it. She had that bearing of the head, that base of the neck, that languorous curve of the hips, those compressed, sensuous lips, that attentive, elusive gaze of Polish women. I thought that this aristocratic liveliness of Polish women, their physical grace, was a way of reacting against the gray ugliness of the countries of Eastern Europe. I thought that this indefinable air of freedom about Polish women was the somatization of their spiritual distinction in the gray, gloomy Europe of post-Stalinist Communism. But I have to admit that this grace, this state of physical grace, of Polish women is universal. It must enable them to preserve their distinction as much in the productive, corporation-minded West as in the productive, bureaucratic East.

But is she really Polish?

I take the initiative and ask her before she speaks to me. It's not a bad tactic, anyway.

"Are you of Polish origin?"

A sunny shadow crosses over her face.

Sunny, I said, for the face lit up, as if lit from inside. Shadow, I said, for her eyes darkened at once. As if being Polish had, necessarily, to bring you both joy and pain.

"Yes!" she says, with a brief smile. "My father died in Buchenwald," she adds; there is an eternal shadow in her eyes.

There. I might have known.

Yet experience should have already taught me that it's seldom you that a person is looking at. It does happen, of course, but it's unusual. Usually, it's the image of something else, of someone else, someone purely imaginary sometimes, that a person sees in you. Today it's the image of the survivor. I am looking at the young Polish woman, who can't be much more than twenty-five. I rapidly calculate the time that separates that autumn of 1970 from that long-ago spring of 1945. Yes, of course, it could be. She must have been born after her father was arrested.

"What right have I to be alive: is that your question?"

She looks at me for a moment. Tears come into her eyes, it seems to me. She lowers her head, hides her face.

She looks up at once, straight and proud, like a Polish woman.

"My father died; he was never able to tell me about it," she says in a strange, thin voice. "I've only got your book, The Long Voyage, to help me imagine what it was like."

She looks me in the eye.

"I do sometimes hate the survivors," she says calmly.

I nod.

"I was born on April eleventh, 1945," she says, "the day Buchenwald was liberated."

My hand brushes over her forehead, her high cheekbones, the lobe of her ear, her shoulder. She doesn't move, she makes no attempt to move away. She must realize that my gesture has nothing male about it: it has no possessive or sexual reference. She must realize that my hand, in a spontaneous gesture, joyful and sad at once, wanted only to touch that flesh that came to life on the last day of our death, to touch lightly that body that measured the distance that separates us from our death: that victory of life over death.

"I love April," I say.

But I go back to what she said before.

"Anyway, you should know that one can never tell one's children!"

She looks at me steadily.

"Not even you?" she asks.

I shake my head.

"No," I say, "one cannot tell one's son, if one has a son. One tells it best to strangers, because one is less involved, less solemn. Besides, your father couldn't have told you about his death. But I can!"

Her eyes widen. Her whole body seems to shudder.

"Did he die in Buchenwald or during the evacuation?" I persist.

She gives a sudden start.

"How did you know he was evacuated?"

A week before the liberation of the camp by the troops of the American Third Army, the SS command brought back into the camp compound all the outside kommandos, at least all those near enough. The roll calls had stopped. Soon food supplies stopped, or almost. The SS command had been ordered from Berlin to evacuate the camp. It had tried to carry out the order. There then began a week of struggles, sometimes overt confrontations, sometimes private meetings between the SS command and the underground resistance leadership, in which the Germans, of course, played a decisive role. The aim of the underground leadership was to keep at the camp, which would be freed by American troops within a matter of days, the maximum number of deportee-resisters. It therefore gave orders to sabotage, or at least to impede to the maximum, the evacuation measures taken by the SS. The SS, consequently, were forced to carry out the necessary measures themselves. Several times, they invaded the camp with armed detachments, in an attempt to remove deportees. On other occasions, certain blocks were encircled, and the inmates moved to the *Appell-platz*, with a view toward departure. But the results of these measures were inconclusive. Only a minority of deportees were sent out on the deadly roads for evacuation.

Some national groups, however, decided to go along with the evacuation. The Soviet prisoners of war, enclosed in special compounds that could be easily surrounded by SS detachments, had decided to set out together, in a compact, organized group, planning to attempt mass escapes on the road. It was a tactic that paid off, to some extent, but only in the short term: the Soviet POWs did manage, on a large scale, to break away from their SS guards—only to fall, some time later, into Stalin's Gulag camps.

The Poles took the same attitude. Their decision to transform the evacuation order into a possible escape to freedom was probably influenced by the opinion, fairly widespread among the deportees, that the camp would end up as a rat trap and that the SS would set fire to the whole camp with everybody inside it. This was an opinion that the underground leadership did not share, having carried out a more realistic, subtler political analysis of the contradictory situation in which the local SS command found itself, caught between its duty to obey Berlin and its desire to prepare for the future, at a time when there was no longer any hope of reversing the tide of war.

Anyway, the Poles had decided to go along with the evacuation. They had turned up on the *Appellplatz*, as the SS had requested, but organized in groups according to a military structure. Moreover, the older ones did not take part in the expedition—only young or fairly young men made up the Polish columns of the Buchenwald exodus—and they left without any luggage, to be unencumbered in their movements, ready either to flee or to fight.

I was on the edge of the *Appellplatz*, with a group of

Spanish comrades from the underground military self-defense group, the day the Poles left. We watched those young, disciplined cohorts. A strange impression of almost wild, irrational joy emanated from them as they moved in a single body to the camp gates. One felt that at any moment they might start singing.

"That's how I saw your father leave, some days before your birth," I say to the young woman from Yale, twenty-five years later. Her eyes shining, she rises to her full height, as if she were looking out into the distance, to the end of the huge *Appellplatz*, at the outline of that young man who had been her father and who was setting out for death, as one sets out for battle.

"So we've seen everything, us Poles," she says, with sad, perhaps desperate pride.

Then, without transition, she sticks her hand into the canvas army-surplus bag that she is carrying slung around her shoulder and takes out a book bound in red.

"Do you know Grudzinski's book?" she asks.

But the book she actually hands me is Gustav Herling's *A World Apart*, which I also happen to be reading at the time. There's a moment of confusion. Then, if I understand her explanations correctly, it turns out that Herling's real name is Grudzinski—or the other way around, I don't know. Anyway, it seems he has published other works in Polish under the double name of Herling-Grudzinski.

I do know Grudzinski's book. I tell her so. In my hotel room in New York, I tell her, I have Herling-Grudzinski's book on my bedside table. I don't tell her about the Bible: it's too early for that. It's not until later, at the end of that Saturday, that I leaf through the Bible, when the first name of the young black girl—"My name is Clytie"—awakens my memories, suddenly reminds me of Jehovah and *Absalom, Absalom!*

• • •

You remembered her, some years later, the young Polish woman from Yale.

It was her birthday, April 11. Her thirtieth birthday, even: April 11, 1975. Thirty years is quite a lot. For her, the young woman of Polish origin at Yale whose name you will probably never know, it was beginning to be quite a long time. But for you, too. Thirty years since your return to life, as they used to say. And what if it had not been a return to life? Thirty years since the last day of your death, you thought to yourself. And what if it had not been the last day of your death? If it had been, on the contrary, the first day of a new death? Of another dream, anyway?

But you remembered her on April 11, 1975, the day of the thirtieth anniversary of the liberation of Buchenwald.

You were watching a literary program on French television in which a number of Parisian intellectuals were taking part, together with Alexander Solzhenitsyn, on the occasion of the publication of *The Oak and the Calf.*

Some time before, you had been watching another program about Solzhenitsyn, without the man himself. You had seen the face of a well-known critic on the television screen. You had seen him purse his lips:

"No," he was saying, "*The Gulag Archipelago* is not a very good book! From a literary point of view, of course!"

It was typical of the strategy of the parasite, whose attitudes are bounded by his own limitations. Khrushchev's report to the Twentieth Congress was not judged to be serious enough, from the Marxist point of view, by people who had adulterated, bastardized, and soiled Marxism for decades, and who had never dared to make the slightest criticism of Stalin, even in Marxist terms, while Stalin was alive and in power. *The Gulag Archipelago* is not well written, is not a very good book, say the same people, or others of their kind. The important thing, in each case, is to obscure what the discussion is really about, the truth contained in it. For if Khrushchev's report was not Marxist—how could it be, anyway, since Marxism doesn't exist!—it was at least veracious. And if *The Gulag Archipelago* is not well written—a question that may be debated until the end of time, like the sex of angels—it is at least well thought out. And well said. Indeed, it is said in masterly fashion. Thought out, with the minds of thousands of anonymous, crazed witnesses, said with the voice of thousands of witnesses silenced forever.

In a dazzling piece written in March 1974, the Italian Franco Fortini analyzed the reasons, admitted or inadmissible, why certain European left-wing intellectuals, having still neither learned nor understood anything, retreated in terror from Solzhenitsyn after the publication of *The Gulag Archipelago*. In that article, "Del disprezzo per Solgenitsin," Fortini showed how "there is a serious hypocrisy in the discourse of those who throw up their hands, with reservations as to the quality of Solzhenitsyn's works," an attitude that serves, in fact, "to bracket out the historico-political content" of those works.

But there was no literary critic on the screen for Bernard Pivot's broadcast on the evening of April 11, 1975.

There was the enormous, truculent truth of Alexander Solzhenitsyn himself. A disturbing, disagreeable truth, to be sure, for most left-wing intellectuals (the right-wing ones, even liberal right-wing ones, are not of interest in this particular context, for although they early understood and declared the truth of the Gulag, that it was a concentrated expression of the reality of Communism, they are, on the other hand, incapable of elaborating a concrete strategy aimed at the destruction of the said

Gulag, and therefore of Communism in its despotic form; although they are, therefore, necessary, often indispensable, allies in protest, they are of very little use in the task of transformation, whereas the hypothetical task of revolutionary Marxism, which is today unthinkable, is not to *interpret* the Gulag and the countries of bureaucratic despotism but to *transform* them)—a truth, therefore, practically inadmissible for left-wing intellectuals, whose task it is, perhaps by vocation, perhaps by the masochism of hope, to square the circle: to keep open the prospect of a union and victory of the left.

But you were looking at Alexander Solzhenitsyn on April 11, 1975, the thirtieth anniversary of the liberation of Buchenwald, and also the thirtieth birthday of the young Polish woman you met briefly at Yale, who reproached you with being alive while being grateful that you were, because you were thus able to speak to her about her father, about that distant past before her birth which had conditioned her life, about that death long ago from which she had not succeeded in distancing herself in her life. You were watching Alexander Solzhenitsyn sweep aside the Parisian intellectuals' delicate, or subtle, objections—subtly marked, anyway, with the seal of guilt—with a broad gesture and a toothy grin. It was the vitality, the capacity for destructive humor of this former zek that struck you above all that evening, as he hit out with his disagreeable truths. You heard him list the truths that were unacceptable to those right-thinking left-wing minds, to the virtuous consciences that strive, in a schizoid way, to condemn the Gulag while approving of its premises—that is, the revolutionary wars that have through the century snatched peoples from imperialist domination, only to throw them into the slavery of the Single Party—and you thought of Franco Fortini's irrefutable article, "Del disprezzo per Solgenitsin": "One shouldn't be surprised that intolerance of Solzhenitsyn should be so widespread, or that contempt for him should be so common. For it is not enough to have made a political judgment on the Soviet Union today or on the policy of the CP. There remains the self-defensive refusal to accept the idea of a historical catastrophe. Out of fear of being confused with the enemies of Communism, one has gone on for so many years *refusing to redefine Communism, refusing its history*. One prefers one's own hopes to the truth. We delude the young because we carry on with our illusions."

You have nothing to add to that.

But no one recalled, during the literary program on April 11, 1975, that a double anniversary was being celebrated. Of course, the birthday of the young Polish woman from Yale was of concern only to you; no one else was even aware of it. There was no question, therefore, of alluding to it. But the other anniversary, that of the liberation of Buchenwald, did not concern only you. It also concerned Senka Klevshin, for example, Ivan Denisovich's companion in the special camp of corrective forced labor, a day Solzhenitsyn described, a day like any other. Senka Klevshin, former inmate of Buchenwald, must have remembered that anniversary, if he was still alive on April 11, 1975. Whatever his real name may have been, Senka Klevshin must have remembered it. Later, perhaps, if he was still alive, he learned that his companion in deportation, the zek Solzhenitsyn, took part in a literary program on French television on April 11, 1975. The coincidence could not have failed to bring a smile to his lips. "Well, well!" he must have said to himself. "It's the day of the liberation of Buchenwald." He must have thought it was a significant coincidence.

So you remember Senka Klevshin, and you begin to watch that very Parisian literary program through Senka

Klevshin's eyes. You may even have known him, the Russian zek hidden beneath that name in a book by Alexander Solzhenitsyn who, some years before, as a *Kazettler* in Buchenwald, had been your companion. You knew many Russians in Buchenwald. Anyway, you must have been close to him on the Weimar road when the armed resistance groups were moving toward that city, after the liberation of the camp. The Russians were deployed to the right of that road, in the forest. But you cannot know whether Senka Klevshin was there. The only thing you know with any certainty about him is what Solzhenitsyn says about him in *One Day in the Life of Ivan Denisovich:* "Senka had really been through the mill. Most of the time he didn't talk. He couldn't hear what people said and usually kept his mouth shut. So they didn't know much about him. All they knew was that he'd been in Buchenwald and was in the camp underground there. He'd smuggled arms in for the uprising."

But it's true, you say to yourself today—not April 11, 1975, but today, as you write these lines—that there are people who deny that uprising in Buchenwald, who deny Senka Klevshin and, by the same token, Solzhenitsyn, who is seen as naïve enough to believe in that legend, and who deny you yourself the right to speak of that uprising, since they decree it did not take place. But do they also deny us the right to remember? Can Senka remember the automatic rifles brought into the camp, secretly, part by part, by comrades in the Gustloff Works? Can he remember the weapons abandoned by the SS that August day 1944 when the camp was bombed by the Americans, and "organized"—for once it's the right term!—by comrades in the underground self-defense groups? And you, have you the right to remember? In a few minutes, when that December Sunday that you are describing here comes to an end—but perhaps it isn't you; perhaps you cannot

completely identify yourself with the Narrator—you will
be summoned by your group leader: there's a military-
alert exercise tonight, a sort of mobilization of all the
detachments—without weapons, of course—that will
have to move around in the camp, in the darkness,
eluding the surveillance of the SS guards on duty in the
watchtowers, in order to join their hypothetical action
stations. But will you have the right to recount this
memory? Now that certain individuals—and the latest to
do so seems to be the distinguished psychiatrist Bruno
Bettelheim—deny the reality of that armed insurrection
in Buchenwald, will you have the right to remember that
early afternoon of April 11, when Palazon—his real name
was Lacalle—who was in charge of the Spanish shock
groups, appeared in front of Block 40, laden with rifles
and yelling, "Grupos, a formar!" and from all the windows of the block, as in a Harold Lloyd film, the Spaniards of the shock groups, who had been piled in there for
hours, spilled out, to grab the rifles and set off for the
positions that had already been assigned them?

You would certainly not deny that the armed uprising
in Buchenwald was not a military exploit, that it did not
change the course of the war. But would the course of the
war have been changed, would the war have been short-
ened by a day, a single day, if Paris had not risen? You
know very well, and Bruno Bettelheim ought to know as
well as you, that armed uprisings of this kind have above
all a political and moral significance. Thus, if the course
of the war was not changed by the Paris uprising, the
political and moral course of French history was profoundly altered by it. The same goes for Buchenwald, you
say. The important thing was not so much the taking of a
few dozen prisoners and the occupation of ground when
the SS had begun their hasty evacuation of the watchtowers and barracks—that is, at the moment when the risk of

uselessly shedding, for the greater glory of the bosses of the groups, the blood of prisoners was minimal, practically zero, a moment perfectly calculated by the underground military leadership—the important thing was to break, if only for a few hours, the fatality of slavery and submission. Power wasn't at the end of your guns that day in Buchenwald, you are well aware of that: it was dignity that was at the end of your guns. It was for that dignity, for that idea of mankind, that you had survived.

And it's strange, you think, that Bruno Bettleheim, a distinguished psychiatrist, a Jew, a former prisoner in Dachau, does not seem to have understood that, in his aptly entitled "Surviving." For Bettelheim is not one of those who reject the reality of the Buchenwald uprising for obscure political reasons, or, rather, for very clear reasons, anti-Communism, pure and simple. Nor is he one of those witnesses who saw nothing because they weren't at any place where anything could be seen, and who deny the reality of what escaped their attention.

No, Bruno Bettelheim is not one of those. His problem, it seems to you, and traces of it are visible throughout his essay "Surviving," is that he cannot forgive himself for surviving. He cannot forgive himself for having been one of the very few Jews to be freed from a Nazi concentration camp. And you understand that feeling. In the spring of 1945, in fact, the *Politische Abteilung* asked the *Arbeitsstatistik* for information concerning a deportee bearing the number 44904. Now, that happened to be your number. Shortly afterward, the *Politische Abteilung* passed on to you a letter from Franco's embassy in Berlin, informing you that Señor de Lequerica had taken up your case and was hoping to reach a positive solution with the German authorities. Someone in your family must have intervened with Lequerica. There were plenty of important people in your family who were well regarded by the

Franco regime. But that's not what you mean. You mean the anguish that overcame you at the idea that these moves might actually be positive, might bring about your liberation. A shameful, terrifying anguish overcame you at the idea that you might abandon your comrades, betray them in a sense, that you might be able to resume your previous life, your life outside, without them, perhaps against them. But, fortunately, those moves by the Spanish authorities came to nothing.

Anyway, that memory enables you to understand perfectly the feeling of guilt that must prey upon the mind of Bruno Bettelheim, a Viennese Jewish psychiatrist, survivor of the genocide of the Viennese Jews, when he speaks of the problems of survival in the concentration camps. You understand very well, but you cannot excuse, for all that, the nonsense he talks about the liberation of Buchenwald.

But you weren't thinking of Bruno Bettelheim on April 11, 1975; you were thinking of Senka Klevshin. You were thinking that you would give years of your life to be able to meet Senka Klevshin. With him, your former companion in Buchenwald, you might at last throw some light on questions that had arisen in your mind about the behavior of the Russians in Buchenwald. You would have been able to tell him what you thought, listen to what he had to say. Eventually, you came to the realization, confirmed by your reading of *The Gulag Archipelago*, that the Russians were so perfectly at home in the world of Buchenwald because the society from which they came had been a perfect preparation for it, for its arbitrariness, its despotism, its rigid hierarchization of privileges, the habit of surviving outside the law, the habit of injustice. The Russians weren't on an alien planet in Buchenwald; they were almost at home, for—and this conclusion had cost you dear, despite the freedom from ideological prejudices that you thought you had reached—the Nazi concentration-camp society was not, as you had long thought, the concentrated, and hence necessarily deformed, expression of capitalist social relations. This idea was fundamentally false. Actually, the essence of capitalist social relations is to be found in the division, the struggle, the antagonism between the classes in a system whose dynamism is based on them: now, the concentration camp suppressed, suspended, at least within its inner compound, any dynamism of that kind. No doubt there were class differences, or at least differences of rank, differences in the consumption of the food needed to survive, in Buchenwald. But that stratification was not based on struggle, exchange, and property, as in capitalist society: it was based on the function, the role, of each individual in a bureaucratic, pyramidal structure, from which resulted an unequal appropriation, as in Soviet society.

In fact, the Nazi camps were not the distorting mirror of capitalist society—even if they were the product of the class struggle, or, rather, the result of the violent suspension of that struggle by the arbitrary action of the fascists —they were a fairly faithful mirror of Stalinist society. And in a camp like Buchenwald, in which politicals, and especially Communists, had the upper hand, the fidelity of that image struck you as terrifying.

As you watched Alexander Solzhenitsyn on the French television screen on April 11, 1975, images exploded in every direction. The imaginary image of Senka Klevshin, the image of that young Polish woman born on the same day thirty years before, the image of Herling-Grudzinski in the camp at Yershevo, reading Dostoyevsky's *From the House of the Dead*, the image of Nikolai, the Russian *Stubendienst* in Block 56, in which Halbwachs and Maspéro lived and died, and Nikolai the Boss, with his gleaming boots and NKVD cap—and now you understood why they were so prized by the young Russian toughs, those caps with their blue edging: they symbolized the real, hidden power of Russian society, the power to which the toughs themselves aspired, in the jungle of the Little Camp in Buchenwald—the image of Ladislav Holdos, the image of Daniel A., with his invincible smile, and the image of Fernand Barizon on the night of that December Sunday.

Fernand Barizon was waiting for me outside the Mutualité. A little while earlier, at the end of the meeting, he had emerged from the crowd.

"Gérard!" he had said.

His hair was turning gray, as were his eyebrows, though they were as thick and bushy as ever. He nodded, smiling.

"I'll never get used to your real name," he said.

"But my name really is Gérard," I said.

He laughed. We both laughed.

People were coming and going all around us, at the foot of the Mutualité platform. I was asked to go and have a drink with some pals from *Clarté*, the Communist students' paper, and the writers who had taken part in the discussion.

"You go, Gérard; don't put yourself out for me," said Barizon.

I didn't put myself out for him, but for both of us, for our friendship. We had begun a journey twenty years before; we had to end it together.

"Are you in a hurry?" I asked.

He shook his head.

"I'm never in a hurry these days, Gérard," he said.

So I arranged to meet him a bit later, in a café on the Rue Saint-Victor. I was going off to rejoin Pierre Kahn, Yves Buin, Bernard Kouchner, my pals from *Clarté*, when Barizon came back.

"You aren't in the Party any more, are you?"

I made a gesture expressing doubt.

"In principle," I said, "I'm still a member of the Central Committee. In fact, I don't think I'm in the Party any more. I'll know before long."

I looked at him, but he showed no reaction.

"Do you mind that I'm not a big shot any more?" I asked, reminding him of the term he had used four years before, during that trip from Paris to Zurich with what turned out to be a decisive stop-over at Nantua.

He burst out laughing, in his usual loud way. "I don't give a shit whether you're a big shot or not!"

He pointed his finger at me. "There's something I want you to know, before we have our talk, Gérard," he said, in a serious tone of voice. "Last spring, some of your guys, I mean some guys from the Spanish Party, came to see me. They told me you were a bastard, and that I should slam my door in your face if ever you showed up. I told them where to get off! That's all I wanted to say. We'll talk later."

He turned and moved away into the crowd.

Why was I so furious that they had done that to Fernand? I was quite well aware that the PCE, as soon as the meeting in the former castle of the kings of Bohemia had ended and I had been removed from the Executive Committee, in April 1964, had contacted all the French comrades I had known in the course of my underground work to warn them about me. That must be what they call vigilance. Why was I particularly shocked that they had done it to Fernand? Because of Buchenwald? Because of our Sundays, long ago, with Juliette and Zarah Leander?

But nothing could negate my having lived through those Sundays with Fernand. *I* had lived through them, not Carrillo. They would never dispossess me of my memory. They would never wipe out the memory of Buchenwald. It wasn't Carrillo who had listened to Zarah

Leander tell us of the desperate, infinite happiness of love, it was I who had listened. It wasn't Carrillo who had dreamed of Juliette in Buchenwald, it was Fernand and I who had dreamed of her.

I watched Barizon move away into the crowd.

"Why are we still Communists, Gérard?"

It was the question that Barizon had asked me in Zurich in 1960.

He had asked me out of the blue, at the wrong moment, at the last minute, at the moment we were about to say good-bye. At the moment when I no longer had time to answer, whatever my answer would have been. We didn't even have time to articulate that question properly, to let that interrogation unfold. But perhaps that's why Barizon had asked the question at that moment, at that particularly inappropriate moment. Perhaps he really didn't want a reply to that inappropriate question. Perhaps he only wanted it to be asked, out of the blue.

Anyway, we were in the departure lounge at the Zurich airport. A female voice had just announced over the loudspeaker the immediate departure of the Swissair flight for Prague. I held out my hand to Fernand Barizon. I was about to go through the nearest passport control. I did not yet know that I would forget all the reasons for that trip to Prague, which seemed so urgent at the time. I did not yet know that my only memory of that trip to Prague was to be of looking at a Renoir painting.

"Why are we still Communists, Gérard?"

Barizon asked me that question just as I was about to turn away. I was rooted to the spot. I didn't even think of giving Barizon hell for calling me Gérard, loud and clear, when I was supposed to be Ramón Barreto, and I was quite obviously no one other than Ramón Barreto, an unknown Uruguayan whom I was embodying for the last part of my trip.

"Come on now!" I said stupidly, rooted to the spot.

It was too late, of course. Too late for that question, or for any other question.

That morning, we had sailed around Lake Zurich talking of Khrushchev's secret report. Opposite Wädenswil, Fernand had asked me his first question, the one about the truth of the report, or, rather, the reality of its existence and the veracity of its contents. Later, opposite Küsnacht, just as the boat was leaving the quay at Küsnacht, I'd told Barizon how Khrushchev and the others had liquidated Beria. I had given him an account of that event, more or less as Carrillo had reported it to me. "Shit!" Barizon had murmured. It was the only comment he had made all morning. The rest of the time, he had confined himself to asking me short questions to spur on my account, to get me to say everything I remembered, everything that was on my mind, in my heart, in my guts, and which actually I didn't always tell myself.

And then, suddenly, at the end of our trip, just as we were about to say good-bye for who knows how long, Barizon had asked that inappropriate question. I mean inappropriate as to time and place. In every other respect, it was the most appropriate question one could imagine. The only appropriate question.

"Why are we still Communists, Gérard?"

That evening, at the Mutualité, during the discussion organized by *Clarté* on the theme "The Uses of Literature," I had tried to answer Fernand Barizon's question.

"What, in my opinion, is the most valid Marxist attitude toward that period of the workers' movement that I shall call, simplifying somewhat in order to make myself quite clear, Stalinism?"

I had thought of Barizon as I had asked that question aloud, before that crowd at the Mutualité, that autumn evening in 1964. I was sitting on the left of Yves Buin, who chaired the discussion. Beside me were Simone de Beauvoir and Jean Ricardou. On the other side of Yves Buin were Jean-Pierre Faye, Yves Berger, and Jean-Paul Sartre.

"It seems to me," I replied to my own question, "it seems to me that the principal element in that attitude is an awareness of our responsibility, or, if you like, our co-responsibility. Here ignorance, real or pretended, is useless, justifying nothing. There are always ways and means of knowing, or at least of *questioning*. We have been too vociferous about the serene conscience, about the bad faith with regard to the extermination of the Jews, for instance, to arrogate for ourselves, now, the excuses of these obfuscating mechanisms.

"Even if we were ignorant, really ignorant, we would still be co-responsible, for that past is our past, and no one can change it. We cannot refuse that past. We can negate it, that is to say, admit and understand it fully, in order to destroy what is left of it, in order to build a future that is radically different from it.

"So, what we need is an active, not an uneasy, awareness of our responsibility. We are responsible for that past because we accept responsibility. We are responsible for that past because we accept responsibility for the future, for revolution on a world scale."

Reading these sentences today, I can easily understand to what extent I was still, in the autumn of 1964, caught up in an inconsistent illusion: the illusion of maintaining and of fostering the values of Communism, despite the Communist Party or even against it. The illusion of liquidating the consequences of Stalinism through revolution, and, what's worse, "on a world scale"! I already knew, of course, that what ought not to have survived in the Communist Party was the Communist Party itself, but I did not yet know, or not yet sufficiently, that no other revolutionary force, no other vanguard, could replace that Party, that type of party: that history was blocked off, in that respect, for an indefinite period, perhaps forever, but at least for the foreseeable future. I already knew—and there was no great merit in knowing it!—that Stalinism was one of the consequences of the defeat of the revolution, but I did not yet know, or did not yet wish to know—perhaps out of fear of breaking my bonds, of being regarded as a "renegade"—that Stalinism also meant the historical impossibility of a resumption of the revolution, that Stalinism, even superficially de-Stalinized, carried within itself the impossibility of revolution on a world scale.

In short, I did not yet know—it wouldn't be long before I did—that world revolution was a historical myth of the same type as that of the universal class. They were equally false and equally effective, each supporting the other, like the halt leading the blind.

"You know, old boy," Barizon says to me a bit later, "you never wrote that book you talked to me about at Nantua, four years ago."

Was it at Nantua? Wasn't it in Geneva, in the buffet of the Gare de Cornavin? I look at Barizon in the café on the Rue Saint-Victor where I have joined him.

Anyway, it's true that I haven't written that book I talked to him about, whether in Geneva or in Nantua.

"The day I saw your photo," Barizon goes on, "last year, with an article on your book—Christ, what a shock it was! I learned your real name at last."

"My real name is Gérard," I interrupted him. "My real name is Sanchez, Artigas, Salagnac, Bustamante, Larrea!"

He looked at me and nodded.

"OK," he said thoughtfully. "Your real name is a false name. The *maquis*, the underground, the struggle: a false

name for that! But try to forget, if you don't want to be too
unhappy from now on."

He was right, I'm sure.

"So, you told me you'd write about a Sunday in
Buchenwald and you'd put me in your story, under the
name of Barizon. I dash out and read your book, but
nothing, nothing at all! No Sunday, no Barizon!" said
Barizon.

We laughed together.

"Anyway," I said, "I must rewrite that book!"

He looked at me, frowning; he didn't understand what I
meant, not yet, anyway.

A bit more than a year before, in April 1963, when the
snow was swirling in the beams of the floodlights in the
Gare de Lyon, I had remembered, in a sickening moment
of illumination, *One Day in the Life of Ivan Denisovich.*

At first sight, the publication of Solzhenitsyn's novel,
and all the attention given to that publication by official
Soviet circles, coming as it did after the Twenty-second
Congress of the Soviet Party, during which the criticism
of Stalin had been not only extended but also made
public, all these events tended to prove, at first sight, the
final victory of Khrushchev's theses. It seemed safe to
infer the possibility that the Soviet political system
would gradually reform itself from the top. Later, in *The
Oak and The Calf,* Alexander Solzhenitsyn was to speak
of that period in biting terms: "After the drab Twenty-first
Congress, which damped and muted the splendid prom-
ise of the Twentieth, there was no way of foreseeing the
sudden fury, the reckless eloquence of the attack on
Stalin which Khrushchev would decide upon for the
Twenty-second! . . . But, there it was—and not even a
secret attack, as at the Twentieth Congress, but a public
one! I could not remember when I had read anything as
interesting as the speeches at the Twenty-second Congress."

Yet appearances were deceptive.

If one did not allow oneself to be confused by the precise circumstances of the power struggle in the USSR and in the upper echelons of the international Communist movement, which had driven Khrushchev to make a new attack on his adversaries at home and abroad by using, pragmatically, Solzhenitsyn's account, the reading of Solzhenitsyn proved in a quite blinding way that the post-Stalinist political system was not reformable. The country of the Gulag would never become that of socialism: such was the conclusion that I could not fail to draw from reading *One Day in the Life of Ivan Denisovich.* In one night, those few dozen pages had managed to make me see what years of experience, from 1956 onward, endless hours of discussion and reading, had failed to elucidate for me definitively. No doubt it was my *Kazettler's* viewpoint on that zek experience that had helped me to understand that one could no longer be under any illusion. The sight of the camps suddenly revealed an inner landscape of ideological impostures, approximations, more or less historical compromises, vague ideas in which I had been floundering since 1956 because of my responsibilities in the PCE, out of solidarity with those who were fighting in the Spanish underground, all those whom I knew, sometimes loved, often respected. No, I did not agree with the opinion expressed by Pierre Daix in his preface to the French translation of Solzhenitsyn's novel, I did not think that "*One Day in the Life of Ivan Denisovich* belongs to the effort now being made to cleanse the revolution of the crimes that sully it, but more profoundly, no doubt, it is a book that aims to give the revolution its full significance." I thought that Solzhenitsyn had quite a different point of view, and that he gave the Russian Revolution its full significance as a historical catastrophe.

I had drawn my own conclusions during the debate that had opened, fairly confusedly, within the Executive Committee of the PCE, after the spring of 1962. The conclusions that I had drawn from it were so far-reaching that here I was, outside the Party—or at least with one foot outside it, my good foot, awaiting the moment, which would not be far now, when I would leave officially, with both feet—in the autumn of 1964, at the very moment I was taking part in the Clarté discussion on the uses of literature.

I had talked of Solzhenitsyn, during that meeting at the Mutualité. "Solzhenitsyn," I had said, "first destroyed the innocence in which we languished. We had come back from the Nazi camps, we were good, the wicked had been punished, Justice and Reason accompanied our steps. Yet, at the same moment, some of our comrades (and perhaps we had known them, perhaps we had shared fifteen grams of black bread with them) were setting out to join Ivan Denisovich somewhere in the Far North, to construct, pitifully, a Socialist City, spreading under the snow the deserted ghosts of its concrete carcasses. There is no longer any possible innocence, after that account, for someone who is trying to live—really live—within a Marxist conception of the world."

Except that, today, I would cross out those last words, for no one knows what a "Marxist conception of the world" is, I have nothing to add to that declaration of 1964.

But a year before, in the Gare de Lyon, in the sudden gust of light snow whose flakes swirled in the beams of the floodlights, I had remembered Fernand Barizon. Actually, it was because of him that I had written The Long Voyage. Because of him and Manuel Azaustre, the Spaniard from Mauthausen I had known in Madrid, on the Calle Concepción-Bahamonde, who had been arrested in

1962 at the same time as Julian Grimau. I had told the story on their behalf, in a sense. But I had not written the book I talked about with Barizon at Nantua or Geneva. I had not recounted a Sunday in Buchenwald. What had I said, anyway? It seemed to me, that day in the Gare de Lyon, that I had still not said anything. Certainly I had not told the most important thing. My book was being printed when I read *One Day in the Life of Ivan Denisovich*, so even before my book appeared, I already knew that I would have to rewrite it one day. I already knew that I would have to destroy that innocence of the memory. I knew that I would have to relive my experience in Buchenwald, hour by hour, with the desperate certainty of the simultaneous existence of the Russian camps, of Stalin's Gulag. I also knew that the only way of reliving that experience was to rewrite it, with full knowledge this time. In the blinding light of the searchlights of the Kolyma camps, illuminating my memory of Buchenwald.

In short, I had not written anything yet.

Not the essential thing, anyway, nothing true. I had written the truth, I suppose, nothing but the truth. If I had not been a Communist, that truth would have been enough. If I had been a Christian, Social Democrat, nationalist—or simply a patriot, as the peasants in the Othe called me—the truth of my evidence would have been enough. But I was not a Christian or a Social Democrat. I was a Communist. The whole of my account in *The Long Voyage* was tacitly articulated, without making it too obvious, without making a fuss about it, according to a Communist vision of the world. The very truth of my account had as its implicit but constricting reference the horizon of a disalienated society: a society without classes in which the camps would have been inconceivable. The very truth of my account bathed in the holy oils of this latent serene conscience. But the horizon of Communism—it's real, historical horizon—was not that of a classless society. The horizon of Communism was, inescapably, that of the Gulag. By the same token, the very truth of my book became a lie—for me, I mean. I could accept that a non-Communist reader would not question what I had written, would continue to lead his private life, if necessary, in the truth of my account. But neither I nor any Communist reader—no reader, at least, who wished to live Communism as a moral universe, who wouldn't simply be perched there, like a bird on a branch—no Communist reader, even if there were only one left, nor I myself, could accept any longer, as such, the truth of my account of the Nazi camps.

Years later, at Yale, it must have been this that the young Polish woman born on April 11, 1945, who showed me Herling-Grudzinski's *A World Apart* after she had talked to me about *The Long Voyage*, wanted me to understand, and wanted to understand herself.

But I didn't talk about that young woman to Fernand Barizon in the autumn of 1964, in that café on the Rue Saint-Victor, for the good reason that I had not yet met her. I simply told him—I was trying to be as simple as possible—why I had to rewrite that book.

Barizon listened to me very attentively.

"Good," he said, nodding. "Write it again, write the book again. But don't forget to put me in it this time! That way we'll stay together, whatever happens!"

We sipped our beer—or white wine or brandy, I don't really remember—and there was a long moment of silence between us.

"You see, Gérard," said Barizon after that long silence, "Communism isn't the youth of the world, that's clear enough. But it was our youth, all the same!"

We silently clinked glasses to our youth.

"A Sunday, hour by hour; that isn't a bad idea," Barizon muttered, a bit later, as if to himself.

As I looked at him, it was the night of that December

Sunday in Buchenwald, in 1944, twenty years before. An
idea suddenly occurred to me.

"By the way, that morning, when you came out shouting, 'What a beautiful Sunday, old friends!' what were
you thinking about?"

We are sitting at the mess table in Block 40. The curfew
will sound any minute now. I was warned a few minutes
ago by the military leader of the underground organization of the PCE that there's going to be an alert exercise,
and we'll get instructions just before the curfew. Fernand
Barizon has been given the same instructions. But I don't
know that. We are talking about something else. We don't
know that we will meet again, after the training exercise
of the combat groups.

We are sitting at the mess table, taking alternate puffs
from a *makhorka* cigarette.

"That morning," said Barizon, "I don't remember."

"You came outside shouting, 'What a beautiful Sunday.' What were you thinking about?"

"About that shitty Sunday, I suppose," said Barizon,
shrugging his shoulders. "What do you think I was
thinking about, with that fucking snow falling?"

Just now, at the end of the Little Camp, as I was
watching the sunset over the snow-covered plains of
Thuringia, Jehovah asked me if I'd had a good Sunday. I
thought of that beech tree, with its almost surreal beauty.
I left the road, I looked at the tree. For a brief moment, I
thought I had discovered some fundamental truth: the
truth of that tree, of all the trees around, the whole forest,
every forest, the world, which had no need of my gaze. I
felt with all the strength of my rushing blood that my
death would not deprive that tree of its radiant beauty,
that it would only deprive the world of my gaze. For a
brief moment of eternity, I looked at that tree with a gaze
from beyond my death, with the eyes of my own death.

And the tree was still as beautiful. My death did not diminish its beauty. Later, I would read an aphorism by Kafka that expressed with perfect precision what I had confusedly but intensely felt that morning, facing the Buchenwald beech: "In the struggle between you and the world, side with the world."

"Yes," I say to Jehovah, "a very good Sunday."